MASS VIOLENCE IN AMERICA

MASS VIOLENCE IN AMERICA

THE WEB

Emerson Hough

ARNO PRESS & THE NEW YORK TIMES

New York • 1969

Reprinted from a copy in the
Columbia University Libraries

*

*

Library of Congress Catalog Card No. 73-90178

*

Manufactured in the United States of America

Editorial Note

NATIONS, LIKE MEN, ARE SOMETIMES INTERESTED IN BURYING THE PAST.

In early 1968, after more than five years marked by political assassinations, racial uprisings, campus disorders, mass demonstrations and the violent suppression of protest, *The New York Times Magazine* asked a group of distinguished scholars to reply to the question, "Is America by nature a violent society?" In answer, University of Chicago anthropologist Clifford Geertz wrote:

> "We do not know very well what kind of society we live in, what kind of history we have had, what kind of people we are. We are just now beginning to find out, the hard way . . ."

The proposition was astonishing but correct: what was least understood about domestic political violence was its role in American history. It was common knowledge that the United States had had a Revolution, a Civil War, some trouble with the Indians and a period of labor-management conflict. But one could search the shelves of the nation's great libraries without discovering more than a handful of works on the subject of violence in American history, and these hopelessly out of date.

Historians had generally ignored or soft-pedaled the history of farmer uprisings, native vigilantism, labor-management struggles, ethnic conflicts and race riots; comparative work in the history of social conflict was particularly weak. Sociologists and political scientists in the grip of "consensus" theory tended to treat episodes of mass violence in America as insignificant or aberrational—temporary exceptions to the norm of peaceful progress. Psychologists and behavioral scientists discussed "mob violence" in terms which suggested that riots, revolts, insurrections and official violence were the products of individual or group pathology. All such interpretations had the effect not only of minimizing group violence in America, but of depriving it of political content—hence, of relevance to the present.

As a result, as late as 1968, the rich, multifarious and often terrifying history of domestic political violence was still largely *terra incognita*. So long as most Americans wished to keep certain skeletons locked away in their closets, few scholars would attempt to open doors. Conversely, once the American people, frightened yet emboldened by the sudden reappearance of intense social conflict, began to ask new questions about the past, so did the scholars.

Our purpose in helping Arno Press and *The New York Times* select and publish significant documents in the history of political violence has not been to compound past errors by overemphasizing the role of conflict in American history. On the contrary, our aim has been to provide materials which will aid in the search for an accurate perspective on the present. MASS VIOLENCE IN AMERICA includes eyewitness reports, government documents and other descriptive and analytic material relating to mass political violence in the United States. These documents not only provide information—they give the "feel" or "flavor" of past eras of civil disorder by evoking the emotional and political context in which revolts took place. Most of them have long been out of print and are obtainable, if at all, only in the nation's largest libraries.

The scope of this series is wide, ranging from accounts of Indian warfare to descriptions of labor-management violence, from narratives of colonial insurrections to reports on modern racial uprisings. It is not, however, limitless, nor were the constituent volumes carelessly selected. The principle of coherence which guided the selections is implicit in the phrase "mass political violence." "Mass" denotes activity engaged in by large groups rather than individuals acting alone; "political" suggests a relationship between such activity and competition among domestic groups for power, property and prestige; and "violence" is narrowly construed as resulting in physical damage to persons or property. In short, the materials reproduced herein are intended to illuminate the resort to violence by American groups seeking to change or to preserve the status quo. Although historical, they are of interest to any who wishes to understand the causes, nature and direction of domestic political violence, whether they be social scientists, historians or just interested Americans.

Of course, we are particularly hopeful that these volumes will prove useful to those now engaged in curriculum-revision and the teaching of high school and college courses in the area of American studies. What Christopher Jencks and David Reisman term "the Academic Revolution" has made difficult demands on all educators, not the least of which is the demand for courses which are both relevant to the condition of modern America and of the highest academic quality. These volumes are meant to provide raw material for such courses—primary source matter which will help both instructors and students to deepen and enrich their views of the American experience.

Most important, the editors and publisher recognize that these volumes appear during a national crisis which is also a crisis of the spirit, a time in which the public response to various manifestations of civil disorder is increasingly governed by anger, fear and hysteria. In such an atmosphere it is important to recognize that one is not alone in time—that such events have taken place before in America and, unless fundamental changes in our social and political life take place, will probably recur in the future. Our fondest hope is that this work, and others like it, will help to keep alive, in a time of growing unreason, the spirit of reasoned inquiry.

RICHARD E. RUBENSTEIN
The Adlai Stevenson Institute
Chicago, Illinois

ROBERT M. FOGELSON
Harvard-MIT Joint Center for Urban Studies
Cambridge, Massachusetts

THE WEB

The Authorized History of The American Protective League

The Web

BY

Emerson Hough

Author of

"The Mississippi Bubble," "54-40 or Fight," "The Magnificent Adventure," etc.

A Revelation of Patriotism

The Web is published by authority of the National Directors of the American Protective League, a vast, silent, volunteer army organized with the approval and operated under the direction of the United States Department of Justice, Bureau of Investigation.

The Reilly & Lee Co.

Chicago

Made in U. S. A.

To
THE UNKNOWN AMERICANS
unnamed, unhonored
unrewarded
who made this history possible

THE CALL OF THE PRESIDENT OF THE UNITED STATES

"It is a distressing and oppressive duty, Gentlemen of the Congress, which I have performed in thus addressing you. There are, it may be, many months of fiery trial and sacrifice ahead of us. It is a fearful thing to lead this great peaceful people into war, into the most terrible and disastrous of all wars, civilization itself seeming to be in the balance. But the right is more precious than peace, and we shall fight for the things which we have always carried nearest our hearts. . . . To such a task we can dedicate our lives and our fortunes, everything that we are and everything that we have, with the pride of those who know that the day has come when America is privileged to spend her blood and her might for the principles that gave her birth and happiness and the peace which she has treasured. God helping her, she can do no other."

THE ANSWER OF THE CONGRESS OF THE UNITED STATES

"WHEREAS, The Imperial German Government has committed repeated acts of war against the Government and the People of the United States of America; therefore be it

"*Resolved, by the Senate and House of Representatives of the United States of America, in Congress assembled,* That the state of war between the United States and the Imperial German Government which has thus been thrust upon the United States is hereby formally declared; and that the President be, and he is hereby, authorized and directed to employ the entire naval and military forces of the United States and the resources of the Government to carry on war against the Imperial German Government; and to bring the conflict to a successful termination all the resources of the country are hereby pledged by the Congress of the United States."

STATEMENT OF THE ATTORNEY GENERAL OF THE UNITED STATES

February 1, 1919

On the occasion of the dissolution to-day of the American Protective League and the final termination of all of its activities, I take the opportunity to express to its National Directors and all other officers and members my personal thanks for their assistance to me and to my Department during the period of the war. I am frank to say that the Department of Justice could not have accomplished its task and attained the measure of success which it did attain without the assistance of the members of the League.

Your reward can only be the expressed thanks of your Government. As the head of the Department of Justice, under which the American Protective League operated, I render you such thanks with sincere pleasure. Upon the occasion of a request from a member of the Committee on the Judiciary of the House of Representatives for an expression of opinion by me as to the adoption of a joint resolution by the Congress of the United States, extending the thanks of Congress to the members of the League, I have urged in strong terms the adoption of such a resolution, as one justly earned by the organization during an extended period of devoted and effective service.

The work of your organization will long be an inspiration to all citizens to render their full measure of service to their country according to her need, without reward, and with abundant zeal.

Respectfully,

T. W. Gregory

Attorney General

AUTHOR'S PREFACE

"Signed!"

The one word, spoken by a young officer of the U. S. Army, a strip of paper in his hand, confirmed to his associates the greatest news the world has ever known. It was the corrected foreword of peace. The armistice had validly been signed by Germany.

In these first days of peace, the streets were full of shouting, laughing, weeping men and women gone primitive. The sane and sober population of America, engaged in sending a third of a million men a month to join the two millions on the front in France, turned into a mob. Their frenzy was that of joy. The war was over.

On the day following the confirmation of the armistice, some who had sat together in a certain room in Washington were scattered. Six thousand resignations of Army officers were handed in within twenty-four hours. The room in which the news of the war's end was thus received was one in the Military Intelligence Division of the General Staff in Washington. There lie the secrets of the Army. All in that room were officers of the Army, or soon to be such. All were volunteers. I may with propriety say that for a time I had sat with those who had ear to the secret voices of the world, in the tensest atmosphere I ever knew.

It was whispers that "M. I. D." heard — the whispers of perfidious men, communicating one with the other, plotting against the peace of America, the dignity of our Government, the sacredness of our flag, the safety of American lives and property. Here sat the authorized agents of the Army, employed to hear such whispers, enlisted to catch the most skilled and unscrupulous spies the world has ever known, the agents of a treacherous and dishonorable enemy.

All those connected with the Military Intelligence Division daily felt also the touch of this great, silent, smooth-running machinery of the Department of Justice, whose governmental mission it was to do detective work on the largest scale this country ever knew. We heard the voice of the War College through the official liaison therewith; also those of the General Staff, the War Department, the Post Office Department, the cable censors, the censors of the Expeditionary Forces. It all worked as an interlocking, vast, silent machine — a solemnly, almost mournfully silent machine, of which America knows almost nothing, the rest of the world nothing at all.

Day by day, in ghostly silhouette, passed sinister figures, themselves silent; those who plotted against America. All the deeds that can come from base and sordid motives, from low, degenerate and perverted minds; all the misguided phenomena of human avarice and hate and eagerness to destroy and kill — such were the pictures on the walls of " M. I. D."

I have spoken of certain essential liaisons against espionage and propaganda. More often seen than any other initials in the desk algebra of " M. I. D." were three initials — " A. P. L." This or that information came from A. P. L. This was referred to A. P. L. for more light. Every questionnaire of a man applying for a commission in the Army was referred back to A. P. L., and A. P. L. took up the question of his unswerving and invincible loyalty. A. P. L. found slackers and deserters in thousands. A. P. L. found this or that spy, large or little. A. P. L., obviously, had a busy mind and a long arm.

Yet if you should look in the Governmental Blue Book for this powerful branch of our Government, you could not find the initials there at all. Very many Americans never heard the name of this wholly unofficial organization which passed on so many governmental questions, was of so much aid in so many ways to the Government. A. P. L. is not and never was a part of any state or national arm, service, department, or bureau. But openly and proudly it has always been definitely authorized to carry on all its letter-heads, " Organized with the Approval and Operating under the Direction of the United States Department of Justice, Bureau of Investigation." These are its credentials.

A. P. L., the mysterious power behind our Government, was no baseless fabric of a vision, as hundreds of Germans and pro-Germans can testify through their prison bars; but it passes now and soon will " leave not a wrack behind." As these pages advance, the word issues for its official demobilization. It was honorably encamped on a secret and silent battlefield, but now, once more to use a poet's word, it has " folded its tents like the Arab, and silently stolen away." It was, and is not. You never have known what it was. You never will see its like again.

" A. P. L." means the American Protective League. It means a silent, unknown army of more than a quarter million of the most loyal and intelligent citizens of America, who indeed did spring to arms over night. It fought battles, saved lives, saved cities, saved treasures, defended the flag, apprehended countless traitors, did its own tremendous share in the winning of the war. It saved America. It did protect. It was a league.

It did all this without a cent of pay. It had no actual identification with the Government. Yet it has won scores of times the written and spoken thanks of our most responsible Government officials. Its aid in the winning of the war can not be estimated and never will be known. Not even its full romance ever can be written. May these hurrying pages save all these things at least in part, though done in the full consciousness that their tribute can be but a fragment of the total due.

The American Protective League was the largest company of detectives the world ever saw. The members served without earlier specialized training, without pay, without glory. That band of citizens, called together overnight, rose, grew and gathered strength until able to meet, and absolutely to defeat, the vast and highly trained army of the German espionage system, which in every country of the globe flooded the land with trained spies who had made a life business of spying. It met that German Army as ours met it at Chateau-Thierry, and in the Argonne, and on the Vesle and on the Aisne. Like to our Army under arms — that Army where any of us would have preferred to serve had it been possible for us to serve under arms — it never gave back an inch of ground. Growing stronger and better equipped each day, it worked always onward and forward until the last fight was won.

A. P. L. has folded its unseen and unknown tents. It will bivouac elsewhere until another day of need may come. Then, be sure, it will be ready. On the day that the American Protective League disbanded, it had no money in the treasury. It had spent millions of dollars, and had brought to judgment three million cases of disloyalty. There, obviously, unwritten and unknown, scattered in every city, and hamlet of America, was a tremendous story, one of the greatest of all war stories, the story of the line behind the guns.

When the men of long or of transient connection with M. I. D. had shaken hands and said good-bye, the National Directors of the American Protective League asked me to stop on and write the history of the American Protective League. And so, in large part, as a matter of loyalty and duty, with millions of pages of records at hand, with a quarter of a million friends I have never seen, who never have seen one another, who never otherwise would know the identity of one another, I began to do something which most obviously and certainly ought to be done. This book is written alike that these quarter million unpaid soldiers may know of one another, and that a hundred million Americans may also know of them accurately, and thank them for what they did.

Before I had done the last page of the strange history, I knew that I had felt an actual reflex of the actual America. I knew that I had been in touch with one of the most astonishing phenomena of modern days, in touch also with the most tremendous, the most thrilling and the most absorbing story of which I ever knew.

EMERSON HOUGH

Washington
District of Columbia
United States of America
February 14, 1919.

CONTENTS

Book I: The League and Its Work

Book II: The Tales of the Cities

Contents

Book III: The Four Winds

Book IV: America

BOOK I

THE LEAGUE AND ITS WORK

THE WEB

CHAPTER I

THE AWAKENING

The "Neutral Cases"— First Realization of the German Spy System in America — Overcrowding of the Department of Justice — The Birth of a New Idea — Formation of the American Protective League, Civilian Auxiliary — Astonishing Growth of the Greatest Semi-Vigilante Movement of the World.

We Americans have always been disposed to peace. We have not planned for war. Our Army has never been a menace to ourselves or to any other nation; our Navy, though strong and modern, never has been larger than a country of our extent in territory and industry admittedly ought to have. No one has feared us, and there has been none of whom we have had any fear. We have designedly stood aloof from entangling alliances. The two great oceans traditionally have been our friends, for they have set us apart from the world's quarrels. An America, far off, new, rich, abounding, a land where a man might be free to grow to his natural stature, where he might be safe at his own fireside, where he might select his own rulers and rest always secure under his own form of government —that was the theory of this country and of this form of government. That was the reason why this country, naturally endowed above any other region of the world, has grown so marvelously fast.

There was reason for America's swift stature. She was a land not of war, but of peace. Rich, she threw open her doors. Frank, free, honest, generous, she made welcome all who came. She suspected none, trusted all, and to prove this, offered partnership in her wealth to any man of the world, under a system of naturalization laws whose like, in broadness and generosity, does not exist. Peace—and the chance to grow and to be happy. Peace—and a partnership in all she had. Peace—and a seat free at the richest table of the world. That was what America offered; and in spite of the pinch and the unrest of growing numbers, in spite of problems imported and not native to our long-untroubled land, that was the theory of American life up to a date four years earlier than this.

In that four years America has changed more than in any forty of her earlier life. But yesterday, young, rich, laughing, free of care, Homerically mirthful and joyous, America to-day is mature, unsmiling, grave, dignified—and wise. What once she never suspected, now she knows. She has been betrayed.

But America, traditionally resourceful, now suddenly agonized in the discovery of treachery at her own table, has out of the very anguish of her indignant horror, out of the very need of the hour, suddenly and adequately risen to her emergency. She always has done so. When the arms of the appointed agents of the law ever have wearied, she has upheld them. She has done so now, at the very moment of our country's greatest need.

The story of how that was done; how the very force of the situation demanded and received an instant and sufficient answer; how the civilians rallied to their own flag; how they came out of private life unasked, unsummoned, as though at spoken command of some central power—that is a great and splendid story of which few ever have known anything at all.

It is a great and splendid story because it verifies America and her intent before all the high courts of things. These men did obey the summons of a vast central power. But it was no more than the soul of America that spoke. It was no more than her theory of the democracy of mankind which issued that unwritten order to assemble the minute men, each armed and garbed in his own way and each resolved to do what he could in a new and tremendous day of Lexington.

It was not autocracy which gave the assembly call to

these silent legions. They mobilized themselves, so rapidly as to offer one of the most curious psychological problems of history. Why did these men leave their homes almost all at once, each unknown at first to the other, in large part each unknown to the other even now? How did it come about that an army of a quarter of a million men enlisted themselves and then offered their services to a government which needed them but never had asked for them? How did it come that—contrary to all European traditions—this tremendous striking-power began at the bottom in our democratic war-born instinct, and worked upward into the Government itself, as a new institution, wholly unrecognized in the constitution of state or nation? Usually the Government issues the order for mobilization. But here the greatest band of minute men ever known in the world mobilized as though unconsciously, as though to some spiritual trumpet call. Having done so, it offered itself to the Nation's heads, saying, "Here we are. Take us and use us. We ask no pay. *We enlist till the end of the war.*"

It was the spirit voice of anguished America which mobilized the American Protective League. There never was a time when America could lose this war. The answer was always written in the stars. Somewhere, high up in the heavens, blind Justice let fall her sword in a gesture of command; and that was all. The issue of the war was determined from that moment. It was certain that Germany, brutal, bloody, autocratic, destructive, would be defeated beyond the sea. Yes, and on this side of the sea.

On this side, much was to be done, more than we had dreamed. Troubled but unparticipating, we stood aloof and watched the soil of all Europe redden with the blood of men—and of women and children. Even we still stood aloof, hands clenched, gasping in an enraged incredulity, watching the sea also—the free and open highway of the world, redden with the blood of men—and of women and children. But still we took no part, though indeed some of our young men could no longer stay at home and so enlisted under some Allied flag.

We held in mind our ancient remoteness from all this. We heard still the counsel against entangling alliances.

And, quite aside from the idea of material profit, we tried to be fair and impartial in a fight that was not yet ours, though every American heart bled with France and Belgium, ached in pain with that of Britain, locked in death grapple in her greatest war—that which must name her still free or forever enslaved. And from Washington came admonition to be calm. President Wilson's appeal went out again and again to the people, and whether or not it ever once seemed to all of us a possible thing for the United States to keep out of this war, at least we sought to do so and were advised and commanded to do so by the chief of our own forces.

Whether or not we all wished to be neutral so many years, we officially and nationally were neutral. Therefore we retained our commercial rights under neutrality. Doing no more than Germany always previously had done, we made and sold arms and munitions in the open markets of the world.

But Germany could not come and get her arms and munitions had she wished to do so. Great Britain had something to say about that. Wherefore Germany hated us, secretly and openly—hated us for doing what she once had done but could no longer do.

The enforcement of blockade made Germany hate us. Germany's psychology has always been double-faced—one face for herself and one for the rest of the world. The Austrian double-headed eagle belongs of right also on the German coat of arms. "What I do not wish to have done to me is Wrong; what I wish to do to others is Right!" That is the sum and substance of the German public creed and the German private character—and now we fairly may say we know them both. The German is not a sportsman—he does not know the meaning of that word. He has not in his language any word meaning "fair play." Nothing is fair play to a German which does not work to his advantage. The American neutrality in combination with the British blockade did not work to his advantage. Hence—so he thought—it was all wrong.

The Germans began to hate America more and more. We did not know, at that time, that Germany had been planning many years for "diesen aufunsangehängten

Krieg"—"this war forced on us!" We did not have any idea that she had counted upon two million German-Americans to help her win this war; that she knew every nook and cranny of the United States and had them mapped; that for years she had maintained a tremendous organization of spies who had learned every vulnerable point of the American defenses, who were better acquainted with our Army than we ourselves were, and who had extended their covert activities to a degree which left them arrogantly confident of their success at war, and contemptuous of the best that America ever could do against her. Germany never doubted that she would win this war. It was charted and plotted out many years in advance, move by move, step by step, clear through to the bloody and brutal end which should leave Germany commander of the world.

Now, in the German general plan of conquest, America had had her place assigned to her. So long as she would remain passive and complaisant—so long as she would furnish munitions to Germany and not to England or France or Russia, all well, all very good. But when, by any shift of the play, America might furnish supplies to Germany's enemies and not to Germany—no matter through whose fault—then so much the worse for America! It never was intended that America should be anything but expansion ground for Germany, whether or not she remained complaisant. But if she did not—if she began in her own idea of neutrality to transgress Germany's two-headed idea of "neutrality"—that meant immediate and positive action against America, now, to-day, and not after a while and at Germany's greater leisure.

"I shall have no foolishness from America!" said William Hohenzollern to the accredited representative of this country in his court—William Hohenzollern, that same pitiable figure who at the final test of defeat had not the courage of Saul to fall on his sword, not the courage of a real King to die at the head of his army, but who fled from his army like a coward when he saw all was lost—even honor. His threat of a million Germans in America who would rise against us was not ill-based. They were here. They are here now, to-day. The reply to that threat, made by Gerard, is historic. "Majesty, let them rise. We have a million lamp-posts waiting for them." And this herein tells the story of how the million traitors at America's too generous table were shown the lamp-posts looming.

The German anger at America grew to the fury point, and she began covertly to stir herself on this side the sea. The rustling of the leaves began to be audible, the hissing grew unmistakable. But America, resting on her old traditions, paid no attention. We heard with sympathy for a time the classic two-faced German-American's wail, "Germany is my mother, America my wife! How can I fight my mother?" The truth is that all too many German-Americans never cared for America at all in any tender or reverent way. Resting under their Kaiser's Delbrueck injunction never to forget the fatherland, they never were anything but German. They used America; they never loved her. They clung to their old language, their old customs, and cared nothing for ours. They prospered, because they would live as we would not live. It would be wrong to call them all bad, and folly to call them all good. As a class they were clannish beyond all other races coming here. Many who at first were openly pro-German became more discreet; but of countless numbers of these, it is well known that at their own firesides and in supposed secrecy they privately were German, although in public they were American. Of Liberty bond buyers, many of the loudest boasters were of this "loyal German-American citizenship." They really had not earned even the hyphen.

Open and covert action was taken by Germany on both sides of the Atlantic to bring America into line. Not fearing America, nor knowing the real America at all, Germany did much as she liked. Outrages on the high seas began. All international law was cast aside by Germany as fully as in her invasion of Belgium. She counted so surely on success and world-conquest that she was absolutely arrogant and indifferent alike to law and to humanity. The militaristic Germany began to show—brutal, crafty, bestial, lacking in all honor, ignorant of the word "fair play," callous to every appeal of humanity, wholly and unscrupulously selfish. We began now to see the significance of that "efficiency" of which our industrial captains sometimes had prated over-much. Yes, Germany was efficient!

The strain between the two countries increased as the blockade tightened, and as the counter-plot of the German submarines developed. Then came the Lusitania. . . . I can not write of that. I have hated Germany since then, and thousands of loyal Americans join in hatred for her. All of good America has been at war with her at heart from that very day, because in America we never have made war on women and children. We are bound by every instinct to hate any nation that does, Turk, German or ignorant savage.

The Lusitania was Germany's deliberate action. She arrogantly commanded us in a few newspaper advertisements not to sail on the Lusitania—as though she owned us and the sea. After the deed, she struck medals in commemoration of it. German church bells rang to glorify it. A German holiday was created to celebrate it. German preachers there and in America preached sermons lauding it. It was a national act, nationally planned, nationally ratified. From that day we were at war. Let those who like, of whatever station, say "We are not at war with the German people." That is not true. The German people, the German rank and file, not their leaders alone, were back of all these deeds and ratified them absolutely on both sides of the Atlantic.

From that day, too, the issue might really have been known. I went into the elevator of a building in my city, a copy of a newspaper in my hand with the black headline of the Lusitania across the page. The German operator of the elevator saw it as I turned it toward him silently. "Vell, they vere varned!" he said, and grinned.

That incident shows Germany in America, then and now, covert, sinister, sneering, confident, exultant. You could not find an answer you would dare speak to such a man. There is no deed that you could do. I pulled together, and only said, "It will cost Germany the war." And so it did.

But we did not go to war; we tried to keep out of the war. The daily page of red horrors fresh from Europe taught us what war meant at this day of the world.

Women naturally did not like the thought of casting their sons into that brutal hell. And then arose the female-men, the pacifists, forgetting their sex, forgetting their country, forgetting the large and lasting game of humanity's good, which cannot count present cost, but must plan for the long game of the centuries.

With the pacifists suddenly and silently rose the hidden army of German espionage and German sympathy in our own country, quick to see that here was their chance! Millions of German gold now came pouring across to finance this break in America's forces. Her high ministers to our Government began their treachery, forgetful of all ambassadorial honor, perjuring themselves and their country. The war was on, on both sides the Atlantic now.

And still America did not know, and still America did not go to war. We dreaded it, held back from it, month after month—some, as it seems to many, wrongly and unhappily even did what they could to capitalize the fact that we were not at war. But the hidden serpent raised its head and began to strike—to strike so openly, in so long a series of overt acts, that now our civil courts and the great national machinery of justice in Washington became literally helpless in their endeavors at resistance.

We were not at war, but war was waged against us in so many ways—against our lives and property—that all sense of security was gone. We offered as our defense not, as yet, our Fleet or our Army, but our Department of Justice. Day and night that department at Washington, and its branches in all the great cities, in New York, Chicago, Boston, Baltimore, Philadelphia, San Francisco, labored to clear the constantly increasing dockets, to keep down the constantly increasing heaps of suspect cases. It was evident that America was hearing from the Kaiser's million Germans in America. But where were the lamp posts?

The Department of Justice found itself flooded and submerged with work in the Bureau of Investigation, collecting evidence against German spies and German lawbreakers. It was plain what efforts now were making to undermine America. But the truth was, the grist was too much for the mill. We had never organized a system to handle covert and hidden war as Germany had done. We had fought in the open when, rarely, we had fought at all. The great mill of Justice clogged up and broke down, not from any inefficiency or inadequacy in average times, but because it never could have been predicted that "Neutrality Cases" such as these ever would be known in our history. In this war, giant figures only have ruled. The world was not prepared for them.

The outrages went on. Germany, confident of the success of ruthless submarine warfare, told us when we could sail, how we must mark our ships—said, sneeringly, "Vell, you vas varned!"

It had very early become plain to all Americans that we could not always submit to this. More and more now we were browbeaten and insulted. More and more also our hearts were wrung at the sight of splendid France, fighting gamely and proudly and silently for her life; at the lists of the gallant British dead; the whole story of the staggering lines of Liberty. It was plain that the great prize of free institutions, of human liberty itself, was about to be lost to the world forever. It became plain that the glorious traditions of America must perish, that her answer to humanity must be forever stilled, that she, too, must be included in the ruin of all the good things of the world. It began also to be said more and more openly that America would come next—that we must fight; if not now, then at some later day, and perhaps without these Allies.

So our war spirit began in the total to outweigh and overtop our peace spirit and our pacifist spirit and our hesitant spirit. We knew we would be at war. Many of us deplored and do still deplore the fact that we waited so long in times so perilous. We lost two precious years; billions in treasure, and what is immeasurably worse, millions in lives. So much for hesitancy.

But now, as bearing upon the purpose of this account of the American Protective League, it is to be kept in mind that for months and years the Department of Justice had been at war with the hidden German army here. And, as the Germans were pushing back the Allies over there, they were pushing us back here, because we were not ready for so unforeseen a situation.

What saves a country in its need? Its loyal men. What reinforces an army called on for sudden enlargement? Its volunteers. What saved San Francisco in its days of riot and anarchy in 1850? Its Volunteers for law and order. What brought peace to Alder Gulch in 1863 when criminals ruled? Its Volunteers for law and order. America always has had Volunteers to fight for law and order against criminals. The law itself says you may arrest without warrant a man caught committing a felony. The line between formal written law and natural law is but thin at best.

There was, therefore, in the spring of 1917 in America, the greatest menace to our country we ever had known. Organized criminals were in a thousand ways attacking our institutions, jeopardizing the safety, the very continuity of our country. No loyal American was safe. We did not know who were the disloyal Americans. We faced an army of masked men. They outnumbered us. We had no machinery of defense adequate to fight them, because we foolishly had thought that all these whom we had welcomed and fed were honest in their protestations—*and their oaths*—when they came to us.

So now, we say, an imperious cry of NEED came, wrung from astounded and anguished America. It was as though this actual cry came from the heavens, "I need you, my children! Help me, my children!"

That cry was heard. How, it is of small importance to any member of the American Protective League, whose wireless antennæ, for the time attuned, caught down that silent wireless from the skies. No one man sent that message. Almost, we might say, no one man answered it, so many flocked in after the first word of answer. No one man of the two hundred and fifty thousand who first and last answered in one way or another would say or would want to say that he alone made so large an answer to so large a call. None the less, we deal here with actual history. So that now we may begin with details, begin to show how those first strands were woven which in a few weeks or months had grown into one of America's strongest cables of anchorage against the terror which was abroad upon the sea.

CHAPTER II

THE WEB

Methods of Work — Getting the Evidence — The Organization in Detail — The Multifold Activities of the League.

It is to Mr. A. M. Briggs of Chicago that credit should go for the initial idea of the American Protective League. The first flash came many months before the declaration of war, although, for reasons outlined, it long was obvious that we must eventually go to war.

The Department of Justice in Chicago was in a terribly congested condition, and long had been, for the neutrality cases were piling up.

"I could get ten times as much done if I had men and money to work with," said Hinton G. Clabaugh, Superintendent of the Bureau of Investigation. "There are thousands of men who are enemies of this country and ought to be behind bars, but it takes a spy to catch a spy, and I've got a dozen spies to catch a hundred thousand spies right here in Chicago. They have motor cars against my street cars. They're supplied with all the money they want; my own funds are limited. We're not at war. All this is civil work. We simply haven't ways and means to meet this emergency."

"I can get ten or twenty good, quiet men with cars who'll work for nothing," said Mr. Briggs one day. "They'll take either their business time or their leisure time, or both, and join forces with you. I know we're not at war, but we're all Americans together."

In that chance conversation—only we ought not to call it chance at all, but a thing foreordained—began the greatest society the world ever saw,—an army of men equipped with money, brains, loyalty, which grew into one of the main legions of our defense. That army to-day probably knows more about you and your affairs than you ever thought anyone could know. If you were not and are not loyal, those facts are known and recorded, whether you live in New York or California or anywhere between.

Once started, the voluntary service idea ran like wildfire. It began as a free taxicab company, working for the most impeccable and most dignified branch of our Government—that branch for which our people always have had the most respect.

The ten private cars grew to two dozen. As many quiet-faced, silent drivers as were necessary were always ready. Word passed among reliable business men, and they came quietly and asked what they could do. They were the best men of the city. They worked for principle, not for excitement, not in any vanity, not for any pay. It was the " live-wires " of the business world that were selected. They were all good men, big men, brave and able, else they must have failed, and else this organization never could have grown. It was secret, absolutely so; clandestine absolutely, this organization of Regulators. But unlike the Vigilantes, the Klu Klux, the Horse-Thief Detectors, it took no punishments into its own hands. It was absolutely non-partisan. It had then and has now no concern with labor questions or political questions. It worked only as collector of evidence. It had no governmental or legal status at all. It tried no cases, suggested no remedies. It simply *found the facts.*

It became apparent that the City of Chicago was not all America. These American men had America and not Chicago at heart. Before long, five hundred men, in widely separated and sometimes overlapping sections, were at work piling up evidence against German and pro-German suspects. These men began to enlist under them yet others. The thing was going swiftly, unaccountably swiftly. America's volunteers were pouring out. The Minute Men were afoot again, ready to fight.

This was in March of 1917. Even yet we were not at war, though in the two years following the Lusitania murders, the world had had more and more proof of Germany's heartless and dishonorable intentions. The snake was now out of the leaves. The issue was joined. We all knew that Washington soon would, soon must, declare war. The country was uneasy, discontented, mutinous over the delay.

Meantime, all these new foci of this amateur organization began to show problems of organization and administration. The several captains unavoidably lapped over one another in their work, and a certain loss in speed and efficiency rose out of this. The idea had proved good, but it was so good it was running away with itself! No set of men could handle it except under a well-matured and adequately-managed organization, worked out in detail from top to bottom.

We may not place one man in this League above another, for all were equal in their unselfish loyalty, from private to general, from operative to inspector, and from inspector to National Directors; but it is necessary to set down the basic facts of the inception of the League in order that the vast volume and usefulness of its labors properly may be understood. So it is in order now to describe how this great army of workers became a unit of immense, united and effective striking power, how the swift and divers developments of the original idea became coördinated into a smooth-running machine, nation-wide in its activities.

Now at last, long deferred—too long—came April 6, 1917. The black headlines smote silence at every American table.

WAR!

We were at War! Men did not talk much. Mothers looked at their sons, wives at their husbands. Thousands of souls had their Gethsemane that day. Now we were to place our own breasts against the steel of Germany.

The cover was off. War—war to the end, now—war on both sides of the sea—war against every form and phase of German activity! America said aloud and firmly now, as, in her anguish, she had but recently whispered, "I need you, my children!" And millions of Americans, many of them debarred from arms by age or infirmity, came forward, each in his own way, and swore the oath.

The oath of the League spread. Not one city or state, but all America must be covered, and it must be done at once. The need of a national administration became at once imperative.

In this work on the neutrality cases Mr. Clabaugh and

his volunteer aids often were in Washington together. The Department of Justice, so far from finding this unasked civilian aid officious, gladly hailed it as a practical aid of immeasurable value. It became apparent that the League was bound to be national in every way at no late day.

All this meant money. But America, unasked, opened her secret purse strings. Banks, prominent firms, loyal individuals gave thousands and hundreds of thousands of dollars for a work which they knew must be done if America was to be safe for decent men. And so the silent army of which you never knew, grew and marched out daily. Your house, your neighbor's, was known and watched, guarded as loyal, circled as disloyal. The nature of your business and your neighbor's was known—and tabulated. You do not know to-day how thoroughly America knows you. If you are hyphenated now, if you are disloyal to this flag, so much the worse for you.

It early became plain to manufacturers and owners of large industrial plants of all sorts that they were in immediate danger of dynamite outrages. Many plants agreed to present to the League monthly a considerable checque to aid the work of safeguarding. Many wealthy individuals gave additional amounts. A very considerable sum was raised from the sale of badges to the operatives, it being explained to all that they were sold at a profit for the benefit of the League. At all times large amounts came in, raised by State or local chiefs, each of whom knew his own community well. On one day in October, 1917, a call went out to 6700 members of the League to meet on a certain evening at Medinah Temple in Chicago, admission to be by credentials only. That meeting was addressed by Chiefs and others. In a short time $82,000 was raised. Later on, certain bankers of national reputation—F. A. Vanderlip of New York, George M. Reynolds of Chicago, Festus Wade of St. Louis, Stoddard Jess of Los Angeles, and others—sent out an appeal to the bankers of America in the interests of the League. This perhaps would of itself have raised a half million more, but it came among Liberty Loan activities, and before it was fully under way, the news of the Armistice broke, which automatically ended many things. But the American Protective League had money. It can have all the money it may need in any future day.

It was not until fall of 1917 that, in answer to the imperious demands of the swiftly grown association, now numbering thousands in every State of the Union, and in order to get into closer touch with the Department of Justice, the League moved its headquarters from Chicago to Washington. Mr. Charles Daniel Frey of Chicago, who had worked out with his associates the details of a perfectly subdivided organization, was made Captain U. S. A. and liaison officer for the League's work with the Military Intelligence Division of the Army, a division which itself had known great changes and rapid development. The three National Directors were now A. M. Briggs, Chairman; Captain Charles Daniel Frey, and Mr. Victor Elting, the latter gentleman, an attorney of Chicago, having before now proved himself of the utmost service in handling certain very tangled skeins. Mr. Elting had been Assistant Chief in Chicago, working with Mr. Frey as Chief. Then later came on, from his League duties in Chicago, Mr. S. S. Doty, a man successful in his own business organization and of proved worth in working out details of organization. Many others from Chicago, in many capacities, joined the personnel in Washington, and good men were taken on as needed and found. It would be cheap to attempt mention of these, but it would be wrong not to give some general mention of the men who actually had in hand the formation of the League and the conduct of its widely reaching affairs from that time until its close at the end of the war. They worked in secrecy and they asked no publicity then or now.

One thing must be very plain and clear. These men, each and all of them, worked as civilian patriots, and, except in a very few necessary clerical cases, without pay of any sort. There was no mummery about the League, no countersigns or grips or passwords, no rituals, no rules. It never was a "secret society," as we understand that usually. It was—the American Protective League, deadly simple, deadly silent, deadly in earnest. There has been no glory, no pay, no publicity, no advertising, no reward in the American Protective League, except as each man's conscience gave him his best reward, the feeling that he had fulfilled the imperative obligations of his citizenship and had done his bit in the world's greatest war.

By the time the League was in Washington, it had a quarter-million members. Its records ran into tons and tons; its clerical work was an enormous thing.

The system, swiftly carried out, was unbelievably successful. An unbelievable artesian fountain of American loyalty had been struck. What and how much work that body of silent men did, how varied and how imperatively essential was the work they did, how thrillingly interesting it became at times as the netted web caught more and more in its secret sweeping, must be taken up in later chapters.

As to the total volume of the League's work, it never will be known, and no figures will ever cover it more than partially. It handled in less than two years, for the War Department alone, over three million cases. It spent millions of dollars. It had a quarter million silent and resolute men on its rolls. These men were the best of their communities. They did not work for pay. They worked for duty, and worked harder than a like number in any army of the world. Some of the things they did, some of the astonishing matters they uncovered, some of the strange stories they unearthed, will be taken up in order in the pages following, and in a way more specifically informing than has hitherto been attempted.

The League totals are tremendous, but the trouble with totals is that they do not enter into comprehension. A million dollars means little as a phrase, if left barren of some yard-stick for comparative measurement. Thus, when we say that long ago the number of suspect cases investigated by the American Protective League had passed the three-million mark, we hail the figures as grandiose, but have no personal idea of what they mean, no accurate conception of the multitude, the nature and the multiplicity in detail of the three million separate and distinct cases. It is when we begin to go into details as to the work and its organization from unit to block, from operative to chief, that we begin to open our eyes.

The government of this country had had thrown on it all at once a burden a thousand times as great as that of times of peace. We had to raise men and money, munitions, food, fuel for ourselves and all the world. We were not prepared. We had to learn all at once the one and hardest thing—one which America never yet had learned—economy. We had to do all the active and positive material things necessary to put an Army in the field across seas—build ships, fabricate ordnance, arm large bodies of men, train them, feed them, get their fighting morale on edge.

Yes, all these things—but this was only part. Our negative defense, our silent forces also had to be developed. We had to learn economy—and suspicion. That last was hard to learn. Just as delay and breakdowns happened in other branches of the suddenly overloaded government, so a breakdown in the resources of the Department of Justice—least known but most valuable portion of our nation's governmental system—was a thing imminent. That was because of the swift multiplication of the list of entirely new things that had to be looked into with justice, and yet with speed. It is not too much to say that without the inspired idea of the American Protective League, its Web spread out behind the lines, there could not long have been said in the full confidence of to-day, "God reigns, and the Government at Washington still lives."

Besides being an auxiliary of the Department of Justice, the League was the active ally also of the Department of War, of the Navy, of the State, of the Treasury. It worked for the Shipping Board, the Fuel and Food Administrations, and the Alien Property Custodian. It ran down, in its less romantic labors, sugar-allowance violators, violators of the gasless-Sunday laws, the lightless-day laws, violators of the liquor laws, as well as the large offenders—the spies who got internment or the penitentiary as the penalty of getting caught. All these large and small activities may be understood by a glance at the report-sheet of any division chief. The heads and sub-heads will show the differentiation. The chart following this chapter will show the method of organizing the League's personnel which was used in practically all the great cities. The table of dates which immediately follows, sets forth in outline the League's early history, and indicates the rapidly broadening character of the League's work.

EARLY DATES OF THE AMERICAN PROTECTIVE LEAGUE

January 25, 1917	First Call by Mr. Clabaugh.
February 2, 1917	Second Call by Mr. Clabaugh (for automobiles).
February 2 to 25, 1917	Automobiles and Plans.
February 25, 1917	Submitted Plan.
March 1, 1917	Plan Endorsed and Forwarded to Washington.
March 15, 1917	Invited to Washington.
March 22, 1917	League Authorized.
March 22, 1917	New York Division Started.
March 22 to 26, 1917	Organizing in Chicago.
March 26, 1917	Chicago Division Started.
March 27, 1917	Milwaukee Division Started.
March 29, 1917	St. Louis Division Started.
April 6, 1917	State of War with Germany Acknowledged.
April 9, 1917	Philadelphia Division Started.
November 1, 1917	Board of National Directors Organized.
November 15, 1917	National Headquarters Established in Washington.

This will close a brief and necessarily incomplete review of the widely ramified nature of that Web which America made over night in her time of need.

There was also a confidential pamphlet, originally sent only to members, which elaborates and makes clear the basic purposes of the League, whose personnel and methods already have been covered. It is given in full as Appendix B. A great historic interest attaches to this document, which tells the complete inside story of the League and the manner in which it first was organized for its work. It is not necessary to say that this now appears before the eyes of the general public for the first time.

Lastly, there is for the first time made public the solemn oath taken by each member of the American Protective

League. Years hence, this page will have historic value. It records one of the most singular phenomena of the American civilization.

THE OATH OF MEMBERSHIP

I, ..., *a member of the American Protective League, organized with the approval and operating under the direction of the United States Department of Justice, Bureau of Investigation, do hereby solemnly swear:*

That I am a citizen of the United States of America; and that I will uphold and defend the Constitution and Laws of the United States against all enemies, foreign and domestic, and will bear true faith and allegiance to the same at all times as a true and loyal citizen thereof.

That I will give due time and diligent attention to such service as I shall undertake to render; and that I will execute promptly and to the best of my ability the commands of my superiors in connection therewith.

That I will in all respects observe the rules and regulations, present and future, of this organization; and that I will promptly report to my superiors any and all violations thereof, and all information of every kind and character and from whatever source derived, tending to prove hostile or disloyal acts or intentions on the part of any person whatsoever and all other information of any kind of interest or value to the Government.

That I will not, except in the necessary performance of my duty, exhibit my credentials or disclose my membership in this organization; and that I will not disclose to any person other than a duly authorized Government official or officer of this organization, facts and information coming to my knowledge in connection with its work.

That the statement on the opposite side hereof, by me subscribed, is true and correct.

That I take this obligation freely, without any mental reservation or purpose of evasion; and that I will well and faithfully discharge my duties, as a volunteer for the defense and preservation of the United States of America.

SO HELP ME GOD

CHAPTER III

EARLY DAYS OF THE LEAGUE

"D. J." and "A. P. L."— The Personal Statement of the Chicago Division Superintendent of the U. S. Bureau of Investigation — Early Days of the League — The Nation Unprepared — Swift Rallying of the Minute Men.

"*Without exaggeration, I think the Chicago Division of the American Protective League did seventy-five per cent of the Government investigating work of the Chicago district throughout the period of the war. It seems to me that this one sentence covers the situation.*"—Hinton G. Clabaugh, Chicago Agent, U. S. Department of Justice.

In previous pages a general outline of the birth and growth of the American Protective League has been given, with a general statement also as to its wide usefulness in the exigencies of the tremendous days of the world war. There will be, however, many thousands of the members of the League, and a like number of the lay public, who will be curious as to the specific and more personal facts surrounding the early days of the organization. Such facts are part of the country's history as well as that of the League, and therefore ought to be recorded, and recorded accurately and indisputably.

Mr. Hinton G. Clabaugh, division superintendent of the Bureau of Investigation of the U. S. Department of Justice, was asked for a written brief, historically covering the joint activities of the Department of Justice and its A. P. L. auxiliary in Chicago during the early period of the war. The admirably comprehensive record which Mr. Clabaugh has furnished appears in this volume as Appendix A.

No statement of facts and figures, however, or of dates and details, can really cover the story of the American Protective League. It has a character and a history which refuse to classify or to run parallel with other organizations. It was an idea born out of a vast necessity, and its growth seemed to be a thing apart from ordinary business methods. Indeed, it sprang into such rapid stature that in large part its officers followed it rather than led it. It was almost sporadic in a thousand towns, so quickly did the achievement of organization follow the realization of the need. Thereafter came the days of national organization, of system, patience, perseverance, and efficiency, which made it a well-knit power in all parts of the country.

It was Mr. Clabaugh's privilege to have lent aid and encouragement in the days when the League was not yet a reality, the early days when all was nebulous, when no one knew anyone else, and when cases were pouring into D. J. that had to be handled in the best way possible and at the first moment possible.

The A. P. L. has always served the regular organization of the law, has always worked with or under the supervision of the D. J. bureau chief nearest at hand, and, indeed, never pretended to do more than that. But this coöperation and interlocking of forces was an easier thing for D. J. superintendents elsewhere, later in the game, after A. P. L. had become an accepted success all over the country.

It was at the very beginning that the greatest difficulties had to be met, and it was during these early troubled days of the League that its history became inseparably linked with that of the Chicago bureau of the Department of Justice. Set down in a seething center of alien activity — for so we may justly call Chicago in the early days of this war — with only a handful of men to rely on, with no laws, no precedents, no support, no help, no past like to the present, and no future that could be predicated on anything that had gone before, Mr. Clabaugh's bureau was the first to get swamped with the neutrality cases — and the first to be offered counsel, friendship, support, help, money, men and methods, all in quality and amount fitted to win the day for him at once. The Clabaugh story, therefore, is the most important one told by any bureau chief, and it is historically indispensable.

It is all very well to have confidence in our government and to believe in a general way that it cannot err and cannot fail, but government in peace and government in war times are two distinct and separate propositions. The sheer truth is that there was absolutely no arm or branch of our government which was prepared for war. In part, we never did get prepared for it, so far as essential equipment of a military sort is concerned. In artillery, in aeroplanes, in various sorts of munitions and of equipment, we were not ready for war when the Armistice was signed. We had no adequate military or intelligence system, and the splendid force built up as M. I. D. was built after the war was begun and not before. In the same way — although, of course, we had the American faith and respect for our courts, believing them to be in some way supernal institutions which could not err and which needed no attention on the part of the people — our judiciary also was unprepared for war. It never would have been prepared for war — never in the world — had it not been for the American Protective League. It is certainly a most curious, almost an uncanny story, how the Minute Men of America once more saved the day, responding instantly to a great national need, not knowing overmuch of this new game, but each resolved to fight — each, if you please, resolving in unheroic and undramatic way — in much the same frame of mind of those men at Verdun who wrote on the page of martial history the clarion phrase, "They shall not pass!"

The enemy did not pass in Chicago, nor in New York, nor in San Francisco, nor in any place between. Not prepared — a whole nation in shirtsleeves at the plow — we became prepared. We fought with one hand, while, with the other, we buttoned on the new tunic for which we had not yet been measured, and in Army, Navy, Aviation, Intelligence, Supply, Motor Transport and Department of Justice, we learned as we fought — and won. The organization of the American Protective League reveals a curious phase of life in this republic. It could not have taken place in any other country of the world.

"A word as to the Chicago organization is in ordor," says the writer of this first report of D. J. on A. P. L.

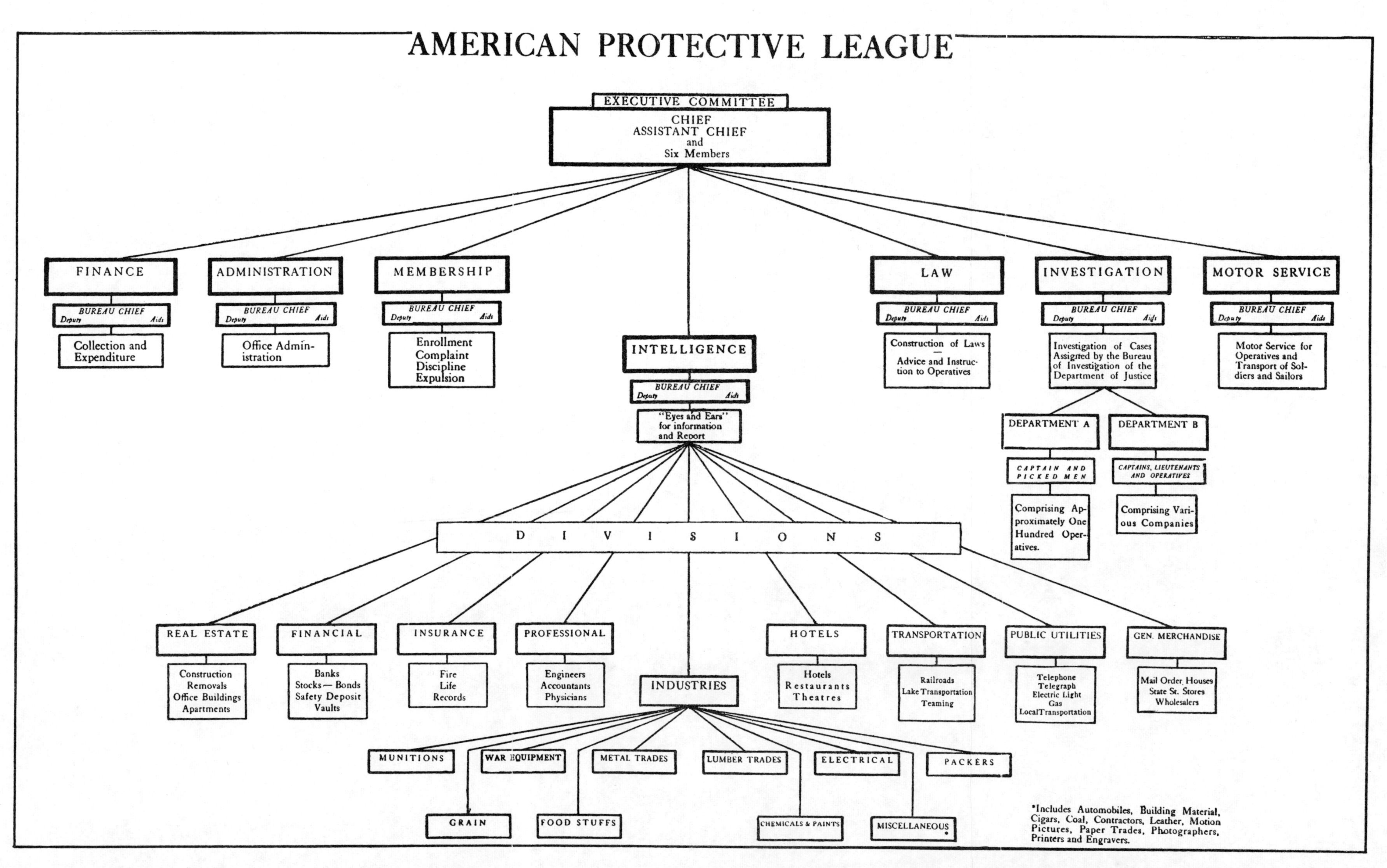
AMERICAN PROTECTIVE LEAGUE
EXECUTIVE COMMITTEE
CHIEF
ASSISTANT CHIEF
and
Six Members
FINANCE
BUREAU CHIEF
Deputy Aids
Collection and Expenditure
ADMINISTRATION
BUREAU CHIEF
Deputy Aids
Office Administration
MEMBERSHIP
BUREAU CHIEF
Deputy Aids
Enrollment
Complaint
Discipline
Expulsion
INTELLIGENCE
BUREAU CHIEF
Deputy Aids
"Eyes and Ears" for information and Report
LAW
BUREAU CHIEF
Deputy Aids
Construction of Laws
—
Advice and Instruction to Operatives
INVESTIGATION
BUREAU CHIEF
Deputy Aids
Investigation of Cases Assigned by the Bureau of Investigation of the Department of Justice
DEPARTMENT A
CAPTAIN AND PICKED MEN
Comprising Approximately One Hundred Operatives.
DEPARTMENT B
CAPTAINS, LIEUTENANTS AND OPERATIVES
Comprising Various Companies
MOTOR SERVICE
BUREAU CHIEF
Deputy Aids
Motor Service for Operatives and Transport of Soldiers and Sailors
D I V I S I O N S
REAL ESTATE
Construction
Removals
Office Buildings
Apartments
FINANCIAL
Banks
Stocks — Bonds
Safety Deposit
Vaults
INSURANCE
Fire
Life
Records
PROFESSIONAL
Engineers
Accountants
Physicians
INDUSTRIES
HOTELS
Hotels
Restaurants
Theatres
TRANSPORTATION
Railroads
Lake Transportation
Teaming
PUBLIC UTILITIES
Telephone
Telegraph
Electric Light
Gas
Local Transportation
GEN. MERCHANDISE
Mail Order Houses
State St. Stores
Wholesalers
MUNITIONS
WAR EQUIPMENT
METAL TRADES
LUMBER TRADES
ELECTRICAL
PACKERS
GRAIN
FOOD STUFFS
CHEMICALS & PAINTS
MISCELLANEOUS*
*Includes Automobiles, Building Material, Cigars, Coal, Contractors, Leather, Motion Pictures, Paper Trades, Photographers, Printers and Engravers.

"The work of the League was presumed to be to report matters of a disloyal nature that came to the attention of the members and to see that they were brought to the attention of the proper Government officials. However, the work of the agents of the Bureau itself increased so rapidly at this time that it was a physical impossibility for the small number to handle the same, and by degrees members of the League who showed aptitude for the work were called upon to assist the agents of the Bureau. *Gradually, more and more work was thrown on the League until practically all complaints coming to the Bureau by mail were turned over to the League for them to investigate.*"

If, during the later months of the war, you had visited the Department of Justice in the Federal Building in Chicago, you would have found extensive and well-equipped offices, ably manned and humming with activity. Yet the Chicago department, though large in personnel and efficient in administration, was greatly overworked in this hotbed of pro-German and enemy spy activity.

After leaving the Federal Building, let us say, you had also decided to visit the headquarters of the volunteer organization in Chicago. Less than a block away from the federal offices, in a stately building given over entirely to the housing of organizations whose sole aim and purpose was the winning of the war, you would have found a set of offices as large, as well equipped, as full of filed records, and of as able a personnel as those of the U. S. bureau. There would be this difference: the latter offices — those of the American Protective League—were run by men who got no pay—and there were almost one hundred times as many of them as there were of the D. J. workers. Yet the two great organizations are parts of the same system, and have worked together in perfect harmony and mutual benefit. Together, they have held German crime and espionage helpless in Chicago all through the war.

Of course, the tremendously expensive operations of so large a secret service organization could be met only by large-handed voluntary giving on the part of private citizens. For instance, the office rent alone of the A. P. L. in Chicago ran into thousands of dollars monthly. It was all carried by one public utility concern, the Commonwealth Edison Company, which turned over the needed space in a building which formerly housed its own offices. It is a part of the private history of the Department of Justice, scarcely if ever mentioned, that long before the idea of the American Protective League was broached — indeed, at the time when we had just severed diplomatic relations with Germany — Mr. Samuel Insull, afterward Chairman of the State Council of Defense for Illinois, called on Mr. Clabaugh and offered financial aid to the Bureau of Investigation. He said: "I know how meager your resources are, and I believe there is a lot of trouble not far ahead. Let me know if you need men or money, and I'll see that you get both." This, of course, had nothing to do with the later organization of the League, nor with the idea on which it is based, but Mr. Clabaugh always has said that Mr. Insull was the first private citizen to his knowledge to offer financial aid to the U. S. Government.

The public has heard more of "D. J." than it has of "A. P. L." for obvious reasons. Of the two great office systems, one has been running for many years as a known part of the Federal Government. The other was two years old, and was always secret in its work and personnel. If it ever were a question of credit or "glory," the palm must go and has gone to the Federal arm, because that is where the dénouements of cases had their home, and where publication of the printable facts originated. A. P. L. carried the evidence to the door of D. J. and stopped. It started cases, but did not finish them.

The public never had more than a very vague idea of the workings of the vast duo-fold machine which held life and property in America so safe in the dangerous days of the war. For instance, the average man reading newspaper mention of Mr. Clabaugh's activities as bureau head, usually thought of him as public prosecutor. He was not that. It was his duty, as it was the League's duty, only to procure testimony. His work was not of the legal branch, and he himself never has been admitted to the bar, although he — with his auxiliary, A. P. L.— has won the largest and most stubbornly fought criminal cases in the history of the country, and is devoutly feared to-day by countless I. W. W.'s not yet arrested.

The story of all these curiously interactive agencies, official and amateur, is indeed the greatest detective story in the world, and it is very difficult to measure it in full, or to visualize it in detail, so simply did it all happen, so naturally, so swiftly and so much as a matter of course. There is no like proof in history of the ability of the American people to govern itself and to take care of itself. Mr. Clabaugh's vivid and accurate story will bear out all these statements, and it is requested that it be read by all who wish a clear and consecutive acquaintance with the history of the American Protective League. Attention is again called to it as printed in full in Appendix A.

CHAPTER IV

THE LEAGUE IN WASHINGTON

Summary of the League's Results Throughout the United States — Report of the National Directors — Facts, Figures and Totals for All the Divisions.

Facts now may be made public property which until lately might not have been divulged. We therefore shall find profit now in studying the central organization by means of which the aroused Americans combined to fight the hidden forces of their unscrupulous enemy. The origin and growth, the general plans and methods of the American Protective League, have been explained; and it will now be well, before we pass on to the specific story of the League's activities, to give some idea of the wide-reaching consolidation of those activities which followed upon the establishment of the National Headquarters.

The report of any official may seem dry and formal, but the records should be made to show how America's amateur Scotland Yard organized to fight the forces of Germany all over America. This portion of the League's story is therefore of great value to anyone desirous of knowing the logical steps by which the League developed into a truly national institution.

The liaison officer of the National Directors, Captain Charles Daniel Frey, made his report and summary of November, 1918, to Colonel K. C. Masteller of the General Staff, Chief of the negative branch of the Military Intelligence Division. This report was a general assembling of the national activities of the League up to the time of the signing of the Armistice. Certain extracts are made in consonance with the general outline above indicated. It should be noted that this report covers only a portion of the League's work in Washington. The Department of

Justice figures, as was to be expected, exceeded those of any other branch of the League's work. The War Department totals were also very high — evidence of service rendered by the League which the War Department always has been very courteous and grateful in acknowledging. Captain Frey's report reads:

SIR: In compliance with your request, we beg to submit the following statement of service rendered the War Department by the American Protective League. As you know, local divisions of the League are in operation in practically all towns and cities of substantial size throughout the United States, and the League has been extended, through a plan of county organization, generally throughout the rural communities. It is not possible to submit to you an accurate classified statement of the aggregate of all of the work done throughout the country. We are able, however, to present a general statement of the activities of the League for the War Department of the United States, with a detailed report of the work of the local divisions in one hundred communities of the country. The total population of these communities is approximately one-seventh of the population of the entire country.

The work of the American Protective League for the Military Intelligence Division of the War Department began soon after the entry of the United States into the war. When the National Headquarters of the League were established in Washington in November, 1917, the National Directors conferred with Colonel R. H. Van Deman regarding a plan for wider service throughout the entire country. One of the National Directors was commissioned in the army, assigned to the Military Intelligence Division and detailed to the work of the League. In April, 1918, a department of the League was installed in the Military Intelligence Division, and since then the work has constantly grown in volume. A Captain in the Military Intelligence is now in charge, and at the present time thirty-six employes are working in the Section.

The increase in the volume of work is clearly shown by the records. Investigations directed by the Section in May, 1918, numbered 819; in June, 1777; in July, 2382; in August, 3617; in September, 6736; and in October, 6604. These investigations were of applicants for overseas service for the Y. M. C. A., Red Cross, Knights of Columbus, Jewish Welfare, Salvation Army, and other civilian organizations; of applicants for commissions and employment in various Departments of the Army, including the Quartermaster Department, Surgeon General's Office, Department of Aeronautics, Ordnance Department, Signal Corps, Army Chaplain Service, Chemical Warfare Service, etc. They also included investigations on counter-espionage matters, German propaganda, deserters, slackers and various other miscellaneous cases, all of which was made at the direct request of the heads of the different sections of the Military Intelligence Division at Washington.

The character of this work differs in no way from that of the Department of Military Intelligence having to do with Negative Intelligence. In the one hundred local divisions referred to, the number of cases investigated and reported upon were 62,888, and upon the percentage basis, the number handled throughout the country would be 440,216.

The League has likewise exerted itself in enlisting the aid of the public in reporting enemy activities, disloyalties and evasions of the war statutes. In various cities, bulletins have been posted in prominent places, including street cars, office buildings and places of public gathering, requesting citizens to report to the American Protective League all such cases coming to their knowledge. Much important information resulted from this practice.

Because of the fact that the members of the League continue to follow their daily vocations and maintain their normal connections with the community, they are afforded unusual opportunities for the investigation of radical organizations of all kinds. The League has been able to introduce members into all of the more important organizations, and to report upon their policies and activities as well as upon the activities of individual members. The number of investigations of this character carried on in the one hundred divisions referred to were 3,645; or 25,515 for the entire country. As most of these were extended, and in many cases involved a complete report upon the local organization as a whole, the figures represent a very considerable amount of work. Under this heading are included investigations of the I. W. W., the W. I. I. U., pacifist organizations of many kinds, the Peoples Council, the League of Humanity, the Non-Partisan League, the Russellites and certain Socialistic movements. Sabotage investigations and conscientious objectors are also included.

In connection with the development of the overseas service of the Red Cross, Y. M. C. A., Knights of Columbus, Jewish Welfare, Salvation Army and other civilian organizations of like character, the necessity arose for the careful investigation of the character, history and connections of civilian applicants to such service. Fortunately, the Military Intelligence finally took over the entire work of passing upon the character and loyalty of applicants, and relieved the League of the responsibility of directly advising the organizations concerned of the outcome of the investigations. The Military Intelligence then called upon the League as its agent to make the larger part of the investigations. By this method the name of the investigator and of the individual responsible for the decision remains undisclosed, and the judgment is in that sense impersonal.

The League likewise made investigations of a large number of applicants for commissions in various Divisions of the War Department, including applicants for Chaplaincies.

Investigations as to character and loyalty reached a very large total. The number aggregates 30,166, including certain investigations made prior to the establishment of the League section in the Military Intelligence Division at Washington.

On January 12, 1918, the National Directors issued a bulletin calling upon all local divisions to make full report upon the rumors, current in their communities, which were harmful to the interest of the United States in the prosecution of the war. As a result of this inquiry, a large amount of information was gathered, complete copies of which were turned over to the Military Intelligence Division for its files.

In view of the fact that a large number of members of the American Protective League enlisted in the military service or were inducted into the draft, the League was requested by the Military Intelligence Division to procure the names of all such men, with their record, in order that the Military Intelligence might avail itself of their services within the military forces if it so desired.

In addition to the foregoing, miscellaneous investigations for the Military Intelligence were carried on in considerable volume. These included cases of impersonation of army officers, visé of passports, bribery, theft and embezzlement, and a variety of other cases. These miscellaneous investigations in the local divisions referred to aggregate 19,556, or 136,892 for the country at large.

On June 5, 1917, the date of the first registration, approximately eighty thousands of members of the League throughout the country assisted at the registration polls, giving advice and assistance to registrants under the law and aiding the officials in all possible ways. In the larger cities, particularly those with large foreign born populations, great congestion resulted because of the ignorance of the law and its provisions on the part of registrants, and because of the difficulty in ascertaining and transcribing correctly their names and other information regarding them. The number of places for registration proved insufficient because of the shortness of the hours, and in many places great confusion resulted. Acting under proper instructions, members of the League in large numbers served as volunteer registrants under the direction of the officials.

On February 6, 1918, the Provost Marshal General and the Attorney General of the United States united in a request to the American Protective League to coöperate with all local and district exemption boards throughout the United States in locating and causing to present themselves to the proper authorities delinquents under the Selective Service Regulations, including those classed as deserters. Thereupon each local division assigned certain members to the Local and District Boards within its jurisdiction. These activities are of many varieties and include the investigation of Board Members, conspiracies and bribery, conspiracies to obstruct the draft, draft evasion in all forms, fraudulent attempts at deferred classification, false claims for exemption, failures to report for examination, failures to report for mobilization, failures to file questionnaires, failures to register, failures to secure final classification, failures to notify local boards of changes in address, failures to ascertain present status from the Local Board, failures to entrain, and all other alleged infractions of the regulations. These investigations made by the one hundred local divisions total 323,349. Upon a percentage basis, the cases handled throughout the country would total 2,263,443, and including the slacker raids, an enormous figure which cannot well be estimated.

Many investigations under the Local Boards were made with extreme difficulty because of the confusion in the spelling of names, inaccurate records and constantly shifting addresses due to the roaming character of the individual. We believe that the Provost Marshal General's office will confirm the statement that the number of delinquents and deserters of this character is very great, possibly exceeding two hundred thousands, a group recruited mostly from laborers, harvesters and the other ranks of homeless unskilled labor. Members of the League have given a great amount of time and energy to these cases.

During the two or three months following the day of first registration, a general effort was made by local divisions of the League in the principal cities to run down those individuals within the draft age who had failed to register on June 5, 1917. In Chicago, a city-wide drive was made during which all stations of the railroads entering Chicago were covered by League operators, and the downtown or loop district was likewise patroled. This was the first organized effort on a large scale to enforce the regulations. Subsequently similar action was taken in other cities.

In the early summer and fall of 1918 many slacker drives were conducted throughout the country. They were made under the direction of the officials of the Department of Justice with the active assistance of the Local Divisions of the American Protective League. Effective drives occurred in Cleveland, Detroit, St. Louis, Philadelphia, New York, Chicago, Minneapolis, St. Paul, Davenport, Dayton and many cities of lesser size throughout the country.

As a result of a single drive in one city, according to the report of the Division Superintendent of the Bureau of Investigation of the Department of Justice, approximately five hundred men were sent to camp as deserters and four thousand delinquents were apprehended. These drives as a whole were carried on with the acquiescence and with the general satisfaction of the public at large, and with the minimum of embarrassment to the individuals concerned. The New York city drive presented an exception where certain difficulties arose.

As a result of these drives, several hundred thousand men were examined throughout the country; tens of thousands who had failed to comply with the requirements of the Selective Service Regulations were compelled to go to their District Boards to make good their delinquencies, and many thousand delinquents and deserters were inducted into the army who otherwise might have escaped service.

Members of the League have apprehended many camp deserters and soldiers absent without leave. They have investigated thousands of requests for furloughs where the soldier claimed illness at home or made other claims. Many fraudulent requests were uncovered by these investigations. These investigations, in the one hundred divisions referred to, number 3,478.

Early in April, 1918, the National Directors conferred with Mr. Fosdick and other officials of the Department of Training Camp activities, and with the officials of the Department of Justice, with regard to developing a plan for the successful enforcement of Section 13 of the Selective Service Act and the regulations thereunder,—the section referred to having to do with the protection of the military and naval forces of the United States from the evil influences of vice and prostitution in the vicinity of the camps. In the one hundred divisions referred to, the number of investigations was 5,866, or in the country at large, 41,062.

In addition to the foregoing, the reports from local divisions indicate that they have made a large number of investigations of a general character for the War Department, including a variety of subjects. Mention should also be made of a considerable amount of service rendered to the Foreign Recruiting Missions in locating slackers and deserters and in making miscellaneous investigations of individuals.

On March 18, 1918, the Military Intelligence Branch of the War Department requested the American Protective League to procure for that Department, for immediate use for intelligence purposes, photographs, drawings and descriptions of bridges, buildings, towns and localities, then occupied by the German forces in France, Belgium and Luxemburg, and likewise in that portion of Germany lying west of a line running north and south through Hamburg. In compliance with that request, National Headquarters issued a bulletin to all Local Divisions, calling upon the entire organization of the League throughout the country to engage in the work, and prescribing a detailed method for carrying it on. The result of the work, and the appreciation of the Military Intelligence Branch, was expressed to the League in a letter from Lieutenant Colonel Coxe, under date of June 11, 1918, in which he quotes a letter from Colonel Nolan, chief of the Military Intelligence Force abroad, to the effect that the material contained much information of value and that "the citizens of the United States who donated the above articles and the League which collected them have done something which definitely helps toward the success of the operations of our army."

Summing up the actual investigations made by the American Protective League in the one hundred local divisions referred to, the grand total of cases reported by these divisions is 448,950. As has been shown, the jurisdiction of these divisions embraces approximately one-seventh of the whole population of the country covered by all of the local divisions of the League, and while some of the work reported by the one hundred divisions is not duplicated elsewhere, yet the reverse is true, and it may fairly be said that the entire number of cases handled by the League for the War Department throughout the country is seven times the above figure, or more than three million.

In conclusion, we beg to state that it has been the policy to coöperate with all local, State and Federal departments in enforcing the war laws of the United States. Our Local Chiefs have been able to establish cordial relations with all local police, sheriffs, fish and game wardens, fire wardens, and other officials whose assistance has been invaluable in many cases, and have likewise gained the friendly interest and support of County and State officials generally as well as of the Judicial Departments.

We have not attempted to set forth in this communication the volume of work done for the Department of Justice.

A very prominent phase of work in which the A. P. L. was of use to the War Department is covered very well by the comment of the Department of Justice regarding the law under which the American Army was raised:

The most important of the war laws is the selective-service act. Cases under this act are of three general kinds—first, the violation of the act by the military eligibles themselves; that is, the failure to register in accordance with the registration system under the draft, the failure to file a questionnaire, the making of false exemption claims, the failure to report for examination, etc. As soon as a man becomes a deserter, he comes under the jurisdiction of the military authorities and is turned over to them. Up to that point, however, if he does not fully comply with the law and the Selective-Service Regulations, he is subject to prosecution by this department. As the main object of the law is the raising of an army and not the filling of a prison, the department seeks to deliver to the military authorities for military service all offenders subject to military service and physically fit therefor, except those who willfully and rebelliously refuse military service and can be subjected to substantial punishment.

The second class of cases concerns the acts of those who, not themselves subject to military service, induce violations of the act, such as making false exemption claims for others, inducing others to resist military service or evade the law. This classification also includes violations of duty on the part of members of the exemption boards.

The third class of cases relates to the violation of those sections which aim to protect training and mobilization camps from the evil influence of the liquor traffic or prostitution within the neighborhood of the camp. The first class of cases has thrown upon the representatives of this department throughout the country an immense amount of work. This work has consisted in part of prosecuting deliberate violations of the law. In far larger measure, however, it has consisted in locating, apprehending, and delivering to local boards or Army officials many thousands of men who for various reasons have failed to appear for physical examination, failed to file questionnaires, etc. *Down to July 1, 1918, the department had thus investigated 220,747 cases of this character and caused induction into military service of 23,439 men.*

A curious personal quality attaches to the study of the work of the American Protective League, which is perhaps attributable to the fact that all the members were amateurs only and altogether unpaid. No doubt, did space and formal limitations permit, a very widespread comment on the personal relations of the members of the League to the League itself would be acceptable to many readers. Within the limits available, however, a certain martial severity and impersonality must be employed. None the less, there ought to be some brief mention made of the work of the National Directors after the establishment of the Washington office. In this connection it is fitting that the names of those men should be mentioned who labored so earnestly and so well to make the work of A. P. L. of vital importance in the winning of the war.

NATIONAL DIRECTORS AND OFFICERS OF ADMINISTRATION OF THE AMERICAN PROTECTIVE LEAGUE

A. M. Briggs, *Chairman*
Charles Daniel Frey
Victor Elting
National Directors — *November, 1917*

S. S. Doty
In charge Bureau of Organization — *February, 1918*

Captain George P. Braun, Jr.
In charge Bureau of Investigation — *June, 1918*

Charles F. Lorenzen
In charge Bureau of Investigation — *September, 1918*

James D. Stover
In charge Bureau of Administration — *September, 1918*

Daniel V. Casey
Editor of The Spy Glass — *May, 1918*

Lieutenant Urban A. Lavery
In charge A. P. L. branch at Military Intelligence — *April, 1918*

Captain John T. Evans
In charge A. P. L. branch at Military Intelligence — *September, 1918*

The enormous growth of the American Protective League in so short a time is sufficient evidence in itself that a vast, pressing need existed for the service it rendered. Indeed, the great local activity of the League became a national activity in record time. Reports piled in from all over the country; the detail of correspondence became enormous; the filing of records an endless task. All at once the National Directors of the American Protective League found they had taken over a business—one of the largest businesses with which any one of them had ever been identified. It would not be too much to say that they worked day and night for a long period. Their task was a very heavy one, but they brought to it a knowledge of large business affairs and a quality of perseverance which saw them through.

The original headquarters of the League were at 1537 Eye Street, Northwest, an old Washington residence—a quaint and none too convenient business home. All the directors lived in the upper part of this building, and such was the crowded and impractical form of Washington life at the time that they were glad to sleep and sometimes cook their meals in the same building where they did their work. Such a thing as rest or leisure were unknown for two years' time. No one who has not been in part acquainted with Washington in war times knows the handicap under which all such work needed to be done. Transportation, living accommodations, clerical help—everything, in that period of the war, became a problem or an obstacle of a very considerable sort. It was faith and enthusiasm which carried these men through, as was the case with their associates all over America.

So, gradually, from this central office, the web of the American Protective League was extended until it reached into every state and territory of the Union, and until each line of communication was one of interchange of intelligence from and to the central headquarters. It is only by reference to the portion of this history marked as "The Four Winds"—showing briefs of reports from all over the Union —that any just knowledge can be gained of the tremendous volume of work done by the central headquarters. Nor does the assemblage offered give more than a mere indication of that volume, because thousands of reports have, for reasons of space, received no notice whatever, unfair as that must always seem to everyone identified with the compilation of this history.

In the fall of 1918, headquarters were moved from 1537 Eye Street to 1719 H Street, Northwest, another old time Washington residence of stately sort, which remained the home of the National Headquarters until the signing of the Armistice and the dissolution of the League itself. Here Mr. Briggs, Captain Frey and Mr. Elting remained until the end of the game in charge of a loyal band of workers. For all of these men, and those associated with them, there remain the recollection of a hectic two years of high speed work, in connection with financial loss to everyone engaged in it.

CHAPTER V

THE LAW AND ITS NEW TEETH

Insufficiency of the Espionage Laws at the Outbreak of the War — Getting Results — The Amended Espionage Act — The Law of 1798 Revived — Statement of the Attorney General of the United States.

If predisposed to alien enemy sympathy, a critic might declare that the League was made up of individual buccaneers, who did high-handed things and escaped punishment therefor only because of the general confusion due to a state of war. Nothing could be more unjust or farther from the truth than such a belief. On the contrary, the League and the Department of Justice as well felt continually held back and hampered by respect for laws admittedly inadequate.

We had matured a great system of jurisprudence, sufficient for ordinary needs. Moreover, when war began, we had passed more laws adjusted to the new needs; but it is a curious fact that, threatened as we were by Germany's perfected system of espionage and propaganda, we had no actual statute by which we adequately could cope with it until May, 1918—more than a year after we went to war, and less than six months before the end of the war.

In the spring of 1918, the National Directors began, under the editorship of Daniel V. Casey, the issue of a League organ or confidential bulletin, called "The Spy Glass." The first number of the publication, in June of that year, took up the amended Espionage Act, which was the base of practically all of the A. P. L. and D. J. work during the war. This amendment rebuilt and stiffened the original Espionage Act of June 15, 1917, which had been found insufficient, and "put teeth in the law," as the Attorney General's office phrased it. "The Spy Glass" printed a digest of the new enactment, which is of essential interest at this point of the League's story as it determined the whole character of the

League's later activities. This summarization of the Espionage Act is printed as Appendix C in the present volume.

Up to the close of 1917, we had had, duly amended, many national statutes covering treason and sedition, foreign and hostile connections, pretending to be an officer, enticing to desertion or strikes, trespassing at military places, falsely claiming citizenship, aiding or counseling offense, wearing uniform unlawfully, conspiracy, neutrality, counterfeiting seals, use of mails, trading with the enemy, censorship, foreign language news items, sabotage, etc., as well as many specific enactments controlling persons liable for military service, and covering the increase of the army, the questions of evasion, desertion, etc. These powers, broad as they were already, were extended under the blanket power of the Articles of War, to cover fraud, desertion, mutiny, insubordination, misbehavior before the enemy, traitors and spies, murder, rape and other crimes, and the general conduct and dicipline of those in military service.

Not even all these laws, however, were found to stand the extreme demands put on the country by thousands of new and wholly unforeseen exigencies. As a matter of fact, one of the most useful of all our laws against enemy aliens and spies was one not up-to-date at all, but dating back to Revolutionary times; that is to say, July 6, 1798![1]

This old law was unearthed by the agents of the Department of Justice. It gave almost blanket powers to the President of the United States, and it was under the President's proclamations, based on that old law, that most of the early internment arrests were made. The old law, long disused, was found to work perfectly still! It was extended in force by the regulations controlling enemy aliens.[2]

It became the duty of the newly organized League to take on the accumulation of testimony under all these new laws; and what that was to mean may be forecast from the comment of the Attorney General of the United States in his annual report for 1918:

> The so-called Espionage Act contains a variety of provisions on different subjects, such as neutrality, protection of

[1] See Appendix D for text of this law.
[2] See Appendix E for text of the President's proclamation for the regulation of alien enemies.

ships in harbor, spy activities, unlawful military expeditions, etc. Most of the cases which have arisen, however, presenting the most complex problems, have been under the third section of Title I of this act, which is aimed at disloyal and dangerous propaganda.

This section 3 was amended by a law which became effective May 18, 1918, commonly called the Sedition Act, which greatly broadened the scope of the original act and brought under its prohibitions many new types of disloyal utterance. The use which our enemies have made of propaganda as a method of warfare is especially dangerous in any country governed by public opinion. During the first three years of the war, the period of our neutrality, the German Government and its sympathizers expended here a vast amount of money in carrying on different types of propaganda, and these activities are a matter of public knowledge. During our participation in the war, section 3 and its later amendment have been the only weapons available to this Government for the suppression of insidious propaganda, and it is obvious that no more difficult task has been placed upon our system of law than the endeavor to distinguish between the legitimate expression of opinion and those types of expression necessarily or deliberately in aid of the enemy. The number of complaints under this law presented to the Department of Justice has been incredibly large.

Such, then, was the ultimate machinery of our national laws when, late, but with such speed as a willing Congress could give after the gauntlet was flung and the issue joined, we began to face in dead earnest the peril of the times. We now had at last a full set of laws with teeth in them. But it was a tremendous burden that the older institutions of our administrative machinery had to carry. In sooth, the load was too much. The machinery buckled under it. We could not do the work we had to get done.

That work was more than ever had been asked of any nation of the world. We had a mixed population of wholly unknown disposition. Some said we delayed going to war for so long because we were not sure our people would back the Government. That, surely, could be the only reason for the delay. All the races of the world were seething in rage and jealousy. We had racial war within our borders. We could not count on our own friends. We could not predict as to what percent of men would be loyal to our flag. We had two million men of German blood inside our borders, guaranteed by their Kaiser to be loyal to Germany. And long before we had gone to war, we had had abundant proof of their disloyalty to us, of their hatred for Britain and France, and their discontent with our own neutrality. We had openly been warned by the German Kaiser that he counted on the loyalty to Germany of many or most of these men. Fear alone held the average pro-German back. But it did not hold back their seasoned spies and the agents who worked under cover. The sudden cessation of pro-German talk which fell when we declared war deceived none but the pacifists. The boasts of German-Americans as to their holdings in Liberty Bonds deceived not at all the men who had sat and listened on the inside; for even at this time the records were piling up—records of private acts and words of treason to America which had been noted by the A. P. L. The full record of German craft and duplicity, of treachery and treason to America, never will be made public. It was alike a loathsome and a dangerous thing.

Obviously, the hands of our Government sorely needed upholding. Who was to do that? Who would apply all these laws now that we had them? Who should watch two million tight-mouthed men whose homes were here but whose hearts were still in Germany? Who could cope with 300,000 spies, in part trained and paid spies, many of whom were sent over to America long before Germany declared the war which was "forced" on her?

That was what the American Protective League already was doing when war was declared; it is what it has done ever since, loyalty, patiently, indefatigably, to an enormous and unknown extent, in an unbelievable variety of detail. If ever you have held its members irresponsible or deemed them actuated by any but good motives, cease to do so now. Beyond all men of this generation they have proven that patriotism is not dead.

The enforcement of the President's proclamation governing the conduct of enemy aliens in this country entailed a tremendous amount of D. J. work, the larger part of which devolved upon the agents of the League. Thousands of investigations of alien Germans were made under its provisions. Numerically speaking, however, the work in that imperatively necessary line yielded to the more thankless labor of slacker and deserter hunting.

The function of the League in all these matters is obvious. No case at law will "stick" unless supported by competent testimony. We have seen that the League was organized for the collection of evidence, and for nothing else. Limited as its power was, it really saved the day for our hard-pressed country. It increased our Army by many thousands of evaders whom it found and turned over to the military authorities. It put hundreds of aliens into internment. It apprehended plotters and prevented consummation of conspiracies beyond number. It kept down the danger of that large disloyal element, and held Germany in America safe while we went on with the open business of war in the field. It is by no means too much to say that much of the Kaiser's disappointment over his German-American revolt was due not so much to any loyalty to the American flag—for of all of our racial representatives, the Germans are the most clannishly and tenaciously loyal to their own former flag—as it was to fear of the silent and stern hand searching out in the dark and taking first one and then another German or pro-German away from the scenes that erstwhile had known him. It was *fear* that held our enemy population down—*fear* and nothing else. It was the League's silent and mysterious errand to pile up good reason for that fear.

At the crack of war, certain hundreds of dangerous aliens were interned at once. They simply vanished, that was all, behind the walls of camps or of prisons. It will be mistaken mercy if we shall not deport thousands more when we shall have the time deliberately to do that. *Fear* is the one thing such men understand. Honor and loyalty, terms interdependent and inseparable, are unknown to them. Too many Germans loved America only because they made money easily here. Their real flag still was across the sea, except as they had raised it here in their churches and their schools.

It was sometimes rumored that many spies were shot secretly in America. That would have been done in Germany—as witness the deaths of Edith Cavell and others. It was not done here. We did not kill a single spy, a single traitor,—more is the pity. By reason of the fact that we had outspied Germany's vaunted espionage, we nipped in the bud none knows how many plots and conspiracies which otherwise would have matured in ruin to life and property.

We did not shoot known spies, but we garroted them in the dark and hurried them to jail. That agency of the law is best, after all, which keeps crime from becoming crime. We did not wait for overt acts—we filled our prisons before the acts were done! That is why the public was obliged to romance as to German spies. They are in jail. The report of the Department of Justice itself, of June, 1918, on these war activities will in this connection prove interesting reading:

> During the period of American neutrality many persons were prosecuted for criminal acts connected with efforts to aid the belligerents. Some of these cases were still pending when the United States declared war on Germany. A very satisfactory standard of success was attained in the ante-bellum prosecutions. Almost before the ink had dried on the proclamation of April 6, 1917, a select company of dangerous Germans were gathered in by the United States Marshals. These prisoners were believed to be potential, and in some cases actual leaders of pro-German plots and propaganda. Subsequent discoveries have quite fully confirmed this belief. Recently a most authoritative document was found to contain among other matters the names of several gentlemen whom the German Government trusted to carry on its work here unofficially after the withdrawal of the official representatives. Of these, all were arrested on April 6, 1917, save one who had already left the country. This disposal of the German leaders had effects which have been continually reflected in the disjointed and sporadic character of hostile outbreaks.
>
> One of the most recent, most novel, and most important of the Department's efforts is the denaturalization of disloyal citizens of foreign origin. Many natives of Germany or Austria, sheltered from summary internment by their acquired citizenship and clever enough to avoid the commission of actual crime, have insulted and injured this government at every opportunity. *Fortunately the naturalization law contains a clause permitting the cancellation of citizenship papers obtained by fraud.* Without waiting for further legislation, which is apparently on the way, the Department has assailed a number of defendants believed to have made fraudulent mental reservations of loyalty to their native countries. Several of these cases have already ended victoriously for the government. More than one defeated defendant has been interned.
>
> Meanwhile the summary arrests have continued. From week to week through 1917 their numbers steadily increased. Since

about the beginning of 1918, the rate has been more nearly constant.

Extremists have advocated the universal internment of alien enemies, somewhat after the English practice. Now, Great Britain interned permanently rather fewer than seventy thousand alien enemies. *The United States would be compelled to intern at least eight hundred thousand Germans and more than twice as many Austrians.* The colossal expense of maintaining this horde in idleness — civilian prisoners of war are far more useless than convicts, because they may not be forced to work — is too obvious to need discussion.

More temperate critics say that there have been too few arrests, too low a proportion of internments, and too high a proportion of paroles. As to the first and second charges, it is a sufficient answer that conditions have improved instead of becoming worse. A policeman's record should not be judged by the number of people he has put in jail, but by the kind of order maintained on his beat

In his annual report, issued December 5, 1918, subsequent to the signing of the armistice, the Attorney General stated that six thousand alien enemies had been arrested on presidential warrants, based on the old law of 1798. Of these, a "considerable number" were placed in the internment camps in charge of the Army. The majority of these were German men and women, with a certain number of Austro-Hungarians. He concludes: "I do not want to create the impression that there is no danger from German spies and German sympathizers. There are thousands of persons in this country who would injure the United States in this war if they could do so with safety to themselves. However, they are no more anxious to be hanged than you are."

The foregoing will show, to any student of the strange and complex situation which has confronted America at home these last four years, the main facts as to the emergencies we met and the means by which we met them.

The surprising thing is that we Americans have not known ourselves! A thoughtful study of the American Protective League is not a mere yawning over phrases of the law any more than it is a mere dipping into exciting or mystifying experiences. It is more than that. It is an excursion into a new and unexplored region in America—into the very heart of America itself.

CHAPTER VI

GERMAN PROPAGANDA

How the Poison was Spread — The Press — The Pulpit — The Word-of-Mouth Rumor — Various Canards Directed Against American Morale — Stories and Instances of the Hun's Subtlety.

Germany made two mistakes—one in beginning the war, the other in losing it. The world has reckoned with her far otherwise than as she hoped. Now she learns what it is to feel defeat. Shrewd as the shrewdest, more patient than the most patient, not lacking courage while victory was with her—yet always showing that peculiar German clumsiness of intellect—Germany fought with trained skill on both sides the sea. The world knows the story of the battles in France. Let us now study the battles fought in silence in America.

In actual practice the various secret methods which the Germans employed in America could not always be defined one from the other. A certain confusion and over-lapping existed between the spy systems and those of propaganda and sabotage. Often one man might practice all three. The purpose of this chapter is to take the humblest form of German secret work in America, that practiced by the least skilled and most numerous branch of her spies—the sort of thing which usually is classified as propaganda.

Let no one undervalue the work of propaganda. No army is better than its morale, and no army's morale is better than that of the people which send it to the front. The entire purpose of enemy propaganda is to lessen the morale either of an army or a people; and that precisely was Germany's purpose with us.

Anything is good propaganda which makes a people nervous, uneasy or discontented. Many of the stories which Germany spread in America seemed clumsy at first, they were so easily detected. Yet they did their work, even though sometimes it would have seemed that the rumors put out were against Germany and not for her. These rumors, repeated and varied, did serve a great purpose in America—they made us restless and uneasy. That certainly is true.

One of the favorite objects of the German propaganda was the Red Cross work. Hardly any American but has heard one or other story about the Red Cross. The result has been a very considerable lessening of the public confidence in that great organization. The average man never runs down any rumor of this sort. At first he does not believe what he hears. At the fourth or fifth story of different sorts, all aiming at one object, he begins to hesitate, to doubt. Without any question, the Red Cross has suffered much from German propaganda. Not that this organization should be called perfect, for such was not the case with any war organization. Not that the Y. M. C. A. work was perfect, for it was far from that. But the point is that all of these organizations, all the war charities, all the war relief organizations, were more nearly perfect than German propaganda has allowed us to believe. The most cruel and malicious statements against the Red Cross, wholly without foundation, were made, with apparent feeling of all lack of responsibility, by German-loving persons in all parts of the country. A complaint came to Washington Headquarters all the way from Portland, Oregon. Comment is unnecessary:

> I am informed that one Bertha A———, who is in the Government service, Bureau of Aircraft Production, Executive Department, Cable Section, office in "D" Building, 4½ Missouri Avenue, Washington, D. C., has written a letter to a friend of hers here that a ward in one of the hospitals in Washington had been set aside for some seventy-five girls who were working in the different bureaus in Washington and had become pregnant since arriving in Washington; and that it was rumored that there were about three hundred in addition to the above who had been sent home for the same reason. Would suggest that she be interviewed. We will look up her antecedents here and if possible secure the letter which she has written or copy thereof. Upon being advised that such a letter had been written, I interviewed the husband of the lady to whom the letter was written, he being bailiff in one of the circuit courts here, and he stated that the quotation as made above was substantially correct.

Nearly everyone has heard the story of the Red Cross sweater which had a five-dollar bill pinned to it for the lucky unknown soldier who might be the recipient. This sweater is always reported to have been sold and to have turned up in some part of America with the proof attached to it. In no instance has there been any foundation for this rumor. A like baselessness marks the stories of Red Cross graft and misappropriation of funds and waste of money. No doubt there was a certain amount of inefficiency in this work; but that the Red Cross was looted or conducted by dishonest persons was never believed to be true even by the German agents who started the stories.

During the time of the influenza epidemic, a common story was that doctors had been found spreading influenza germs in the cantonments. It was reported, as no doubt every reader will remember, that two doctors had been shot in one post. Sometimes the story would come from a man who got it from an enlisted man who had been one of the firing squad who had executed several doctors in this way. There was not a word of truth in any of this. The inoculation propaganda was German propaganda, pure and simple. It might not seem clear how such mendacity could be of direct help to Germany; but it had this result—it made American mothers and fathers more uneasy about their sons. It made them want to keep their boys at home.

The powdered glass rumor was one of the most widely spread instances of German propaganda. Who has not heard it divulged in secrecy by some woman, with the injunction that not a word must be said about it? A German nurse had been detected putting powdered glass in the rolled surgical bandages in the Red Cross work rooms. She had disappeared before she could be arrested, and she had not left her name. That mysterious German woman who worked with the Red Cross is still absent. The rumors of powdered glass in bandages have been practically groundless—only one division, that in upper New Jersey, reports any case of that sort actually run down. The charges of powdered glass in food sent to the soldiers or put in tinned goods have been found equally baseless. Two cases of glass found in food stuffs are authentically reported,—both accidents, and the glass was broken and not powdered.

The charges of poisoned wells around cantonments was another canard. Rumors came out that horses, and men also, had been killed by the poisoned water. The entire investigating force of the United States has found one case of poisoned water in a horse trough in West Virginia—and no horse drank of it. The charges about poisoned court-plaster were proved to be equally groundless—indeed, they would seem to be of small reason in any case, because, if Germany was putting out the court-plaster, why should she speak of it; and why should America put it out at all? The psychology of it is this: anything which makes the people feel uneasy or anxious is good propaganda for the enemy.

Stories were spread very widely at one time that Canada and England were not practicing food conservation—that we were shipping our food to England and she was eating it without reservation, whereas we were denying ourselves sugar and butter. Perhaps you had best talk with someone who lived in England during the war as to the truth of that. It was one of the many German lies. There was the charge that the price of gasoline was due to the fact that the Standard Oil Company was dumping and wasting large quantities of gasoline. There was nothing in that, of course.

The report of Polish pograms, general Jew killing expeditions by the Poles, were magnified and distorted, all with the purpose of making both the Poles and Jews dissatisfied with the conduct of the war. Continually these anti-Ally stories got out, and always they were hard to trace.

This form of propaganda, spread by word of mouth, was the most insidious and most widely spread of all forms. It was, of course, made the more easy by the excited state of mind of the people during war times. You will remember that you yourself bought more newspapers than you ever did in your life—you looked for new headlines, new sensations, all the time. At home, your wife also was eager for sensations, for the news, for the gossip. It was ready for her and every member of her family, and her neighbors and neighbors' families. The spread of a rumor is not governed by the laws of evidence; and hearsay testimony rarely is given twice the same—it always grows.

Into this form of German propaganda came spite work against German-Americans who themselves were loyal. A great deal of League activity had to do with running down rumors against persons declared to be pro-German. Sometimes these things were found baseless; and again enough pro-Germanism was found to warrant a stern rebuke.

Sometimes, public speakers, well trained in their tasks, put out propaganda which at the time seemed an innocent statement of facts. To the Lake Placid Club of New York came a certain "Belgian officer" who spoke very good English, and who purported to be able to tell all about the war. He made a long speech, regarding which many members of the local Red Cross complained bitterly to the American Protective League. This man's talk, while purporting to be that of an ally of this country, was really German propaganda. He denied or justified German atrocities, deplored Red Cross knitting, declared it would take ten million Americans to beat the Germans; that they were going into a hell of vermin, dirt and disease; that our army as yet was difficult to find. There was a German orchestra at the Club, supposed to have come from the Boston Symphony Orchestra. They all applauded vociferously when the speaker made such statements as, "After the war there will be a day of reckoning." Further details, which proved that this speaker really was spreading German propaganda, led to his being traced to New York. He was found to have worked at different times in Iowa, Kansas, and elsewhere. The last report was that he was supposed to have sailed for his native country.

There was no way, shape nor manner in which Germany did not endeavor to embarrass us. She had, besides her carefully trained public speakers, her secret workers who had assigned to them definite objectives. For instance, it was known that the negro race would furnish a considerable number of soldiers for our army. A very wide German propaganda existed among the negroes in Georgia and Carolina, and in such northern cities as Indianapolis, where large numbers of that race were located. A certain German was indicted under seven counts for this manner of activity. It was proved that he had told a great many negro privates in the army that they would be mutilated if captured, and that they were going to starve to death in France if they ever got across. The horrors of war with the American forces were pointed out to these simple people; but, on the other hand it was explained to them that if they would work for the German interests, they would be allowed to set up a government of their own in America if Germany won the war! They were told Germany loved the negroes and believed in their equality with the white race in every way, and would support their government when once her war was won! One such secret German worker among colored soldiers and civilians was M. F——— of New York, indicted under seven counts in June, 1918, under the new Espionage Law. F——— put out much the same story to frighten the negroes and make them discontented—wholesale mutilation at the hands of Germans if they were captured in France. He declared that their eyes would be gouged out and their ears cut off. He also said that Germany was allowing our transports to reach Europe unharmed because she wanted a lot of Americans in France, where, after cutting off their supplies, she intended to starve them all to death.

This looks like making out a bad case for Germany—but softly. F——— also said that, on the other hand, Germany did not want to kill the negroes if they would not fight; that if only they would work for Germany's interests, they should have their own country and their own government. Stories like this were circulated in the South and among cities in the North with a heavy negro population. F——— was the first propagandist to be caught with the goods. He was talking much with colored privates in the draft army.

Of course, a prime object of propaganda was to obstruct the draft and to prevent the shipment of munitions. It largely failed, as everyone knows. But still it cannot be said that Germany did not invest such money well as she spent on her secret pro-German propaganda in America. She knew that she had ruined Russia by propaganda. We might further have learned the danger of propaganda as a weapon had we heard the rumor that Germany herself had her collapse hastened by propaganda which Great Britain managed to spread among her people. It is a matter of history that German propaganda caused the Italian debacle in the first Austrian advance into Italy.

Nor is it to be believed that Germany has ceased in her

propaganda. She does not believe herself defeated even now. The undying occult spirit of the old Teutonic Knights still lives to-day in America. Now, you will begin to hear attempts to make us dislike England, attempts to incite Ireland to revolt against England, attempts to make us dislike France, stories that England and France owe us much for everything they gave us in the way of equipment, aeroplanes, munitions; stories that we will never get back any of the moneys we loaned to the Allies; stories of how simple and innocent the German people are, how anxious they are to be friendly to America. That is all propaganda. By this time we ought to know how to value it.

Of course, the German language papers in this country were hotbeds of propaganda and sedition. Some of them were suppressed by the censorship, some by the indignant American people who informed the courts of justice. Most of them by this time have become tame since they have seen the penitentiary sentences imposed upon the more outspoken of these German editors living in America. These foreign language papers were prominent in New York, Chicago, Milwaukee, Pittsburgh, Philadelphia, and other cities. They show the strength of German sentiment in America. Every one of them was a center of propaganda, at first outspoken, then more careful. The great majority of these papers, in order to protect their business investments, tried to cover up when they found which way the wind was setting. The censorship officers were flooded with complaints against these papers. For instance, there came all the way from Indianapolis a complaint against a paper printed in Baltimore, Maryland, "The Bavarian Weekly." A. P. L. had many extended translations of articles printed in this paper, the general tenor of which was a laudation of Germany and German methods. One wonders what Germany would have done to any American newspaper printed within the confines of Germany which might have expressed such hostile sentiments against the country harboring it.

In addition to these, there were, of course, the English language papers which for one reason or another were covertly or outspokenly in favor of Germany. Papers all the way from New York to Pueblo, Colorado, were bought or were attempted to be bought outright by German capital.

The most sensational scandals of this sort came out of New York.

It is known that in many towns the German element undertook to sow seeds of discontent in the minds of savings bank depositors. Rumors got out—no one could tell where they started—to the effect that the United States Government was going to confiscate all the savings of the people; that the bonds would never be paid off. Of course, all this was absurd, but it had its effect upon servant girls and others who were loyally putting their savings into the securities of the government. It cost a great deal of time and expense to run down such rumors.

The pulpit was a recognized part of the German system of spy work in America, as has elsewhere been noted. It is not just to accuse all Lutheran ministers of desecrating the cloth they wore. There are good Lutheran ministers who are loyal Americans without question. At the same time it is true that more charges have been brought against pastors of the Lutheran church, and charges of more specific nature, than against any other class or profession in our country. There are scores and hundreds of such reports which came into the National Headquarters of the A. P. L. from all parts of the country, more especially those parts which have heavy German settlements. These are so numerous that one cannot avoid calling the Lutheran pulpit in America one of the most active and poisonous influences which existed in America during the war. A sample report comes in from the Chief of the A. P. L. at Armour, S. D.:

> I have reported on five German Lutheran preachers of this vicinity. They are all of the same stripe — profess loyalty, but actions speak otherwise. It seems strange to me that they have such an anxiety to get into active war work in the army and navy.

In yet another and longer specification, the same chief states:

> I am becoming concerned about the large number of reports I get locally regarding German Lutheran ministers in this part of South Dakota. They are attempting to obtain

positions of trust in Government work in the army and navy. *I would not trust one of them in this part of the State. We have had trouble continually with the German communities where these ministers are located.* Twenty-nine were convicted from Tripp. . . . Our Government might as well choose men from Berlin as to select German Lutheran ministers from this part of South Dakota. It seems to me that the A. P. L. should investigate and see what is inducing all these German Lutheran ministers to apply for Government positions. If even one succeeds in obtaining an appointment, it would be an opening.

This matter went before the Military Intelligence Division in Washington and received proper handling there.

A report from Osage, Iowa, came in against a certain priest in another Iowa town. The entire record of this man is given, besides other details regarding his parentage, his education, and his conduct of his church. "Previous to the entry of the United States into the war, he upheld Germany in all particulars. Since war has been declared, he has been more careful in his speech. A service flag was dedicated in our village, which consists of but one street. The ceremonies were held in front of this man's house. He did not attend the services. The next Sunday he roasted his congregation for giving money toward the flag and told them they should give quite as much to the church. A committee of five men visited him and invited him to subscribe to the Third Loan."

One of these clerical gentlemen who have remained loyal to the Kaiser, though not to Christ, is the Reverend John Fontana, Lutheran clergyman of New Salem, North Dakota. He was convicted for preaching sedition, and got a three-year sentence in a Federal Court. This did not deter his likewise loyal Kaiserliche congregation. By a vote of fifty-seven to twenty-two the members decided to continue him as their beloved pastor. Yet this is what Judge Amidon said to Fontana when he was arraigned,—words which ought to be printed in large letters and displayed prominently in every street of every city of every portion of America. The Judge said to the prisoner:

You received your final papers as a citizen in 1898. By the oath which you then took, you renounced and abjured all allegiance to Germany and the Emperor of Germany, and swore that you would bear true faith and allegiance to the United States. What did that mean? That you would set about earnestly growing an American soul, and put away your German soul.

Have you done that? I do not think you have. You have cherished everything German and stifled everything American. You have preached German, prayed German, read German, sung German. Every thought of your mind and every emotion of your heart through all these years has been German. Your body has been in America, but your life has been in Germany. You have influenced others who have been under your ministry to do the same thing.

There have been a good many Germans before me in the last month. They have lived in this country, like yourself, ten, twenty, thirty, forty years, and they have had to give their evidence through an interpreter. It has been an impressive part of the trial. As I looked at them and tried, as best I could, to understand them, there was written all over every one of them, "Made in Germany." American life had not dimmed that mark in the least.

I do not blame you and these men alone. I blame myself. I blame my country. We urged you to come; we welcomed you; we gave you opportunity; we gave you land; we conferred upon you the diadem of American citizenship—and then we left you.

When we get through with this war, and civil liberty is made safe once more upon this earth, there is going to be a day of judgment in these United States. Foreign-born citizens and the institutions which have cherished foreigners are going to be brought to the judgment of this Republic. That day of judgment looks more to me to-day like the great Day of Judgment than anything that I have thought of for many years. There is going to be a separation on that day of the sheep from the goats. Every institution that has been engaged in this business of making foreigners perpetual in the United States will have to change — or cease. That is going to cut deep, but it is coming.

It must be pointed out that in spite of this charge of the judge, and in spite of the sentence of this minister of the gospel, his flock remained loyal to him and invited him back to preach when he got out of jail!

It has always been charged against the Germans in America that they were the most clannish of all the foreigners coming to settle in this country. They, longer than any other people, retain their own institutions, their own language, their own customs. In parts of the country there are schools which teach the German language more than they do the English—a practice which, in all likelihood, will be discontinued when the troops come back from France and Germany. Without any doubt or question, pro-German school teachers were German propagandists, usually of the indiscreet and hotheaded sort.

From Terre Haute, Indiana, comes a complaint regarding Miss Lena Neubern—that is what we will call her—a hot socialist and worse, who was a school teacher. Miss Neubern had two brothers in that city who refused to allow an American flag to be placed in front of their store, or to allow their clerks to attend the parade of the Third Liberty Loan. A committee of citizens called on them and told them "in strong term what was expected of them." Miss Neubern taught her school children, Americans, that the "Kaiser was just as good a man as President Wilson; that the United States was in this war, not for democracy, but for commercial supremacy; that the United States was as greedy as Germany; that we were controlled by England, always the enemy of the United States." Miss Neubern refused to allow the Star Spangled Banner to be sung in her room, and did all she could to hinder the sale of Thrift Stamps among the children, though in other schools large numbers of stamps had been sold. This active and intelligent young woman pleaded guilty of this charge and was dismissed by the school board. One wonders whether the German Government would have stopped at the dismissal in a similar instance!

Another form of German propagandist might have been found higher up in educational circles. The faculties of our great universities have always been made up in part of a class of men who are of the belief that intellect and scholarship are best shown by eccentricity and radicalism. More than that, we had a number of actual Germans in our university faculties in America. Since it is the proposition here to deal in concrete facts and not in mere general assertions, let us print something which came in, embodied in the report from Champaign, Illinois.

Champaign, Illinois, is the home of the University of Illinois, and for some reason university towns seem to act as chutes for all sorts of independent thought. There are two strong German settlements in Champaign County, and a very strong German settlement in the city, where many residents have shown very pro-German tendencies. These German settlements have their own German schools, taught by their German Lutheran ministers under the pretense of teaching religion. Sentiment became so intense that the local A. P. L. Chief was requested by the Government to close these schools if possible. Some of them have reopened since the armistice. In such localities the Germans have been very independent and often quite outspoken, so that it was necessary in many cases for the A. P. L. to use influence to prevent violence to them. There were only one or two cases where the citizens got out of control, although many citizens of German descent refused to buy bonds and made disparaging remarks regarding the war.

The A. P. L. Chief says: "We were confronted with the problem of ousting five alien enemies at the University of Illinois, two of them regarded as dangerous. We also had to handle a cook at the aviation barracks, an alien enemy who was deliberately wasting food. We convicted the wife of a German minister in the Federal Court for making disloyal remarks. We had some difficulty with Russellites, Mennonites, and radical Socialists, but all have been kept in hand. Our organization consists of seventy-five members, but about twenty-five of us have done most of the active work." A good and worthy twenty-five.

The reference to Russellites and Mennonites covers two regions of great A. P. L. activity. Pastor Russell, as he was known, passed away from this scene some time ago, but he left behind him seeds of discord. He was perhaps not so much disloyal as he was eccentric and fanatical in his mental habit. His book, "The Finished Mystery," was so open a plea against war that it was proscribed by the United States Government. A. P. L. operatives ran down a great deal of so-called pro-German talk which originated in the Russellites. An instance of this comes from Coloma, Michigan, which reports: "Radical socialists became active during August, 1917. Acting under instructions from the Department of Justice, we put all of these meetings out of business in the territory of our jurisdiction. No more socialist meetings of any kind here. We got information which resulted in my calling upon certain Russellites. Collected five books of 'The Finished Mystery,' and some copies of the 'Kingdom News.' Russellites were watched, and they promised to discontinue activities until after the war. They have done so."

It is not to be denied that the following of the radical banner among all nations of the world is an increasing one and one which will demand great care on the part of the governments on both sides of the Atlantic. Bolshevism is the great threat of the day, and we shall have to meet it in America as it must be met in Germany and Russia before there can be any lasting peace.

At times some of these radicals have got caught in the jaws of the amended Espionage Act, as for instance, Eugene V. Debs, the veteran Socialist candidate for the presidency, who was given three concurrent sentences of ten years each. Early in the fall of 1918, Dr. Morris Zucker, a well known Socialist in Brooklyn, was arrested on a charge of sedition and locked up. He is said to have declared that the stories of German atrocities committed by German army officers were not true and that they were circulated by capitalists in this country to further their own purposes. Dr. Zucker was of the belief that American soldiers are "make believe" soldiers. On September 6, 1918, in Philadelphia, Joseph V. Stillson, secretary of the "Kova," a Lithuanian newspaper, was caught by the Espionage Act and sentenced to three years' imprisonment at Atlanta.

In Chicago, in December, 1918, there began the trial of Victor L. Berger, Congressman-elect from Milwaukee, for violation of the espionage act and conspiracy to obstruct the United States in prosecuting the war with Germany. With Berger, four other Socialist co-defendants were arraigned: Adolph Germer, National Secretary of the Socialist party; J. Louis Engdahl, Editor of the *American Socialist;* William F. Kruse, Secretary of the draft-evading organization of the anti-war Socialists, and Irwin St. John Tucker, a radical Episcopalian rector.

The trial before Federal Judge Kenesaw M. Landis lasted for more than a month and resulted in a verdict of guilty against all of the defendants. On February 20, 1918, Judge Landis sentenced the convicted men to twenty years' imprisonment in the federal penitentiary at Fort Leavenworth, Kansas. In sentencing the men, Judge Landis said:

> Their writings and utterances fairly represent the consistent, personal campaigns they conducted to discredit the cause of the United States and obstruct its efforts. By no single word or act did they offer help to the country to win the war. It was a conscious, continuous plan to obstruct the country's military efforts. What has been said in this courtroom by the defendants is but an apology by them for obstructing the country's effort.

The convicted men were granted an appeal to the United States Circuit Court of Appeals by Judge Samuel Alschuler. In the upper court the defendants were compelled to give their personal pledge to Judge Alschuler that neither by word or act would they do any of the things for which they have been convicted, pending the final disposition of the case. It should be understood and remembered that these men were convicted not for their personal or political beliefs, but for violation of a law of the United States.

A. P. L. reports show that Lake Mills, Iowa, had a state senator who advised young men that they could not be forced to cross the water to fight, nor forced to buy Liberty bonds. He also was alleged to have obstructed the United War Work campaign by telling a client that he did not need to assist. He was connected with the Non-Partisan League and promised the farmers that they would secure control of the Legislature. Affidavits to this effect were handed to "D. J." The Non-Partisan League was well investigated in that neighborhood. The organizer of the local chapter was forced to buy bonds and stamps and to remain inactive until Peace was declared. "He moved away and never came back," says the local chief.

In another Lake Mills office, there was found by American Protective League operatives a picture drawn by a rather good amateur artist depicting a single German blowing to pieces the head of an American column of troops. Investigation showed that this picture was drawn by a clerk in a local store. He was drafted and is in France, and the report regarding him is filed with "D. J." His original drawing is in the possession of the National Directors of the A. P. L.

A League report, simple and direct, which comes from Todd County, Minnesota, is one of the best and freest expositions of our system of government and the character of our citizenry that may be seen in many a day. The college professor would be valuable who could write a clearer or more useful paper. Says the report:

> The Germans of the country are about evenly divided between the Catholic and Lutheran faiths. The Scandinavians are practically all Lutheran. The German Catholics, in general, allied themselves with loyal element; but a majority of the Lutherans, both German and Scandinavian, gave evidence of pro-German sympathies.
>
> To complicate matters at this time, a political movement under socialist leadership showed great activity. The movement was organized under the name of the Non-Partisan League, with its platform built of essentially socialistic planks. The League attained a membership of approximately 1,200 in the summer of 1918. Its representatives and organizers held meetings in every neighborhood and solicited memberships. In the early days of our entry into the war, they demanded the cessation of hostilities; declared that it was a rich man's war; denounced conscription, and were guilty of numberless seditious utterances. Many of the greater lights of the League came into the country and delivered addresses, among whom were Townley, Lindbergh, Bowen, Randall and others. The burden to the cry of these men was the iniquity of "Big Business" and the wrongs of the farmers. As a remedy for all these economic evils, the socialistic schemes of the League were offered, and found acceptance among a greater number than would have been thought possible.
>
> In June, 1917, the Todd County Public Safety Commission was organized. The loyalist element began to assert itself. A system of education was inaugurated to offset the propaganda of the Bolshevists. The better newspapers lent their aid, and the Red Cross and other war activities were pushed. Many public meetings were held, and many outside speakers assisted in the work. The Public Safety Commission made itself felt by many arrests. Some were fined for seditious utterances, and some were held to the Grand Jury. Conditions in the

county were such that, while indictments were preferred by the Grand Jury in the state courts, it was impossible in some flagrant cases to secure a conviction by the petit jury. Such relief as was secured was through the state courts. So far as this county was concerned, the federal courts were useless.

Just how far the war is going to affect American politics in the future is something that many a politician in America would be exceedingly glad to know. It may be that there will be some public men, unworthy to be called representatives of the American people, who will cater now, as before the war, to the German vote. We should beware of such men, for all they can do will be to advocate that very propaganda which to-day is matter of execration all over the country.

There have not lacked men, who, more especially before we declared war, have boasted of their German birth and openly made that their main argument for office. In a large Ohio city such a man ran for the mayoralty and polled a very considerable vote. He said many times publicly that he would not subscribe to any Liberty Loans and was not in accord with our govervnment. He was very bitter in his denunciation of all who did not side with him. He proclaimed himself a hyphenated German proud of his native origin. He spoke before the German Sängerbund of his city and before delegates of the German-American Alliance—and he spoke in German—a democratic candidate for mayor in an American city of the second class! He uttered that old and familiar and useless plea—dangerous in America to-day—"One can't forget the blood that flows in one's veins." Part of his campaign argument was this: "I personally hope that the war in Europe will be a draw; but if there must be a victory, if I must choose between intelligent Germany and ignorant Russia, there is but one place for me to cast my lot, and that is with the Kaiser. If I felt otherwise, I would not be human." What he should have said was, if he had felt otherwise, he would not have been German. He concluded his remarks with the statement that if he became mayor, "Whatever interference there has been in the past with such an organization as I am now addressing, there will be no such interference when I become mayor." But he did not become mayor.

It is only of late that we have heard much of the Non-Partisan League in America, even in this day of leagues, societies and alliances, but it has had growth and political significance in certain of the Northwestern States. It would not be true to charge the Non-Partisan League with disloyalty as a body, but certainly it would be yet more foolish to say that all its members, in the North-European part of the United States, had been loyal to America in this war, or free of sympathy with Germany. Read the A. P. L. reports—they are not all shown in these pages—of its manifold activities in sections where the Non-Partisan League is strongest. Draw your own inferences then, for then you will have certain premises and need not jump at any conclusion not based on premises.

We may take its reports from Dakota and Iowa as fairly good proof of the accuracy of the foregoing statements. Let us, for instance, examine as a concrete proposition the report from Mason City, Iowa. It is done simply; yet it leads us directly into the heart of the problem of America's future and face to face with the basic questions of courage in business and social life which must underlie the future growth of our country. A story? It is all the story of America.

This report, quite normal in all ways, would represent the usual type of report from a nice, average agricultural city, were it not for certain phases of the work it represents. There were 24 alien enemy cases; 97 disloyalty and sedition cases; 21 cases of propaganda, and eleven I. W. W. cases and other forms of radicalism. The state of society reflected by these figures is best covered in the words of the report itself:

> In ante-bellum times there existed a more or less well-grounded opinion that in this vast western farming region the melting pot had most nearly accomplished its task and that here, if anywhere, was a truly American community. The citizen might be of English, Irish, Scotch, Scandinavian, German or French birth or ancestry, but he was primarily an American. This belief was based upon the fact that here all American institutions and customs received hearty support, that the pepole encouraged to the limit the American liberty

of thought and action. American politics in our region was relatively free from the corruption encouraged by a large percentage of ignorant or apathetic voters. In fact, the population of this region is enlightened, temperate, and prosperous — a condition most favorable if not essential to the proper and full development of a real Americanism.

What did the war bring out? Previous to the advent of America into the war there was, on the whole, a true neutrality. There were sympathizers and partisans of both sides and there was an even greater class of interested spectators who marveled at the stupendous feats of the armies of both sides. The American declaration of war was gladly acclaimed by the pro-Allies, cheerfully accepted as a call to duty by the great mass of interested spectators. It immediately engaged the support of the majority of those previously pro-German, leaving a very small minority of pro-Germans to carry on the propaganda against the American and Allied cause.

It was to deal with this small minority that we organized in May, 1917, and began to select and swear in A. P. L. operatives.

Among matters which called for constant vigilance, the Non-Partisan League came in for a share of our attention. At the time of the entry of the United States into the war, Iowa was being covered with literature for and against this movement, the leading force against the Non-Partisan League being the Greater Iowa Association. The State Council for National Defense considered that it was not for the good of Iowa for this fight to continue, and passed resolutions asking both factions to discontinue their efforts until after the war. The Greater Iowa Association readily acceded to the request, but the Non-Partisan League persisted in its propaganda, and the Council for Defense deemed it wise to take a hand in fairness to the Greater Iowa Association.

But the foregoing mild report does not tell the full story in all of its acrimonious vehemence. A local agricultural journal came out in red head-lines across its cover page, "Iowa's Reign of Terror!" The editor, in that and subsequent issues, printed perhaps 50,000 words of condemnation of those not included among his own constituents, sidetracking alfalfa and Holsteins wholly for the time. He says:

To-day in Iowa there is a veritable reign of terror, which has been encouraged among ignorant and irresponsible people,

> by men and organizations who should and do know better, but who are playing upon passion and prejudice for ulterior purposes. More harm is resulting from this assumption of authority by private individuals, without the shadow of moral or legal right, than by all the pro-German propaganda or real disloyalty in the state. And the worst of it is that it defeats the very purpose which is used to excuse it — the purpose of uniting all our citizens whole-heartedly and sincerely behind the Government's war aims. Already this rule of passion, freed from legal restraint, has resulted in the excess of mob violence, of injustice and wrongs towards loyal and patriotic citizens, whose whole lives will be embittered by the brutal intolerance of a few. Our boasted freedom and liberty and love of fair play are being made the victims of methods no better than those of the despoilers of Belgium, from which they differ not in quality but only in degree.
>
> Right to-day in Iowa, men in positions of leadership and responsibility are fomenting and encouraging this spirit of mob rule and terrorism, which is wholly outside the pale of law, and which will result in such a spirit of lawlessness that we will all pay dearly for it in the years to come. The Greater Iowa Association and its allied organizations are among those which are helping to create this atmosphere of dangerous suspicion and distrust, especially towards farmers' organizations in Iowa, which is bound to result in bloodshed and lynch-law if it is not quickly checked. The Greater Iowa Association boasts in its monthly publication that it has already spent $20,000 in helping to put down the Bolsheviki of Iowa (its usual expression for the loyal and conservative farmers of this state) and that it will spend $180,000 more (a total of $200,000) for this purpose if necessary. Its sentiments are approved and applauded by its sycophant organizations, such as the Des Moines Chamber of Commerce, in its official monthly bulletin, which it proclaims is "the mouthpiece for Des Moines."

Tut, tut! Obviously, Mason City leads directly into a pretty political mess. Willy-nilly, friends of the A. P. L., if not members of the Non-Partisan League, are pushed into ranks assigned to enemies. We may mildly animadvert on the fact that it is the members of the Non-Partisan League who largely buy the journal from which the foregoing quotation is made. It has had a long and honorable history, but is perhaps not so disinterested as the A. P. L. It does not, however, go to war with the A. P. L. so much as with the Greater Iowa Association, which presently voted the editor out of membership. The American Protective League might have been drawn into politics if it had lived much longer—perforce would be and ought to be drawn. One thing is sure, if a man must cater in business to a class which has disloyalty inborn and ingrained, that man is not catering to America and a great future for her.

It is all a question of the high heart of the gentleman unafraid—individual courage, clear-headedness, honest self-searching. That is as true for the native born as for the naturalized citizen. Perhaps for all these warring Iowans, some of whom were zealous and interested, there might very well, in these grave, troubled days of our country and of all the world, be put on the wall of our house the old Bible motto: "Blessed are the pure in heart."

You ask, indeed, what shall we do with all these chameleon propagandists, these foreigners? How shall we classify them — as Americans or as enemies? Who *is* the American?

It is simple to answer that. It is he who himself knows in his own soul whether or not he is done with the damnable hyphen which has almost ruined America, and yet may do so. Liberty Bonds and public speaking do not prove Americanism. Not even service stars in a window make a man American. Blessed are the *pure in heart,* of Mason City or of Des Moines, of the Greater Iowa Association or the Non-Partisan League, of the Peoples' Council, of the A. P. L., or of German or American birth. And when individual American courage is common enough to make a man fight pro-Germanism until it is dead forever, one thinks we shall indeed see God manifested again in the great civilization which once was promised for America. It can be had now in only one way, and that way will cost dear. If you are interested in your son's future, see to it that he—and you yourself—shall be pure in heart. We want and will have no others for Americans to-day or to-morrow.

CHAPTER VII

THE GERMAN SPY CASES

The Great Spy Cases — Details of German Propaganda — Finances and Personnel of German Forces in America — The Diplomatic Fiasco — Notorious Figures of Alien Espionage Uncovered — The Senate Judicial Investigation.

To gain any adequate idea of the amount of the activities which centered in New York would mean the following out of countless concealed threads leading all over the world and covering the United States like a net. We never knew until we were well into this war that, long before we dreamed of war, our country was infested by vast numbers of the paid spies of Germany; that these worked under a well-established, and now well-known, organization; that the highest German diplomatic representatives were a part of the system; that leading financial figures of New York were figures in it also, and that the whole intricate machine was differentiated like a great and well-ordered business undertaking. It was an elaborate organization for the betrayal of a country; and that organization, like the armed forces of Germany in the field, was beaten and broken only by the loyal men of America, resolved once more that a government of the people should not perish from the earth.

Let the scene shift from New York—whose defensive organization has been outlined—to the national judicial center at Washington, the seat of our intelligence system and of those courts of law which have in charge the national affairs. There, for many months, a few men have sat and watched pour into their offices such proofs of human perfidy and depravity as can never have been paralleled in the most Machiavellian days of the Dark Ages.

The daily press of the United States acted under a voluntary censorship during the war, even while it saw pass by such news as never before had it seen in America. Now and again something of this would break which obviously was public property and ought to be known—the notorious transactions of von Bernstorff, von Papen, Dr. Albert, Boy-Ed, Bolo; such crimes as the blowing up of the international bridge in Maine; the mysterious fires and explosions whose regularity attracted attention; the diplomatic revelations regarding Dumba and Dernburg and their colleagues, which finally resulted in the dismissal of the clique of high German officials whose creed had been one of diplomatic and personal dishonor.

The stories of German attempts to control several New York newspapers; their efforts to buy or subsidize some thirty other journals in all parts of the country; the well-known subsidizing of certain writers to spread propaganda in the press—all these things also necessarily got abroad to such an extent that the United States Government could not fail to take cognizance of it. At length, charges came out linking up a Washington daily with wealthy commercial interests of a supposedly pro-German nature, and a great deal of acrimonious comment appeared in all parts of the country. Washington resolved to investigate these charges. The process took the form, in the late fall of 1918, of the appointment of a sub-committee of the great Senate Judiciary Committee, which popularly was known as the Overman Committee.

The work of this committee, which summoned before it officers of the Attorney General's establishment in New York, agents of the Bureau of Investigation in Washington, of Military and Naval Intelligence in Washington, and all the larger figures of the accused or suspected persons implicated in what now had become a wide-reaching national scandal, was continued over many weeks. The proceedings were made public regularly, and at last the readers of America began to get, at first hand, authentic ideas of what menace had been at our doors and inside our doors. It was before this Overman Committee that many of the great New York cases in which A. P. L. assisted passed to their final review.

Perhaps the most important single witness called before this Senate committee was Mr. A. Bruce Bielaski, Chief of the Bureau of Investigation of the Department of Justice at Washington. Mr. Bielaski was on the stand for days at a time, and his testimony came as a distinct shock to those of us who heretofore had known little or nothing about the way in which our covert forces of espionage were combating those of Germany. It will not be needful to follow the records of the committee from day to day throughout the long period of its sittings, but some of the more important revelations made by Mr. Bielaski first may be brought to notice.

It was brought into the record, for publication later by the State Department, that there was a regular system of secret messages between Count von Bernstorff of the Imperial German Embassy at Washington, and the Berlin Foreign Office, by way of South America and Stockholm. All this time the Imperial German Ambassador was posing as a great friend of America, while in reality he was the chief of the German spy system in America—an example of all that a nobleman should not be.

It was shown by Mr. Bielaski that the German consul in Chicago, Reiswitz, suggested as long ago as 1915 that German interests ought to buy the Wright aeroplane factories in Dayton, Ohio, in an attempt to stop the shipment of aeroplanes to the Allies. Something stopped the shipment—let us suppose that it was not the efficiency of Germany so much as our own inefficiency, deplorable as that admission must be.

Nothing came of this attempt, nor of the attempt to control the Bridgeport Projectile Works, in any very conclusive and satisfactory fashion for Germany. A year later von Bernstorff begins to complain that German propaganda has not been producing much result. He cuts free from the German publication, "Fair Play," and declares that he would be glad to be well quit of George Sylvester Viereck's "Fatherland." He asks his imperial government to give him $50,000 more, with which he would like to start a monthly magazine in the United States. This was the beginning of those general revelations which exposed alike the clumsiness of German diplomacy, and the endeavor of German espionage as against our own.

Reiswitz was declared by Mr. Bielaski to have advised

the continuance of the "American Embargo Conference," which was set on foot to create opposition to our shipment of munitions to the Allies. He signified that this ought to be used as an influence to swing German voters in presidential elections. Mr. Bielaski brought into the record the "Citizens' Committee for Food Shipments," which was supported by Dr. Edmund von Mach of Cambridge. It had been organized in the home of a prominent New York citizen.

There was brought in the record also the name of a newspaper correspondent—more is the pity for that—who had letters from Count von Bernstorff and Captain von Papen, military attache, declaring that this man was in the service of Germany and Austria. The syndicate employing this man, as is well known, cancelled his contract as soon as his real character and his pro-German attitude were revealed.

The record also declared that a former correspondent of the *Cologne Gazette* in Washington, notified by the State Department to leave this country, had been in close wireless communication with a German paper in Rotterdam.

All of these revelations began to implicate certain Americans prominent in business and in politics, so that at once the transaction by the Senate Committee became the biggest news of the time, one recrimination following another and one explanation another in rapid sequence. The Committee, none the less, ground on, and produced original papers which proved German methods beyond a doubt. Two code dispatches from von Bernstorff to the Berlin Foreign Office were put into the evidence, one of which was dated November 1, 1916, and stated: "Since the Lusitania case, we have strictly confined ourselves to such propaganda as cannot hurt us if it becomes known. The sole exception is perhaps the peace propaganda, which has cost the least amount, but which also has been the most successful."

Again von Bernstorff states that it would not seem desirable for him to be held responsible for any articles in the subsidized newspaper, "when, as now, we are in a campaign of the bitterest character which is turning largely upon foreign policy."

Mr. Reiswitz of Chicago was on hand with estimates for his excellent master at all times. In regard to the Embargo Conference, he wrote in the first year of the war: "It would require an estimated amount of $6,000 or $7,000. The contemplated continuation of the enterprise would, in accordance with my opinion, be favorable to the entire German vote, and would facilitate influencing German voters." So we have at once the first indication of the truth that the great German population of America is to be handled for the particular purpose of advancing Germany's interests, not only in America but all over the world.

Mr. Bielaski read into the record documents alleging that the American Press Association was contemplated as desirable for German control. A memorandum by Dr. Albert, financial expert, stated that he would obtain a thirty day option on the American Press Association for the price of $900,000, with an additional $100,000 for news service. The memorandum in full was introduced before the Committee.

Professor von Mach was stated by Mr. Bielaski to have been active in behalf of interned prisoners, largely by way of his press agent, whom he supplied with inspiration. Von Mach was later brought before the Committee to explain in person as best he might certain publications which he had put out in other form.

Mr. Bielaski stated that German interests advanced to the Bridgeport Projectile Company $3,400,000, and that these interests got back $1,000,000 of this money by selling a large part of the company's product to Spain.

Mr. Bielaski mentioned a society known as the "American Truth Society," organized in 1910 and reported to have been financed by the German government, to what extent was undetermined. One record of a transfer of $10,000 was shown.

Records which had been taken from the office of Wolf von Igel showed that scarcely a ship sailed for a neutral country which did not carry a German agent. There were at least two American newspaper men who had been bought outright by Germany. Blackmail was not above the consideration of some of these fellow-conspirators.

Amounts of $1,000 to $5,000 had been paid to subsidize one paper which was dropped by the embassy. The owner then threatened the embassy that if he did not get any more money he might allow the paper to go into bankruptcy, and the ensuing publicity would show the subsidy. Dr. Albert was authorized to settle with this man to keep him quiet—he paid something over $3,000 in this instance. Continually there rose a loud wail from Dr. Albert and von Bernstorff, "Stung!"

There were some recriminations between journals in America as to the nature of the "news" sent in by American foreign correspondents located in Germany. It was sometimes offered in explanation of the pro-German attitude of certain of these correspondents that it was natural that a man resident in Germany should hear one side only of the case. Others, more especially after the Senate revelations, were disposed to think there might be other valuable considerations moving correspondents thereto. Indeed, names and dates and prices of perfectly good correspondents are now on record with the Overman Committee.

The Bielaski testimony was strengthened by that of Major Humes and Captain Lester of Military Intelligence. Incidentally, the attempts of Germany to embroil us with Mexico were shown. Very interesting testimony was brought out from Carl Heinen, an interned German, formerly a member of the Embassy staff, and a former consul general at Mexico City. Major Humes of M. I. D. put in the record the relations of Felix A. Somerfeld, an alien enemy who was an alleged Villa agent in New York, showing that in eight months Villa had received nearly $400,000 worth of rifle cartridges from Somerfeld, who was closely associated with the German agents, Carl Rintelen and Friedrick Stallforth, a prominent German banker in Mexico. The drafts on certain trust companies were produced as part of the evidence.

Heinen's deposition was subscribed to by F. A. Borgermeister, Dr. Albert's confidential secretary, before he was interned at Fort Oglethorpe. This disclosed the disposition of $33,770,000 that passed through German hands. This money was obtained in loans from New York banks, or through the American agents of banks in Germany.

Secretary of War Baker had commanded Captain Lester of Military Intelligence to make public some of the secrets of this division which heretofore had been reposing in the silence of the tomb. Captain Lester testified to the confession of a former German officer, who admitted having been sent here as a propagandist. This man told the federal officials that in June, before the Archduke Francis Ferdinand of Austria was assassinated, the German government was plotting the war. Captain Lester quoted this man as saying that in the middle of June, 1914, Bethmann-Holweg sent out inquiries to various scientists, professors and other intellectual persons to learn whether they were ready for foreign service in the event of war. There were one hundred and thirty of these who were told to be ready for instant call to service in North and South America, Japan and China, as directors of propaganda. They met in the Foreign Office in Berlin, July 10, 1914, and three weeks later sailed from Copenhagen for New York under charge of Dr. Heinrich F. Albert. In order not to arouse suspicion, most of them traveled steerage.

Captain Lester, after a long day of testimony, referred to the "Golden Book"—a book in which German-Americans wrote their names after they had contributed to a German War Relief fund. This book was to have been presented to the Kaiserin. The purpose of this book, in the belief of Captain Lester, was to get certain prominent German-Americans signed up as loyal to the fatherland, without letting them know they were doing it.

Captain Lester, in later testimony before the Overman Committee, said that of the one hundred and thirty trained and educated German propagandists sent out nearly a month before the war started, thirty-one landed in the United States two weeks after hostilities had started in Europe. They became the starting point of an organization comprising between 200,000 and 300,000 volunteers, in large part German-Americans, who were secret spies in this country and who reported regularly to German consuls and agents in widely scattered centers of the German spy system in the United States.

It may cause a certain horror and revulsion in the hearts

of the American public when they realize that a quarter of a million secret German agents were working here in America all the time against us — just about as many as existed of loyal Americans under the unseen banner of the American Protective League. The American public now can begin to understand something of the bitter battle which was fought between these two secret organizations — the quarter million German spies who lived here, and the quarter million loyal American citizens who made this their home and this their country.

Captain Lester showed that the group sent to America had definite instructions. One was to deal with commercial matters, another with political, and a third leader was to take up the South American and Mexican relations. General headquarters in New York were at 1123 Broadway, arrangements having been made for these quarters in advance. The Hamburg-American Company, whose status toward us in the war is now notorious, took charge of the first work of the German Press Bureau. The original artist in this labor was replaced by a newspaper man, whose salary from Germany was later discovered to have been $15,000. A former major of the United States, once a newspaper man, was declared to have been hired at $40 a week to report to these German headquarters any confidential interviews he might have with Washington officials.

The Lutheran church propaganda was brought definitely before the Overman Committee. Dr. Albert and Dr. Fuhr had this form of propaganda in charge. Captain Lester said that there are about six thousand Lutheran congregations in the United States, with a membership of nearly 3,000,000, and that the propaganda was directed through pastors who had been born in Germany, or were alien enemies, or were of German parentage. There were over one thousand two hundred individual cases investigated. Readers of these pages will recall a few instances of the work of the American Protective League in looking into these many instances of disloyalty. Captain Lester said: "We have found in localities that the word had gone down the line to groups of clergymen that they were to preach sermons in favor of Germany, and that this had been done. I investigated a case in New York where the clergyman admitted to me he had received instructions to preach such a sermon. From August, 1914, to April, 1917, in hundreds of Lutheran churches, the continuous preaching was in favor and hope of German victory.''

It transpired that British Military Intelligence had in possession a great mass of documents taken by General Allenby in the capture of Nazareth. These were found among the effects of that Major Franz von Papen who once had been military attache in Washington, and whose name has become more or less familiar through some of the disclosures regarding von Bernstorff and his activities.

These papers, added to those taken by our own Intelligence officers from prominent Germans this side the water, go to build up the tremendous and tragic story of a nation's shame. Germany had a widely spread and elaborate plan to ruin this country. She failed. The proofs of her failure are now before the public, and they run very wide. They do not leave us feeling any too comfortable or any too sure regarding our own country. It is not pleasant to have listed, as part with the German records, those of our great newspapers which, in the German belief, might be classed as '' neutral or favorable to Germany.'' It is not pleasant to see the names of newspaper men once held honorable and loyal, but now condemned to have had the itching palm and to have received German gold. There is nothing pleasant about the whole sordid, abominable story, nothing clean, nothing satisfying, nothing honorable. But it shows that when we had this sort of work to do, we did it thoroughly and accomplished the mission on which our men were sent out.

Some of the most sensational testimony was that brought out by Alfred L. Becker, Deputy Attorney General of New York, who had in charge a great many of the big espionage and treason investigations in that city, which was the American home and headquarters of the German spy army.

Mr. Becker told of his own investigations, at the instance of the French Government, in the case of Bolo Pacha. The latter was executed as a French traitor, but was shown to have gotten Germany money in this country to the extent of $1,683,000. As is well known, Bolo had raised this money to purchase the Paris *Journal.* This paper, however, did not change its loyalty to France, so there was a loud wail on the part of Germany's head spies that they had been swindled once more.

Mr. Becker produced many British secret service documents showing the elaborate governmental arrangements in Berlin to establish and maintain spy systems, both before and after the war. These documents listed, as agents, journalists, college professors, bankers, business men, consular attaches, and others of all ranks. Mr. Becker showed that a former German reservist, later an auditor of accounts in New York City, was told as early as 1909 that he would be valuable in case of war as a German propagandist in the United States. It was intended to get a good system of distribution of German " kultur " established in America. Then there could at once be put before American readers such stories as that systematic attempt made in 1917 to advance the idea that Germany was on the verge of revolt and that the Kaiser soon would be overthrown. The German censor was back of the dissemination of these reports, it being maintained to paralyze the prosecution of the war in this country, where we had the pleasant theory that the German Kaiser and the German people were not at one as to the war.

Mr. Becker also went into many transactions of Ambassador von Bernstorff, showing him to have been quite willing to buy the Paris *Journal* with German money if need be. He placed in the record correspondence which showed that when Dr. Dernburg left Germany for the United States in August, 1914, the German government deposited 25,000,000 marks with M. M. Warburg & Company of Hamburg, which Mr. Becker stated was for propaganda purposes in the United States. Dr. Dernburg brought to this country a power of attorney from the Imperial Secretary of the Treasury, which gave him the distribution of the fund. Of this fund, $400,000 was turned over to Dr. Albert, head of German finances in New York, by Dr. Dernburg.

Mr. Becker gave a long list of banks which had participated in the sale of German bonds in this country, these banks being located in the principal cities of the east and west. He named as well the chain of banks in which the German government opened accounts for certain purposes. He showed the credentials brought from the German chancellor by Dr. Dernburg to large financial institutions in New York, which were made repositories of German funds. The letter to one such banking firm in New York, from Warburg & Company of Hamburg, establishing the German credit of 25,000,000 marks, was made a part of the record, also the power of attorney enclosed by Dr. Dernburg to the New York repository.

Mr. Becker mentioned the underwriting of German bonds by a New York concern to a total amount of $9,908,-000. The proceeds were deposited with a trust company in New York to the order of the Imperial German Government, and were checked out by von Bernstorff and Albert for deposit in the chain of banks above referred to. It was the intention to make these banking institutions favorable to the German ideas, and unfavorable to the American bond sales. An initial deposit was made with the Equitable Trust Company of $3,350,000; the Columbia Trust Company had an initial deposit of $750,000; the Chase National Bank was alleged to have had an initial deposit of $125,000. As the proceeds of the German war loan notes accumulated, the deposits in certain of these New York financial institutions were increased. In order to avoid any legal complications, the German government opened a blind account so that Dr. Albert could go on with his operations without any fear of detection by anyone desiring to bring legal action against him. These figures will give the reader some idea of the extent of the German finances. *All this money — and many times the amounts above mentioned — was spent for the one and only purpose of German propaganda and spy work in the United States.*

Major Humes took Dr. Edmund von Mach over the jumps in his cross-examination before the Overman Committee. Von Mach came in for a gruelling by Senator Nelson and others of the Committee when he attempted to speak in justification of German practices in war. He did his best to carry water on both shoulders, but had a very unhappy quarter of an hour. He was followed and preceded on the stand by certain literary gentlemen, college professors and others, who undertook to explain to the Committee utterances they had made in print or elsewhere which were charged to show disloyalty to the interests of the United States. It is impossible to give in any sort of detail the vast extension of the testimony before this Committee, or to mention the many widely extended forms of the German activities that ran in this country during the war. Perhaps we may summarize the German attitude, as well as in any other way, by citing the opinion of that delectable gentleman, the Count von Bernstorff, ambassador of the Imperial German Government at Washington, in his communication to the Foreign Office in Berlin, in explanation of his activities in the United States:

> It is particularly difficult in a hostile country to find suitable persons for help of this sort, and to this fact, as well as the Lusitania case, we may attribute the shipwreck of the German propaganda initiated by Herr Dernburg. Now that opinion is somewhat improved in our favor, and that we are no longer ostracized, we can take the work up again. As I have said before, our success depends entirely upon finding the suitable people. We can then leave to them whether they will start a daily, weekly, or a monthly, and the sort of support to be given. In my opinion, we should always observe the principle that either a representative of ours should buy the paper, or that the proprietor should be secured by us by continuous support. The latter course has been followed by the English in respect of the New York ———, and our enemies have spent here large sums in this manner. All the same, I do not think that they pay regular subsidies. At least, I never heard of such. This form of payment is moreover inadvisable, because one can never get free of the recipients. They all wish to become permanent pensioners of the Empire, and if they fail in that, they try to blackmail us.
>
> I, therefore, request your Excellency to sanction the payment in question.

By way of general summary, it may be said that a well-defined organization long existed in our country, districted with the usual German exactness. German Naval Intelligence had charge of destruction of our shipping, naval sabotage, etc. Boy-Ed, naval attache at Washington, was to have handled this. The notorious Rintelen, who seemed to have operated independently in New York, confined his activities rather to the making of bombs to be concealed on ships, to the incitement of strikes, munition embargoes, etc. Dr. Scheele, one of the three most prominent spies in America, was relied on to devise means of burning ships at sea. His method of bomb manufacture is spoken of later.

What is equivalent to our Military Intelligence Department in Germany, in turn took up the question of sabotage in our ammunition works, and of getting contraband stuff into Germany. Scheele, who was taken in custody by the United States, declared that this country was divided into military districts, and that supplies of arms and ammunition were gotten together. He even declared at one time that he knew of 200,000 Mauser rifles stored in a German club in New York City. He was taken there by Government officials and located the place where the rifles probably had been stored, although they had in the meantime been removed.

Von Papen, military attache at Washington, had much the same work for the army that Boy-Ed had taken on for the navy. He often appears in the revelations of the German spy system, as in the plot against the Welland Canal, and the Vanceboro bridge, for which Werner Horn was arrested. Von Papen had the charge of the Bridgeport Projectile Company, which was intended to disorganize our manufacture of munitions. He had some sort of charge of Scheele, the German chemist spy, who is, perhaps, the best known example now remaining on American soil of the German espionage system.

Special commissions to spread disease germs were sent to this country, as perhaps A. P. L. reading will have indicated. A good deal of this work failed because so many of the German spies were interned early in the war, and there has been no good opportunity since to replace these men properly, the war having traveled too fast when once America was in it.

But what, perhaps, has shocked and horrified Americans more than anything else (and it cannot be too often iterated) was the knowledge that long before this war Germany had a vast system of spies all through America. This system of international spies was originated almost a generation ago by the Prussian War Office. There were supposed to have been about 30,000 spies in France before this war was declared. England also was well sown with such persons in every rank of life. We had our share.

Dr. Scheele told the Department of Justice when he was taken in charge that for twenty-one years before the outbreak of the European war he had been stationed in Brooklyn as a representative of the German government. His "honorarium," as he called it, was $125 a month. He had been a German major, yet owned a drug store in Brooklyn. A couple of months before war was declared by Germany, he was told to get rid of his drug store — that is to say, to mobilize in America for the German purposes in the coming war. He said the drug store was doing very well. Others of these fixed spies got salaries about like that of Scheele, a retainer of $1,000 nominal salary being more frequent. In charge of all these lesser regular spies, who had been absorbed in the American citizenship, were the consuls and the high diplomatic officials of the Imperial German Government in our country. It would be a very great deal to hope that this system has been actually extirpated. That it did exist is true without any doubt or question.

Any A. P. L. man whose work was identified with the larger eastern cities will note many points of contact of the A. P. L. with D. J. and M. I. D. in the testimony brought before the Overman Committee. It is, of course, not too much to say that A. P. L. was at the foundation of much of that testimony itself. Many of the facts above brought out are of record in the A. P. L. files.

In yet another line of Government work, the League has been very useful — that of coöperating with Mr. A. Mitchell Palmer, Custodian of Alien Property, whose statements, made elsewhere than in the committee, constitute a rather valuable extension of the committee's information.

Reference was made before the committee to the Bridgeport Projectile Company. Mr. Palmer some time ago announced that he had taken over 19,900 of the 20,000 shares of the capital stock of that concern, and that there had been reported to him other property of approximate value of $500,000 held by it for and in behalf of Germany.

In a statement accredited to him, Mr. Palmer again bared the efforts of that malodorous quartet, Count von Bernstorff, Dr. Albert, Dr. Dernburg and Captain von Papen. It was the obvious intent of these to use the Bridgeport Projectile Company to prevent the manufacture and shipment of arms and ammunition to the Allies. The taking over of the stock of the Bridgeport Projectile Company, and the report by the company of the property owned by the German government, with the disclosures incident thereto, followed many months of persistent investigation.

It was planned to have this corporation buy up all the available supplies of powder, antimony, hydraulic presses, and other supplies and materials essential to the manufacture of munitions. The plan also involved the negotiation of contracts with the allied Governments to supply them with materials of war, apparently in good faith but in reality with no intention of fulfilling them. The ultimate expenditure of approximately $10,000,000 for this purpose was contemplated.

In a cable from London printed in the American press on the morning of January 15, 1919, a statement was given from a German newspaper quoting Dr. Dernburg, the German propagandist who was expelled from America some years ago. Now Dr. Dernburg comes out in the Vienna *Neue Freie Presse* and states that Germany is depending upon " a certain drawing together of Germany and the United States." He believes that nothing should be done which will " give foundation for a lasting alienation of the two peoples." He finds the Allies in victory somewhat difficult in their terms, so that Germans turn their eyes and expectations toward America, " and feel sure that their expectations will not come to grief." He goes on to say that Germany needs raw materials for the revival of her industries, needs credit, and also a market. He looks to America for all these, and says: " A fear of German competition does not exist in America in the same degree as in France and England. The hatred against the German people does not exist since the dynasty has been overthrown, and it is quite possible that America will transfer English and French debts to Germany in order to give her money, for America seeks not destruction but justice. Our two countries will be brought together, and as rivalry is out of the question, this coöperation will take a more tolerable form than in the case of our neighbors." He goes on to say: "A careful economic policy, I think, will secure Germans sympathy, thereby providing economic help for our German industries, now in collapse, and possibly awaken stirring echoes in two million Americans of German origin. . . . America will have other interests in Germany allied with her by interest and by service rendered to Germany; so taking all these points of view together, one may well consider that the earliest possible reconciliation between Germany and America will be good for the future of the world and will be welcomed by the German people."

The human mind with difficulty can conceive of anything indicative of more brazen effrontery than the foregoing. That is the statement to-day of one of the arch-traitors planted in this country by Germany. No doubt, it may awaken a "stirring echo" at least in the hearts of the quarter million of German spies who worked with Dernburg here.

The great danger to America is her unsuspiciousness. Having lived half a century cheek by jowl with these men, although in ignorance of their real quality, we are expected to go on living with them on the same terms that existed before the war. Great Britain, sterner than we, definitely has announced her intention of deporting German aliens — she intends to take no chances. What the French will do is a foregone conclusion. German "kultur" is begging at the doorsteps of the world.

Mr. Palmer, custodian of alien enemy property, can complete the story. For instance, there was loose talk around New York in the early days of the war that under one tennis court in New Jersey there was a gun emplacement from which New York could be bombarded. It was said that a German-owned factory building had a gun emplacement built into its floor with the same amiable intention. Custodian Palmer points out that there really was a concrete pier in the port of St. Thomas, Virgin Islands, with a concealed base suitable for heavy gun mounts. That pier now belongs to the United States Government. Before the war it was the property of a steamship company organized by wealthy Germans, of whom Emperor William was one. Its office was in the headquarters of the German spies in New York. After the United States went to war, the pier was sold to a Dane to cover the ownership. The Dane could not meet his note when it came due, and Mr. Palmer confiscated the pier immediately as German property.

Mr. Palmer stated, long before the Overman Committee began its testimony, that Germany, years before she started this war, had undertaken to plant on American soil a great industrial and commercial army. She believed she could keep America out of the conflict, for she had her organization in every state of the Union. It reached across the Pacific to Hawaii and the Philippines and up to Alaska; in the Atlantic it was found in Porto Rico, the Virgin Islands and Panama. Industry after industry was built up, totaling probably two billion dollars in money value, and billions more in potential political value.

"Germany had spies in the German-owned industries of Pittsburgh, Chicago, New York and the West," says Mr. Palmer. "She fought the war when we were neutral on American soil by agents sent here for that purpose."

St. Andrew's Bay, not far from Pensacola, Florida, is a very fine harbor, the nearest American harbor, indeed, to the Panama canal. Mr. Palmer shows that this was wholly controlled by Germans, who were organized in the form of a lumber company and who had purchased thousands of acres of timber nearby. The wealthy owner of the German property never saw it. A concealed fort had been constructed there, and right of way on the shore had been purchased. Not even the Government of the United States could have obtained a terminal on St. Andrew's Bay unless it did business with the owner in Berlin. Such being the case, Custodian Palmer did not buy it at all — he simply took it in and added it to his list of more than two billion dollars' worth of German-owned property taken over since the war began.

There were German spies in our chemical works, metal industries, textile concerns, and in every line of our commerce. They had a fund, mentioned at different times in the Overman Committee testimony, which was somewhere between thirty millions and sixty millions of dollars — all of it to be used in propaganda, subsidizing, subornation and destruction.

There were three or four German firms in America which had much to do with the German declaration of war. They were instrumental in piling up the gigantic quantities of American metals, to prepare that country for its onslaught in 1914. There were great stocks of copper accumulated in America to be sold to Germany after the close of the war. The actual ownership of these things was so very carefully concealed by a masquerading interchangeable personnel that it required months of investigation to get at the real facts and to discover that the real owner was Germany itself. In taking over these metal businesses, Alien Property Custodian Palmer broke the German control of the metal industry of America. It has been intended to wipe out these industries so completely that they cannot get a start again.

The New York *Times* of November 3, 1918, printed a quarter-page story in regard to some of these revelations which should be made not only a part of the record of the Senate Committee but of the records of America itself:

> When on April 6, 1917, America declared war on Germany, there was in New York as American representative of the Deutsche Bank of Berlin, a German by the name of Hugo Schmidt. As the world now knows, it was the Deutsche Bank which financed the von Bernstorff-Bolo Pacha plot to debauch France, which formulated a scheme to corner the wool market of the world, a plot the object of which was to gain control of the after-the-war trade in South America, and which, through its agents in this country and South America, was keeping tab on the political situation in this hemisphere for the Foreign Office in Berlin. How these plots and numerous others were planned and how they were to be carried out, was disclosed in a great mass of documents which will go down in history as the "Hugo Schmidt Papers."
>
> Despite the fact that he was one of the first of the Kaiser's subjects to be arrested after this country entered the war, and

despite the fact that he knew the all-important nature of the papers, Schmidt failed to destroy the documents. He acted on the theory that the United States Government would not take them, and so he catalogued them and stored them away in his private office at Broadway and Rector Street, and in his living quarters in the old German Club in West Fifty-ninth Street.

It was the plotting of Bernstorff and Bolo Pacha, with Adolph Pavenstedt, the enemy alien banker of New York, acting as a go-between, that caused the seizure of Schmidt's papers, with the unmasking of scores of German political and trade plots, involving financial backing mounting into the hundreds of millions of dollars.

The revelations which have followed the seizure of these papers have filled pages in the newspapers of the United States and the rest of the world, and yet the story has not yet been half told. The new chapters in a story, which has been pronounced by Federal officials among the most interesting of all the disclosures brought about as a result of the great war, will be issued by Deputy Attorney General Alfred L. Becker, the man who exposed Bolo.

The seizure of millions of dollars worth of German-owned property in this country has been made possible, to a large extent, by Mr. Becker's seizure of Schmidt's papers. But for its conclusive evidence of the true ownership of certain great properties, the Government of the United States would have had an almost impossible job in ferreting out the trade footholds of the Hun in America. To-day the Government is in control of great woolen mills, of huge plants now engaged in the manutacture of munitions of war, of splendid ocean-going steamships (not those of the Hamburg-American and North German Lloyd lines), which, until Schmidt's papers were studied, were supposed to be neutral or American owned; not to mention numerous other important plants, all of which were proved to be of enemy ownership and of which a majority have already been auctioned off to bona fide American ownership and control.

Aside from what the future may disclose as a result of a further study and investigation of Schmidt's papers, the following summary, prepared in the office of Mr. Becker, shows in a condensed form the results obtained to date as a result of the seizure of the German banker's books and other data:

1. Part of documents that helped in the conviction of Bolo Pacha.

2. Furnished evidence upon which Hugo Schmidt and Adolph Pavenstedt were interned.

3. Furnished evidence disclosing German plot to hoard

wools and other textiles for German account; furnished evidence enabling the Government to take control of Forstmann & Huffmann Company, and proving conclusively the German ownership of the Botany Worsted Mills.

4. Furnished evidence upon which Eugene Schwerdt was interned.

5. Furnished key of the secret telegraphic code of the Deutsche Bank, which since has been used by all the intelligence bureaus throughout the world to decode wireless and cable messages as well as correspondence.

6. Furnished information to compile an index showing approximately 32,000 subscribers in America for war loans of the Central Powers.

7. Disclosed payments of moneys made by the German Foreign Office to their diplomatic representatives abroad, notably to the German Minister in Buenos Aires, about 8,000,000 marks ($1,600,000); to the German Minister in Mexico, about $178,000; to the Minister at Port-au-Prince, Haiti, $120,000, etc.

8. Disclosed the payments made by the German Foreign Office, through the Deutsche Bank, to its diplomatic representatives in the United States, von Bernstorff, Boy-Ed, von Papen and Albert, to carry on different methods of German propaganda and frightfulness, as well as commercial aggression.

9. Disclosed extensive plans for the control of South American trade by German interests, and showed German methods of keeping a close scrutiny on the political situation of the several South American republics.

10. Disclosed means adopted for carrying on German business in enemy as well as in neutral countries, and gave to the authorities the names of the German agents in every neutral country in the world.

The arrest and internment of Schmidt and Pavenstedt was a direct result of the exposure of Bolo Pacha. Pavenstedt is the former head of the banking house of G. Amsinck & Co., and for years was among the best known of the Kaiser's subjects in New York. The Schmidt papers disclosed him as an intimate of von Bernstorff, Dr. Albert, Boy-Ed, and von Papen, and as the man to whom Bolo went immediately on arrival in this this country in the late winter of 1916. Pavenstedt negotiated for Bernstorff the financial part of the conspiracy which resulted in the payment to Bolo out of the funds of the Deutsche Bank in this country a sum totaling about $1,700,000.

It was also disclosed that immediately following the outbreak of the war, Boy-Ed and von Papen hurried to New York to establish propaganda and plot headquarters as per instructions received from Berlin. Boy-Ed, like Bolo, first sought Pavenstedt, who found room for the German naval attache in his own office in the bank building. Later, when the newspapers began to print stories of the questionable operations of the German naval and military attaches, they moved to other headquarters, the transfer being made "for reasons of policy," at the suggestion of Pavenstedt.

The story of Bolo is known to every one, and it is not necessary to point out how the Schmidt papers led to that traitor's arrest and subsequently to his execution by a French firing squad.

Here is an A. P. L. case which is recommended to the attention of those who write short stories of a detective nature: It has to do with a beautiful adventuress, who among other things was known as a countess. Let us not give the real name. We will call her Mrs. Jeannette Sickles, alias Countess De Galli, alias Mrs. Dalbert, alias Rose La Foine, alias Jeannette McDaniels, alias Miss Ellen Hyde, alias Jeannette La Foine — we need not give more of her names. The records of this case show that she was entangled with an employe of the Adjutant General's office, a night clerk, whose duties were to sort the mail. This clerk under examination admitted that he knew this lady, admitted that he had become very fond of her — was, indeed, in love with her; said she had kissed him and given him divers manifestations of her affection; said he had met her often at hotels in the presence of others; said she came to him for advice about certain unfair treatment which she thought the Department of Justice had given her; said he was going to marry the lady if he had a chance, as he had found her a very congenial woman. The writer of fiction can easily fill out the details. The adventuress was intelligent, beautiful and accomplished. She was working close to many of our Government secrets; it would be her fault if she did not learn a great many things about this country and its government.

It was stated that this particular Government clerk was known to be a socialist; was corresponding with Emma Goldman. Other charges were made against him, not redounding to the credit of his moral character. He was rated as being a man slovenly in his looks and "with no moral and mental stamina." In short, the field was pretty good for the purposes of German espionage. Pages could be written covering the activities of this particular emissary. She was one of a certain type who will work anywhere for money. During the Red Cross drives in Washington, she was suspected by some of the operatives who were working for the United States Shipping Board. It was discovered that she was working in that department, also, as a welfare worker "under very mysterious circumstances." She was cared for.

There was a certain gentleman by the name of Dr. Frederick August von Strensch, who was arrested by the Department of Justice on testimony furnished by operatives. The worthy doctor might have been regarded as practically innocent — all he planned was the invasion of Canada and Mexico by German reservists located in the United States. This man had long made America his home. He was arrested on a presidential warrant. Along with him, there was arrested a certain dazzling stage celebrity represented to have been a countess in her more private life in Europe. A mass of correspondence was taken with these people, revealing the fact that 150,000 German reservists were to be sent to Canada, about the same number into Mexico. Definite plans were mentioned referring to the assemblage of 25,000 men on the Canadian border. This one plot alone, if mentioned here in detail, would give all the data necessary for a sensational thriller in detective fiction. But it is not fiction. This sort of work actually went on within our country. Not only in this instance, but in many others, a deliberate and extremely dangerous attempt was made to embroil us with other countries.

When the merchant submarine "Deutschland" arrived in this country on its celebrated voyage, a part of its cargo consisted of thirty-three thousand pounds of tungsten, scarce in this country, but of value in making certain high grades of steel. After considerable sleuthing on the part of operatives, this tungsten was traced to a concern ostensibly American, but really owned altogether by Germans. The way in which the identity of these steel manufacturers was concealed is proof of the ingenuity and resourcefulness of the master criminal minds of the world. As showing the thoroughness with which Germany works, one of the accused stated that when he came out of Germany to confer with his associates, the German censors destroyed all his papers, examined all his clothing, and stripped him and washed him with a solution of alcohol to eradicate any message which he might have painted on his skin! They were not above a suspicion on their own part. The Alien Property Custodian took over, as a result of these investigations, the Becker Steel Company, whose plant was located at Charleston, W. Va. The details of this case are extremely voluminous.

The passport frauds have long been " old stuff " in the American journals, and need be no more than referred to here. At the time German reservists were needed in the Old Country (there were more than a thousand very useful officers here who were much needed in the German army), the question of passports came up. These men could not get U. S. passports, so a general system of forged passports was set on foot in which the highest diplomatic officials of Germany in America did not scorn to take a hand. It was their idea of honorable service, one supposes. Certainly, von Bernstorff — whom we kept in this country long after he should have been kicked out — employed a go-between who arranged and carried on a very considerable traffic in foreign passports. The ordinary price was about twenty dollars,— small business, truly, for an ambassador, but von Bernstorff, von Papen, von Weddell, von Igel and others worked together in this thing until the Department of Justice men got too hot upon their trail. A long and intricate story hangs upon this. It is enough to say that the frauds were unearthed and the lower and middle class operatives in the frauds were put away. Von Weddell, the most important of these conspirators, took ship for Norway. However, the ship on which he sailed was sunk by a German U-boat,— tragic justice in at least one instance.

Another of the well known German enterprises against England and her Indian empire was brought to light in the so-called Hindu Plot — also very well known through newspaper publication. It came to a focus in a trial in

San Francisco, in which one Hindu leader shot another and was himself shot the next instant in the court room by a deputy marshal in attendance — a fact which perhaps lingers in the public memory even in these exciting days. The Hindu plot, reduced to its simple and banal lowest common denominator, consisted in a more or less useless intrigue with certain more or less uninfluential citizens of Hindu birth. One phase of the activities was the purchase with German money in New York of several hundred thousand rifles and several million cartridges, which were to be shipped in a vessel from the Pacific Coast to meet a certain other vessel far out in the Pacific for transfer of the cargo. That cargo was to be delivered where it would do the most good to any Hindu gentleman disposed to rise against the British authority. It is a long and rather dull story — how everything miscarried for our friends the Germans and the Hindus. The rifles never were delivered; the conspirators were brought to trial; the conspiracy was ended. And at the end, in a court room, and because he himself had a weapon in his hand, we got one Hindu Hun at least.

As a mere trifle, it may be mentioned that Joseph W———, an Austrian subject, was arraigned in the Enemy Alien Bureau at New York, charged with having in his possession a United States navy code book. W——— was said to be a "collector of stamps." He had in his possession a map of South America, and a list of warships of the Brazilian navy. He had also certain sheets of paper carrying mysterious characters made up of letters and dashes. He said he had been a piano player and was taking music lessons by mail.

Lt. Christian S——— was before the Enemy Alien Bureau at the same time. He was once six years in the German army as an officer of the Uhlans. One day S——— called on United States Marshal McCarthy and asked him to help him get a job. He returned to find out if the marshal had found a place for him, and when the marshal said he had not, the German showed anger and remarked: "This is what makes us disloyal!" Marshal McCarthy arrested S——— and arraigned him before Perry Armstrong, assistant chief of the Enemy Alien Bureau. In answer to questions, S——— said he did not approve of German-Americans, that he approved of the sinking of the Lusitania and endorsed what the Germans had done in Belgium. He was committed to Ludlow Street jail pending further investigation.

Last May there was arrested in New York one Gustave B. K———, of whom it was said: "Not only is he an officer of the German army and an intimate friend and adviser of von Bernstorff, von Papen, and Boy-Ed, but he is also a confidant, it is said, of the Kaiser and the Crown Prince. Though he has lived in the United States twenty years, he is still a German subject and is said to have paid out large sums of German money on Boy-Ed's account, having had as much as $750,000 for that purpose in one New York bank at one time."

It is enough! Further details would be revolting. Enough has been shown to develop some idea of the tremendous centralization of these international spy activities on the eastern seaboard of America. It was with these that the cities of New York and Washington had the most to do.

CHAPTER VIII

THE SPY HIMSELF

The Perverted German Mind — Stories of Brutal Indifference to Innocent Victims — Treason, Treachery, and Unmorality Hand in Hand — The Authentic Story of Dr. Scheele — Twenty-one Years a German Spy in America — The "Honor of a German Officer."

Comment has been made elsewhere in these pages on the curiously perverted nature of the German intellect. It would not be truthful to call all Germans unintellectual or unscientific, for the reverse of this is in part true. But continually in its most elaborate workings, the German mind displays reversions to grossness, coarseness, and bestiality. Perversions and atrocities seem natural to their soldiers. These restrictions apply often to men in high authority. The German officer was perhaps even more a brute than the German private.

Take the case of the man Thierichens, Captain of the *Prinz Eitel Friedrich*, which was interned at Norfolk in March, 1915, after a successful career of six months as a commerce raider. For a long time Captain Thierichens was hailed in this country as a sort of naval hero; he received the admiration not only of men but of women. It was only after a considerable career in adulation that the tide of public estimation turned in regard to this man. His private correspondence was investigated, and it was found that he was carrying on correspondence with women in this country which showed a depth of human depravity on his part which cannot be understood and may not be described.

This phase of German mentality was manifested also in the highest diplomatic representatives that that country sent abroad. These men had no sense of honor or morality, but curiously enough, they were not aware of their own lack. They performed the most pernicious acts of treason, and yet were never conscious they were committing any crime. Von Bernstorff, Dumba, von Papen, Boy-Ed, Bolo Pacha, Rintelen and Dr. Scheele—such a record of treachery never has been known in all the history of diplomacy; such a wholly devilish ingenuity, such an intellectual finesse in conspiracy, such a delicate exactness and such a crude brutality in destruction, never have been manifested on the part of any other nation in the world. The flower of centuries of civilization in Germany's case had been merely a baneful, noisome bloom, and not the sweet product of an actual culture. The efflorescence of the German heart is the fungus of decay. Feed them? Why should we feed them? Trust them? Why should we trust them? Spare them? Why should we spare them? Receive them? Why should we receive them? Believe them? Why should we ever believe them?

A fine band of conspirators was uncovered by investigations of attempted atrocities against our eastern shipping. There was a man named Robert Fay who had invented a ship bomb, and who had all the German money he needed back of him. His machine was a sort of tank which he fastened to the rudder post just below the water line of a ship which was being loaded and which stood high in the water. As the vessel was loaded, it would submerge the tank and leave everything out of sight under water. Fay had worked out one of the most ingenious devices which any of the investigating Government engineers had ever seen.

His scheme, as Mr. Strothers describes it in his book, "Fighting Germany's Spies," was to go under the stern of an ocean steamer in a small boat and to affix to the rudder post this little tank. Of course every reader will know that in steering a ship the rudder turns first this way, then that. Fay had a rod so adjusted that every time the rudder moved it turned a beveled wheel within the bomb just one notch. A certain number of revolutions of that wheel — which of course would be very slow and gradual — would turn the next wheel of the clock one notch. This would gear into the wheel next beyond it. The last wheel would slowly unscrew a threaded cap at the head of a bolt which had, pressing upon its top, a strong spring. When the cap was loose the bolt would drop and it would act like a firing pin in a rifle, its point striking upon the cap of a rifle cartridge which was adjusted just above a small charge of chloride of potash. Below the potash there was a charge of dynamite, and below that again a charge of the tremendous explosive trinitrotoluol — the explosive known as "T. N. T."

Suppose the device adjusted to the rudder of a steamship on some dark night in New York harbor. The cargo is loaded on the ship; inch by inch the ship sinks down, and this contrivance, spiked on the rudder post, is lost to sight. The ship steams out to sea. Every time she swings to change her course, every time the rudder is adjusted gently, a notch in the leisurely clock trained below her stern slips with a little, unheard click. Far out at sea — for what reason no one can tell — without any warning, the whole stern of the ship heaves up in the air. The water rushes in; the boilers explode. The ship, her cargo, her crew, her passengers, are gone.

Well, it cost but little. A few dollars would make such a bomb. Von Papen looked it over. He did not object to the cost; indeed, Germany did not scruple to spend any sum of money of the millions she sent to America, provided it would produce results. But von Papen was not sure of this; he did not think much of it. He declined it. As to the immorality of it, the frightfulness of it — that never came into his mind at all.

One recalls reading the other day that Great Britain had shot only fourteen spies. We did not shoot one in America.

The Federal grand jury in New York on December 6, 1918, returned indictments charging treason against two men who already were in the Tombs awaiting trial on an earlier charge of conspiracy. This was the first actual treason trial since we entered the war. The men were Paul Fricke of Mt. Vernon and Hermann Wessells, an Imperial German Government spy, former officer of the German navy, then domiciled in America. Their co-defendants in the conspiracy trial were Jeremiah A. O'Leary, the Sinn Fein agitator; John T. Ryan, a Buffalo lawyer; Mme. Victorica, also an alleged German spy; Willard J. Robinson, an American, and the late Dr. Hugo Schweitzer, one of the best known German business men in New York.

It was alleged that the activities of Wessells had to do with "ways and means of secretly placing explosives, or securing other persons secretly to place explosives, on wharves located in the United States, on ships and vessels in ports of the United States, and plying between ports of the United States and other countries; to blow up, injure, and destroy the same, and cause fires thereon, and thereby hinder and hamper the prosecution of the war by the United States against Germany."

The final overt act charged was that in July, 1917, Wessells requested "information as to ways and means of importing toy blocks from Switzerland," his purpose being to find "ways and means of secretly and clandestinely introducing into the United States explosives and ingredients of explosives concealed in toy blocks."

Had any of these toy blocks come into the hands of innocent children, what matter to a mind which would regard the Lusitania sinking as justifiable war? What difference would it make to a man hiding T. N. T. in a child's toys whether he killed babies in Flanders or on the high seas or in American homes? Such men are unmoral. One would call treason one of their lesser crimes.

There was in New York City a certain German whom we will call von S———. He was an inventor of a machine called an aeromobile, which, however, he said he would not sell to any government but that of Germany. He was arrested by agents of the Department of Justice, charged with uttering disloyal, scurrilous and profane remarks against the Government and military forces of the United States. He is a German-born citizen of the United States. Enter now another citizen of the United States who spoke as good German as von S——— did and who posed as "an official representative of the German Imperial Government in the United States." This latter gentleman said he wanted to buy the S——— invention for the Fatherland. S——— turned himself inside out, saying among other things: "Everything is fair in war — gas, poison, the bomb, the knife — we must stop at nothing. Germany must triumph over her enemies. I would not hesitate to destroy a whole city for the good of the German cause." After S——— had been allowed to talk sufficiently, his new friend, who proved to be an A. P. L. operative in disguise, caused his arrest by an agent in the Military Intelligence Division. S——— was struck speechless when he found he had been trapped. He was held in ten thousand dollars bail at the examination and committed to the Tombs in default of surety. Would he have been admitted to any bail at all in Germany in similar circumstances?

Out in a great city on Puget Sound, the Minute Men Division of the American Protective League, after an exhaustive investigation covering several months, arrested a certain man whom we will call Johnson. He was charged with conspiracy to doctor steel and iron in the Seattle ship-yards with a powerful chemical, intending to commit wholesale murder by wrecking troop trains. He was a pattern-maker employed in a ship-building plant when the Federal officials arrested him as an alleged German spy. At the time of his arrest, he had in his pocket a bottle containing a violent explosive. His scheme was to apply a strong acid to steel and iron in the shipyards, which would destroy these metals by eating them away. He planned to place acid on iron about to be melted, so that the resulting steel products would be valueless and the ship-building program delayed. He was charged with undertaking to damage the more delicate bearings of the ships, so that they would be useless after putting out to sea. It was part of his scheme, as developed by the operatives, to place acids in the journal boxes of cars, with the intent of destroying them while they were under way. The A. P. L. operatives claimed to be conspirators with him. When one of them pointed out that such a wreck would cost a large amount of life, the accused is said to have replied: "Well, what's the odds how we kill them, and what's the difference whether we kill them over here or over there?" That man, like many now behind bars, had no moral sense at all.

Not all of these agents of Germany were men of the mental shrewdness of their great spy leaders. Johnson picked out a fellow worker and felt him out for a long period of time as to whether he would be safe as a confidant. This particular fellow happened to look like a German, and to talk like one. He also happened to be an A. P. L. operative. The accused, who is charged under the Espionage Act, does not yet know the identity of the man who informed against him.

"There was one old German in my district," says the report of a New York state chief, "who had spent thirty years in our region, surveying. He had been an officer in the Franco-German war, and was a recognized expert in real estate values, appraisals, etc. When we went into the war, he made public a little statement telling of his German origin and of his American citizenship. He came under the suspicion of some, and I looked into the matter. One of his men remembered hearing the German say, twenty years ago, when under the influence of liquor, that he had been a German spy in the war with France; he also remembered the German's story of a horse he had used, which he had trained to run, trot or walk at certain definite paces. By keeping track of the different gaits, as he jogged along in his buggy over France, he would measure certain localities and compute distances—information which proved valuable later. It was need of such information that made Germany send out secret surveying forces when she was preparing to attack France. We put this man under surveillance but could get nothing on him except that he tried to learn when transports sailed. Apparently he had done all his work before the war began, just as he had in France before the other war."

An ingenious and dastardly instance of spy work and sabotage was recently uncovered in Detroit. Anton G——, a skilled workman employed in a factory making airplane fuel tanks, deliberately planned an aviation accident. He took a tank which had been condemned because the bottom sump casting had been riveted into the wrong position, cut the rivets, properly adjusted the casting and soldered it in place, replacing the cut rivets so that the tank appeared O. K. for use. It passed the plant's inspection, and was installed in a plane before its dangerous character was detected. G—— has given up the making of airplane tanks for the duration of the war — and longer.

Of all the individual spies located in America, one of the most noted and most able was that Dr. Scheele elsewhere mentioned as a Brooklyn druggist. Dr. Scheele was taken in Cuba by the United States Government after he had fled the country just ahead of the hounds. This accomplished student and practitioner of villainy was one of the finest chemists Germany ever produced — a descendant of a family of chemists. He was a major in the German army. That this man had intellect is beyond any question — he had more than that; he had genius. He was one of the finest examples of the great development in Germany of commercial chemistry. Men such as he have rendered services valuable beyond any price in almost all ranks of commerce, and Germany's military orders were to get them at any price, all of them, for German-controlled concerns. Such men have helped give Germany her tremendous and powerful place in the commerce of the world. This unique genius in research, this ability to divine elemental secrets, allied with the hard working, abstemious, thrifty, free-breeding traits of the German people, made that nation very strong in her position among the world forces.

But here again comes in the proof of the assertion made in regard to the debased activities of the German nature, not only in its emotional manifestations but in its intellectual processes at well. Perhaps the one thought which will awaken the bitterest resentment and the most long-lived suspicion in the American mind against the German citizen is the revelation of the fact that German spies lived among us so long as accepted citizens, made their business successes here, profited by our free-handed generosity, while all the time they were agents of Germany and traitors to the United States.

In the preceding chapter, reference was made to some of these long-term spies, as they may be called — men who were sent out on their iniquitous missions even in time of peace. The best known of these men is Scheele, who, when apprehénded, was trying to get to Europe. Now he is hugging the deputy U. S. marshal in whose custody he is, for fear some German will kill him for turning state's evidence and revealing the whole secret German spy system in the United States. This man is the most interesting of all the known spies.

In brief, Scheele came over to this country quietly, a man quite unknown, just twenty-five years ago. For twenty-one years, up to the outbreak of the war, he received regularly $125 a month as his "honorarium" from the German Government. He was one of the fixed location spies — one of very many. He went into business, opening a drug store in a New York suburb, and he prospered there. He was not alone. There were many of his people about. He met more than one prominent German living in New York City — most of whom now live in Fort Oglethorpe. In these influential circles, in continuous close touch with Berlin, supplied all the time with money from Berlin, Scheele was appraised at his true worth as a possible agent of destruction.

Came to him, therefore, one day, a captain in the service of the North German Lloyd Steamship Company. This man carried a card. From whom? No less than von Papen, a man accepted as bearing the credentials of a foreign government, entitling him to courtesy in our own country — von Papen, one of the master plotters located on this side of the sea. Scheele was asked to invent some sort of infernal machine by which ships could be set on fire after they had left port and were on the high seas. That was all. If innocent persons died, what matter? It must be a secret sort of thing, this machine, which could be distributed without creating a suspicion. It must be efficient. It must be small. It must work without much mechanism. And it must be deadly sure. This was the sort of warfare — allied to bestiality in France and Belgium, and red ruthlessness on the high seas — that was to make Germany loved and revered in the whole world, as now, amazingly enough, she asks us to be — we, her American brothers "with whom she has no quarrel."

Very well, the order was accepted by Scheele. It was simple for this man, a mechanical and chemical genius. Of course, he needed some materials. Where should he get them except among fellow Germans? And were not the entire interned crew and corps of officers of the interned German steamships, which were lying in the Hudson, available for his purposes? Scheele got all the lead and tin and like material he needed there. The Scheele cigar bomb, as it came to be called, was only three or four inches long and an inch or two in diameter. Inside of it was a thin partition made of tin. In a cavity at one end was placed a certain chemical; in the other end, divided from it for the time being by a partition sheet of tin, was a strong corrosive acid. When the ends were sealed the work was done.

It was relatively simple to put two or three of these in a pocket and casually go aboard a ship, or through the influence of simple and kindly German neighbor people, have someone else go aboard the ship and drop such a bomb into a coal bunker; or better, among the cargo. The bomb needed absolutely no attention on the part of anyone. Scheele, a competent, thorough, painstaking German scientist of Germany's highest and best type, left nothing to chance. He experimented from time to time, and verified his experiments. He knew how thick to make that partition of tin. He could make it of just such a thickness that the acid could eat through it in two or three or four days, so that if a certain steamship carried that bomb on the high seas for two or three or four days, in the course of time the acid would eat through the tin. Then, in the combination of the chemicals, heat would be generated and a fire was absolutely certain.

These things sound like the invention of a diseased mind — like the romance of some excited intellect concerning itself with unreal and impossible events belonging in another age — another world than ours. But they are true, actually true. Scheele, backed by these influential Germans in New York, backed by the diplomatic representatives of the German Government itself — we might as well say by all Germans also — actually did these things in this country.

Not one, but many ships broke into flames in mid-Atlantic. Sometimes the damage was not complete, but quite frequently the loss of a merchant ship was absolute. We cannot tell how many millions of dollars of the world's property were lost in this way through the activities of this one perverted mind. Our censorship took care of some of that. Those losses of foodstuffs, of fuel, of clothing, had to be paid for by someone. They were subtracted from the world's useful supplies. Who paid for them? You and I and all the taxpayers of America paid for the losses. One does not know how much Scheele himself got out of it — not very much; for, two months before this war was "forced" on Germany, Scheele was ordered to sell his drug store, and did so — though he complained he was doing very well in it. His salary is not known to have been raised.

One of the astonishing and disgusting developments of this war had been the knowledge gained of the unspeakable depravity and degeneracy of the German mind. There are in the Government records at Washington countless cases of German officers who, over their own signatures, have written things so foul and filthy, so low, lewd and bestial, that no pen on earth ever would rewrite them save one of their own sort. The Huns were not clean-minded fighting men, but in large percent animal-like, low, cruel, cunning, unscrupulous, unchivalrous even in their most arrogant ranks. This explains out of hand the atrocities in Belgium and France and shows what atrocities were waiting for America had this war been won by Germany.

Germany fell because she was rotten in heart and in soul. That was why she fought foul — because she *was* foul, foul to the core. It was an amazing and an abhorrent "kultur," this which she offered to the world. It is no wonder that her ways of warfare were cruel, merciless, unchivalrous; no wonder that she crucified men and tortured women and children until there is no human way ever of squaring the account with her. She no longer belongs on the clear avenues of the world, and the one epitaph she has earned is the one word, "Unclean!" History has not usually recorded such statements. No. And history has not usually been in the way of discovering such truths.

It was this Dr. Scheele, an upper class German who lived here twenty-five years as a spy, who, under German Government order, started this friendly plan against America. You cannot call that military genius. You cannot call such a man a soldier. His is simply an instance of perverted intellect. It is not even to be dignified by the term malicious. It is unmoral, base, intellectually obscene, as Thierichens was emotionally obscene.

But Scheele himself, now grown old — for he was a major when he came to America twenty-five years ago — is to-day a pleasant man of genial manner. He used to visit the home of one of his guards — to whom he stuck very close in his walks on the street, the guard having told him he would kill him on his first step toward escape — and there he always was kind to the children. "He was such a nice man," said the guard's wife — "so courtly." He is a very egotistical man, and it requires a certain playing up to his vanity to get him to talk freely. Yet he has talked freely, and has given much valuable information to the United States. The men who accompany him in his city walks would dearly love to drop him out a high window or see him try to escape. They do not love him.

But Scheele loves himself. Asked one time as to some statement he had made, he took offense at suspicion of his veracity. He, twenty-five years a spy in America, a state's-evidence man at last against his original country which he thus betrayed in turn, at this imputation slapped himself on the chest and said: "On my honor as a German officer!" Great God!

In his statements he was not often found tripping. For instance, when he said that 200,000 rifles for German revolutionists were stored in a German club in New York, its searchers did find evidence that rifles had earlier been stored there, but later removed. Scheele was taken from Washington to New York to point out these rifles. He would not go with less than four men as a guard. He is always afraid some German will kill him. Oh, yes, he is still alive. The secret men of the United States know where he is. He can be seen. He will talk. He is an elderly, kindly-looking man now — a man who speaks of his "honor as a German officer!"

The story of Scheele's ferreting out is of itself a strange and absorbing tale, which shows how our own men were on their guard. To begin with, his cigar bombs did not work infallibly — perhaps the motion of the ship would slop the acid away from the tin partition so it would not cut through quite on schedule. One or two bombs were found on shipboard. One or two were found unexploded in the coal when ships were unloading at Bordeaux. The bombs were traced back to New York. Dock laborers had been bribed to put them aboard ships sometimes — and sometimes were ashamed to do so and dropped them into the water instead. Men who can decipher code can run a trail like this. Scheele soon was located.

But Scheele had fled long before. Why? Whither? The Imperial German Government knew Scheele was going to be caught. The large spies of the German embassy promised to pick Scheele up at Cuba — where he had taken temporary residence under the practically German custody of a Spaniard who kept him in a castle which also was a prison. And so it came to pass that when the embassadorial train of the Imperial German Government was kicked out of America and all these big spies were named openly, and all the news of that big spy system began to break, von Bernstorff, von Papen and company sailed for Germany — but they did not take any chances. They did not stop at Cuba.

Scheele was abandoned by his people — he was an actual prisoner in Cuba. He was bitter. He might talk under a third degree. An A. P. L. man of New York Division, Richmond Levering, now Major Levering, U. S. A., went to Cuba, got access to Scheele, took him to Key West, took him back again to Cuba — but took him back to an actual prison. Then, finding he had no place in the world, and no friend whose protection he could not buy, he sold his "honor of a German officer" to the United States, and in return, he is still alive, having paid as the price of life the full story, so far as he knows it, of the German Imperial spy system from Wilhelmstrasse to Brooklyn Bridge.

And there you have a spy, a real one, a man who planned murder and arson on the high seas, death to unknown hundreds of men, women and children; the man who invented the mustard gas that tortured and killed our boys and those of our allies on the line in France, and whose perverted intellect did none may know what else of subtle crime " on the honor of a German officer."

Scheele made many revelations which never heretofore have been made public, because they were humiliating and shocking to us, and showed how completely we had been befooled for years. He said: " We knew all you had, everything, and we used all you had. You invented the submarine — and we used it, not you. You invented the airplane — and we used it, not you." (Which is true, as our boys in the Argonne battle would testify.) " If you had had new gases, we'd have got them. We had four men for years in your Patent Office, and you never knew it. We knew every invention useful to us. We had a man in your army secrets, one in your navy."

" But how could you do such things — how could you have men inside of our Government in that way? " interrupted the man to whom he was unburdening himself.

" Good God! " said Scheele, " we've got them in your Congress, haven't we? "

It is enough. And now comes Dernburg and believes that Americans will hail the " new understanding " between Germany and America! He believes that we shall be very good friends, now that the war is over.

CHAPTER IX

HANDLING BAD ALIENS

Dealing with Dangerous Propagandists — High and Low Class Disloyalists — The Alleged Americanism of the Kaiser's Kultur-Spreaders — A Few Instances of A. P. L. Persuasions.

In the early days of the A. P. L., Mr. Bielaski, Chief of the Bureau of Investigations of the Department of Justice, issued an explicit letter of warning and advice to all League members as to their conduct regarding aliens. The Attorney General often publicly denounced lynchings. The Bureau of Investigation always counseled prudence and full justice to all. Surely, the aliens, the unnaturalized, the strangers and visitors of other races than our own, caught in this country with or against their will by the declaration of war, can offer no complaint regarding the fairness and generosity of the treatment accorded them. These enemies of ours, these spies, propagandists and pro-Germans, had better treatment than they deserved then and better than they deserve now. We have been too temperate, too fair, too lenient with them. The moderation of the A. P. L. work, indeed, all our Government work, with traitorous persons living in America, has been a matter of astonishment to all the European nations, who perhaps knew more of the alien enemy type than we did ourselves.

A reference to the table of reports of all division chiefs will show that investigations for "disloyal and seditious utterances" far outnumber those under any other head. The truth is that Germans and pro-Germans generally were mighty cocky in their talk in this country. Arrogant and assured that Germany was going to win this war — for which, as most of her amateur and all of her special spies knew, she had been preparing for many years — they talked as though they owned America and might say or do what they liked at any time or place they pleased. As against this offensive conduct, the A. P. L. showed two phases. First, it saved many a German life, perhaps of little worth, by preventing large and free-handed lynchings; and in the second place, it exercised so potent an influence on openly sneering and boasting pro-Germans that very soon they ceased to talk where they might be heard. That any such persons ever changed very much in loyalty, that they ever gained any more love for our institutions or felt any less love for those of Germany, the author of this book, after reading some thousands of A. P. L. reports of investigations, frankly does not believe. That it was *fear* of justice in one or another form which quieted them, this author frankly does believe. And that *fear* only is going to hold down such citizens in the future, he believes with equal frankness. In their hearts, these people have learned no new principles, although in their conduct they may have learned new counsels.

America handled her racial war problem as though she were afraid of it. There is small ultimate benefit in that. The only reconstruction policy—political, commercial or industrial—by which America really can gain, is one which is going to say: "This country is America. It has but one flag." It is time we laid aside our old vote-catching methods, our old business timidities, and quit ourselves like men. Indeed, it is impossible to get in touch with the mass of the A. P. L. testimony and not to feel bitter and more bitter toward the traitors who have been left immune under our flag—not to feel sure and more sure that we have handled them too gently and to our own later sorrow. All this is written in absolute deliberation, with a certain feeling of authoritativeness. It has been given to few men to read the mass of testimony which the writing of this book necessitated. To do so was to sit in touch of the greatest reflex of the real America that perhaps ever has existed. We deal here not with theories, but with actual, concrete facts.

We do not give authorized figures as to the alien enemies interned, but it is sometimes said that we interned only about five thousand aliens, that we paroled a very large number, deported a few, and revoked citizenship for only two. It was said that the close of the war would set free a great many of these persons who will resume their residence, if not their former activities, in America. It is true that we have not executed a single German spy. That is an astonishing commentary on our laws and our Government in times such as these. Let those who are wiser than the writer of this book can claim to be after the extraordinary experience of studying the real America, pass on the wisdom of such leniency in its bearing on later Bolshevism in America. Other nations certainly have acted otherwise. Sometimes they have smiled at us as the easy mark of all the nations.

Certainly, however, whatever may be the personal belief of many citizens of this country, our public documents prove the wish of our Department of Justice, all its Bureaus and all its auxiliaries, to be just and more than just, generous and more than generous, to those not in accord with our laws and institutions,—a strange contrast for the reflection of those "simple and kindly" folk who for four years have exulted in the outrages Germany has wrought upon the world, and who for four years have given the world the most detestable examples of treacherous espionage.

At times we did teach some of those gentry that there was a God in Israel. If as yet we have deported few or none of those interned aliens—all of whom, and a hundred thousand more, surely ought to be deported—if we have received back into our tolerant friendship those who have been for some time warned out of our Government zones, at least we have trailed down certain of the more active cases of Kultur spreading in America. Space confines us to very few of those, chosen almost at random from the thousands at hand in the records.

The chief centers of alien enemy activity in this country, as might have been expected, were the great industrial towns and cities. It was in these places that the A. P. L. fought its hardest fights and achieved its greatest triumphs.

The great city of Seattle was no exception. The report of the splendid work it did all through the far Northwest ought by every right to appear in full. We must be content, however, to extract from the Seattle record a couple of interesting incidents of trailing aliens.

The first suspect was a German who had changed the spelling of his name. Outer appearances were in his favor. He resided in a good part of Seattle, in a good bungalow, and showed all the insignia of the Red Cross, Liberty Loans, etc., in his windows. He was unassuming in his manner and openly talked patriotism. However, as the case proceeded, it was found that he associated with a domestic of a citizen, and that this domestic collected Canadian bills and sent them to Canada. Tracing this clue, the suspect C——— was found to have come from Canada where he had been interned. He had made his escape and come to the United States without permission. He had a covert postoffice box in the name of Joe M——— (his real German name was K———), and he had been an alien enemy agent of Germany. He was arrested by an A. P. L. man, brought before Federal officials and later was interned for the period of the war.

In the possession of this man there was found a long list of names of Germans, all of whom were afterwards found to have served in the German Army, but who were now corporals or privates in the American Army. These men were stationed mostly in forts on Puget Sound. Through these men, C——— had a well established system leading into the Navy Yard of Puget Sound and the forts protecting the harbors. There was taken into custody a photographer, T———, who had in his possession photographs of nearly everything in and about Fort Worden. T———, who was associated with C——— in some manner, was given a hearing and released on ten thousand dollars bail. The money was immediately put up by Germans then under suspicion at Fort Townsend. At about this time, T———'s house took fire and burned down. One trunk was saved, of which he quickly took charge when released on bail. There were other arrests made in this case, regarding the final issue of which nothing can be said at this writing. So much at least for the gentle and unassuming Mr. C———, quiet citizen.

Seattle had another case which ended in an internment,

that of Gus S———, whose story is succinctly covered in the words of the Seattle Chief:

Early in January, 1918, our organization was requested by the Department of Justice to get a line on one Gus S———, generally believed to be a German who worked along the water front dismantling boats and storing the material, which he afterwards sold for junk. Operatives H——— and B——— were detailed on this case, and confirming the suspicions of the authorities, it was established that S——— had a cache in a remote district of the Sound where he buried the stolen articles until they had accumulated in sufficient quantity that he could sell them wholesale.

It was found that he had four points established on the Sound as headquarters; one of them situated about forty miles north of Seattle where he could dodge in and out among the numerous islands on the Sound and evade the authorities.

On the morning of January 9, 1918, one Dr. W——— voluntarily appeared at the office of the American Protective League, 615 Lyon Building, stating that he was a German and had done considerable intricate work in the Government and that he was anxious to serve our organization. W——— was immediately placed under investigation, and it developed that he was a German alien enemy, and was in the habit of violating his alien enemy permit. It was also discovered that he owned and occupied a houseboat on the East Waterway in the ship-building district, in the prohibited zone on the water front. This place was visited and examined. Our operatives found documents proving that W——— was an alien enemy and a Reserve Officer in the German Army. He had on board the houseboat an extensive chemical laboratory and a complete chemical library in the German language; also technical books on wireless and other matters of military importance. The chemicals were seized, sent to the Immigration Department and examined by a chemist. W——— was placed under arrest, given a hearing, and ordered interned for the duration of the war.

It developed that W——— had communicated with S——— and warned him of his approaching arrest, and that S——— had departed north in his boat. The League officers immediately got in touch with their organization in Skagit County, and operatives were detailed to watch for S———. When he came into the Flats, they apprehended and placed him under arrest and seized his boat. On board was found quite an arsenal of assorted makes of guns. The examination took place at the time an opportunity was being given alien enemies to register as such, and this opportunity was given S——— at the Immigration Station. S———, however, maintained that he was an American citizen; he could not produce papers but his explanation was as follows: That he had filed his declaration to become an American citizen and that, by reason of his activities against the law, he had been arrested and sentenced to serve six years in the penitentiary at Walla Walla; that while he was serving out his sentence, the date for him to appear for examination and acquire his second papers had expired, and that on account of his inability to appear, this automatically made him an American citizen. Therefore, he refused to register as an alien enemy. At the conclusion of the hearing, S——— was ordered interned and sent to Utah.

S——— had, for the previous six weeks, been hovering around the depot tanks of the Standard Oil Company. From the association of W——— and S——— and the facts that were disclosed in the investigation, there is no question in the minds of the officers of the organization but that they were about to cause an explosion at this plant as well as at one of the shipyards.

Yet another good report from the Seattle Chief covers the case of M. J. B———, alias W. J. H———, who apparently was unable to keep all his life as secret as he might wish. We cannot improve upon the report of the Chief as it was written:

B——— appeared in Seattle early in December, 1917, and took rooms at the P——— Hotel. From his acts it was immediately noted by our operatives at the hotel that B——— was receiving packages under the assumed name of W. J. H———, which name he explained to the clerk was used as a code. He received no visitors except two persons of foreign birth, and it developed that upon going to the hotel he was without ready money to sustain his expenses. Within a short time, however, B——— was found to have not only sufficient funds to maintain his daily expenses, but quite a surplus, which he was using lavishly. He claimed to be a working man, but his hands, dress and facial appearance were certainly those of a man who was accustomed to appearing in society, and taking life rather easy.

Following certain suspicious activities on the part of B———, an investigation thereof disclosed the fact that he was having considerable correspondence with Germans in the

United States, and that he had the names and addresses apparently of every German in the United States. It further developed that he had cards made in Seattle, representing himself as being connected with a bank in Detroit. He was placed under arrest and sent to the Detention Station in the Department of Immigration to establish his nationality and status. He claimed to have been taking orders for a toy balloon concern on W——— Avenue, the proprietor of which stated that B——— had worked for him on a commission basis, but that his total commissions for the first year would amount to about $86.00, approximately. This was the merest trifle compared to the totals believed to have been spent by the subject, and he evidently had some other source of income than that derived from toy balloons.

The subject was well educated, spoke four or five languages, and it developed that he had formerly held a commission of lieutenant in the Austrian army. B——— was a sketch artist, very clever, and in passing through the country, was accustomed to make landscape scenes of various places of interest from a military standpoint — which sketches, together with certain puzzle sketches, were believed by the officers of the organization to be for the purpose of furnishing information to the enemy.

The specific charge was thought by him to be that he was an I. W. W., and he requested the permission of the Immigration authorities to address a letter to a friend, which permission was given. This letter, which, of course, was censored by the authorities, addressed a German at Bremerton, close to the Navy Yard, and complained of his arrest as an I. W. W. He informed this friend that he had done a great many things which he "had been ordered to do," but that he was not, nor had he been, requested to be an I. W. W., and he requested aid for his release.

A very complete examination was made of B——— and his entire movements since arriving in this country. It developed that he was born at Frankstock, Moravia, in Austria; that he was twenty-four years of age, had had military training, had just completed same prior to departing for this country, and was a Second Lieutenant in the 54th Royal Imperial Infantry. He was in Hamburg and Paris during 1914, and just prior to the outbreak of the war, he came to New York, passing through England on this trip, since which time it developed that he had been receiving money from Germany, and had been operating in the cities of Hoboken, Pittsburgh, Cleveland, Chicago, Seattle, Helena and Spokane. Regardless of the fact that he was heir to an estate in Austria and was supposed to have reported to the consul (Austrian) in Seattle, he claimed he had not done so.

In explanation of the alias, W. J. H———, he claimed to have adopted that name simply because his name was funny. It developed that B——— had been previously arrested and released, and had in his possession documents covering his entire experiences, as well as information concerning his particular case. Certain documents, undoubtedly codes, were taken from B———, and the only information or explanation he would give concerning them was that they were puzzles. The subject was well acquainted with the German element in each of the towns he had visited, many of whom were held under suspicion by the authorities. It further developed that he had made frequent visits to the ship-yards and to the Navy Yards, and that he was intimately associated with certain leaders of the order of the I. W. W. He was ordered interned, and sent to Utah.

It never was urged against Seattle that she displayed anything but live wire characteristics, and it is too bad that we may not delve deeper into the Seattle files. The Chief adds: "We have many other cases, perhaps of more importance." The existing records bear out the assertion. But we must dismiss this big center of activity with only a brief summary of tables showing six months' work of the Minute Men Division of the American Protective League for Seattle. The situation revealed by this summary, astounding as it is, and humiliating as it must be to make the admission, is one that finds a parallel in the experience of every great industrial center in America during the war.

TABLE OF CASES INVESTIGATED BY THE SEATTLE DIVISION OF THE AMERICAN PROTECTIVE LEAGUE

Report for Six Months, May 1 to November 1, 1918.

Alien Enemies	399
Aliens and Citizens Living in Luxury Without Visible Means of Support	36
Anti-Military Activities	23
Bomb and Dynamite Cases	14
Passport Applications	1,114
Loyalty Reports to Government	707

Alleged Deserters	93
Destruction of Foods	8
Disloyal Citizens	677
Disloyal Government Employees	35
Draft Evaders	86
Incendiarism	4
Food Regulation Violators	239
Liberty Bond and Red Cross Slackers	938
I. W. W. Agitators	1,198
Pro-German Radicals	990
Sale of Liquor to Soldiers and Sailors	64
Alleged Spies or German Agents	451
Seditious Meetings	91
Seditious Publications	53
Seditious Utterances	449
Wireless Stations	21
Naturalization Cases	386
Jurors	542
Miscellaneous	624
Total	10,042
Total number of arrests made	1,008

There came up in the Birmingham, Ala., Division the character investigation of R. E. S———, a lieutenant in the United States Army, reported to be in the Military Intelligence Department, foreign service. This man lived in Birmingham several years before the declaration of war, and moved with the best people. He always seemed to have enough money for the demands of society, although his business was limited in its earning capacity. He attended a training camp and received a commission, but after he had arrived in France, the War Department requested an investigation through the League. The result shows that danger existed at all times from German explosives even in the most jealously guarded places. Below is given the substance of the investigation. The first operative reported:

I have known S——— for several years, and have always been impressed with his pro-German tendencies. He lived in comparative comfort, belonged to all of the clubs and moved in the best society. He never appeared to be lacking in funds in spite of the fact that the income from his position, and later his business, did not warrant his living in this manner. It was understood that he had no investments producing income. I have thought for the past four years that he received money from the German Government, and have so expressed myself on many occasions.

Before we entered the war, S——— was very bitter in his denunciation of England for going into it. He claimed Russia and France were responsible and that Germany was fighting for her life. He stated that England would rue the day she went in, and that nothing could stand against the Kaiser and his great war machine. He considered the Kaiser the greatest man on earth and the German people superior to all others. He justified the invasion of Belgium as a war necessity and the ravages of that country and of invaded France on the same grounds. He gloried in the sinking of the Lusitania, and stated that all who lost their lives on it deserved to do so. He criticised the general policy of our government and President Wilson.

When we entered the war, S———'s whole attitude changed and immediately he was anxious to fight for his country. He attended the first Officer's Training Camp at Ft. McPherson, Georgia, but was discharged in a short time. He was bitter about this and stated he had not gotten a square deal.

I have discussed S——— on many occasions with a great many of my friends, and the consensus of opinion is that he is entirely too pro-German to be in our Army in any capacity. Many think he is an agent of the German Government. Personally, I feel that he is an extremely dangerous man. I would not care to serve in the Army under him as an officer, and I would like to see him placed in such a position that he could not possibly do us harm.

Another operative said he did not think S———a safe man to have in the United States Army. In his presence, S——— approved the sinking of the Lusitania, and said that the people who lost their lives had no business on the ship. He also stated that he had two brothers in business in Germany before the United States entered the war. Operative said that S——— was strongly pro-German in his sympathies. He regarded him as a dangerous man—particularly dangerous if he was in the Intelligence Department. Operative stated that he had no confidence whatever in S———'s loyalty. He stated that S——— admired Germany and thought the Germans were the greatest people on earth.

A third operative prefaced his statement with the remark that he was a warm personal friend of S——— and did not want to do him an injustice. He did say that S———, before the entry of the United States into the war, was intensely pro-German. On being asked if he would like to be a private in a company commanded by S——— and pressed for an answer, he said: "Well, I would like to know my captain hated the Germans a whole lot more than S——— does." He further said that if S——— were to be captured, he would very soon be on friendly terms with his captors.

Follows a statement of an operative who had known S——— for twenty-five or thirty years, and had been on the terms of the best friendship for several years past:

> Prior to the entry of the United States into the war, S——— was rabidly pro-German and expressed himself freely on any and all occasions. He thought that Germany was all-powerful and had nothing to fear from the Unted States. He favored the German U-Boat policy, and said: "I am damn glad of it!" when he read the newspaper notice of the sinking of the Lusitania. He said furthermore that the people on the ship got just what was coming to them, and they had no business being on it. S——— seemed to be thoroughly imbued with the idea that the Germans are supermen, and that they could do anything. He regarded the Kaiser as the greatest man on earth. He took all the German papers in the country, and received German propaganda from some source unknown. When he went to the Officer's Training Camp in Atlanta, he wrote a card to one of his friends here asking him to forward his mail but not to forward any newspapers. He was a constant reader of papers of German tendencies. He stated in conversation that the United States had no Navy, and that the safest place for its ships was in our harbors; that there was more danger to our sailors from our own ships than from anything else. He seemed to have a great deal of information concerning the armament and equipment of the United States as regards cannon, small arms and vessels, together with the number of men in our Army and Navy. Mr. R——— did not know where he got the information nor what he did with it. S——— knew all the local anarchists and wild-eyed citizens of German and Russian nationality. One day S——— was talking on the street with a friend when a rough, unkempt, hobo-like man passed them. S——— asked his friend to ex-

cuse him a moment as he wanted to speak to that man. He conversed in German with the man for several moments, and on his return said: "He is a Russian anarchist, and he told me that a revolution is brewing in Russia and that the Germans will not have to fight the Russians much longer." He always expressed great pleasure at any news which was favorable to Germany. He did not think the United States had any business entering the war. He has relatives in Germany now.

When asked the direct question if he thought it advisable for S——— to be in the Intelligence Division of the Army, operative said:

I would not want to be in a company which he commands, and I believe it highly dangerous for him to be in the Intelligence Department. I believe if he was captured by the Germans, he would have nothing to fear.

The report of this operative further says:

S——— had a twin brother engaged in the tea importing business in New York. In July, 1917, the twin brother referred to said that he would not fight the Kaiser, that he was a German. He was even more rabid than the subject of this report. It was rumored here for some time that S——— was a German spy but there was never anything definite to verify the rumor, though he was very active in gathering all sorts of information regarding the material resources of the United States. He cultivated the acquaintance of the amateur wireless operators here, and was a fairly expert telegraph operator himself. Mr. R——— stated: "If S——— is in the Intelligence Department in France, it is an extremely dangerous thing and might cause a terrible disaster."

After S——— went to Washington last fall, and after he had received his commission in the United States Army, he wrote a letter severely criticising the United States War Department for inefficiency. His strictures were of such a nature that B——— said to R——— that he was very sorry that he had read it. S——— and B——— burned the letter. This letter criticised the methods of the War Department, stated that things were badly handled, and that our preparations for war were inadequate and inefficiently managed. This letter was written after S——— had received his commission as First Lieutenant in the United States Army and was stationed in Washington. A German friend admitted that S——— was violently pro-German before our country entered the war. He said that Germany had a right to sink our ships after giving us warning of the restricted zone in which German submarines were operating. He justified the sinking of the Lusitania, and expressed no sympathy for the people who lost their lives, stating that they got what they deserved as they had no business on the ship. He justified the invasion of Belgium as a war necessity, and condoned Germany's violation of her pledge to preserve the integrity of Belgium because it was a war measure. S——— regarded the Germans as a superior people, and admired the Kaiser greatly. He was much opposed to the entry of the United States into the war, said that he was so sorry that we had gotten into it, and that it was not our affair but England's.

It has been thought advisable to take these widely separated cases and to give them in detail rather than to present summaries of a large number of cases which may or may not have resulted in sentences or internments. An examination of these instances will show the fairness and shrewdness with which the League's Chiefs and Operatives worked, as well as their unflagging interest in the work offered them. It also will be apparent that a single investigation might involve a great deal of patient, hard work.

CHAPTER X

THE GREAT I. W. W. TRIAL

Story of the Greatest Criminal Prosecution Known in the Jurisprudence of America — The Lawless Acts Leading up to the Arrests — Methods of Violence Used by Members of the I. W. W.— Sabotage and Terror — Chief Figures of the Trial — Incidents from the Inside.

The greatest trial with which the American Protective League was identified was the genuine *cause celébrè* known all over the world as the I. W. W. trial. It began in the Federal Court for Chicago, presided over by Judge Kenesaw M. Landis (the same of fame in the Standard Oil case), on April 1, 1918, and ended with ninety-seven convictions and sentences in one lot. The case was concluded at two in the afternoon of August 30, 1918.

The trial lasted for five months. The preparation for it covered two years or more. The record is said to be the most elaborate and complete ever prepared in any case at law. The case was by no means a Chicago or Illinois case, but was a national and indeed an international one. The documentary and other evidence preserved in the rooms of the Bureau of Investigation in Chicago is so voluminous as to pass belief, and it includes more proof of the depravity of the human mind than any like assemblage of written and printed material known to man. It is the record of the attempted ruin of this republic.

With this great case, the American Protective League had been connected practically all the time from the date of its own inception. It had men shadowing the suspects, men intercepting their mail, men ingratiating themselves into their good graces, men watching all their comings and goings, men transcribing and indexing the reports, men looking into the law in all its phases as bearing on these cases. No one knows how many A. P. L. operatives, in all the states from Michigan westward, worked on this case for months before an arrest was made. There were fifteen lawyers, all of them members of the League, not one of whom got a cent of pay, who worked for a full year helping the Bureau of Investigation to brief the evidence. There you see the A. P. L. in action.

For months and years before the arrests, the Industrial Workers of the World, as they call themselves, had been notorious for their anarchy and violence. Countless acts of ruthlessness had marked their career; millions and perhaps billions in property had been destroyed by them; their leader had been tried for the murder of a governor of a Western state, though acquitted. Nothing lacked in their record of lawlessness and terror, and they were inspired by a Hun-like frightfulness as well as a Hun-like cunning which for a time both excited and baffled the agents of the law in a dozen Western States.

The I. W. W. as an organization began, according to their Secretary and Treasurer, W. H. Haywood, in 1904, in an amalgamation agreed to by officers of the Western Federation of Miners and the American Labor Union. The theory of the band, reduced to its least common denominator, was that of striking terror by secret acts of violence. Their ethics were precisely those of the barnburner, who works in the dark. What was their reason for their acts? None. They all had had their fair chance in America—more than a fair chance. But, because some men had wealth, they thought they also should have, and if it was not offered them free, then they would show their resentment by destroying wealth and injuring those who had it. Their plea was the wish to "aid the laboring man." God save the mark! They did more to hurt the cause of labor than could have been done in any other way in the world. They stained the name of this republic so black that the most rabid labor unions in Europe protested and disowned them. And they got their reward for that; or at least some of them have, and more will have before the tale is told.

Sabotage and strikes were the common methods of the I. W. W. organization, which at the time of the trial numbered over 100,000 members, mostly scattered in the West in many trades. They managed strikes in widely scattered parts of the Union, and as they grew bolder, they planned in war times a general strike of all branches of labor, all over the United States. They first began work among the lumber-jacks, then among the miners. They meant to include all harvest hands in harvest time, all agricultural labor, indeed, labor of every sort. It was the plan to demand a six hour day and $6.00 a day, even for all farm labor; which, as all Americans now carrying the war prices of living can see, would inevitably have raised the price of food unspeakably had it succeeded. When opposed, they wrecked and burned and ruined, maimed, murdered.

"Big Bill" Haywood, the I. W. W. leader, execrated "military preparedness." He called sabotage—that is to say, secret industrial wrecking—the "weapon of the disinterested." Perhaps in peace times our fatuousness as a people would have caused us to pay small attention even to the series of I. W. W. outrages. We would have absorbed the discomforts and the crimes in our old careless, cowardly way. But now we were at war. We were making ships and airplanes, cannon and small arms and munitions and clothing and equipment. We needed the labor of every loyal man as much as we needed money and soldiers. And it was about this time that Frank H. Little (an I. W. W. leader who was lynched in Butte, Montana, soon after) wrote a letter to the general board of the I. W. W., demanding that the board should take action against the draft law requiring service in the Army.

This, coupled with the evidence of strikes, and the prospect of paralysis in many essential government activities, was going too far. It was known that the I. W. W. intended to get at the marine workers, then all allied industries. That would have meant the end of the war, or of our activity in the war.

Now, therefore, these arrogant and lawless men, never else than malcontents, became traitors. In order to work out to the quotient of ruin these vague theories about the "rights of man," they cast aside what shred of patriotism they ever may have had to cover their nakedness of manhood, and declared themselves ready to cripple and leave helpless before her merciless foe this republic of America, whose whole theory from the foundation has been that of the rights of man, who fought in all her wars for the rights of man and has asked only in this peace the recognition of the rights of man. Ah, they were so wise, these ruffians!

But now they ran against our espionage law and its new teeth. Secretly watched for months by the many agents of the Government and its auxiliaries, the I. W. W. was at last found with sufficient goods on it to warrant the movement of the law's forces. The charges were made that I. W. W. members had violated the espionage act; that they had fostered strikes to delay the output in war munitions; that they had spoiled industrial material; that they had been guilty of acts of violence against men not of their views; that they had violated the postal laws; that they had violated the statutes against conspiracy. The indictments were framed on those general lines, and the long arm of Uncle Sam, not that of any state or county or city, reached out for the accused.

By this time the agitations of the I. W. W. had covered Montana, Arizona and Colorado, were reaching into Utah and Nevada, and had Minnesota and Michigan next on the list. But *pari passu* with the I. W. W. activities had gone on those of certain other alphabetical organizations, to wit, D. J. and A. P. L.

Mr. Clabaugh, the storm center of the Chicago Bureau of Investigation, worked long months with the Government attorneys. Mr. Frank Nebeker, the trial lawyer, was an assistant U. S. Attorney General of Salt Lake City, and he was on this case for over a year. It was he who directed the raids. He was assisted by Mr. Claude Porter, of Des Moines, Iowa, U. S. Attorney for the Southern District of Iowa—now Assistant to the U. S. Attorney General in Washington. Mr. Porter came on as Special Assistant in place of Mr. Frank C. Dailey of Indianapolis, who had resigned. These men and their aids brought together, as has been said, the most elaborate legal records ever known. *That they had the evidence* is proved by the results of the trial—ninety-seven convictions out of the ninety-nine accused and tried. The A. P. L. *got the evidence.*

These men and Mr. Clabaugh were all in conference with U. S. Attorneys all over the country from Detroit west, and in conference with the governors of many states as well. Everything was kept secret. Then, one day, a wire flashed across the country which set the law afoot. At the same moment, two o'clock, Central time, on the afternoon of September 5, 1917, one hundred I. W. W. offices were raided. The Web had done its work! One hundred and sixty-five frightened insects struggled where but now a like number of arrogant and boastful traitors had strutted free. At one time Mr. Clabaugh took down to the Department of Justice in Washington a large trunk full of papers—incriminating documents once property of the I. W. W. It would take such reading of these unspeakable documents by all the American public as these officers of the law gave them, before America ever could know what foul sort of traitors she has been welcoming here at her own table.

Some of these arrested suspects were bailed out, others held in prison. Of the total arrested, ninety-nine were brought to trial. The case began before that staunch fighting man, Judge Landis—who had a son in the U. S. aviation corps himself—on Monday, April 1, 1918, and a month was spent in selecting a jury. In all this work, the A. P. L. was active, and more than once its men choked off alleged illegal enterprises—for the defendants were desperate now. The opening statement was made by Mr. Nebeker on May 2, and examination of witnesses followed for six weeks, when the Government rested till Wednesday, June 19. Mr. George Vandever, for the defense, made the opening statement on Monday, June 24. Judge Landis charged the jury Saturday, August 17. The jury brought in its verdict in fifty-five minutes and on one ballot. The statements of the prisoners were taken on Thursday, August 29, and sentence was passed by Judge Landis at 2:00 P. M., August 30, 1918.

The jury had needed but little time for deliberation. The judge in reading his instructions, dismissed the fifth count of the indictment, charging a conspiracy to violate the postal laws of the United States. After telling the jury that it had exclusive domain over the determination of the facts of the case, while it must take the law from the Court, Judge Landis said it was within the province of the court to give his opinion regarding the evidence.

"But in this case I shall not do so," said the court. "I shall submit it to you free from expression of my own judgment. Your decision shall be the last and only one on the question of fact."

He then explained the law of conspiracy at considerable length, after presenting a brief digest of the substance of the indictment. He announced that it was unnecessary to prove explicit agreement to enter a conspiracy against the defendants if there was circumstantial evidence that such a conspiracy existed, judged by the facts and the actions of the defendants.

"Mere passive knowledge of the criminal activities of other persons is not sufficient to establish a conspiracy," he instructed. "Some participation, coöperation, must be shown to establish the connection of any defendant, and by evidence of fact and circumstances independent of the declarations of other people,—that is, by evidence of the defendants' own acts. Until such evidence is introduced, the defendants are not bound by the declaration or statements of others. But after it is shown he is a member of the conspiracy, he is so bound, providing the acts are in furtherance of the common purpose."

The court also instructed that if any defendants entered the conspiracy after it started, knowing its purpose, they were equally guilty as if they had been of those who originally conspired, but he tempered this by suggesting that they might all have been guilty of minor conspiracies in different places, and he stated that if these were not related to a common purpose, they were not guilty under the indictment. He also announced that they might all be guilty of the acts of violence set forth in the indictment, and yet, if these were not related to a common conspiracy, they were not guilty in the charge in the case.

Both sides professed satisfaction with the instructions. The sentences of the Court sent Haywood and fourteen others, his principal aids, to the penitentiary for twenty years. Thirty-three men got ten years, the same number got five years; twelve men got a year and a day, two men got off with two days in jail, and two had their cases continued. There was well nigh a train load of them that started for Leavenworth federal penitentiary the next day.

The Department of Justice could not find handcuffs enough in the city of Chicago to accommodate all the prisoners on that train!

The total time covered by these I. W. W. sentences amounts to eight hundred and seven years and twenty days. The world is deprived of that much-too-independent work in a time when the world needs honest labor. Haywood's boast that there are 100,000 uncaught and unrepentant I. W. W.'s in the United States alone is all the proof needed of the nature of the men thus put away.

These men, like most under-cover criminals, were cowards. Haywood's face went white when he heard sentence passed on him. The prisoners, but lately sneering and arrogant, now sat overwhelmed. Their friends and adherents also were stunned. The court room was filled with armed U. S. Marshals and A. P. L. men, all unknown and all ready for trouble. There was no trouble. Dead silence was in the room. All bail was cancelled, of course, and the march to jail began.

What did the Government prove against the I. W. W.'s? That they had been guilty of almost everything a depraved mind could invent in the way of crime. The public is already conversant with the argot of the band. The "sab cat," or worker of sabotage—secret destruction of property—was a title of pride among them. "Wobblies," "high jacks," "scissor-bills," "bundle-stiffs"—all were part of the personnel put in evidence. A "clock" was divulged to mean a phosphorus bomb, intended to be fired by the sun and set a wheat stack ablaze.

These men spiked a great many spruce trees so that mill saws were ruined on the logs. They killed vineyards in California, and claimed to have burned $2,000,000 worth of wheat in that state alone. They not only burned wheat in the stack, but sowed spikes to damage reapers. They dropped matches and bits of metal in threshing machines. They put emery in delicate machine bearings. In canning factories they mixed the labels, so that grades were vitiated for the vegetables sent out. They polluted or poisoned canned goods with dead rats and the like in factories where they worked. No doubt also they set forest fires, and beyond doubt caused explosions that destroyed hundreds of thousands of dollars in property. They did this to terrorize their own country in its day of peril. They were not worth the name of men. You can not make citizens out of such creatures. *Fear* is all they understand.

Their literature was a continuous blasphemy. Cursing the name of the Savior was nothing to their writers. They put lime in men's shoes and burned their feet to the bone. They had a special sort of club they used in attacking "scabs." It had short, sharp nails driven along it, painted the color of the club so they could not easily be seen. The victim would catch at the club to wrest it from his assailant. It was then jerked through his hands, often tearing out the sinews, always scarring and often maiming him forever. Always they were cowards. To injure and not destroy was part of their religion. "Strike while you work" meant to disable a machine for a while and so to stop work for the crew or for the whole plant. "Feed the kitty more cream" meant to use more emery on bearings, to do more dirt in factories, to wreck and mar and mutilate more cunningly and covertly—and to escape by feigning the innocent laboring man. If they were not all Huns, they had the foul Hun imagination, and also the methods of the Hun.

By December of 1918, the trial of a half hundred more alleged I. W. W. men was progressing at Sacramento, California. The attempt of the prosecution there was to show a nation-wide plot against the Government of the United States. And again, A. P. L. had the evidence ready, ticketed and tabulated, for A. P. L. covers all of the United States and not merely one part. On January 16, 1919, forty-six of the defendants were convicted.

If we have 100,000 I. W. W. members such as these yet among us, and internment camps full of Germans and pro-Germans, would there not seem need for a house cleaning? It is time now for a new American point of view. We are not going to allow America to be used as it has been by these men. *Fear* at least they shall understand.

CHAPTER XI

THE SLACKER RAIDS

How the A. P. L. Made Patriots — Chasing the Slacker — Teaching the Love of the Flag — Incidents of Western Raids.

Even had Mr. Bryan's famous prophecy come true, that a million armed men would spring up over night and so end at once any trouble America might presumably experience in going to war, there still would have existed a vast deficit in our Army, which at the time of the Armistice had more than two million men armed and on the soil of France, almost as many in training, and ten times as many listed as army material if needed—although, to be sure, they had not sprung up either armed or equipped, as perhaps France or Great Britain could testify. The new draft ages of 18 to 45 swept in a vast additional army under the latest conscription act, although the first registration, those of 21 to 31, had set on foot our first American forces—as fine soldiers as ever stood on leather.

A great many phrases are made in time of war about war itself, and most of these come around to the ancient recruiting sergeant's inviting motto recounting the glory of dying for one's country. The Napoleonic wars were fought on the death-or-glory basis; but Napoleon got his troops by rigid conscription. We fought this war on a more sober basis of necessity. Most of us who are old enough and wise enough to study human nature and world politics knew that commercial jealousy, and not any abstract theories about democracy and the rights of man, lay basically under this war, as they have lain under most other wars. And the boys of the world—youth being resilient, of high pulse and low blood pressure, and believing, as youth always does, that nothing wrong can happen to youth and hope—were called on once more to fight the wars of the world, as the boys always have been asked to do.

Youth and middle age volunteered, old age itself volunteered, but the truth became obvious that our volunteer army would not spring armed over night in sufficient numbers. In fairness, we passed our draft acts, euphonically termed "Selective Service Acts," it being intended that this action should bring America to its focus, and should put under arms warm and lukewarm lovers of our flag alike. As it seems to this writer, that originally was unfair only in that it made the maximum service age too low. It cast the burden of the war on the boys, the young men, most of whom had never felt hate against any country, and knew little about the causes of this war; for soldiers often do not really know why they fight.

Under the weak American pacifist propaganda, there lay much human nature and very much more of shrewd German propaganda. Germany always has had this country sown with spies and secret agents, as we have shown, and always has counted very largely on the German-American loyalty to the flag of Germany. That very able spy, Prince Henry of Prussia, brother to that now very contemptible but once very arrogant coward, William Hohenzollern, carried back to his royal brother the most confident reports regarding potential German forces in America. He was especially well received in Milwaukee and Chicago, where he was met and welcomed by officials not unmindful of the value of the German vote.

We find all these influences enlisted to aid and abet any natural reluctance of boys to go to war, boys of the noblest and bravest souls, who none the less had mothers to weep over them, sisters and sweethearts to hold them back. So there became apparent, in more cities than one, the truth that a great many young men had not registered, had not filled out questionnaires, were deserting, or were in some way evading the draft.

Very naturally, an intense feeling grew up against these draft-dodgers and slackers, a feeling based on the fair-play principle. If one man's son must go, why not the next man's, especially as that next man might be a secret pro-German trying to protect his blood as well as his property?

But the blood had really nothing to do with the real question between the government and the man needed with the colors. The law was the law, and it played no favorites after the exemption boards were done. The fit man of proper age must show himself.

Orders went out, in the summer of 1918, from the Department of Justice to throw the net for slackers. That meant the immediate mobilization for police duty not only of many soldiers and sailors, many policemen and all the force of the Bureau of Investigation, but also of the entire personnel of the American Protective League. With the exception of the I. W. W. cases, the aid the Chicago division of the League gave in the great raids of July 11, 12, 13 and 14, in 1918, was its most important single contribution to the welfare of the country. The New York slacker raids (of a certain publicity), those carried on also in Philadelphia, San Francisco, and many other cities, were all so similar in method, that the story of the Chicago raids will describe them all.

The big slacker drive in Chicago meant the mobilization of the entire League membership, and over 10,000 men were enlisted from this organization alone as operatives in the slacker search. These men interrogated over 150,000 suspects, and seized over 20,000; and they inducted into the army, as willing or unwilling patriots, around 1,400 young men of that one city who otherwise would not have served. At one time they had herded on the great Municipal Pier over 1,100 men, all of whom had to pass the night there. Countless motor cars and wagons carried loads under guard. A big tourist motor-bus was requisitioned also, and all the street cars were packed. Hundreds of men were crowded over night in the rooms of the Bureau of Investigation in the Federal Building. The courts and jails were jammed. Vacant store-rooms were filled with prisoners. Mothers, wives, sweethearts, sisters, brothers and babies made the Federal Building an actual bedlam when they rallied to the attempted rescue. But the grist ground on through, and the guilty were found and dealt with. Most of the young men were glad enough to exchange a bed on a stone floor for one in an Army tent. No doubt, most of them made good soldiers afterwards. They were rather passively than actively disloyal—and all of them were young.

No announcement was made of the plans of the Government. The word was passed silently that at a certain hour the hunt would be on. Once begun, it was prosecuted with energy and system. All the current ball games were visited, and the crowds were told to file out at a gate, where each suspect was asked to show his registration card. Motion picture shows were treated in the same way, the perfect districting and subdividing of the League's force making all this synchronous and smooth. Cabarets and all-night places of all sorts were combed out. All the city parks were patrolled at night, and many a young man was taken from his young woman companion in that way. Members of the League even donned bathing costumes, and swimming out among the bathers at the beaches, plied their questions there! They took in over one hundred slackers out of the wet in that way.

At a thronged boulevard crossing in the loop district, every motor car was stopped. A. P. L. operatives met every incoming railway train and were at the gate of every train leaving the city. Countless homes and shops were visited. Sunday picnics in the suburbs were inspected, every theater and public building, every "L" road station and steamboat landing was investigated and guarded by men who made but one remark: "Show me!" On one night of the four, 7,000 men in a short time were gathered, held and taken to the police stations. Factories, stores, saloons, the open streets, all yielded up their toll—many innocent, many loyal, many negligent, many culpable and many disloyal evaders who were trying to dodge the draft.

In a vast wave, the vigilantes of Chicago, whose existence was suspected by almost none of these, swept out into the open. The guilty and the lukewarm alike, the innocent and ignorant conscript and the veiled enemy alike, got the largest and swiftest lesson in Americanism this country ever had had up to that hour. It showed a certain element that under the careless American character there are vast capacities for self-government and a stern respect for law and government. Many a pro-German has known in his soul since last July that about the most uncompromising autocrat he ever met was a simple man bearing not a scepter but a little badge.

In general, the raids met with no resistance, and though there was confusion there was no disorder. The people took it well, as might have been expected. Loyal Americans would not object, disloyal ones dared not. The general working out of the widely-scattered raids was admirable. As to the rapidity and thoroughness of the League's work, it never has done better anywhere, because by this time it had grown into a well-drilled and perfectly-organized body of constabulary. As covering the public attitude of this city towards the raids—similar raids were met with worse receptions in other cities — a great daily, the *Chicago Tribune*, printed the following editorial comment:

> The object of the roundup of draft registrants was, of course, to find those who are evading the law and bring them into the service. But the results of the drive go considerably beyond that. It has proved the splendid spirit of the community.
>
> Americans do not like to be interfered with by officials. They are not accustomed to it, and they resent it in normal times, even when it is quite justifiable. But though it has been by no means convenient to be stopped on the way to work, interrogated, sent back home for credentials, or taken in custody pending investigation, there has been in this roundup a general good-natured acceptance of the process, and in the vast majority of cases, a cordial co-operation with the authorities.
>
> A part of the credit for this undoubtedly belongs to the tact and good sense shown by the draft authorities and the volunteers of the American Protective League, who deserve congratulation upon the skill with which they have accomplished a by no means easy task with a minimum of friction and a maximum of thoroughness. But if the authorities showed good spirit, the public met them half way, and the total experience proves the excellent morale now existing. Whatever is necessary to get on with the war is accepted without complaint. Virtually everybody wants to help. Furthermore, the number of slackers found in proportion to the number of men questioned is gratifyingly small.
>
> The young manhood is sound. As it is called on for service small or great, it will respond promptly and spiritedly.

There are two distinct points of view as to the slacker raids, so called, and criticisms as well as praise have come to the A. P. L. for its part in them all over the country. Naturally, no miracle was wrought in human nature. The families of the men who were hid or shielded were no more loyal after their men were taken than they had been before. The conscientious objector experienced no stiffening of fiber in his flabby soul. But even these would have felt otherwise towards the slacker drives had they known all the truth. Ask the men themselves who were inducted into the army what they think about it now. Nine-tenths of them will say that they are ashamed that they had to be asked twice to go into the army. The other one-tenth is the better for having gone, whether or not they will confess so much. As a saving influence, a mere reclamation enterprise, the slacker raids were a vast agency for the public good. They were not man-hunters, but man-savers, these men who conducted the raids.

Just one instance of this truth must serve for all the many communities who engaged in this work and who caught, in all, perhaps, a half million men for examination, and held a tenth of all they caught. It is only a little anecdote, but it makes the best answer possible to all the critics of the Selective Service Act.

A gentleman came into the National Headquarters with certain papers in the way of reports, and announced that he was the Chief of the Akron, Ohio, Division. He offered the usual apologies—by this time more or less familiar at the book desk—that he had been able to do so little when he had wanted to do so much in the work of the A. P. L. "But there is one thing that I wish you would put in this book," he said, "to show people what this League has done in the remaking of men. I don't care whether you say another thing for Akron, but I want to tell this story of a man we saved.

"A young woman came to my office and complained of her husband. 'I am almost desperate about Joe,' she said to me. 'He drinks and drinks, and hangs around the saloons. He hasn't given me a cent in eight months, and I don't know what to do. I—I love him. I don't want him to go. But do you think the army would do him any good. He doesn't do anything for me and our baby.'

"'The army will see,' I said to her. So I went and found her husband—in a saloon, drunk, shabby, dead to all pride and all ambition, about as poor-looking material for a soldier as you ever saw. 'That's Joe,' said his wife, when I brought them together in my office.

"Well, I sent Joe to jail to think things over. When he was in his cell, his wife took him in a tray full of good things to eat, some hot coffee, and all that sort of thing. I went with her. 'You see,' I said to him, 'how much your wife is doing now for your support—more than you have done for her in a year. What do you think about it now?'

"Well, he was inside the draft age, and we sent him into the Army. We saw to it that his wife got her share of his pay—the first support he had given her in many months.

"I forgot about this case, so many others came in. The days went by until not so long ago. After the armistice was signed and just before I came down here, some one knocked at my door. There came in a smiling young woman, neatly dressed, a neatly dressed baby in her arms. And with her was a tall, grinning, brown-faced, hard-bitten, well-set-up young man, in the uniform of the United States Army. He had a sergeant's chevrons on his sleeve. I did not know any of these people.

"'That's Joe,' said the young woman. Then I remembered it all. It made me feel rather funny—I couldn't really quite believe it.

"'He does not drink,' said the wife. 'I am so glad he went into the Army.'

"Well, maybe you think I'm not glad of my share in remaking a man like that. It paid me for all my work and worry in the League. I believe that our Division would have made good if it had not done anything more than just what it did for Joe."

One does not know of any better summary of the slacker raids than that conveyed by this simple little story from one chief out of very many hundreds.

CHAPTER XII

SKULKER CHASING

Hunting Bad Men — Deserter-Catching in the Southern Mountains — Tricks of the Slacker's Trade — Running Down Unwilling Patriots — Some A. P. L. Adventures — Death of a Deserter — How a Southern Ranger Brings Them In.

One of the earliest recollections of the writer's boyhood is that of seeing his father busily engaged in molding bullets for his rifle on a certain Sunday morning—at that time the old muzzle-loading rifle was still in use. The old gentleman was with the Army Recruiting Service in the Civil War, in a branch which at times was obliged to look after men who were evading the draft or unduly prolonging their furloughs, or who belonged to that detested group of conscientious objectors and obstructionists who at that time bore the local name of "Copperheads." Some of these men had ambushed and killed two of the Army men sent out to bring them in, and as others of the force then took up the matter, it was deemed wise to be alert and well armed. The murderers were duly apprehended and dealt with.

At that time we had a United States Secret Service whose annals make interesting reading to-day—as, for instance, the burial by Secret Service men of the body of John Wilkes Booth, the assassin of President Lincoln. That final resting place to this day is known to very few men. There was, however, in Civil War times no Military Intelligence Division, no censorship of the mails or cables, no real system of espionage, and certainly no A. P. L. We had less need then than now for such extensions of the arm of Justice, because then each army was fighting an honorable foe—though both were mistaken foes—and be-because our country then was not populated so largely with unassimilated and treacherous foreigners. There was some spy work in that time on both sides, as in any war; but for the most part, clean, straightaway fighting was the main concern of both sides; and that war was so fought that such a thing as honor did exist and could survive for both combatants.

The Civil War had as one of its worst results the fact that the rich new West and Northwest, then opening up with the early railroads, came to be largely settled soon after the war by a heavy foreign population, instead of by young Americans who must otherwise have marched out at the head of the rails, and not at the head of armies from which so many of them never returned. Had there been no Civil War, there would have been less of loose immigration. Without that war, there would be no Non-Partisan League in the Northwest, no German Alliance in the Middle West, no Bolshevism in the cities of the East. Nevertheless, even in that day of honorable warfare, when men met foemen worthy of their steel and not cowardly assassins, there existed men who had the craven heart. There were deserters then as there always are in war,—and sometimes they were sought out by men who molded bullets of a Sunday morning, and who, having started out after their men, did not come back until they had found them.

To-day also we have deserters and slackers—let us say, perhaps, with better color of excuse than in the old days, because in some of the more remote districts of the United States, far from the confusion of the crowded city life, in sections where the world runs smoothly and quietly and men are content, there existed no definite and concrete local reasons for a man to go to war with a foe across the sea of whom he knew little or nothing. Secure in the only American part of America, sometimes the Southern mountaineers, for instance, resented the draft because they did not understand it. The bravest of the brave, ready to fight at the drop of the hat, and natural soldiers, there were among them many whose fathers joined the Federal Army in the Civil War. They volunteered for that—but they would not be drafted for this foreign war. They made a brand of conscientious objectors—rather, say, ignorant objectors—who were dangerous to go up against in the laurel thickets or the far-back mountain coves. Very often, these men, when they learned how the flag of this country had been insulted, how our women and children had been murdered on the sea, were eager to join the colors, and never again were they deserters or slackers—only fighting men.

To this form of military evader among the simple outlying people of the southern hills, there must be added a great many deserters of foreign descent all over the country, caught in the Selective Service Act. Some of these had imbibed no real loyalty to America in their home associations; much too often their environments were those of other countries and not this. They heard another speech than ours used as a "mother tongue"; daily saw customs of the old world maintained, and not those of the new world taken on. They had small heart for the war because their loyalty to this country still was crude and unformulated. Many of the foreign-born troops who fought so well in France first joined our colors, not because they wished to, but because they had to, the law leaving no option. After that, they learned the fierce love of a real soldier for the real flag of a real country. Perhaps their wounds and their deaths may teach their surviving relatives in America not to remain foreigners, but to become Americans—and not foreigners masquerading as Americans. Some of our best soldiers had fathers who had taken the German oath never to renounce fealty to that famous "War Lord," chiefest coward of them all, who had not courage to die at the head of his army.

There was also in this war, as in all other wars, a certain percentage of the sullen and rebellious, of the weak and cowardly, men of no mark and no convictions in any cause, men who never rise above themselves and their selfish concerns in any situation. Beyond these, again, was a small class whose natural home longings or home bewailings or home pleadings led them to desert. Because of many reasons, then, a certain percentage of deserters marked this war as every war.

In the eyes of the law this was every man's war, and all must get under and back of it with no exceptions. A deserter was a deserter. Some were dangerous men, and some no more than yellow slackers. We could not in these pages give a great many instances of either type. One A. P. L. report, however, that comes from Birmingham, Alabama, is peculiar in that it gives details regarding several investigations and arrests of deserters.

One of the most remarkable cases handled by the Birmingham Division was that of Dan D——— of Tuscaloosa County, who deserted from the regular army of the United States on November 27, 1917, and was not captured until September 1, 1918. Information having been received by the Chief on the 23rd of August, 1918, that Dan was hiding near Reno Mines, he immediately ordered a number of his men under Special Agent M——— to go after the deserter. The trip was taken in automobiles on the afternoon of August 23, and through very heavy mist. Arriving at Reno Mines, some information was given the party as to the location of the man's home, which proved to be a four-room boxed house in front of which and about sixty feet away was a small frame barn about twenty by thirty feet, built of rough plank, with four horse stalls in the main building and some cow stalls in the lean-to shed.

A careful search of house and barn failed to show any signs of the missing man, his parents and sister denying any knowledge of his whereabouts. The mother said, "The last I hear'n of Dan was a letter from Long Island two months or more ago," and she remarked, "Of course, you 'uns know he was home on a furlough last November." A request to produce the letter was met with the reply, "The chillun tore it up."

The search of the barn was again renewed by the men, and the loft was searched with the aid of a ladder from the outside. It was found to be filled with fodder, hay and grass, and prodding with poles and forks convinced the parties that there was no chance for any one to be hiding under same.

Very much mystified, and yet satisfied by the demeanor and sullen manner of the father, mother and sister that Dan was somewhere close, the Special Agent divided his men, leaving part of them to watch, while the others sought for outside information.

Mr. W———, a Deputy Sheriff of Tuscaloosa County, had been trying to locate Dan for ten months, and had watched continuously as much as ten days at one time, both house and barn. A number of searches prior to the arrival of the A. P. L. squad, made in and around the mines of the different operating companies, had given no clue. One thing was certain, however: nearly everybody in the district was related to him, due to the intermarriage during several generations of the people, and, as usual, there were some of his own kin-folks who would "shore like to see him pulled."

At last, the patience of the party being exhausted, and feeling sure that Dan was somewhere, either about the house or barn, the father, William D———, and the mother, and a sister, who had denied any relationship to Dan, were told positively either to surrender him or go to jail. They asked for time, and it was refused. They pleaded for the officers to come again to-morrow. This also was refused. After pleading again to give them till afternoon, they finally asked one of the League operators to a conference behind the house with the mother and father. They then renewed their pleadings for time, but finally agreed to show the hiding place of their son and deliver him to the party, as they now realized that the "U. S. was a blame sight stronger than kin-folks who were liable to split on you at any minute."

The father was then accompanied to the barn. He knocked on the wall of the barn and said, "Come down, son!" Almost immediately a wide plank in the floor of the barn loft, almost over the heads of the astonished men, mysteriously arose from its resting place, revealing the most unique and simple hiding place imaginable. It was nothing more or less than a box, about as large as a good sized coffin, in which there were bed clothes, food and water. The box was cut to fit the joists, hiding all joints, and being apparent from below as a part of the loft floor. It was covered with fodder and hay above, the occupant using one loose plank of the box as his trap door. When occupied, it would naturally be as tight as any other part of the floor. Later, the party saw a hole dug out under the cow stall which he had occupied until his more palatial quarters in the coffin box had been provided.

The District was noted in years gone by as the "favorite stamping ground of Jim Morrison and kindred outlawed spirits." Most of the inhabitants of the surrounding country are employed in the mining of brown iron ore, which is taken out of large open cuts and washed by machinery and shipped to the furnaces of the Birmingham district. Nearly all of the labor, black and white, are the descendants of small farmers of Tuscaloosa County and the southern part of Jefferson County. Many of them still carry on farming in a small way, and the region has long been famous for its smooth and creamy "moonshine," which in some mysterious way still continues to be made. It was for many years a favorite pastime of old Judge Shackelford, who lived and died in sight of the D——— home, to mix his corn juice in an old sugar bowl while dispensing justice in the good old way. Shortly after the events narrated here, the sheriff of the county was murdered in cold blood on the village street by one of the outlaws of the section.

Two other interesting cases handled by the Birmingham Division concerned two brothers, S——— and R———. S——— deserted from Camp Pike, Arkansas, October 5, 1917, and R——— from Camp Mills, N. Y., September 25, 1917. The peculiar part of the case was that while S——— was listed as a deserter, the War Department had no record of R——— deserting, though they were advised that he was in this section of the country and efforts were made to check the records. While their desertions took place the latter part of 1917, it was not until August, 1918, that Operative No. 202 of the Birmingham Division received confidential information that both men were in Shelby County, Alabama, making moonshine whiskey, which they were selling to the miners and also to citizens in Bessemer, Alabama, a town thirteen miles southwest of Birmingham.

A party was organized to go after them, but unfortunately missed them by four days, the brothers and their family having moved elsewhere. Operative continued giving the case active attention, and finally information was secured that the brothers were in Coosa County, Alabama.

Arrangements for automobiles having been made over long distance, a party of A. P. L. men, six in number, headed by Agent Crawford of the Department of Justice, left Birmingham at 3:50 P. M. Thursday, November 7 (the day made famous by the premature Armistice celebration), arriving at Goodwater about 6:00 P. M.

After supper they were met by two 100 per cent American volunteers with automobiles, and were driven about five miles beyond Goodwater. The latter informed them of the danger of arousing these parties by going over the regular road, on account of dogs barking, so they left the machines about two miles away from the cabin they were seeking and detoured over a large hill, in the dark and cold, to get to the cabin. The report says:

> The humorous part of it was that, in spite of our precautions, the "hound dawgs" treed us about a mile from the place and certainly let forth unearthly baying. By the time we reached and surrounded the cabin, the entire household was aroused. Again we seemed doomed to disappointment, for we were informed that the parties we sought had left there just four days before—the same length of time by which we missed them in Shelby County.
>
> After exploring the country in the immediate vicinity we finally secured a tip that the brothers were near another town about forty miles away, so we regained the machines and returned to Goodwater, arriving there about 10:30 p. m. Feeling that perhaps some word might reach the parties that we were after them, if we postponed the trip, our drivers, after much discussion finally agreed to drive us to Kellyton, Alabama, about ten miles from Goodwater, to a man who ran a jitney line. It was the coldest night of the year, with only the stars as light. Finally we reached Kellyton, shortly after midnight, and while two of us were arousing the jitney man the others collected leaves and firewood and in a few minutes had a roaring fire by the roadside to warm our frozen extremities.
>
> Until we acquainted the jitney man with the urgency of the matter, he demurred about getting out in the cold, saying he had only two Ford cars and would have to depend on a thirteen-year-old son to drive the second car of the two. He was persuaded to take us over the thirty miles of rough country roads, with our drivers rather uncertain of the correct route.
>
> We reached Wadley, Alabama, about five o'clock in the morning. Some coffee filled a long-felt want and in a few minutes

we were ready again. Further investigation, at Abanda, developed the fact that the two suspects were with their family, who had just moved in a country house about a mile distant from the town. This house was in a hollow, off the road, well shielded from view, and the surroundings made it an ideal place for those seeking seclusion. Bearing in mind the fact that in the rural districts most every one is suspicious of strangers, we duly surrounded the house about 6:30 A. M. At a signal the house was rushed and the men were in the center passage of the house before the occupants were aware of their presence. Hearing the noise, the mother opened the door to one of the rooms and looked out. Seeing these strange men, she tried to close the door, but was prevented from doing so by one of the men who stuck his foot in the opening. On being questioned the mother denied that the boys were there.

The house was the usual country cabin, with rooms on each side and a hall down the middle, so while the two members were forcing the door where the mother was, Agent Crawford broke in the door across the hall and discovered the two brothers on pallets on the floor. They were promptly covered before they had a chance to use their pump guns, though search revealed three of the guns fully loaded and placed for convenient use. Also, an extra box of cartridges was found with the top off. Had it not been for the quickness with which we worked, trouble would doubtless have ensued, as the reputation of these men was that they shot first and asked questions afterward. One member of the family had the reputation of killing at least two men and had they been given a chance they would have resisted.

The boys were ordered to dress and placed under arrest. Both of these men were big, strapping fellows, weighing about 175 pounds apiece, and each of them six feet tall. They had no dependents, so there was absolutely no excuse for their failure to serve their country. It usually is the case in the rural districts of the South that nearly everyone is related to everybody else, and all are "quick on the trigger" if they think their relatives are being sought. It is interesting to mention that the house where we captured the brothers had new barbed wire fencing almost completely surrounding it, as if they expected a little trench warfare of their own. Though we have handled numerous other cases, I believe the circumstances surrounding this particular one will long linger in the memory of those composing the party.

The Local Agent of the Department of Justice at Birmingham had many times received information that there were a number of deserters and delinquents in the swamps of Pickens County, Alabama. The local office there being unable to cope with the situation, on Monday, December 10, a D. J. man, Robert B———, went to Gordo to secure information as to the location of these men. The information was secured. Mr. B——— then proceeded to Tuscaloosa where he called the Special Agent over long distance phone asking that eight A. P. L. men be sent to join him in Tuscaloosa. Eight picked men of the A. P. L. assembled, and with three high power automobiles, left Birmingham at 9:00 A. M., December 11, arriving in Tuscaloosa at noon. At four o'clock the party left Tuscaloosa, going to a point two miles from Gordo where deputy sheriff D——— met the party. D——— was thoroughly familiar with the surrounding country.

Leaving the automobiles about two miles from the first house that was to be covered, the party very quietly surrounded the house, not overlooking the barn and out houses. They had been informed that the alleged deserter had been staying at this house, the owner being his step father. The whole place was searched, no evidence being found. The step father and young brother were put under arrest. This, however, failed to accomplish the desired result. The mother was in her bed, an old-time, worn-out umbrella beside her. Before the Assistant Chief could catch her hand, a heavy blow was accurately placed on his head, the old lady remarking, "I am damn tired of all this foolishness!" She was gently relieved of the umbrella and convinced that the bed was the place for her.

A younger daughter, about the age of fifteen, left the house at this time by a back entrance and ran a mile to another step brother's house, with the evident intention of notifying her step brother who was wanted. This was the undoing of the A. P. L., as far as this deserter was concerned. Another step brother of the deserter, however, was placed under arrest, handcuffed and brought to jail for harboring a deserter. Operatives discovered notices that had been put on different houses in the locality of this deserter, one of them reading: "You are talking too damn much. The first thing you know the sun will rise under your house."

The party then proceeded to the house of another deserter. The house as usual was surrounded. One of the operatives discovered an open window with a blind, the window being about two feet square. While a search light and a good gun guarded the entrance, Agent B——— and an A. P. L. operative crawled through this opening in the room. After awakening the occupants, a deserter and the mother of another deserter were found. The deserter was forced to dress. The mother was closely questioned regarding her son, and finally agreed that if she would be allowed to go alone, she would bring him to us. This was agreed to. She was watched and in about fifteen minutes she brought her son, who was a deserter, and also her husband. It was discovered that the son and father were sleeping in a ditch about one hundred yards from the house. They had bed clothing, and slept in the open air with the sky for a roof. These two also were handcuffed and brought to jail.

The most interesting case on this trip was the capture of another deserter who had been away from camp for over a year. He and his wife, it is alleged, had sworn that he would never be taken alive. The information was that they had bought a lot in the community cemetery where they were to be buried together. Arriving at the house of the deserter at 2:15 A. M., the house was covered and each operative given detailed instructions. The deserter was called to the open door, and was warned not to offer resistance, as his house was fully surrounded. When told he was wanted by Uncle Sam's men, he opened his door and offered no resistance, stating that he had made up his mind to surrender to government officers, but not to the local officers. Judging from the weapons that he had by his bed, he evidently meant what he had said. He too was handcuffed and brought to jail. The total mileage of this trip was two hundred and sixteen miles, all without a scratch to car or man.

Lexington, North Carolina, was in this same mountain country which furnished so considerable a number of deserters during the war. It is a strange thing to say, but perhaps the largest numbers of deserters were found in the most American and most loyal part of the country—that is to say, the South, where there was almost no alien population. The only pure-bred American population in the United States was the very element which seemed unwilling to support the war! This, however, is a statement which needs full explanation. Let the Chief of Lexington make that explanation in the story of one case.

Tom B——— was a Tar-Heel tie hacker and lived in the mountains of North Carolina, twenty-six miles from a railroad. He could neither read nor write, but was straight and strong, and to see him swing a broad-axe was worth a trip into the mountains. When Tom heard of the draft he did not understand it. He had led a life of peaceful seclusion. There were two old Germans over at the railroad that ran a store, but Tom could work up no enthusiasm about crossing the Atlantic to kill people of that sort. But the draft came and many of Tom's meantime friends disappeared. It seemed inexplicable to him. He did not want to go to war with anybody and did not understand why there was any war. The solution of his problem at last came to him.

His people had come to these mountain fastnesses because there they found that liberty of thought and action which all our early Americans longed for; but now into that freedom of action there came some intangible influence which he could not understand. Tom simply resolved to march into the forest as his great-grandfather had done. He "stepped back into the brush" for the duration of the war. For him this was the only natural solution for a problem he did not understand. In this way he could escape what seemed to him oppression and impairment of the liberty which he held more dear than life. So he made the usual arrangements. Food would be left for him at a certain spot by his people. If anyone came in looking for Tom, his people would put up a smoke signal so he would understand. Meantime, Tom continued his work in a tie camp, his squirrel rifle leaning against a tree. When he finished his work, he "stepped back" into deep laurel and was lost as though he had gone up into smoke. His decision, having been taken, would remain unshakable even unto death. He said, "I reckon I made up my mind, and I'd ruther die here than in Germany."

Let us consider the situation. Here is Tom B———, an

American of native blood, afraid of nothing that rides, walks or swims, willing to fight his weight in wildcats to defend the freedom and liberty of his native hills — and he is a fugitive from justice. Now, how can the A. P. L. save that man from the consequence of his folly?

He was saved. As soon as the Chief heard of Tom B———'s disappearance, he packed his timber cruising kit and went out into Tom's country. At night he reached the cabin of Uncle John Coggins, who knew everybody in that neck of the woods and whose word was law. Uncle John knew what was up, but he said nothing — only kept his small blue eyes fixed on the visitor. After they had finished their meal, the two went out and sat on a log in the sun, in the middle of a clearing where no one could approach without being seen in time.

"I understand," remarked the Chief casually, "that Tom has stepped back into the brush."

No sign from Uncle John that he had heard anything. Tom's name was not mentioned again.

Then the talk was shifted to the war and other things. The chief tried to explain to Uncle John the problem of raising the army. He tried to bring home the war, across the thousands of miles of sea and land, to this old man sitting on a log in the western North Carolina mountains. He pointed out the purpose and the manifest fairness of selective service, taking all alike from all ranks.

Then they talked about the weather and the crops and the soaring price of corn "likker" and the growing scarcity of good white oak timber. The Chief went away. Uncle John, when he said good-bye, understood perfectly why the visitor had come to his cabin.

Several days later Uncle John appeared in the office of the Chief. He drew up a chair and remarked, "Howdy," and sat gazing at the other man with about as much animation as an Egyptian mummy. Only his little snappy eyes under the bushy brows told of his alertness. The conversation was again about the weather, the crops, the soaring price of corn "likker" and the growing scarcity of good white oak timber. At length Uncle John hitched his chair closer.

"I kinda tho't you all mought wanter know 'bout Tom

B———," he said. "I've done been out whar Tom is a-settin' back, an' he seed how hit is—an' he's a-comin' in!" The Chief of the A. P. L. nodded. The thing was settled. They smoked for a time, discussed the weather, the crops, the soaring price of corn " likker " and the growing scarcity of good white oak timber. Tom's name was not mentioned again. The Chief spoke quite casually of a few details that would naturally attend Tom's " comin' in." Uncle John said he would attend to those matters. A little later he went away. And by and by Tom B——— came in and joined the Army.

These Southern leaders understood the mountain people. Their method of work was infinitely more simple than sending a posse out into the brush to round up a desperate man who knew how to shoot to kill. There were characters who needed other methods; but among the boys in the mountains, ignorance and aloofness were the common causes of their "stepping back into the brush." To have called any one of them afraid to fight would have been the deepest insult possible to men of their race. Once in the army, they did fight—the records of the Army will speak as to that. There never were better or braver soldiers in the world, nor men more loyal and devoted to their country.

Olympia, Washington, had an interesting case of a deserter named G———, whose father made the statement that anyone who took the boy would have to come shooting. The house was searched but the boy was gone. The A. P. L. operative later became a game warden, and while traveling in the country ran across an empty cabin. As it was known that the boy's father had taken out a trapper's license, they thought that perhaps this cabin might be occupied by the deserter. It was in a swamp, built under overhanging trees, so it was almost impossible to find. There was no trail to the cabin, as the boy did not go in and out in any regular way but took different paths to avoid discovery. The operative and an associate went into the woods, found G———'s line of traps, followed them up and captured him in the woods. This deserter's family would not buy Liberty bonds but said they would save their money for ammunition. The prompt and vigorous action of A. P. L. closed a case which was notorious in the vicinity.

A study of the reports of operatives engaged in League activities at the busy Birmingham Division, and indeed all over the country, shows an astonishing lack of anything like personal violence. It never could be told, however, where such an instance might break out. Only two or three cases of killing in the course of duty are recorded in the thousands of cases handled. One of these comes from a quiet little farming village, Morris, Illinois, about the last place in the world where anything of the sort might have been expected. It resulted in the shooting down, in the uniform of our Army, of Private A. J. K———, Company D., U. S. Infantry, a deserter from Rock Island arsenal. K——— had escaped from confinement at Rock Island with Corporal George S———. Acting Sheriff S———, who also was Chief of the A. P. L. at Morris, accompanied by Chief of Police A———, had been advised to be on the lookout for two deserters who were reported to be bad men.

The two men were on top of a box car when a train pulled into town, and were accosted by the Sheriff. They claimed to be government guards, and were asked to show their papers. A weapon was seen in S———'s pocket. The other man, still on the top of the car, covered the two peace officers and ordered them to keep away or he would shoot. At last the Sheriff managed to get the drop on him before he fired, but meantime the train began to pull out, so no shooting ensued at that time.

Morris wired Joliet to arrest the soldiers when the train got in. The man hunt now was on, because other officers down the valley reported the men wanted for desertion. The two fugitives left the train at Durkee's Crossing and hid in the woods near the tracks. The Sheriff got a posse and following down the track, located the men and surrounded the wood where they were concealed. The chief got up to S——— unnoticed, covered him with a rifle and told him to come along, which he did. He then asked S——— where the other man was.

Just then, K———, who had not been seen, called to the officer to drop the gun or he would shoot. Some threatening talk ensued on both sides and K——— advanced, the officer still commanding him to drop his gun as he was under arrest. K———, in turn, demanded that the chief should drop his rifle, holding him covered fair all the time. The Chief then called for his men to fire. Patrolman Wm. M——— fired on K——— with his rifle, and K——— dropped. He did not die immediately, and was taken to the hospital in Morris that night. The patrolman's bullet passed through his left shoulder, cut through the lung, and lodged near the heart. K——— refused to talk. His companion talked more freely, and said that K——— was bad and had had a shooting difficulty in West Virginia. They had both been in confinement, and had escaped with the intention of going back to West Virginia. He said that K——— "was the best shot in the regiment, and was a 'killer.'" That the A. P. L. Chief was not himself killed is nothing less than a marvel.

CHAPTER XIII

ARTS OF THE OPERATIVES

The Midnight Camera — The Way of a Man and a Maid and a Dictagraph — Secret Inks and Codes — Stories of the Trail — How Evidence Was Secured.

It already has been stated that the American Protective League had no governmental or legal status, though strong as Gibraltar in governmental and legal sanction. The mails are supposed to be sacred—the Postmaster General has sworn they always shall be sacred. They are sacred. But let us call the A. P. L. sometimes almost clairvoyant as to letters done by suspects. Sometimes it clairvoyantly found the proofs it sought!

It is supposed that breaking and entering a man's home or office place without warrant is burglary. Granted. But the League has done that thousands of times and has never been detected! It is entirely naïve and frank about that. It did not harm or unsettle any innocent man. It was after the guilty alone, and it was no time to mince matters or to pass fine phrases when the land was full of dangerous enemies in disguise. The League broke some little laws and precedents? Perhaps. But it upheld the great law under the great need of an unprecedented hour.

A man's private correspondence is supposed to be safe in his office files or vault. You suppose yours never was seen? Was it? Perhaps. It certainly was, if you were known as a loyal citizen—a true-blood American. But the League examined all of the personal and business correspondence of thousands of men who never were the wiser.

How could that be done? Simply, as we shall see. Suppose there was a man, ostensibly a good business man, apparently a good citizen and a good American, but who at heart still was a good German—as hundreds of thousands of such men living in America are this very day. This man has a big office in a down-town skyscraper. He is what the A. P. L. calls a "suspect." Let us call him Biedermacher.

About midnight or later, after all the tenants have gone home, you and I, who chance to be lieutenants and operatives in the League, just chance in at the corridor of that building as we pass. We just chance to find there the agent of the building—who just chances also to wear the concealed badge of the A. P. L. You say to the agent of the building, "I want to go through the papers of Biedermacher, Room 1117, in your building."

"John," the agent says to the janitor, "give me your keys, I've forgotten mine, and I want to go to my office a while with these gentlemen."

We three, openly, in fact, do go to Biedermacher's office. His desk is opened, his vault if need be — it has been done a thousand times in every city of America. Certain letters or documents are found. They would be missed if taken away. What shall be done?

The operative takes from his pocket a curious little box-like instrument which he sets up on the table. He unscrews a light bulb, screws in the plug at the end of his long insulated wire. He has a perfectly effective electric camera.

One by one the essential papers of Biedermacher are photographed, page by page, and then returned to the files exactly — and that means *exactly* — in the place from which each was taken. The drawers and doors are locked again. Search has been made *without a search warrant.* The serving of a search warrant would have "queered" the whole case and would not have got the evidence. The camera film has it safe.

"Pretty wife and kids the fellow has," says the agent of the building, turning over the photographs which the simple and kindly Biedermacher, respected Board of Trade broker, we will say, has in his desk. He turns them back again to exactly — *exactly* — the same position.

"Good night, John," he yawns to the janitor, when they meet him on the floor below. "Pretty late, isn't it?"

The three men pass out to the street and go home. Each of them in joining the League has sworn to break any social engagement to obey a call from the League headquarters at any hour of the day or night. Perhaps such engagements have been broken to-night by some or all of these three men. But no one has "broken and entered" Biedermacher's office.

In Central office some data are added to a card, cross-indexed by name and number also, and under a general guide. Some photostats, as these pictures are called, are put in the "case's" envelope. Nothing happens just yet. Biedermacher still is watched.

Then, one morning, an officer of the Department of Justice finds Mr. Biedermacher in his office. He takes from his pocket a folded paper and says, "In the name of the United States, I demand possession of a letter dated the 12th of last month, which you wrote to von Bernstorff in New York. I want a letter of the 15th of this month which you wrote to von Papen in Berlin. I want your list of the names of the United Sängerbund and German Brotherhood in America which you brought home from the last meeting. I want the papers showing the sums you have received from New York and Washington for your propaganda work here in this city. I want the letter received by you from seven Lutheran ministers in Wisconsin telling of their future addresses to the faithful."

"But, my God!" says Biedermacher, "what do you mean? I have no such letters here or anywhere else. I am innocent! I am as good an American as you are. I have bought a hundred thousand dollars' worth of Liberty bonds, some of each issue. My wife is in the Red Cross. I have a daughter in Y. W. C. A. I give to all the war charities. I am an American citizen. What do you mean by insulting me, sir?"

"John," says the officer to his drayman, "go to that desk. Take out all the papers in it. Here's the U. S. warrant, Mr. Biedermacher. Rope 'em up, John."

John ropes up the files, and the papers go in bulk to the office of the U. S. attorney on the case. Now, *all* the evidence is in possession of the Government, and the case is clear. Biedermacher is met quietly at the train when he tries to get out of town. Nothing gets into the papers. No one talks — secrecy is the oath. But before long, the big Biedermacher offices are closed. Biedermacher's wife says her husband has gone south for his health. He has — to Oglethorpe.

You think this case imaginary, far-fetched, impossible? It is neither of the three. It is the truth. It shows how D. J. and A. P. L. worked together. This is a case which has happened not once but scores and hundreds of times. It is espionage, it is spy work, yes, and it has gone on to an extent of which the average American citizen, loyal or disloyal, has had no conception. It was, however, the espionage of a national self-defense. It was only in this way that the office and the mail and the home of the loyal citizen *could* be held inviolate. The web of the A. P. L. was precisely that of the submarine net. Invisible, it offered an apparently frail but actually efficient defense against the dastardly weapons of Germany.

It must become plain at once that secret work such as this, carried on in such volume all across the country — three million cases, involving an enormous mass of detail and an untold expenditure of time and energy, were disposed of — meant system and organization to prevent overlapping of work and consequent waste of time. It meant more than that — there was needed also good judgment, individual shrewdness and of course, above all things, patience and hard work.

For instance, John Wielawski is a deserter reported to National Headquarters missing from Camp Grant, Illinois, possibly hiding in Chicago. The order goes to the Chief in Chicago, who hands it to the right district lieutenant. The latter finds in his cards the name of an operative who speaks Wielawski's native tongue. The latter goes to the neighborhood where Wielawski lived, inquires especially in regard to any sweetheart or sweethearts Wielawski may have had. It is certain he left some ties somewhere, that he has been seen, that he has written at least a line, or will write. His running down is sure. The League has found thousands of deserters, located thousands of men who had refused to take out their second naturalization papers, thousands who were skulkers and draft evaders. They could not escape the Web which reached all across America, unseen, but deadly sure.

The great average intelligence of the League members alone made the extraordinary results possible. These were no ordinary hired sleuths of the mysterious detective type, gum-shoe artists with a bent for masks and false eyebrows. On the contrary, the officers and operatives were men of standing, of great personal intelligence and sober good sense. They dropped their private affairs, in which they had been successful, to obey the League call at any time. They studied their new duties regularly and faithfully, as best they could — and they learned them.

The methods of such men varied widely. They had attended no outside school, had no special governmental training. Their success depended on the natural alertness of the American character. For instance, one gentleman prominent in the work, we will say in New York, was sent after a draft evader whose name, racially considered, did not tally with his personal description. The operative found his case originated in a foreign part of the city. His man had originally lived in a certain flat. Some boys played ball near by. The operative strolled by to watch, engaged two or three in conversation. Yes, a dark man — some said he was a Turk — had lived there. He had moved, they didn't know where. He used to work in a laundry, they thought. Very well, a Turk and a laundryman would naturally be found in some other laundry, possibly near his own people. The case was carried on until, in a laundry in another part of the same city, a new man was found — he had a new name, but the same face. Eventually he was put where he belonged.

The psalmist of old voiced his complaint that there were three things in the world which he did not know, three things which he could not find out: the way of a ship upon the sea, the way of the serpent on a rock, and the way of a man with a maid. The trouble with Solomon was that he seems not to have owned either a geometry, a microscope or a dictagraph. These used respectively in connection with the problems described above might have helped him out considerably.

A. P. L. operatives at Nyack, New York, had Solomon beaten by a city block. They installed a dictagraph in a room frequented by one A. L——, who was impersonating an officer, declaring that he was " Chief of the Secret Service from New York to Boston." His game was to advertise for women to engage in espionage work, saying that the Government would pay a big price and would also buy clothes and hats for the operatives and put them up at the best hotels. It was suspected very keenly that Mr. A. L——— was neither employed by the Government nor acting as an officer and a gentleman ought to act. He did not know anything about the deadly dictagraph which A. P. L. had placed in this apartment. Hence, he conversed quite freely with a certain Mrs. U———, who had answered his advertisement and at whose apartment he was paying a call. They seem first to have talked about the apartment itself, the conversation going as follows:

Mrs. U.: Isn't it nice? I'm crazy about it. He is a curio dealer, the owner of the apartment. Here is the dish closet. Here is the kitchen. Look and see the bedroom. I haven't got my bed linen yet. Sit down and I'll talk to you. Oh, I've got to get rid of this hat; my head aches.

Mr. L—: Oh, what a nice lamp.

Mrs. U—: Isn't it lovely? See, you can turn the lights on here. Look, this is the telephone downstairs. There's one thing; they are very strict here. You have to be careful. Sit down there.

(*Pause of a minute.*)

Mrs. U—: I can't swallow a pill to save my life. Now, I'll tell you what I have to say. Do you know I like that picture? I think it must have been a calendar. You know he said he would buy me anything I wanted. He is some kid, that boy. This is just like the headache I had two weeks ago. I had such a headache. All day Sunday I was in bed and I couldn't get any relief. It's just the same old way all along. It is so trying. Now, I want to hear all about your trip. I am terribly interested. Tell me all about it.

Mr. L—: Now, tell me exactly what you told him.

Mrs. U—: Sit down. Here's what I told him.

Mr. L—: What's his name and all about him?

Mrs. U—: Well, the first time I met him he told me all about the story of his life. Then, some time after that I met him again. "Hey, kid," he said, "you know a lot of people in Wall Street; take me down there and introduce me to some of them." I said: "I have a friend who is very well connected." Well, I saw him again and I told him that I had met you, and that you were right close to the Government and were in touch with the Government offices and you got inside news. Of course, I didn't tell him that you were in the Secret Service of the Government. You don't want me to tell him that, do you?

Mr. L—: No, not at all. I'll decide what I want to tell him.

Mrs. U—: Do you think he could be a spy?

Mr. L—: Yes, he could be. He acts just like one. He acts like a perfect damn fool.

Mrs. U—: Well, how do they act?

Mr. L—: They act just this way. That's their game.

Mrs. U—: Oh, I get so excited about your work.

Mr. L—: Yes; you know, if you were to catch a spy like that, it would be worth $5,000 to you.

Mrs. U—: $5000! Would it really? Who would pay that?

Mr. L—: The Government.

Mrs. U—: Oh, it's so exciting! You must think me silly, but I can't help getting all excited about this Secret Service work! And you're the head of it, too, aren't you?

Mr. L—: I am not the head of it all. I am only the head of certain branches. You know there are different branches.

Mrs. U—: Which are you in?

Mr. L—: In the Treasury Department.

Mrs. U—: In the Treasury Department?

Mr. L—: Yes, I'm the head of the Treasury Department and three other Departments besides. Four of them altogether. There are seventeen different branches, you know; I have full charge of this one.

Mrs. U—: No wonder you're so busy! Well, have you caught any spies lately?

Mr. L—: Oh, yes. We get them right along. I got forty last week.

Mrs. U—: You know, we have known each other a long time now, haven't we? You know, it's funny how you meet people through advertisements. Nearly everybody that I met in a business way I met through advertisements. And everybody that I met that way turned out to be a factor in my life! I met a good friend of mine, a girl, through an ad. And then, I have got some very good positions through advertisements. And then, I met you through that ad in—let's see—was it the "Times"?

Mr. L—: No, the "Herald."

Mrs. U—: Tell me about that girl that you said you had that was so good. Is she still catching spies?

Mr. L—: Yes; she got fourteen last week.

Mrs. U—: Gee! She must have worked overtime. . . . Did she have to do what you wanted me to do?

Mr. L—: Oh, yes, you see she was crazy about the work.

Mrs. U—: Gosh, you know that is very interesting to me. How many girls did you get from that advertisement? I guess you think I am a fool, but I get so interested, and I like to have you tell me all these things.

Mr. L—: Oh, I don't remember. You know, I think the spies would take to you and I don't blame them. I know I would.

Mrs. U—: Do you think they would like a red-head? Is there any demand at all for them?

Mr. L—: Oh, I couldn't see all of them.

Mrs. U—: I guess you're busy now with all these German submarines around, aren't you?

Mr. L—: Oh, yes, indeed; very busy. They are very dangerous people.

Mrs. U—: Do you always have to teach those girls that you have in the Secret Service? You know I have been reading all about this spy work and this Secret Service thing since I saw you. I am so much interested. They go by numbers, don't they, instead of names? Well, if I was in the service, would you look up all about where I was born, and who my people were, and everything like that? Would you do that to see if I had any German blood? I'll tell you why I ask it, because the Y. M. C. A. people told me that they would have to look me up very carefully and that they would have to find out if any of my people were born in Germany. . . . How long have you been in the Government Secret Service?

Mr. L—: Twenty-five years.

Mrs. U—: Twenty-five years! Oh, dear, and no one would ever know that you were in it.

Mr. L—: Come here—oh, you're just a little kiddie.

Mrs. U—: Oh, now, wait a minute, just wait a minute!

The operatives who were listening to this partially reported conversation in the janitor's room did not wait even a minute. They broke down the door and arrested Mr. L———. He was turned over to the United States Secret Service and arraigned before the Assistant District Attorney. His activities as an employer of espionage agents thereupon ceased abruptly. He was a cheap and dirty imposter.

It was found in hundreds of cases — and the knowledge

was invariably suppressed — that an alien suspect's sudden and mysterious shifts and changes, his suspicious and watchful conduct, his evasive acts, all had to do with nothing more than the fact that the man had a mistress or so in another part of the city. The woman in his case very often was not the woman in the case at all, for there was no case, so far as the League was concerned. But countless men were quietly warned. Often with tears they implored the secrecy which was given them. There are hundreds, perhaps thousands, of men in America whose private lives are known to the League and not known in their own families. There is yet to be known the first case where any advantage ever was taken of the unintended victim caught in the general meshes of the Web; but it may be interesting for any of those of guilty conscience who by chance may read these lines, to know that their lives are filed away, cross-indexed, for future reference in the vast archives of the Department of Justice at Washington!

The extent of these "woman cases," as they were known, is very considerable, and the per cent of suspect spy cases which simmered down to a petticoat basis is a very large one. A great part of the work of the League was done in finding the woman, if not in searching for her specifically. The League brought up from the deep-sea soundings of its steel meshes all the sordid and unworthy phases of human life on the part of both men and women. But while combing out the discards of human intrigue, the League often found the evidence it really sought. This was without fail used mercilessly and coldly.

One case, handled by the Central Division in Chicago, we may call the Otero case. Word came from El Paso that a certain prominent Mexican, a revolutionary and political leader with aspirations for a very high office in that republic, had come into the United States and was headed north, probably for Chicago. Nothing was known about him and his purpose excepting that his name was given. The League at once began making inquiries about Senor Otero. It was found that he was traveling in a special car. Obviously, therefore, he was a man of money. Ergo, he would go to a good hotel, and he probably would make a reservation in advance. Inquiries were made by telephone at all the leading hotels in Chicago, which in practically all cases were members of the American Protective League. Senor Otero was found to have reserved a large suite at the Blackstone, and had made the time of his arrival known. From that time on, he was in the hands of the American Protective League, although he never knew it. The boy who took his bag at the door was an A. P. L. operative, the bellhop who responded to his summons was an A. P. L. operative, his waiter at table was A. P. L., his night taxicab driver was A. P. L. In fact, the A. P. L. put Senor Otero to bed and woke him up in the morning, followed his activities during the day and knew what he was doing all night. It was not discovered that he was engaged in any plot against the peace of the United States, but was apparently active in the more pleasant task of spending some money he had gotten hold of in Mexico. If relatives or friends of the Senor Otero would be pleased to know how he spent it, the nature of his associations in Chicago by day — or night — and if they can persuade the Department of Justice to advise them, they can find the entire record of his stay in Chicago. Had he been engaged in any suspicious acts against this country, his return to Mexico might not have been so peaceful.

If an A. P. L. man knew the chemistry of any synthetic or invisible ink, he would not make the secret public any more than would M. I. D. Many devices for making and using these inks, however, are very generally known, although it is believed that Great Britain and France have gone farthest in classifying and developing them. A piece of a necktie has been taken from one German, a corner of which, snipped off and put in a glass of water, would make an invisible ink. A shoestring has been known to do the same thing, a small piece of it making enough for a letter or more. A shirt-stud has been described by a foreign operative, which, when unscrewed and dropped into a glass of water, would do the same thing and leave no trace. With what chemicals were these articles treated in order to make the ink? Ah, that is another matter. If the author knew, he could not tell. One thing is sure, it is not likely that the most inventive writer of "detective" stories could imagine anything more ingenious or more baffling than some of these well-known methods in use by our own men.

Mr. Byron R. Newton, collector at the port of New York, gave out a curious story on the work done by the Customs Intelligence Bureau, created as a lookout for smugglers and others. This service was employed in searching ships, examining baggage, looking out for explosive bombs, invisible writing, and so forth. Mr. Newton's story appeared in the New York *Herald* of July 14, 1918, and from it one incident may be taken.

> Through the Boarding Officials, a passenger who arrived the other day has furnished interesting material for the Intelligence Bureau investigators. The passenger, who for some time had been a resident of Germany, although an American citizen, said he had been approached in Dresden by German agents and asked if on his return to the United States he would obtain military and other information of interest to the Imperial German Intelligence Bureau. He was furnished with a code to be used by him for forwarding information to Germany and also with a formula for manufacturing an *invisible ink*, and with paper to be treated by a special process for correspondence. The passenger, in evidence of what he stated, offered four collars to the customs officials. They appeared to be ordinary negligee collars of cream-colored material—double, turn-over collars, medium height, such as many men wear with sport shirts or for informal occasions. The passenger explained the purpose of these collars as follows:
>
> "I take a soup plate and I put boiling water in it and let it stand for about a quarter of an hour, after which I throw away the water. The plate being warm, I place one of these collars in it. I pour over the collar one hundred grams of boiling water and let it stand for half an hour. Then I wring out the collar, and the water that remains is my invisible ink. They call it 'pyrogram.' It looks like water, it is not poisonous and it can be drunk.
>
> "I wash my hands, since they are wet with this ink, and take the paper and fold it crosswise and begin the letter, writing two fingers from the edge. I let it dry, and then take a glass of water and put about one teaspoonful of ammonia in it. With a piece of wadding dipped in this solution of ammonia and water, I rub the paper both ways, and thus prepare it on both sides. After this I place the paper in this wet condition between blotting paper and under heavy books or a trunk for three hours. You will not be able to recognize the

paper any more. It looks like foreign writing paper, very thin and glazed. I can write anything I choose on this letter now. When they get the letter and develop it the writing appears positively black. I head the letter 'Dear Bob' and they know it is a code letter. When I am through with the letter I use the word 'Schluss,' because in developing it, they want to know if they have the entire letter, and that word ends it up."

This passenger also told the examining officials that in carrying addresses without an address book, the German agents usually take a bone button of an overcoat or a large button of some sort and on the reverse side scratch the address with a diamond, sometimes also scratching instructions which they cannot carry in their heads. After this they treat the button with shellac, or, as they call it in Germany, "spitituslak." That fills the crevices and dries rapidly. On reaching the destination, they use pure alcohol to wash off the shellac. They also write addresses on this paper and work them into leather buttons.

Cipher and code are part of the education of certain intelligence officers, but into a discussion of these matters we may not go, as they are secrets of the American Government. Our own experts were able to decipher and decode all the secret messages bearing on the great German plots in this country, but this was not usually A. P. L. work. Of course, the lay reader, or more especially the A. P. L. member, may know that a cipher means the substitution of some symbol, or some number, or another letter, for each letter of the alphabet. Or the real letters may be transposed, one to stand for another, in such a way that only the sender and receiver may understand. That looks hard to read? Not at all. It is easier than code. It is said that any cipher message can be unriddled in time.

A code is a scheme agreed on by which the two parties substitute certain whole words for the real words of the message. A code message might seem wholly innocent—let us say, just a simple comment on the weather. But suppose "bright and fair" meant in code "The Leviathan sailed this morning," and suppose the *Leviathan* were a transport carrying twelve thousand troops to France! Unless the de-code artist is indeed an artist, he cannot know what interchange in ideas had been agreed upon for interchanged words; and there are not twenty-six letters, but 26,000 words which may be transposed in meaning. The big German spy work — that is, the chain of messages that passed between the German Embassy in America and the Imperial Headquarters in Berlin — was done in enciphered code. They had first been written in German before coding, and after coding, the code was put in cipher. None the less, we read them, and von Bernstorff, Dr. Albert, et al., are no more on our soil.

This is specialized, expert work of the most delicate and difficult sort, and is not for the average amateur. Sometimes the latter had more enthusiasm than knowledge in his ambition to be a real sleuth, and in such cases, perhaps something amusing might happen, where zeal did not jump with discretion.

BOOK II

THE TALES OF THE CITIES

CHAPTER I

THE STORY OF CHICAGO

The Birthplace of the American Protective League — Center of Enemy Alien Activities — Focus of German Propaganda and Home of Pro-German Cults and Creeds — Story of the League's Work and Workers.

The unvarnished story of the growth and accomplishments of this League is the greatest proof in the world of the ability for self-government of intelligent, educated and thinking men. The American Protective League was made up of sober citizens who had something to protect. It was no one man, no one set of men, no one city, which makes it great. The real credit belongs to the unclassified and unsegregated Little Fellow.

We had in this war the usual amount of self-seeking. Our first pages abounded in pictures and praises of our great men, born of God to do wonders in ships, supplies, aeroplanes and armies. Some of them worked for a dollar a year. Some of them earned that much, many a great deal less. The scandals of this war are as great as the scandals of any war, when you come to know the truth about them. But there is no scandal attached to the plain, average citizen in this war. It was he, the real democrat and the real American, who won this war for us.

There is no charge of vain-glory, no charge of inefficiency and self-seeking attached to the story of Chateau Thierry and Belleau Wood and the Argonne, where died thousands of Little Fellows become great in making good. Neither is there any scandal attaching to the unknown men, the unnamed Little Fellows who " made good " back home behind the lines — the men who usually get lost after any war when the glory is being passed around by the politicians and paid historians.

There is, in a work such as this, no such thing as dividing or apportioning personal or local credit or approbation. Names, portraits, credits, praises — nothing of these is desired or may be begun, for there could be no end; and besides, one man is as big and as good as another in A. P. L. The League existed in countless communities all over the country — so many, it is not possible even to name a fraction of them. There is not even the possibility of mentioning more than a few of the greater centers of the work, and that in partial fashion only.

In this plan, perhaps, the city of Chicago naturally may come first, because, as we have seen, it was there that the League began. Besides, in this great Western hive of all the races, there are far more Germans than there are Americans. Have you not heard that astounding utterance of a sitting Mayor to the effect that Chicago is "the sixth greatest German city on the earth"? One also has heard an earlier Mayor of Chicago say that in his political plans he cared nothing at all for the American vote. "Give me the Austrian and the Italian and the Polish vote," he said; "but above all, give me the German vote!" Perhaps he would not be so outspoken to-day.

Among the unassimilated rabble who make a certain portion of Chicago's polyglot politik-futter, there are perhaps more troublemakers than in any other city of America. It is our own fault that they make so much trouble, but they do make it and they have. Bolsheviki, socialists, incendiaries, I. W. W.'s, Lutheran treason-talkers, Russellites, Bergerites, all the other-ites, religious and social fanatics, third-sex agitators, long haired visionaries and work-haters from every race in the world — Chicago had them and has them still, because she has invited them, accepted them and made them free of the place. Cheap politicians have done the rest; mayors who care nothing for the American vote.

This was the situation when we declared war. We then heard less about the "duty" the foreign-born had reserved when they swore (and then forgot) their solemn Delbrücked oaths of renunciation of all other allegiance, and of loyalty to America alone. But underneath this smug oath of faith to America, all too often the Teuton and his kin, the Kaiser's friend and sympathizer, still hid unchanged. To-day, as thousands of them read these lines, they know that this is the truth.

When we went to war, the militant Chicago Germans did not change — they simply submerged, German fashion; that was all. Then Chicago dropped her paravanes — spread down her WEB — to guard against under-surface attacks.

Once firmly established, the Chicago Division grew by leaps and bounds. On March 22, 1917, the first definite steps were taken toward the formation of a compact organization. Captains were appointed by Mr. Briggs, and these in turn organized their own working squads. Mr. Clabaugh was now beginning to get some of the assistance he so sorely needed.

Then, on April 6, came war. Followed the days of swift expansion and organization which have been covered in the preceding pages. Every day saw new men enrolled, big men, men eager to contribute time, money, experience, brains, energy and faithfulness. This is the story of the whole League, and this is Chicago's story, too.

On April 10, Mr. Charles Daniel Frey was appointed a captain in the Chicago Division, and shortly afterward, Mr. Victor Elting came into the organization as an appointee of Mr. Frey. Two months had now passed since the first Chicago operative had gone forth on an official mission. Chicago Division was demonstrably a success. Yet something more was needed. Work was piling up faster than personnel. It was now patent that Chicago must have a larger, stronger organization — an organization under direct executive control which would do its work with efficiency and business-like despatch. System was needed; speed was needed — and men. On May 22, as a first step in the reorganization, Mr. Briggs appointed Mr. Frey as Chief of the Chicago Division and Mr. Elting as Assistant Chief.

Mr. Frey and Mr. Elting thereupon developed a comprehensive plan of organization for the Chicago Division — a plan which was adopted in its main outlines by almost all of the large cities. Chicago was divided into zones, and an Inspector was appointed to direct and supervise the work in each zone. Bureaus were established covering the whole range of League operations. Bankers, railroad men, merchants, professional men — leading men from every sphere of activity were placed in charge of bureau work for which they were especially fitted.

The League was now a going concern in Chicago. That it should become national in every sense of the word was inevitable. In October, 1917, Mr. Frey and Mr. Elting joined Mr. Briggs in Washington and, in conference with the Attorney General of the United States, it was decided to establish National Headquarters in the Capital. The three men who were responsible for this great step became the national directors of the League. Pending the appointment of a Chief and Assistant Chief for the Chicago Division, Mr. R. A. Gunn, who had made a most efficient record as an Inspector, was appointed Acting Chief.

On January 26, 1918, Mr. John F. Gilchrist was appointed Chief of the Chicago Division, a position which he continued to hold until September 21, 1918, six weeks before the Armistice. Under his wise leadership, the organization gained in strength and numbers and influence, and handled, in wholly admirable fashion, the many difficult problems which arose during nine of the most trying months of the war. The Chicago unit, at the close of 1917, numbered 4,500 active members and about 2,000 industrial members. At the time of the Armistice, these numbers had been increased to 6,142 active members and over 7,000 members in the industrial division.

Upon the resignation of Mr. Gilchrist, a committee plan of executive control was adopted, and Mr. R. A. Gunn was appointed Chief. Mr. Gunn's report to D. J., covering the work of the Chicago Division almost to the period of the Armistice, will give at least a partial notion of what was accomplished, and should, therefore, be summarized:

> The greater part of the work of the organization is, of course, the work assigned from the Bureau of Investigation, with such complaints as are received from our own members, both active and industrial, and a number that come through the mail. We receive an average of 175 D. J. cases daily. Our reports when turned in are viséd by the Chief of our Bureau of Investigation, and those deemed ready for prosecution are turned over to the Special Agent assigned, and by him are taken to the District Attorney for active prosecution. I believe that our co-operation with the Bureau has been

active and I think, helpful, at all times. We have furnished A. P. L. men used for special work, such as under-cover investigations in the County Jail and in the Internment Camps. Through our organization, which covers practically every banking institution, mercantile, industrial and manufacturing plant, every profession and trade, in the entire Chicago district, we have furnished special and specific information from among our own members, which the Bureau of Investigation has generously intimated could hardly have been secured from any other source.

At its own expense, A. P. L. furnished three competent stenographers for a period of three months to systematize, card and index the 18,000 male German alien enemies, registered by the United States Marshal. During the "drives" of the Red Cross, many rumors and derogatory statements concerning the work of the Red Cross were spread broadcast through the country. A. P. L. ran down hundreds of complaints, secured many convictions, and handled the entire investigation of the Red Cross until quite recently, when they added a Bureau of Investigation of their own. The propaganda has practically ceased.

Work in co-operation with the Local Fuel Administrator was always active. Beginning with the fuelless Mondays, A. P. L. placed at his disposal some 3,500 men for checking up violations. On the lightless Monday and Tuesday night, A. P. L. had out the entire active organization checking violations of this sort. Again, on the order of the Administrator that no gasoline should be used on Sundays for pleasure, the entire organization was called on for service. During the wheatless and meatless days, also, the entire organization was called on to check and report violations among the restaurants, hotels and other places.

Chicago received daily from M. I. D. at Washington an average of twenty-five cases for character and loyalty investigations of civilians and officers going into foreign service. This work alone required the services of a Bureau Chief and five clerical assistants at headquarters.

Following the bomb explosion at the Federal building (where, by the way, A. P. L. mobilized within half an hour 1,700 men for duty if called upon), the officials of the United States War Exposition called on the organization for help. For eight days, an average of two hundred and fifty A. P. L. men mingled with the crowd both afternoon and evening with a view of preventing panics and of detecting and forestalling any outrage.

Next in volume to the work from D. J. was that which came

in under the Selective Service Act in connection with the draft problem. In addition to the locating of registrants, the division, on request, conducted investigations on a number of Local Boards, and also investigated thousands of cases involving deferred classifications, where the result of the investigation placed the registrant in Class 1-A and made him available for immediate service.

At the specific request of the commanding officer of the local branch of the Ordnance Department, Chicago division conducted a total of 536 investigations of officers and employees of the Ordnance Department in Chicago. Similar work was done for the Bureau of Investigation.

Chief Gunn concludes his simple and convincing narrative with a few division figures:

In conclusion I would say that at the headquarters of our units we employed sixty-six stenographers and clerks who were directed by thirty-one able men who gave their entire time, days, nights, and often Sundays, without one penny from our Treasury, to the direction of this work. In addition to this, we maintained eighteen captain's offices, the average monthly expenditure of each being in the neighborhood of $300. Exclusive of this, our average monthly expenses were about $7,000, which money was raised both from our own membership and from subscriptions of individuals and commercial houses.

We have been insistent at all times that our men should set a patriotic example to all others in accepting active service when liable or able. This is evidenced by the fact that five hundred and fifty of our members are now in the service. I have no hesitancy in saying that for loyalty, ability, judgment, and willingness to serve their country, I do not know, nor do I believe there can exist, a more splendid body of men than is contained in the membership of our Division of the American Protective League.

Follows the statistical record of the work accomplished by the Chicago division of the American Protective League up to January 21, 1919:

Neutrality cases investigated	43,026
War Department—all branches.	
Character and loyalty investigations	3,739
American Red Cross.	
Character and loyalty investigations	115
Illinois Volunteer Training Corps.	
Character and loyalty investigations	141

War Risk Insurance cases	230
U. S. Bureau of Naturalization cases	3,905
Draft investigations	30,440
Food Administration cases.	
Food investigations	12,637
Sugar investigations[1]	179
Fuel Administration cases.	
Coal investigations	3,263
Lightless Night investigations	1,500
Total investigations[2]	99,175
Number of men temporarily detained for examination of Registration and Classification Cards during the Slacker Drive of July, 1918	200,000
Delinquents apprehended and forced to appear at local Draft Boards	44,167
Deserters apprehended and sent to Military Camps	1,900
Record compiled for the U. S. Marshal for Alien Enemies; number of entries	18,000
Escaped criminals apprehended and turned over to Police Department	38
Blue Slip Summons issued	726
Automobile license numbers registered on first Gasless Sunday	129,204
Photographs, maps, postal cards of views of Germany sent to War Department	9,525

But it is from the notebooks of the operatives, recording varied activities all in the day's work, that we get the real reflex of the A. P. L. We cannot forego giving a few extracts from the stories of Chicago captains.

Let us take at random the summary from S———, captain of District No. 11, where there were fifty-six members — forty active operatives, under a captain, two lieutenants and a legal advisor. This district covers a large portion of the most German section of Chicago, part of which is loyal and part very much otherwise. In six months, during the last year of the war, there were 512 cases assigned to the district by headquarters, and the district turned

[1] A direct result of the sugar investigations was the saving of millions of pounds of sugar, and the donation to the American Red Cross of thousands of dollars by violators.

[2] In addition to the above, hundreds of jewelry store investigations were made for the purpose of obtaining information regarding alleged price discrimination against soldiers and sailors; also, hundreds of investigations of tailors, clothing stores and department stores in the interest of Army uniform regulations.

in to headquarters 298 complaints. Character and loyalty investigations to the number of fifty-three were made, necessitating from five to fifteen interviews each. In the slacker drive, July 11-13, a total of 1,744 individual cases were interviewed and disposed of in this district. Between 9:00 p. m. and 4:00 a. m. one night, eighty-one I. W. W. investigations were handled.

The total number of cases on record in this district for the six months is 3,842, which, if averaged, gives sixty-eight cases to each operative, but as only forty were active, the average should be figured as nearly eighty cases per capita. There is not figured in the foregoing about one thousand interviews which were necessary in making up reports to different departments of the Government on factories, saloons, garages and other buildings and structures, which might come under the head of miscellaneous services.

The activities of the operatives of District No. 11 were not confined to the boundaries of their own district. An illustration will show what is meant. A deserter was being protected by all branches of his family. Operatives spent nights interviewing every ascertainable relative and friend. Nothing could be learned except that the various members of the family, male and female, were so mixed in their sex relations that apparently no two of the opposite sex were living together in a legally permissible way. A chance lead pointed to a couple living in the country ten miles beyond the city limits. An hour's interview with the man and his consort, the two being examined separately, resulted in the chance mention of Norfolk, Virginia. Being pressed on this remark, the man hesitatingly declared he had had letters from Norfolk from the suspect who was working there and that he, the witness, would himself write to Norfolk at once and get definite information. The operatives agreed cheerfully to the proposition. On their return to the city, a telegram was immediately dispatched to Norfolk. By the time the letter from the "loyal" relative reached Norfolk, word was received that the deserter was located and taken into custody. The action of this little drama was staged entirely outside of District No. 11.

During the "heatless days" two operatives from the same district entered a saloon. They found it warm, the heat coming from a large radiator in the middle of the room covered by a table. The proprietor claimed he was unable to shut off this heat without shutting off the heat from rooms above where he had lodgers. The operatives went to the cellar and found no attempt had been made to shut off the heat from the saloon. Returning to the saloon, they investigated a back room, which was also heated, and where they found four men playing cards. The proprietor claimed these men were his lodgers and that this was their sitting-room. A search was made and evidence found which proved these men to be conducting a regular clearing-house of information for the enemy's use. Leads were discovered that spread in many directions and made the case one of the most important handled by the District. A camouflaged saloon radiator was the starting point.

Each operative discovered that the badge he wore bred a feeling of respect or fear for the authority of Uncle Sam which was quite marked. Seldom was an attempt made to dispute its meaning or to take exception to the request or direction made under its authority. The most desperate characters showed a meekness and a docility that was surprising. The only explanation reasonable is that the United States has from the start of the war shown the world and its own people that it meant business, and that in playing with the authorized agencies of the Government, criminals were not playing with politicians or officials who might be influenced, but with the newly and sternly roused sense of American loyalty which would brook no traitor or near-traitor under the Star and Stripes.

District No. 13 had an interesting case handled by Lieutenant McR——— and Operative L———. They searched the room occupied by the suspect and found two handbags and several suit-cases filled with clothing and some chemicals. They interviewed the subject. His registration card gave his serial and order number, and draft board status which was Class No. 5 Austrian. The operatives went back to report this to the Inspector, and upon returning found that the subject, his wife and sister had fled. By calling upon the different taxicab companies in the neighborhood, it was found that they had used a yellow taxicab to move their effects to an apartment several miles distant. A raid was immediately organized. Four men and two detective sergeants went to the new address, and the apartment was surrounded. One of the men saw a figure which appeared to be a woman, attempting to cross the area between the two buildings from one third story window to another, and he called to her to stop. One of the men inside the building, hearing the call, put his head out and found the subject on the window sill of the adjoining building in a very embarrassing position. It was not a woman, but the suspect, in woman's clothes! He was hauled in and put under arrest. In the meantime an analysis of the chemicals had been made and they were found to consist of materials for the manufacture of enough explosives to blow out another end of the postoffice building. Information was received from the League at New York to the effect that he was a very dangerous enemy alien.

This same District landed another good case. One morning a traveling man heard a little girl say to a small boy playmate, "We have a fine piano in our flat," and the boy finally answered, "That's nothing, we've got a German spy in ours." The traveling man turned a complaint in to the Department of Justice and in due course it came back to our district to be investigated. The operative had little to start with. Finally he asked a little girl if she had ever heard any boy make such a remark. By merest chance, she happened to be one of the children who had overheard the boy, and at once pointed out where he lived. The operative then went to the apartment and questioned the boy's mother, telling her that he was getting a list of boarding-houses in that district for directory purposes and, of course, asking her the names and occupations of all lodgers. He noticed that one of the names was German and after he had finished his list he asked her if he might see the accommodations. When he reached the German's room, he saw a trunk of foreign make. He opened it and found lying inside on top of the clothing a cartridge belt filled with loaded cartridges. This he noticed had seen much use and was worn smooth. He also found papers, drawings, a Lueger pistol and several other things which an alien enemy is not supposed to enjoy during war times. The landlady stated that the man was a draftsman in the Federal Building. It was subsequently found that the drawings were plans of the Municipal Pier and the Federal Building. About five o'clock the next morning, several Federal officers took the man down to the Bureau of Investigation and found that he was an enemy alien in the employ of the German Government. Within twenty-four hours he was on his way to Leavenworth under an order of internment.

Women are not enlisted in espionage work for M. I. D. and were not employed as operatives in the Chicago A. P. L. — with one exception. Many a suspect has found " Mrs. B " fatally easy to look at and listen to — even easy to talk too much to!

Here is a " Mrs. B " case. The subject, Miss W———, during the year 1912, met a Mr. and Mrs. M———, Americans, who were in Paris with their two children, a boy ten and a girl twelve. Miss W——— told them a story of having quarreled with her family, who were quite wealthy, and said she was seeking a position that would bring her to America. She produced unquestionable references, and returned with the M——— family to the United States. After remaining in their employ for six months, she took a course in nursing in B——— Hospital in Indianapolis. She graduated from this hospital, came to Chicago with letters of introduction from the faculty, and became engaged here as governess in the home of a wealthy family on Lake Shore Drive. In April, 1917, she applied to the Chicago Telephone Company for a position, asking to be sent to France in their next unit. She told a confusing story in reference to her age, brought about a suspicion, which was followed by an investigation. " Mrs. B." was given the assignment. Miss W——— gave up her position as governess, took a room on the north side of Chicago near Wilson Avenue. She was closely shadowed night and day, and was found to be in continual communication with doctors and nurses. During the time she was waiting to hear from the Chicago Telephone Company in reference to the application she had filed, she also filed an application with the American Red Cross. Here she gave practically the same references, and told the same story. Investigators from the American Red Cross were advised by the Department of Justice that they drop their investigation for the time being. "Mrs. B" proved that this woman was the medium through which tetanus germs were being delivered to certain doctors and nurses, who in turn were to spread them through our cantonments and hospitals.

District No. 8 lies in the extreme southern part of Chicago. "The Gold Coast" of this territory, lying along "The Ridge," is a strictly residential district, but a veritable melting-pot of foreigners has sprung up in the neighborhood of the mammoth factories and mills in the suburban towns of Kensington, West Pullman, Roseland, Riverdale and South Chicago proper, east of the Southern Division Gold Coast. In this modern Babel there are fifty or sixty different nationalities. Even a short season with such a racial hodge-podge as exists in and around Kensington is almost equivalent to a trip around the world. Practically the only work in this community (Districts 41 and 47) consisted of draft evasions and pro-Germans. The last named were kindly but positively reminded that our country was at war. The operatives in this Gold Coast district were practically all business men, being recruited from banks, business houses, schools and the ministry. It was no uncommon thing to have two ministers, one of them a leading "dry exponent," go out with a squad of men through saloons and pool-rooms, picking up suspects and evaders. During the four-day raid in July, one of the captains working out of Draft Board No. 22 remarked: "I just sent out the vice-president of our bank. I commanded him to look up one of these draft cases and he went right to it without question. That man holds the mortgage on my home, and I am bossing him around as though he were my office boy!"

Another captain tells something more of this foreign part of the city, Districts 39, 40, 42, 46 of the South Division. This comprises the large territory on the lake, at the extreme southern end of the city, and has in it a large harbor and river which is lined with elevators, shipyards, and important steel industries of all kinds. The population is mostly of foreign origin, anything from a descendant of the Pilgrim Fathers to a Tartar from Siberia. Poles, Austrians, Serbs, Swedes, Germans and Italians predominate, and many of the A. P. L. operatives were recruited from this source, thereby giving access to all tongues. This division captain says:

> The magnitude of the shipping and the enormous steel industries, together with a population of from ten to twenty thousand aliens, has rightly given this district the reputation of being one of the most difficult in Chicago. Thousands of these people speak no English, and are living here under foreign customs. Two local draft boards are in this district, 19 and 20, and naturally many cases of draft evasion were found. After the first general registration, we were called upon to investigate about 1,200 cases under this head, a large percentage of them being cases of men who were really willing to comply with the regulations, but who had been badly advised by their more erudite countrymen. As we always have a large "floating population," we naturally experienced much trouble in tracing this class.
>
> That small things often lead to large affairs, we discovered many times. One night a Pole came home, went over to the side of the room, took a large crucifix from the wall, broke it across his knee, and told his wife who stared at him big-eyed with horror, that that ——— thing was no good any more and that he had no place for it. The woman, who like most of her nationality, was intensely religious, was quick to see that her man was not drunk, and was shrewd enough to determine to find the cause of his action. On quizzing him, she found he had joined a new Polish Church which taught many new things, so she asked if she could not go to that church. He took her there, and she learned of the notorious Pastor Russell and his teachings, heard the doctrines of non-resistance preached, and learned of a service to be held to persuade young men never to fight or shed blood under any circumstances. She reported what she learned, and made such a positive and specific affidavit, that we resolved to see how much truth it contained. So, when we discovered that services were being held in their church, and that the congregation contained a great many young men of draft age, evidently Poles, we took a chance and called the wagon.
>
> We arrested the entire congregation during the services, confiscated copies of "The Finished Mystery," a proscribed

> book, and practically moved the contents of the church to the police station. Here we found much seditious literature, and obtained statements from many of the congregation, which were sufficient to cause quite a stir. At present, seven of the leaders of this church from Brooklyn are sojourning at Fort Leavenworth. We feel, here in southern Chicago, that the breaking of that crucifix led to a nation-wide investigation of a dangerous propaganda.

This same captain, in closing his report, makes the following observation:

> Some of the striking phases of this work are the real friendships engendered by our associations with each other. Here the measure of a man is his loyalty and sincerity, his judgment, his grit, and his personal sacrifice. When you can find as many real and true Americans as this organization contains, you need never have worries as to whether this country is going to be safe.

Central District of Chicago is that important region covering the great business district, out of which some four hundred men, under four captains, regularly worked all over the city. This is not one of the residence districts, so that the squad of operatives who reported to this branch were far scattered throughout the city for most of the twenty-four hours. The personnel of this district embraced lawyers, doctors, bankers, printers, dry goods merchants, insurance men, mechanics, railway trainmen, traveling salesmen, actors, and all kinds of employed persons. A great many members belonged to the prominent clubs of Chicago. There were interpreters who understood all of the continental languages. There were both rich men and poor men included in this membership. There were boys in the twenties and men of sixty-five. It had come to be the practice of all the interlocking branches of our Governmental defensive organizations to call up Central District for men needed on some particular work. It had been the headquarters squad, and had sent men all over Northern Illinois, and sometimes out of the State.

There was a school of instruction for new operatives in this district in which new men are taught the elements of the League work, the elements of espionage laws, and other war measures. They were instructed, also, in the fundamentals of shadow work; the details of the selective service regulations; the principles of law and evidence, and other subjects proper to the activities of the League. There were seven words taught to every operative, applying equally well to complaints and to reports — guide words in investigations. If these seven words were borne in mind at the time of making complaint or investigations, or in writing up the report, an operative would be fairly well assured of embodying the information desired. These words are: "Who," "Which," "What," "Why," "When," "How," and "Witnesses."

Every care was exercised by the operative not to approach the subject himself or to allow him to know he was being investigated. There were countless Chicago Germans and pro-Germans investigated, ticketed, tabulated, and filed away, who to this day do not know that they ever told anybody anything about themselves. Many of these Prussianized Chicagoans to-day wear heavy frowns and look aggrieved.

In order to save his time, each operative was taught how to use the regular city channels of information. If he got a name without any address, he was taught to go to the nearest telephone directory or city directory. Sometimes a telephone number was known and the name of the party unknown. Reference to the numerical telephone directory sometimes covered this. Sometimes the business of the subject might be known and his address unknown, in which case it might be found by reference to the classified business telephone directory, or the city directory. A subject might be doing business in the city and living in the suburbs. Countless suburban telephone directories were always in the central office for such reference.

In every great city a directory gives a concise arrangement of the personnel of the various departments of the U. S. Government; state and federal officials, their titles, their room numbers, their buildings, can be found in this way. In this way, also, all the officers of the city government can be found; the rooms where the court of this or that judge are located, etc. The state offices, including hospitals, etc., can be found in these directories.

A wide range of useful information concerning the city and its environs was given to novitiate operatives in this Central District. This information was of incalculable benefit to new members of the League when once their active investigating work began. The A. P. L. training school was a very important cog in the Chicago machine, and made it possible for the district to do more work per capita and better work than would otherwise have been possible. Indeed, the training for an operative was not bad training for a newspaper reporter. What is said regarding this work in the Chicago district might apply in very considerable part also to the work in other large communities.

Operatives were obliged to take all sorts of roles. At times they acted as waiters or clerks, and sometimes they impersonated lawbreakers themselves. One of them succeeded in impersonating an I. W. W. so well that at a meeting he was covering he was asked to contribute to the I. W. W. cause — and did so! Another ingratiated himself into the good offices of the I. W. W.'s so well that he was permitted to take notes at one of their meetings with the understanding that he was a newspaper man representing one of their own papers.

The Southwest Division in Chicago is only another corner of darkest Europe. In this section, however, were located a good many foreign-born operatives, who affiliated well in that region and did their work thoroughly until the closing days of the war. Their grist included some curious and interesting cases.

There was, for instance, a certain person called Panco, the Fry Cook, long wanted by the Department of Justice for anarchistic and seditious utterances. The Department had been hunting Panco for months but could not find him. Four Southwest A. P. L. operatives went after Panco. Two of them became members in a waiters' union in which Panco was known to belong. They could not find their man, who did not seem to report often at the headquarters of that union; so they gave out reports everywhere that Panco was a dead beat and would not pay his union dues! This came to Panco's ears. He showed up at headquarters to deny this impeachment. He got thirty years.

A Lithuanian lecturer was described as about to deliver a seditious harangue in the village of Cicero, near Chicago. The Southwest Division sent out several motor cars with picked men ready for trouble. They found a hall crowded with foreigners who were listening to a much bewhiskered man, clad in shabby tweeds, who was demonstrating at a blackboard on a platform, and was speaking in some unknown tongue. At last one of the operatives who had been taken along as an interpreter began to laugh and said, "Let's go home, fellows; we've got the old bird wrong. He ain't talking anarchy; he's giving a lecture on sex control!"

An unusual amount of shrewdness should be credited to some of these operatives. It was a mere guess, for instance, on the part of such a man that the figure "8" — the final figure on a foreign birth certificate — had been changed to a "5." If this were true, it meant that the suspect would come within the draft age, although otherwise his story was perfectly straight. Suspicion is not evidence, so the Department of Justice was about to release this man. The latter had remarked to someone that his father lived in Indiana. The operative went to the phone and pretended to call up the father in this town personally, with the intention of inducing the suspect to eavesdrop on the phone conversation in the next room. After a while the operative turned to the suspect, his hand over the receiver, and said: "Well, we've got the information we wanted. What have you got to say?" Completely fooled, the suspect confessed! He was inducted into the army.

A certain colored draft dodger was discovered to belong to a staff of colored waiters in a certain hotel. The head waiter, very pompous and very shiny, refused to allow a search. The A. P. L. declared that if the suspect was not forthcoming he would arrest every waiter in the place and carry them off in the wagon. This brought out the suspect. He's in the Army now.

A certain Mrs. L——— called the Red Cross a bunch of grafters and crooks, said Ambassador Gerard was a traitor and a liar, said the President was the greatest traitor since Jefferson Davis and made other interesting remarks. She repeated these statements before a U. S. Marshal and was held in $5,000 bond. Then she became more abusive and was held in $5,000 additional. She kept on until her bond amounted to $25,000, and was then asked if she did not think it was time to stop talking. She did. As she could not raise the bail, she was sent to Cook County jail, where she remained till the Armistice was signed.

Chicago at times handled other live stock than that commonly seen in the stockyards. On August 5, 1918, the sixth enemy alien special to Fort Oglethorpe carried fifteen persons for internment. The train was to pick up eight more at Indianapolis. On the following day, it seems, the Chicago Symphony Orchestra had seven members who groaned while they were playing the Star Spangled Banner. They explained their frame of mind before a judge, who taught them very much better manners. On August 7, Lieutenant Friederick Walter S——— of the German army, who for a month had worn a United States uniform at Camp Grant, had his naturalization papers revoked, and got interned for the period of the war. On September 1, among ten aliens shipped to Fort Oglethorpe, one was a munition manufacturer who had been just at the point of receiving a very fat United States order. He had been filling contracts for Germany before we went to war.

On November 17, 1918, the radicals and socialists of Chicago held a great meeting in the Coliseum. There were about 12,000 present. It is not necessary to go into details regarding their action beyond saying that they gave over the Chicago Socialist party, body and breeches, to Bolshevism. Here in Chicago, one of our centers of the civilization of America, these men declared themselves in sympathy with Russian anarchy. In America, the land of hope, they declared themselves in sympathy with hopelessness, despair and destruction. Some of the speeches were made in the German language — a tongue which we ought to forbid to be used in public, on our streets, in our printed pages, and over our telephone wires to-day. These speakers, in the Hun tongue, openly deplored contributions to our War funds. They hailed with much applause such speakers as Victor Berger, who publicly gloried in the four indictments pending over him. In short, the meeting came dangerously close to being disloyal. We shall be so mild as this in comment, since being a member of the Socialist party is not *per se* a disloyal act, and not all Socialists are of the radical wing.

Much pleased with the sound of their own voices, these gentlemen now concluded to hold a public street parade, with red banners and the usual Bolshevist appurtenances. They went to Acting Chief of Police Alcock, and asked for a permit to parade in the streets. They said they wanted to carry the red flag, and they asked police protection. Note the reply the Chief of Police made to them:

> My friends, I won't give you police protection at all, nor try to do so. Do you know what you are up against? There are 12,000 A. P. L. men in this village who are opposed to this sort of thing, and my men don't want to get in wrong with any 12,000 A. P. L. men. We work with those people and not against them. They work with us and not against us. Believe me, the best thing you folks can do is to cut out the parade.

The representatives of the proposed parade could not get back to their headquarters fast enough. They cut out the parade.

As late as November 21, Chicago was still running enemy alien specials for Fort Oglethorpe. This consignment included a cook, also a Highland Park riding master who had been over-curious in regard to matters adjacent to Fort Sheridan. Twenty others were to be picked up later down the line — all after the Armistice had been signed.

On November 23, Fred I———, said to resemble the Crown Prince very much in his personal appearance, was fined five thousand dollars, whether for seditious utterances or for his resemblance to the Crown Prince does not appear, and is immaterial. Either would be enough.

On November 26, nine men were given free transportation from Chicago to Fort Leavenworth. One of these was a Dunkard preacher who got ten years for saying, "I'd kill a man rather than buy a Liberty bond." He will have time to think that proposition over.

These straws will show well which way the wind blew in Chicago for the last year or so. Much to the disappointment of the Kaiser and one or two mayors, Chicago seems to be but very imperfectly Germanized after all. As for setting down the full tale of the A. P. L. activities in this city, it would be a thing impossible of accomplishment. The world knows how Chicago does the things she considers proper to have done. The American Protective League in Chicago worked in the well-known and well-accredited Chicago way. To thank the men who did this work, or even to mention their names, would cheapen them and their work. They did not ask thanks. They were Americans and were citizens.

CHAPTER II

THE STORY OF NEW YORK

The Focus of German International Espionage — Center of Foreign Population — The Great Plots — Governmental Concentration — How the A. P. L. Web Helped Collect Traitors — Details of the Organization — A Metropolis Loved by a Country.

The great American metropolis was the storm-center of America in the war. The heart of the great and intricate system of German espionage, the controlling financial body of Germany's spy army, was there; the treacherous diplomacy of Germany centered there. Moreover, our shipments of men, munitions and supplies largely centered there, and that was the general point of departure of our troops bound overseas. Naturally, therefore, our Government concentrated in and around this danger spot its strongest protective measures for our troops and their supplies. Literally, it was plot and counterplot in New York; war and counter war; espionage and counter espionage.

Such a story as that cannot be covered by the printed page. No volume can describe New York's part in the war, for that man does not live who knows or ever will know all that went on in New York in war time. New York herself never will know how she was endangered and how she was protected.

Until war broke out, New York was much like London. Grown indifferent to her vast foreign element, she was disposed to let these people meet and march, preach and pray and then go home again, red flag and all. No great world city can have a homogeneous population, nor can any such population be governed as a whole. New York accepted the fact that she was one of the centers of the world's transient life. Her entire business prosperity is built up on the transient trade. With an amused indifference, New York allowed her visitors to meet and march, preach and pray, amuse themselves so long as they liked, so long as they paid for their privilege of passing through. She had long since ceased to analyze her population, but has entertained it instead, regarding it with neither fear, shame, pride nor alarm. She was truly a metropolis.

But when war came, New York realized that she was not only a metropolis but a commercial center and a place where human beings lived. She had tall buildings. A brick shot off the top of the Woolworth Building would certainly jar a man below if it fell upon him; and the Woolworth or other buildings might easily be hit by naval guns of a hostile fleet lying comfortably off shore. The funk of New York and other eastern cities was never felt at all in the central portion of the country. When the submarines began to show what they could do, New York awoke to a sense of real danger. She faced the fact that, although she was foreign in population, she must become American if America was to endure. Then New York turned her face no longer toward Europe, but toward America and since that time has been more beloved by America than ever she was before.

It was imperative that the vast protective agencies of the national Government should focus here at the gateway to the Atlantic. Military Intelligence, Naval Intelligence, Cable Censorship, Mail Censorship, the Department of Justice, War Trade Intelligence — each of these and all the various war boards and branches of war activities must center in the metropolis inevitably. The machinery for protecting the invaluable shipping of men and munitions was as elaborate and perfect as the Government could make it. Every force was rushed to the danger line in New York.

In so complicated and overburdened a series of Government enterprises it early became obvious that there was need for an auxiliary such as the American Protective League. The organization was duly made and widely extended. It was natural none the less that it should be very much overshadowed by the greater volume and greater importance of the agencies of the Government's judicial and war work, which were massed in the great city. But the A. P. L. was there, active as elsewhere, and perhaps more useful than in any other city in the country, because it had to do there with larger risks than offered in any other city.

In the period of its work in New York up to the time of the Armistice, the A. P. L. division was thought to have covered some 300,000 cases in all, which is far and away the record for America. Such figures as these mean, of course, that to single out any one case or a few cases would be only to repeat cases the like of which already have been described for other points; and besides, it would not in any sense give an idea of the extent of the data handed over to the United States departments on A. P. L. initiative or on government request. It seems wiser to let the great national or international cases, which have become publicly prominent through Government activity, stand for the minor story of New York.

These *causes celébrès* have in great part been made public in the newspapers,—and in a great many instances made yet more public by the testimony of the witnesses of the Federal Attorneys before the Overman Senate Committee in Washington. It certainly could be said of the great city that she produced more sensations in espionage than all the rest of the country combined. A. P. L. was not concerned in all these matters, although in some of them it played its part.

The first chief of the New York Division was a lawyer, John H. Hendrick, who had charge of the small beginnings in April, 1917, but who in the following month, was succeeded by Richmond Levering, special agent of the Department of Justice. Mr. Bielaski, Chief of the U. S. Bureau of Investigation, approved this appointment, Mr. Levering later becoming Major in the U. S. Army. In early June, Mr. E. S. Underhill, an Agent of the Department of Justice, was detailed to take charge. The work now began to grow somewhat. In October, 1917, League affairs were placed in the hands of an operating committee. On January 3, 1918, the committee was abolished, and Mr. E. H. Rushmore was appointed Acting Chief. In May, 1918, Mr. Rushmore became Chief of the Division.

New York Division, like others, at first was organized

along trade lines, which was found to be impracticable. Then the Southern and Eastern Federal Districts of New York were divided into zones. The Borough of Manhattan contained eight zones, each under an inspector. The Borough of the Bronx was placed in charge of a deputy chief, and was divided into nine sub-divisions. The Borough of Brooklyn and Long Island was also in charge of a deputy chief, and subdivided into eight districts, each in charge of an inspector. The outlying districts were formed into zones, using county lines as boundaries, and each of these zones also was under the charge of an inspector. All the inspectors appointed a sufficient number of captains, who had under them lieutenants in charge of squads.

It will be seen that this is rather a complicated organization, and indeed it could not be swung as a unit in the matter of its records, because of the diverse reporting system required.

The work of the Division Headquarters on Nassau Street was efficiently handled by twenty volunteer members who acted as Bureau Chiefs in the matter of assignment of work. Headquarters had about fifty file clerks and stenographers in its force, and in addition operated six zone offices, all of which were used exclusively for these zone workers, and all of them fully equipped with office facilities and help. The Division expended something over $75,000, all of which was raised by individual subscriptions of members of the League and their friends.

A. P. L. in New York had all sorts of cases. Chief Rushmore thinks about the most important was that concerned with A. L———, intimate friend of Jeremiah O'Leary, on trial for treason. This case was turned over to the League by Division Superintendent DeWoody of D. J., who asked the covering of all railroad stations, ferries and steamship lines or other possible means of entry into New York in order that L——— might be apprehended. A rather meagre description of the suspect was given. Information had reached the Department that L——— had left New York when O'Leary forfeited his trial bond and did not appear in court for trial on charge of treason. L——— was thought to be on his way back to New York. A. P. L. put out about one hundred operatives on this case, and stopped hundreds of passengers who might have resembled him and asked them to identify themselves. This came to nothing. Other operatives interviewed the man's wife and were convinced L——— was in town. An operative of A. P. L., accompanied by a D. J. man, therefore shadowed one of L———'s intimate friends, with the result that L——— himself finally was located in Brooklyn and apprehended. He was taken to the New York office of the Department of Justice and there gave information as to O'Leary's whereabouts. The latter man, who had jumped his bail bond, was immediately apprehended in the West and brought on to New York, where, at the last writing, he was waiting trial on the charge of treason.

The A. P. L. shadow work in the foregoing case was so good as to elicit a letter of praise from D. J. in Washington to Mr. DeWoody. The latter disclaimed the credit and gave it to the A. P. L. operative "who performed a remarkable feat in a continued and difficult shadow."

The Division Chief himself writes something regarding a matter which has brought up considerable other writing at different times from many different sources.

> The story of the much discussed slacker raid in New York is known to every one, but we might give some details. In August, 1918, Mr. Bielaski, in Washington, advised the National Directors of A. P. L. that he was anxious to conduct a New York slacker raid similar to that in Chicago. The National Directors conferred with Mr. De Woody, the D. J. Agent in New York, who talked the matter over with Martin Conboy, Director of the Draft for New York City. The National Directors also went to the New York Division of A. P. L. and left a tentative plan based upon the Chicago arrangement, which was submitted to Mr. DeWoody, who, later, with these others, worked out a plan for the raid which was to come off on September 3, 4 and 5.
>
> Arrangements were made to obtain the Sixty-ninth Regiment Armory in New York and the Twenty-third Regiment Armory in Brooklyn, and about 1,000 sailors and 750 soldiers from posts in New York City were obtained for assistance in the raids. Two American Protective League operatives were detailed to each of the one hundred and eighty-nine local boards in New York, and two to each police station. There were seventy-five operatives on duty in the Armories in New

York and about fifty in Brooklyn. There were ten special agents of D. J. in Brooklyn and twenty in New York. Mr. DeWoody prepared printed instructions to be used by the sailors, soldiers and A. P. L. operatives in the work.

The system used on the streets was to interrogate a man, and ask for his registration card and his final classification card. If he had none, he was taken to the nearest police station, where he was questioned further by the operatives in charge, and if thought to be a delinquent, was then sent by a motor car to the armory to be held. From that point his local board was communicated with by telephone or telegraph, and the true status of the man obtained at the earliest possible moment. In these raids, there were apprehended 21,402 men, of whom 756 were inducted into the service. There were found 2,485 men who were delinquents from their local boards.

Up till December 11, 1918, there were 45,150 filed cases of a general nature in the New York Division: 3,610 civil service case, 2,920 passport visés, 471 passport cases, 2,507 overseas investigations, 2,539 investigations of officers' commissions, and 29,680 cases connected with selective service matters. This makes a total of 86,877 cases.

It is to be noted that the above numbers apply to folder numbers only, and many folders contain more than one case, some of them as high as 250 cases. For instance, the investigations of a jury panel would be carried all in one folder under the name of the trial on which that jury was to sit. The figures in selective service matters are the actual number of cases turned over to the League at the time they started work with the various local boards. Subsequent to this date the A. P. L. officers in charge of the work at the various boards were given thousands of cases which they reported directly to the board, there being no file in the office in such instances. The A. P. L. Chief of New York therefore thinks it a very conservative estimate to say that the number of individuals investigated by the New York Division would run between 300,000 and 400,000. All these cases in the New York office system were filed alphabetically under the name of the person or firm to be investigated; for that reason definite figures could not be given in any summary. As League operatives became better acquainted with the Chairmen of the Draft Boards, more and more cases would be turned in directly to the Local Boards, which left the files incomplete also in cases of this character.

On Long Island, near New York, there were several large military camps, including Camp Mills and Camp Upton, and several aviation fields. The A. P. L. zone inspectors in charge of Nassau and Suffolk Counties, together with the Deputy Chief, in charge of Long Island, coöperated closely with the Intelligence officers of these camps. A. P. L. quite often was of assistance in locating deserters from these camps, it being the usual thing for an officer to telegraph A. P. L. to pick up the pursuit.

A. P. L. also investigated a great many cases for the camp authorities at Camp Wadsworth, Spartanburg, South Carolina, because this camp was occupied for some time by the New York National Guard. Sometimes the League would be asked to investigate the statement of a man who wanted a furlough because his family in New York was sick. A great many fraudulent requests of this kind were discovered. The War Department detailed a special officer to handle cases of deception of this character, and A. P. L. turned over to him a great deal of information of this nature as well as many reports which had come in to A. P. L. of the sale of liquor to men in uniform. Captain Peiffer, the officer in charge of this work, at one time investigated some thirty hotels in New York City. For more than two weeks these hotels were covered by A. P. L. operators. This officer had a lieutenant detailed to watch liquor and vice matters on Long Island, who made his headquarters at Hempstead. A. P. L. officers coöperated with this lieutenant in every way and gave him much assistance in closing up saloons and hotels that came within the five mile limit of the various camps.

Military Intelligence Division, of the General Staff, sent a great many character and loyalty investigations of overseas cases, officers' investigation cases and a large variety of cases of special investigation of both positive and negative nature, to A. P. L. in New York. A separate department was established in New York headquarters exclusively to handle the cases coming to New York Military Intelligence in Washington. Within the seven months ending December 11, 1918, the New York office received

5,046 cases of the types above mentioned. Perhaps a man going overseas would give from one to ten references, say an average of four references to each case, which would mean the interviewing of more than 20,000 individuals at the request of the War Department in Washington. The men who did this work did not get a cent for it. The territory covered by the Division extends from Poughkeepsie, New York, to Montauk Point, Long Island, a distance of about 200 miles. The cases would be scattered all over this territory, and very often the same case would require two or more investigators.

Beside all of these rather heavy duties in connection with the big government work, A. P. L. had daily requests from the Intelligence Office at Governor's Island, the Port of Embarkation at Hoboken, and the various other Intelligence Offices in and around New York City. Every possible assistance was rendered these various officers. It was impossible to classify all of this work in the files, so that the entire number is not available.

As the perfectly interlocking system of intelligence of the A. P. L. in the great city became known, the agents of the Department of Justice and the officers of the various Military Intelligence services got in the habit of calling on headquarters at A. P. L. for all sorts of information. Quite often they would call regarding some case which needed looking into at a town a long distance away. The name of an A. P. L. division at that point would be given, and the case turned over to the latter by telegraph. Thus it is easy to see that the web of New York, expanded into the web of A. P. L. all over America, was of almost incalculable benefit to all of the U. S. Departments concerned in any way with the war.

The New York office has conducted some part of the investigation of almost every alien enemy that has been interned in that part of the country. Just how much value the work of the League has had in these various internment cases, it is difficult to tell. Department of Justice has sometimes been rather haughty and lofty in regard to its humbler auxiliary. When New York A. P. L. has inquired of D. J. as to the outcome of a certain case, sometimes the answer would be that " proper action will be taken in due time," the inference being that D. J. did not want to be bothered by questions. A like vagueness quite often enshrouded cases turned over to Military Intelligence. A. P. L. might investigate fifty men for commissions and never know even whether any of them got a commission.

The offices of the United States Attorneys in both the Southern and Eastern districts of New York were greatly overworked, and had a very inadequate staff of assistants. It was necessary, in many instances, for A. P. L. to take cases that should have gone to a Federal Court, before some local magistrate on a disorderly conduct charge.

In brief, the story of A. P. L. in New York City is very satisfying indeed. How fortunate for Military Intelligence, the Draft Boards, the Department of Justice and other war branches that they had an A. P. L. to help them out, and to do that for nothing! Had this not been the case, it is not too much to say that these branches of our war activities would also have broken down as so lamentably did other portions of our war work — ordnance, equipment, airplane work, etc., all of which suffered from not having a quarter million of men at hand to do the work for nothing and do it right. The truth about this war never has been known and never will be printed. A lot of it lies in the files of the A. P. L.

In the course of the last ten months, according to the Military Intelligence Bureau, New York Division probably had more investigations entrusted to it than would in peace times be made throughout the entire country. Since the A. P. L. men were of the highest type, with all the advantage of education and wide experience, their ready adaptability can be taken for granted. But even with the high average of ability of the League officers and operatives, the notably fine record of the New York Division would not have been possible had there not been a most thorough and up-to-date business system. And such was actually the case.

A full series of blanks, the use of special cover sheets, of different colors, and the employment of case covers corresponding to the cover sheets, so simplified the filing system and the record of the case itself as to save a great deal of time and eliminate a great many mistakes. For instance, the case card would be buff in a case of a "commission" investigation, green in an "overseas" investigation and pink for special cases. The card is kept clipped to its cover sheet until a case is assigned. When it has been assigned, notation is made on the card and cover sheet, and the individual record card of the man to whom assigned. The case is then sent to the operative, and the case card filed alphabetically under his name in the "out" box. A separate record card is maintained for each investigator or district officer. It is thus possible to locate a case at once, by looking up a name of the subject in the "out" box of case cards, and to locate what cases are in the hands of any investigator by looking up his record card. An equally thorough system was employed in the handling of reports as they came in.

Without a most efficient system for transacting the business of the League, the most hopeless confusion must have obtained among that seething mass of conflicting human activities. Mere bulk of paper is an incomprehensible thing, and no one who has not seen the masses of reports coming in, even to the minor offices of the League, can understand what the handling of the *three million* A. P. L. investigations really meant in office work alone.

The Army is divided into the Staff and the Line; otherwise, the Office and the Field. A similar division may be made in the American Protective League. The men handling the records in the central office are more or less unhonored and unsung. Upon the other hand, the operative who puts on false eyebrows and a beard and goes out to stalk a suspect is apt to seem far more the heroic figure, although what he really is doing is no more than getting something for the office to file. Neither branch of the activity ought to be overlooked.

The New York A. P. L. conducted investigations for the Department of Justice under three heads; the State Department under two heads; the War Department under five heads; and also the Navy Department, the Alien Property Custodian, the Civil Service Commission, the War Trade Board and the U. S. Shipping Board, as well as the Treasury Department under three different heads.

When one pauses to reflect on these different classifications of the work and the different ramifications of the League's operative forces, one is pretty nearly ready to admit that without a perfect office system the whole thing would have been jolly well messed up inside of a week. This amateur organization sprang into being almost over night, a smooth-working, modern business machine, which rendered invaluable services at no cost at all. When you stop to think of it, this is one of the most wonderful phenomena of American business life.

The total membership of officers and operatives in the New York Division numbered over four thousand five hundred substantial business and professional men, chosen from every field of activity. They were classified and reclassified to such an extent that, from speaking any required language on earth to expert knowledge in any profession on earth, aid could be furnished on demand. Two significant facts stand out in comparing New York with other cities. The first, the rather smaller number of men; the second, the rather small amount of money spent in the work. It is due to the excellent business system of that division that the cost per case was kept so low, for New York runs more cases to the operative, and more to the member, than any other city in the country.

CHAPTER III

THE STORY OF PHILADELPHIA

Splendid Record of a Ship-Shape Office—A Model Organization and the Way it Worked — Stories of the Silent Soldiers — A Banner Report.

The City of Brotherly Love gives us pause. Is it indeed the truth that Americans do not know their own country? The story of the American Protective League, covering some millions of typewritten words, some hundreds of thousands of pages of typewritten copy, might be called one of the largest and one of the best histories of America ever written. It offers no pretense at deductions, but only an abundance of facts, objective and not subjective, concrete and not abstract. Popular impression hath it that the city founded by good William Penn is a simple and quiet sort of community, where life goes on lawfully and all is ease and comfort, peace and content. The facts do not seem to bear out this supposition. Philadelphia was as lawless as the next city during war times, possessed of as many undesirables and offering as many urgent problems in national defense. Tucson, Arizona, reports peace. Philadelphia is bad and borderish!

Among the many hundreds of reports coming in during the closing days of the American Protective League, there are some which run forty, fifty, or seventy-five pages of single space type. A very few of such reports would make a book the size of this one in hand. It has been, let it be repeated, with a most genuine regret that such work had to be condensed by the press. The Philadelphia report, for instance, covers ninety pages, and is an absolute model in every way. Indeed, a visit to the Philadelphia A. P. L. offices would have left any visitor certain of the high level of efficiency which has been attained by that division in every phase of its work. There was not a neater, better-systematized or smoother-running division in all the League than that in bad and borderish Philadelphia. The installation in that city was not so large as some. A Swiss watch is not so large as a Big Ben clock, but the latter does not keep any better time and makes much more noise about it.

It being impossible to print all of the Philadelphia report, it is quite in order to give rather a full summary of it, that we may correct the old impression regarding Philadelphia as a place of peace. The tabulated records cover only eleven months, from December 26, 1917, to November, 1918. In that period, 18,275 persons were examined, not counting those who were released in the big slacker raids. In order that the lay reader may have a perfect idea of the many different heads of activity in any one of these great offices, the Philadelphia table is offered in full, precisely as sent in:

Department of Justice Cases.

Alien Enemy Activities.		
a. Male	1,575	
b. Female	177	1,752
Citizen disloyalties and sedition. (Espionage Act)		880
Treason		1
Sabotage, bombs, dynamite, defective manufacture of war material		78
Anti-Military activity, interference with draft, etc.		91
Propaganda.		
a. Word of mouth	509	
b. Printed matter and publications	75	584
Radical organizations.		
I. W. W., Peoples' Council, League of Humanity, and all other radical organizations, including pacifist and radical "socialists"		377
Bribery, graft, theft, and embezzlement		66
Miscellaneous, including naturalization and jury panel	350	
Impersonation of U. S. or foreign officers	21	371

War Department Cases.		
Counter-Espionage for Military Intelligence.		
Selective Service Regulations.		
a. Under local and district boards (All individual investigations of delinquents and deserters and of those charged with any violation of selective service regulations.)	5,384	
b. In Slacker raids	3,726	
c. Of local and district board members	47	
d. Work or fight order	18	9,175
Character and Loyalty.		
a. Civilian applicants for oversea service	1,013	
b. Applicants for Commissions	61	1,074
Training camp activities	6	
(Under Sections 12 and 13 of Selective Service Law Regulations, p. 355.)		
a. Liquor	587	
b. Vice and prostitution	860	1,453
Camp desertions and absences without leave		175
Collection of foreign maps and photographs for Military Intelligence Bureau—Pieces of matter (about)		1,500
Navy Department.		
Counter-espionage for Naval Intelligence, including:		
Wireless	42	
Lights	9	
Other signalling to submarines, etc	7	58
Food Administration.		
Hoarding	33	
Destruction	1	
Waste	21	
Profiteering	6	61
Fuel Administration.		
Hoarding	25	
Destruction	0	
Waste	20	
Profiteering	5	50

Department of State.		
Visé of Passport	6	
Miscellaneous	1	7
Treasury Department.		
War Risk Insurance Allotments, Allowances, Frauds, etc.	53	
Miscellaneous	2	55
United States Shipping Board.		
Under National Headquarters Bulletins Nos. 11 and 12		26
Federal Investigation.		
Hog Island		407
Miscellaneous		33

The beginnings of the A. P. L. in Philadelphia lay in a meeting of fifty business men, who came together April 9, 1917, and organized as the Philadelphia Branch of the A. P. L. From that time on, varying fortunes and different personnel attended the League activities. On December 26, 1917, Mr. Mahlon R. Kline, who for years had been in charge of the Claim Department of the Philadelphia Rapid Transit Company and had been engaged in secret service work in other corporations, was appointed Chief of the division. In February, 1918, there came in with Mr. Kline, Mr. Frank H. Gaskill, formerly Superintendent of the Franklin Detective Agency, who also had been associated with the Claims Department of the Rapid Transit Company. Although no pretense is made of naming all their associates, it should be mentioned that to these two men must be accorded a great deal of the credit for the last year's work.

Naturally the question of finances came in early. In January, 1918, Mr. Horace A. Beale, Jr., president of an iron company, volunteered to purchase any furniture and office equipment which might be necessary. This brought out the need of a permanent fund, and Mr. Beale was one of the League's staunchest supporters along these lines. There was put before the members of the Chamber of Commerce a plant protection system which has been in practice in many American cities. Factory owners paid into the treasury of the League twenty-five to one hundred dollars a month, which, for a time, covered the running expenses of the office even in its growing condition. When this income became inadequate, Mr. Kline with the Executive Committee later arranged for an expense account through the War Chest Fund of $3,000 a month.

There was a handy little cabinet made up by the Bureau Chief in charge of slackers and deserters, which contained the following card index information: Names, addresses and telephone numbers of members to be counted on at any hour; names of members taking assignments in the several districts; names of members willing to accept assignments in any section. This cabinet contains the address and telephone numbers of all members owning yachts, motor cars, etc.; also a record of members speaking the following languages: German, French, Italian, Spanish, Yiddish, Hungarian, Swedish, Russian, Dutch, Pennsylvania Dutch, Danish, Portuguese, Chinese, Polish, Greek, Esperanto, Laplandish, Korean, Japanese, Austrian, Slavish and Latin.

The League in Philadelphia did not attempt secrecy. On the contrary, it openly availed itself of the services of the newspapers, and had the confident backing of all the great journals. It did not always go out after its man personally, but saved a great deal of time by inventing a little form letter which read as follows:

> Mr. John Doe:
>
> Kindly call at this office immediately upon receipt of this letter with reference to a matter of great importance. Bring this letter with you and ask for Mr. Bouton.
>
> Respectfully,
>
> American Protective League.

This was the letter sent out to draft evaders. It was thought at first it would not work, but, as a matter of fact, it brought in a stream of men who otherwise would have needed to be found. Once in the office, the rest was easy.

At the time that Mr. Kline came into the League there were 1,225 members. Additional members were selected with great care, but politics, religion, lodge affiliations, and so forth, were not factors in the working of the League.

There were on February 7, 1919, 3,440 members of the A. P. L. in Philadelphia, all working for purely patriotic motives.

The training of operatives under the skilled secret service instruction available in the division offices resulted in losing a good many men to the Department of Justice forces, who were not slow to recognize the value of good, well-trained men when they saw them. There were many departments of the United States Government which lie under deep debt to-day to the Philadelphia office of the American Protective League.

The Philadelphia work was perhaps most famous through its great system of drives. That city is indeed the original drive center, and there, better than anywhere else, perhaps, may be seen the working of a thoroughly differentiated system of drag-nets. There were a number of these raids which may be summarized briefly.

The first was a small affair conducted on May 17, 1918, which took in a couple of roadhouses where uniformed men were buying liquor.

The second raid was conducted on July 15, 1918, when about 2,000 members swooped down on the Tenderloin district of Chester, Pennsylvania, arresting about four hundred persons, mostly of the lowest type. About ninety per cent of these prisoners were convicted for bootlegging or crimes of a worse character — denisons of the section known as Bethel Court and Leiper's Flat, which the officers call the worst hell-holes they have ever seen — "such places as make the Mexican border look like a Sunday School picnic," says one. In this tough district many desperate characters were met who were quick to use weapons; but the agents of the law sustained practically no personal injuries.

Other raids followed, the sixth taking place on August 2, 1918, at Woodside Park, an amusement place which was filled with slackers. Two hundred A. P. L. members and agents of D. J. surrounded the place and handled in all 2,000 men, out of which more than three hundred were detained.

The seventh raid was August 6, 1918 — the great slacker raid on Shibe Park, at the time when there was a crowd of 8,000 men gathered to witness the Jack Thompson-Sam Langford prize fight. There were twenty agents of D. J., two hundred A. P. L. members and one hundred Philadelphia police. They examined over 2,000 men between the ages of twenty-one and thirty-two, and held one hundred and forty-one as deserters or evaders.

The eighth raid, August 15, 1918, was set at Atlantic City, N. J., and is considered the daddy of them all. At that time four pleasure piers were raided, and more than 60,000 men, women and children were handled without commotion. Preparations for this raid were left to Mr. Gaskill, since he had done so well with other raids. In the call for the assembly the members did not know where they were going — they got sealed directions. At 10:00 P. M. sharp, the entrance and exit guards took up positions and refused to allow any males to leave the pier without showing classification cards, if within draft age. The other squads of from fifty to seventy-five men were instructed to proceed to the ocean end of the pier, form a solid line and sweep all men within the above mentioned ages, found without papers, to a point at the board walk end of the pier where they were detained until the work had been completed, after which they were transferred to the armory for further examination. There were about seven hundred men apprehended in that raid and sixty real slackers. It was an all-night job, the members from Philadelphia arriving home about seven o'clock as quietly as they had slipped out of town.

On November 6, 1918, the Olympia Athletic Club was raided, and out of the 8,000 men who had gathered to witnessed the Dempsey-Levinsky prize fight, more than 1,000 were detained, thirty-six of which proved real draft evaders. This bunch of fight fans was handled by one hundred and twenty-five A. P. L. members, forty police, and twelve agents of the Department of Justice.

The signing of the armistice on the eleventh of November ended the slacker raids, but having its hand well skilled by this time, the A. P. L. went on with vice raids and picked up a great many people who had not complied with the draft laws. On November 20, 1918, Chester, Pa., was again raided and an additional forty-two prisoners apprehended. The next three days were put in with Tenderloin raids for bootleggers, of whom sixty were sentenced to nine months' imprisonment.

It is probable that the Philadelphia division has worked out the raid matter as exactly as any other division of the country. The Chief had a carefully-drawn diagram or map made, showing the system by which the men were stationed. It is a good instance of the Web of the Law. The chart shows fifteen squads of men traveling north and south, east and west, in a systematic covering of a bootleg territory 10 by 15 squares. Therefore, one squad travels north on one street and south on another street, while the squad working on opposite sides to them travels east and then west in the same manner. This makes it absolutely impossible for an offender to operate without an agent seeing him. It was often noticed that a bootlegger approaching a uniformed man would be almost instantly surrounded by one or two or even three squads who closed in to make the arrest. Philadelphia had the hunting of the bootlegger down to a fine point.

Mr. Todd Daniel, Superintendent of the Department of Justice for Philadelphia, has always been an ardent admirer of the A. P. L. In return, the League has supplied him on request with fifty to one hundred motor cars each month, and investigated as many as 1,000 cases which his staff would have been unable to handle. No wonder he admires them.

Surveillance such as this kept property damages in and around this great industrial center at a minimum. The Eddystone Munition Plant explosion occurred previous to the organization of the League. The Woodbury Bag Loading Plant, Woodbury, N. J., was so well covered that although a great many attempts to cause explosions and set fires were made with bombs and inflammable materials, they all failed of their purpose. No one can tell how much property loss was averted through the work of the Philadelphia division. It would be invidious to quote any, and hopeless to quote all, of the many letters of approval received from persons high in Government, political and commercial circles, complimenting the division upon its efficiency.

Needless to say, Philadelphia had her own share of *causes celébrès.* One of the most unique and interesting of these was that of the Philadelphia *Tageblatt,* a German daily newspaper prosecuted under the charge of seditious and disloyal utterances. In the fall of 1917, a raid was conducted by D. J. and A. P. L. upon the headquarters of this paper, at which time many files, books, papers, and so forth, were seized, with the result that warrants were issued for the editor and all his staff. When they were called for trial, members of the division were again used for the purpose of investigating the jury panel, as well as for the procurement of evidence essential to the case. In one item, this work took the form of securing through banking members, proofs of certain signatures without which the Government's case would have been crippled.

These men were tried for treason, but were discharged for lack of evidence. They were subsequently prosecuted under a charge of conspiracy to hinder voluntary enrollment and for violation of the Espionage Act. On the latter charge, they were found guilty. Louis Werner, the editor, and his associate, Martin Darkow, got five years' imprisonment each, Herman Lemke two years, Peter Shaefer and Paul Vogel, one year each.

The *Tageblatt* had been warned often against its unseemly utterances, but to no avail. It was a sheet of no great consequence, and about fifteen years ago was anarchistic. Then it turned to Socialism. When war was declared, it was outspoken against the Allies. After the declaration it became more cautious, but its columns were full of propaganda. It had no telegraph or cable service, but its policy was dictated by the selective choice of its editorial staff. Louis Werner was a naturalized citizen born in Germany. Darkow was a non-registered alien enemy and wrote the editorials. The president was Peter Shaefer, the treasurer Paul Vogel, and the business manager Herman Lemke. The trial for treason lasted only ten days. The second trial, for conspiracy, was more successful from the viewpoint of the law. Upon the stand, both Werner and Darkow were insolent. They will have time to think over all these matters in quiet for a while.

Red Cross frauds attracted some attention on the part

of the League in Philadelphia, which investigated all sorts of fanciful rumors, as well as several schemes of fraudulent or nearly fraudulent or unworthy nature. One of these, purporting to collect for a central hospital, seemed at first to have merit; but when advertisements appeared offering solicitors a highly lucrative connection, the A. P. L. agents discovered that this was for the purpose of raising about $1,500,000 — out of which a commission of twenty per cent was to be paid to the solicitors. A halt was called on this, but the same people got busy again about three months later with a campaign purporting to collect $1,000,000 for the care of "crippled negro soldiers." There was a fund of about $10,000 which had been contributed by colored persons. Some of the people connected with this movement were well-meaning and absolutely disinterested; yet in the background were others who appeared to be out for the coin. The campaign was closed down again. This is but a sample of other affairs of the same sort.

One of the notable Philadelphia affairs was that of Norman T. W———, scholar, patent attorney, chess expert and draft evader. This case originated in Washington where he failed to appear for examination or to turn in a questionnaire. He asked to have his examination transferred to Philadelphia, so the whole matter was transferred to Philadelphia. On July 15, W——— was mailed his order for induction into the service and was told to report July 24, but he did not appear. Philadelphia A. P. L. then took on the matter.

W——— was the son of respectable Philadelphia parents and of good connections. Without doubt, he and his brother were shielded by their relatives and friends as long as possible. On November 8, the Philadelphia Division of the A. P. L. wired Washington stating that W——— had been apprehended. On November 16, 1918, he was sent to Camp Dix.

The public has some notion of the great plant for ship construction erected at Hog Island, near Philadelphia, by the United States Shipping Board. All sorts of stories came out regarding affairs at this shipping yard, and the charges were so direct and well-supported that Congress finally investigated the matter. The Philadelphia Division of the A. P. L. had some part in this investigation, which had to do with charges of extravagance, graft and waste of public moneys. There was one item, the employment of thousands of jitney drivers, which was severely criticised. These cars were employed by the Emergency Fleet Corporation to transport their workmen from their homes to the Island, since it was thought the regular transportation lines could not handle them. The charge was made that large amounts were collected by the jitney men from the Shipping Yard without rendering any service; the shipping yards, in turn, charged these amounts back to the Government. There were thousands of reports turned in by the operatives to D. J. on these "jitney cases." It was found that a good many men in authority were in the habit of ordering the drivers, after they had brought them down to the Shipping Yard, to go back home and place themselves at the disposal of the members of the families of the foremen or officers — the Government thus supporting a large number of private automobiles for salaried persons. The entire matter quieted down when the increased cost of tires and gas deprived the jitney drivers of their profits, and when competition came on through the installation of better service and equipment by the Philadelphia Rapid Transit Company.

There was no branch of the A. P. L. activities in Philadelphia so carefully handled as that having to do with the I. W. W. and other radical organizations. There were five Locals found and fifty-one revolutionary clubs with a total membership of 5,000, ninety per cent of whom were of foreign birth, absolutely opposed to all government and ever ready to overthrow law by revolutionary tactics.

The A. P. L. made a raid upon one club solely for the purpose of seizing literature and files. As a result of this, fifty I. W. W. agitators were dismissed from shipping yards and government plants. Some of these were in the Government Bag Loading Plant at Woodbury, in the shipping yard at Bristol, and in the Emergency Fleet Corporation at Hog Island. All these Philadelphia radicals contributed heavily to the defense fund of the I. W. W. members who were on trial in Chicago.

It was thought desirable to find any possible connection of German interest with these radicals. At one meeting the discovery was made that two men appeared and made a contribution to the foregoing defense fund. They came from a Fairmount German singing society — where they sang anything but American patriotic airs. The League kept close watch on all these radical organizations, so close that they have not dared to make any outright break. The slightest step out of the proper path would mean an immediate reckoning with men who have been rather stern in matters of justice.

After the *Tageblatt* case, which was the first case in the entire country resulting in a conviction under the indictments which were brought against Werner and his associates, the Grover Bergdoll case of mysterious disappearance is perhaps Philadelphia's greatest contribution to detective literature. Indeed, there is still chance for a good detective in Philadelphia who can give bond for the production of the body of Grover C. Bergdoll, college athlete, wealthy young man-about-town, skillful mechanician, student of law, X-ray experimenter, radical editor — and draft evader. The Bergdoll brothers, Grover and Irwin, are known as the "slackers de luxe." They were sons of a wealthy brewer, and having money, it seemed to them that they need not respect the law. They had shown their contempt for it before the draft reached out for them. Grover C. did not register, and Irwin failed to file his questionnaire. A. P. L. was set on their trail, but the young men had both disappeared. From that time until now neither of these men has been apprehended. Grover C. Bergdoll was seen in Mexico, was alleged to have been in the West on a ranch, was reported to have been in Spain, was said to have been seen in Western New York, and was reported also to have been in Philadelphia twice. Sometimes he would send a card to the newspapers just to tantalize the public, or to the officials whom he knew to be after him. Well, money is a present friend in times of trouble. For a time the Bergdoll mystery will remain a mystery. One of these days the life of the Bergdoll boys will fail to interest them. One of these days the law will lay its hands on them, and they will have to settle with the country which they have slighted and scorned and whose citizenship they do not deserve.

It may have occurred to readers of these pages that there was not enough blood and thunder stuff pulled off by the operatives of the A. P. L. It is quite possible that the Department of Justice men have had the harder load to carry in these more violent affairs, because quite often they are obliged to make the actual arrest, on warrants under evidence obtained by the A. P. L. One Philadelphia incident resulted in the killing of the man sought — a negro desperado who carried several aliases but was best known in the saloon district as "Porto Rico."

On Friday, November 8, two men of the League, in trying to locate a suspect, found two colored men in military uniform whom they followed. These gave up the whereabouts of two of their companions who were in a certain house. When found, these men claimed they had been drugged and robbed by some colored women there. It had been their present plan to wait there in the darkness until the women came back and then to kill them. The whole scene was in a tough part of town where the uniform of the United States does not belong.

Out of these proceedings the operatives got the address of four other men, one of these Porto Rico, who were supposed to be in the habit of robbing colored soldiers and other men in uniform. A certain saloon was visited by the operatives, and a few minutes after they appeared, a burly negro entered and was accosted as "Porto Rico" by the owner. The two operatives were C. H. Keelor of the League and Mr. Sprague of the Department of Justice. Keelor tapped Porto Rico on the arm and asked him for his card. The man got into action at once, kicked Keelor in the leg and struck Sprague, knocking him down. He made a leap to the open and pulled a heavy revolver, starting to retreat northeast on Lombard Street.

Operative Logan was on the opposite side of the street, and he now closed in. There was a shot fired, perhaps by a friend of Porto Rico. The latter raised his revolver and took aim at Sprague. Sprague was armed with a heavy holster gun and beat the negro to the shot, killing him with a bullet through the heart. Porto Rico fell, his revolver dropping from his hand, and such was his vitality that for a long time he struggled to reach the gun as it lay close by him. Sprague was cleared in court, as he shot obviously in self-defense. Charles Seamore, alias John E. Manuel, alias Porto Rico, was a notorious gun man. Beside his revolver he carried a razor and a number of 38-calibre cartridges. His registration card showed that he had registered under a false name. In almost the same place a little while later a Philadelphia policeman was shot by a negro, who in turn was killed by a lieutenant of the police department.

In May, 1918, Major C. N. Green, U. S. Engineers, came into the League Headquarters of the Philadelphia Division and said he wanted assistance in organizing secret service work for plant protection and that he had been directed to the A. P. L. offices. Out of this later grew the connection of the A. P. L. with the Woodbury Bag Loading Plant.

At first there were about one hundred buildings on the 1,800 acres of unfenced land, about two hundred men being engaged in guarding the place. An organization of proved men had been made, which went directly into Government service. Five strikes were settled and no serious labor trouble resulted. It seemed marvelous that no disaster occurred in this plant. Time and again enemies attached time bombs to powder cars on their way to the munition plant. These cars were all stopped on an outside siding and searched, sometimes as many as thirty in one night. One time a bomb was found and two sticks of dynamite. A great deal of oily waste was found, which was no doubt attached in the hope that it might be set afire and so cause destruction of the car. There were two hundred and ten arrests made under charge of disorderly conduct, and one hundred under charge of trespassing. In each of these cases a conviction was secured. About two hundred violators of the Selective Service Act were put under arrest, and, as has been stated, thirty-five members of the I. W. W. were removed from the premises. More than one hundred and ten Austrians and Hungarians were discharged, and about two hundred aliens sent to the Department of Justice for examination. Over 1,500 investigations of suspects were made by the League, largely of men whose names seemed to proclaim them of German extraction. The record of this plant is unique, it probably being the only plant that has had so low a record of fires, explosions and accidents in all the history of our war work.

Guards often found people endeavoring to do damage. One such man had piled up scrap lumber and rags and was touching it off when fired upon by the guard. Two other attempts were made to destroy another one of the buildings. Not content with protecting the property from without, the A. P. L. even protected it from within. Charges were made of extravagant prices paid by the Government, a fact which strongly indicated graft somewhere. A corporation had made a bid to furnish boxes at $450 each, delivered. This bid was refused. Volunteer workers were called on to make these boxes. The work was done on Sunday, double time being paid — each man receiving $14 a day — and even with such labor charges, it was found the boxes could be turned out at $17.25! This particular expenditure of money was stopped by the artless Ordnance Department. One or two chiefs were dismissed on the strength of reports from the A. P. L. of inefficiency, graft and irregularities.

This, then, all too briefly and lamely done in review, is the story of Philadelphia, which operated one of the very best amateur detective agencies the world has ever seen and which was a credit not only to Philadelphia itself but to every operative of the A. P. L. wherever he was located in the United States.

It only remains to say that in the monthly report for December, 1918, the Philadelphia Division turns in forty-eight bootleggers additional, two hold-up men, and nine soldiers absent without leave. It furnished D. J. in that month six hundred and forty-five men and sixty-five cars, investigated in that month two hundred and fifty-two draft evaders, seven hundred and forty-three cases from D. J. and various branches of the A. P. L., and 1,812 office assignments and Washington investigations. The Division closed the month of December, after the Armistice, going strong, with a membership of 3,438.

On the last day of the year, and after Philadelphia had

finished all its reports for the year, there was a bomb outrage in that city in which lawless persons blew up the homes of three citizens. A call to the City Hall brought out every available detective and policeman, and houses of other prominent men were placed under guard for that night. Once more the drag-net was put out to take in the lawless and all those of Bolshevik tendencies. The outrage was of such a nature that the Philadelphia papers carried editorials almost appealing to the American Protective League not to disband. Truly it will be missed in that city and in many another city of America. In this bomb outrage the lives of women and children were endangered. What are we to think of America for the future if at will the superintendent of police, a judge of the court, and a president of a chamber of commerce are to have their houses blown up as an act of vengeance of wholly irresponsible people such as no doubt committed this crime!

Early in January, 1919, Mr. Frank H. Gaskill, Assistant Chief, was promoted to be Chief of the Philadelphia Division for its closing days, Mr. Mahlon R. Kline resigning in his favor. The demobilization banquet of Philadelphia Division A. P. L. was held on the night of February 5, 1919, and it was as fine and ship-shape as all the other activities of the Division. It was hard for these men to say good-bye. Indeed, it is quite probable that many of the old Philadelphia A. P. L. members will organize, under another name, for purposes somewhat similar.

CHAPTER IV

THE STORY OF NEWARK

Big Division of Northern New Jersey—Hot-Bed of Spydom and Anarchy — Cases from the Files — Guarding the Gate to the Sea.

Northern New Jersey was recognized as one of the riskiest regions of the United States. Time out of mind, American readers have noted, with the short-lived American anger, the many newspaper tales of Paterson and anarchy, of New Jersey and New Thought, of socialistic ranters hailing from this or that semi-foreign community, in one of the oldest states in the American union, whose battlefields in our first war for freedom are spread on many glorious pages of our country's history. The battlefields of Jersey are different now, and are not so glorious. Still, a few men, as patriotic as those in Revolutionary days, have done their best during this war to keep their country safe. The work of the Northern New Jersey Division, which has been in charge of Mr. W. D. McDermid, as State Inspector, is reassuring.

It is proper to point out that the Northern New Jersey Division, being one of the first of the A. P. L. to be organized, operated on lines different from those of almost any other territory. Its district covers one-half of the state, including the vitally important Port of Embarkation. Under a single central office, it combined over one hundred municipalities, most of which would ordinarily have had a separate headquarters organization, but which for local reasons had all been consolidated in one division.

There was abundance to do, and there were plenty to be watched. There could, for example, be furnished several hundred instances of sabotage in this manufacturing district of Northern New Jersey — sabotage either detected in advance, or thoroughly investigated afterwards. This was so common in the hundreds of plants in that District that it became for the Northern Division, for the most part, a matter of routine. A great deal of the work of this character ultimately was handled by the Plant Protection Division of the War Department.

In upper New Jersey, as in the State of New York, the Governmental departments reached out and rather overshadowed, in glory at least, the patient and less known efforts of the A. P. L. Newark frankly complains that quite often sufficiently vigorous action was not to be had by the officers of the Department of Justice, even after full evidence had been handed to it by the A. P. L. Some A. P. L. men even go so far as to claim that D. J. would not only crab an act, but claim a glory! Our State Inspector voices this in occasional comment:

> In particular reference to two cases of ours, it is a source of great disappointment and a great deal of harsh criticism that the Department of Justice has seen fit to take the position toward our evidence that it has. Their indifference has led us to secure a number of clean-cut convictions in state courts under local laws. These, of course, have not the scope of Federal laws, under which these cases might very much better have been prosecuted We feel that in common justice to the work of the A. P. L., some such comment as this should be made.

There was abundant fire behind some of these New Jersey smokes, be sure of that, and many rumors of the class commonly pooh-poohed at by M. I. D. and D. J. were made good. Three actual samples of powdered glass in food were found; two actual cases of Red Cross bandages containing deleterious substances also were found; there was one instance of insidious printed propaganda distributed by means of knitted work; and there was a very distinct trail of Sinn Feiners working in conjunction with the enemy. To these may be added such instances of investigation as are given below.

Mr. X, a minister of the gospel, was very offensive in his pacifism. He refused permission for the display of an American flag in his church, or even a service flag, and would not allow the church to be used for Red Cross work.

He was forced to resign, his particular brand of piety not seeming to track with the creed of his congregation. The quality of his pacifism may be judged from the fact that he excused the Germans for their atrocities, saying that if France and Belgium had not resisted, there never would have been any atrocities! This man applied for a position to go to France in Government war work. His application was refused.

It is, of course, well known that the U. S. troops in large part sailed from the vicinity of the City of New York, or upper New Jersey. Of course, also, all the preparations for this war, all of the expense of it, all the time and trouble of it, focused exactly on the number of troops we actually could get on the way. The utmost secrecy was maintained by our Government as to the number of troops, the ships that carried them, and the time and place of sailing. The mother of a boy on his way to France did not know he had sailed until a curt card from the other side of the water told her that he was in France. Practically all the people of the United States, however, accepted this secrecy as a necessary war measure — that being obviously and permanently necessary in this war, where the risks of the sea included the danger of the German submarine.

Naturally, also, the German spies on this side of the water would do everything in their power to learn precisely the facts which our Government sought to conceal — the number of troops going over, the times of sailings of the transports, and so forth. Naturally also, our system of espionage — the divisions of Military Intelligence, Naval Intelligence, Department of Justice, and the auxiliary work of the American Protective League — would do all they could to prevent German espionage from attaining its own purpose in regard to this knowledge.

When the Government seized the Port of Embarkation at Hoboken, much interest was shown in the former Hamburg-American and North German Lloyd line steamers located there. There were numerous rumors that these boats were to be blown up by the Germans. Of these, the largest was the *Vaterland,* which was re-christened *Leviathan.*

All this section, along the Jersey Palisades, near Hoboken, is strong in sympathy for Germany. Nearly all of the population is from Germany or of German parentage and here was this steamer, the biggest of all the boats, and long the pride of the Germans. It was not to be expected that the New Jersey Germans would feel pleasant about its present status. These local Germans boasted that they had been through these boats after our Government took them over. They told stories of what the Government was doing with them and what they were going to do themselves so that the boats would never sail or never get across. The history of other ships which took fire in mid-ocean, or were blown up by concealed explosives is referred to elsewhere. It always was sufficient to make the sailing of any transport a matter of great uneasiness.

An A. P. L. operative wanted to know what these Germans were doing regarding the *Leviathan.* Of course, the boat was supposed to be absolutely guarded against entry by any stranger. This man, however, went to the gate and asked for the Commandant by nickname. The guard supposed he must be a friend of the Commandant, because of his familiarity, and naïvely let him through. The operative walked up and down the pier wondering how he could get on board, for he saw guards at the gangway. There was a pile of mailbags on the dock, so the operative stole over that way, picked up a mail sack and threw it over his shoulder. Near the gangway there was a group of soldiers and sailors engaged in an argument. As the operative approached, they separated, and he went through. He was dressed in civilian clothes, and had on a derby hat, but these did not seem to be suspicious facts. The operative walked on up the gangplank unmolested, and roamed all over the boat from top to bottom, still carrying the mailbag. Having done what any German could have done in the same circumstances, he started out, but near the gangway was stopped by a man who wore a watchman's badge, and who spoke with a noticeable German accent. This man stopped the operative, who, upon being asked where he was going, replied that he was going off the boat. The watchman told him to get off in a hurry. He was still carrying his U. S. mail sack, which he replaced on the pile where he had got it. After that, he strolled out to the street again, satisfied that the guard around the *Leviathan* might have been a trifle more airtight.

As a matter of fact, while the sailing dates of the *Leviathan* were jealously guarded, bets were made by the Germans on her sailing time out and back. Word came to an A. P. L. man that the *Leviathan* was going to sail at 12:15 the next day. As this came from German sources, it seemed a useful thing to have the Government alter the sailing hour. The operative in this case strolled around in the vicinity of the *Leviathan's* pier and talked with sailors, who freely told him the sailing hour. Then, in order to mystify the Government officers, the operative called up a certain Department and said over the 'phone that he was an Intelligence official of the Imperial German Navy, and wanted to know if it was true that the *Leviathan* was to sail at 12:15 the next day. This caused some excitement. The operative then told whom he was, explaining that he had got that knowledge himself the previous evening. As a result, the sailing hour was changed several hours, and the *Leviathan* got off safely.

Again, there were a great many rumors regarding the numbers of troops carried by this big transport. We did not want Germany to know how many men we really were shipping, and we rather thought that no one ever could know. An A. P. L. operative was able to make a very close guess under rather singular circumstances. Since he could have done so, perhaps a German spy might have done as much had he an equally sharp wit.

This instance really started in a practical joke. The jokers suggested to a certain young husband, who had to sit up late several nights with a crying baby, that he might pass the time counting the cars of troop trains which passed in front of his house. In all seriousness, the young man did do this, checking each car by the bumps it made on the railroad frogs. He really counted in this way with very fair accuracy the number of cars carrying troops for the *Leviathan's* sailing. As everyone knew about how many troops were in each car, this operative figured that there would be about 12,000 troops. This was reported to the Government, but was never checked out, so that

A. P. L. still wants to know whether they were good detectives or not.

There was a member of the Division who sold automobile tires. A Naval officer came to him to buy a tire, and wanted to know if the tire could not get to the boat that afternoon. This salesman suggested the next morning at noon. The officer innocently said that he would have sailed by that time. He also named his boat, the *Leviathan*. This salesman asked how it would do to have the tire ready when the ship came back, and asked how long it would be. The officer said sixteen and a half days — which tallied with the former *Leviathan* record of seventeen days. The salesman also learned that the stop at Bordeaux was from forty to seventy-two hours. Incidentally, he also learned that the boat carried 12,000 troops, had five hundred officers and a crew of fifteen hundred.

This figure of 12,000 troops checks perfectly with the A. P. L. estimate made by the baby-carrying member. This tire-hunting officer of the boat also told a great many things which he ought not to have told anyone. He told the means used to protect the *Leviathan* against U-boats, saying that the ship depended mostly on her speed. He said the ship drew only forty-two feet of water, so it had not been necessary to dredge the channel at Bordeaux. The operative then asked the officer how late he could receive the tire, and was told about two hours before sailing. "You can refer to your local newspapers and figure on fifteen minutes after the tide begins to go out," he said. This, of course, was so that the boat could get the benefit of the ebb tide in warping out.

From these facts, both the Military and Naval Intelligence were able to stop such leaks of information, and stiffened up the guarding of ships and cargo, besides giving, in many ways, a far greater degree of protection to the task of embarkation. It is thought that the League investigations caused recommendation to be made regarding more secrecy in regard to embarkation. The Armistice cut off these matters. Sufficient has been shown here, however, to indicate how an enemy might sometimes get information.

There did not seem to be much to start with in this case

which originated in Northern New Jersey, nor indeed was there much left of the case by the time it was finished. Yet the case itself had the makings of quite a big affair. A report came in that Otto B———, starter for the X. Y. Z. Transit Company, was pro-German. Such reports came in all the time, so that there were usually fifty or sixty cases in the zone. Two days later came in more facts from operative C-123. He had gotten pretty thick with Herr B——— by saying that Germany seemed to be gaining, and that this news would please his wife, who was German herself. Herr B——— was much pleased to learn this, and went on to unbosom himself. Several such meetings enabled C-123 to learn pretty much everything he desired.

Herr B——— wanted to do something for the Fatherland and the Kaiser. He was sure he could do something if he had some help. The one danger was that, in talking to almost anybody, Herr B——— might be talking not to a representative of the Kaiser but to some one who would report him to the United States Secret Service. Operative C-123 agreed with him as to this, and gravely told him he ought to be very careful. But he said he knew a man that could be trusted, and he would bring him around so that they could talk it over, and perhaps the two of them could do something for the Kaiser.

The name of this new man was Schultz. He had been in Mexico organizing the United States Germans who had fled to Mexico. He had been a member of the Dantzig Dragoons, and had traveled all through Germany, and his experiences in the Army there had gotten him his place as German propagandist of Mexico. He was a member of the Imperial German Espionage System — and he had his Wilhelmstrasse card to show it. He always carried it pinned to his underclothing. It was a great day for Otto, the train dispatcher. At last he had some trusted fellow-Germans in whom he could confide! He and Schultz talked bombs and that sort of thing until midnight. Herr B——— told Schultz: "You can depend on me — I am the real stuff — I can get a thousand men back of me since I know I have got a man from the German Government here."

Talks between these three gentlemen were going on in fine shape at the time the Armistice was signed. As a matter of fact, Otto B——— is still flagging trains at the old railroad crossing, and the League is recommending his prosecution and the revocation of his citizenship, because it certainly had proof of his unfitness to live in the United States. It hardly seems necessary to add that "Schultz" was an A. P. L. operative also. His "credentials" were made in the United States and not in Germany, having been copied from those captured on a real agent of the Kaiser.

There was another near-case, one which almost became a real one, in Northern New Jersey Division, which, at the first, looked like scores that had preceded it and scores that followed it. It had to do with one K———, reported rabid against America, although employed in doing essential Government work. This might have been a spite case, or a case of remarks made before we went into the war, or still more possibly something said before the amended Espionage Act was passed. However, member C-891 went out on the case to see what he could find about K———.

The latter had a factory of his own, and when found, seemed to be disposed to talk. The operative speaks a perfect German, and has a German look. The two got on handsomely. The operative was surprised to find that K——— talked so freely and to a stranger. Another member of the League, C-1378, also of German parentage, went with C-891 a few days later to visit K——— again. That gentleman was more bitter than ever against America. He said, among other things, that if he heard that President Wilson had been shot, he would be so glad that he would celebrate it by getting too drunk to see. And there was very much more talk of that nature.

A few days later, K——— had cause to regret his disposition to talk. He was brought before a United States Commissioner on a warrant, and spent a good night in jail before he could find bail. The next day, he being a man of means, he engaged a lawyer. The Armistice ended these activities, as it did so many others. The hearing was held on the morning of November 7—the first news of the Armistice, later confirmed. Since that time, A. P. L. of

Northern New Jersey has heard nothing about Mr. K———. With a couple million others, he has been allowed to sink back to our citizenship — just as poisonous, just as unregenerate, just as little fit to remain in this country. It was understood that D. J. laid down a rule that testimony secured in conversations such as the foregoing was not a basis of prosecution. Perhaps it would have been better to wait until Mr. K——— had really shot somebody or blown up a ship or so.

Of active sympathizers with the enemy, Northern New Jersey did not lack. A thousand cases could be given. One will serve. In July, 1918, the office learned of suspicious activities on the part of some of these sympathizers. A Mr. E——— was told by Miss G———, a young woman of foreign birth, that the people she lived with had active connections with the enemy. Especially was this true in the case of one S———, who had Central and South American relations. This latter man was found to be of American birth and German parentage — which, in a good many cases, would leave him German. He had been a traveler, and a son of his had been born in Kingston, Jamaica, although this son was at present in the U. S. Army. This Mr. S——— was found to be identified with a New York concern which had sent him to Jamaica to get the release there of a man jailed by the English authorities for alleged implication in the coaling of German raiders at sea. That did not look any too good for Mr. S——— of itself. He also had in his employ a stenographer whose husband, a Mr. W———, had been employed in an alleged poisoning of the reservoir at Kingston, Jamaica.

These things led up to the case of the subject, who will be called P———. This man had lived with S——— for a time. P——— came to this country from Germany in 1907, and applied for his first naturalization papers — please note the date — August 1, 1914. He was thirty-five years of age, well educated, unmarried, and without dependents. He had served in the German Army, but was not a reservist. In his alien enemy questionnaire, he left out the name of one of his previous employers, which was found to have been an importing concern with a German name, with connections in Kingston, Jamaica, doing business in Central and South America. This German concern had many different names. Some of its personnel were interned at Panama. A member of the concern had been interned in the United States for alleged provisioning of German raiders at sea. This made the stage set for a rather interesting investigation. Operatives discovered that the principal men of this concern were at large, and were doing business under yet another name. They also discovered that this Mr. S——— was affiliated with the work in a downtown office building in New York City.

During 1912, or earlier, Mr. S——— had introduced Mr. P——— to the President of an iron and steel concern, who took him into employ as Treasurer and gave him a block of shares. The alien enemy P——— seemed to get along pretty well for a time, but got in wrong with the firm through a transaction which they did not approve. The Secretary of the firm was very friendly to the alien enemy P———. This Secretary was found to be connected by marriage with one of the foremost electrical inventors of the age, who had been very active in the development of devices for our Army and Navy. Observe that this man was a particular confidant of the unnaturalized German P———, formerly of the German Army.

The original Mr. S———, who had acted as a voucher for P———, had stated that he could get money to the enemy, through the War Department. His father had stock in a concern which was taken over by our Alien Enemy Custodian. The not very mysterious Mr. P——— removed during June, 1918, leaving New York without notifying the Chief of Police, as is required. He was located doing business in an office in down-town New York City as a broker, although his name was not listed in the telephone directory. He was apparently trading under the name of L. P. & Company. The A. P. L. has found that his mother is living in Germany and is reported to be wealthy. P——— has pretended that he was a traveling salesman, which he was not. He endeavored to avoid meeting people whom he knew while residing in northern New Jersey. His residence was located in another state.

This case also shows how much sometimes may be discovered by way of a tangled skein, even if no one is shot at sunrise. Mr. S——— was visited at his office by an A. P. L. man, who did not make himself known. He was very much exercised over the fact that the place of his business was known. He requested that his personal and business relations should not be linked up together. Mr. P——— is still in business in New York, no doubt waiting for the next war.

Northern New Jersey was the field for many reports of mysterious signal lights along the seacoast. Most of these stories had small foundation, but at least one of these would have come to something had not the Armistice cut off the investigation. In this case, operators were sometimes out for hours watching for the flashlights, and once a squad of military reserves lay on watch practically all night around a suspect's house. They discovered night signaling with a search-light and calcium-light at different places over the Northeastern part of Bergen County, and there seemed to be evidence of a system of signaling extending from the Hudson River in New Jersey, across Bergen County up into the Ramapo Mountains and the Greenwood Lake district in New York. The observers used surveying transits for spotting the lights, and by means of this instrument, were able to obtain the angles of the lights. These angles were then plotted, and the intersection points gave approximately the location of the light. This work resulted in the location of three individuals, but at about this time the Armistice ended the signals and the apparent necessity for watching them. There had been discovered, however, some real foundation for a signal light scare in this district.

Ridgewood had another strange case — a German who claimed to be so sick that he could not live long — who wanted to go back home in order to die in the dear old Fatherland. Medical examination showed that he probably would die sometime, but the A. P. L. examination led to the refusal of his passports, it being believed that he might carry something to Germany besides fatal disease.

Newark, the capital of Northern New Jersey Division, had a very baffling pro-German case where it was difficult to find anything on which a legal prosecution could be brought. The facts were such as resulted in the social ostracism of the family, so that their disloyalty, after all, had a certain punishment, although it did not hit the crime. H——— and his wife were members of a Presbyterian Church, and were so openly pro-German that everybody ceased to have anything to do with them. At a luncheon given at the H——— household the favors distributed to a dozen ladies consisted of nice pictures of Kaiser Wilhelm. One of the guests then suggested that it would be a nice thing to sing the Star Spangled Banner, which did not please Mrs. H——— at all. The head of this household was educated in Germany, and married a German woman whose relatives were high in the German army. They had a daughter who was engaged to an American, but the latter broke off the engagement on account of the pro-Germanism of the H——— family. The social ostracism really amounted to isolation, so that it was impossible to hear of any disloyal utterances which would warrant governmental action, nor indeed any utterances at all. The town was through with them.

Northern New Jersey probably has the laziest slacker in the world. His name is M———, and at one time he resided in New York. He had an Emergency Fleet classification card, but only worked two or three days out of the week and spent most of his time at home in bed. He thought he would rather go South where the climate was better. He was rated as so lazy that he was shifted from one government job to another — and that certainly is going some, in view of what is sometimes done in government service. He was so lazy that he used to go to bed with his shoes on, and would leave his light burning all night because he was too tired to put it out. This champion rester carried a registration card, but he had been given limited service on account of calloused feet. From the description of him, it is difficult to see how his feet got calloused; but at least that is what the report says.

New Jersey had a very blood-curdling citizen who dwelt in Newark under the name of H. B———. He carried an American name although he was born in Italy about forty-two years ago. He came to America thirty years ago, when he was a small boy, in order to escape punishment for having killed a priest. He never dared to return to

Italy, but remained an alien in this country and an enemy to about everything going. He was a very ardent I. W. W. man, and declared that there were enough I. W. W. men in the Army and outside to blow up the country if they liked, — a very good example of the flourishing Bolshevik element in America. Mr. B——— claimed that he had stabbed a detective in Providence, R. I., a year or so ago during an I. W. W. celebration; hence he did not like to visit Providence either. He told how in another place he had cut out a man's intestines, and when asked if the man died, remarked: "What in hell do you suppose I am here for?" This pleasant gentleman often went to Paterson and New York to attend I. W. W. meetings there. He hoped that "every —— ——— soldier the U. S. sent over would be blown up by submarines and drowned like rats, and that if any did get across, he hoped the Germans would choke or shoot them to death." He said he would like to get his fingers on President Wilson's throat. It was his pleasant practice to tear American flags from the coats of persons wearing them. His home was searched, and some clock-works were found without any dials and hands, such as have been known to be used with bombs. It seems that nothing was done with the bloodthirsty Mr. B——— after all, and he is still at large.

In so complex an office as that of the Northern New Jersey Division, which much resembles that of New York City, Newark alone cleared over 9,013 cases, of which twenty-five per cent were for the War Department, forty-five per cent for the Department of Justice, other divisions of A. P. L. work fifteen per cent, and original cases with New Jersey A. P. L. fifteen per cent. Most of this work was for D. J., but there was much coöperation with officers from Naval and Military Intelligence, not to mention the local boards. This great division has a tangible record of 4,563 cases of the second class, those handled entirely in local units, making a total of 13,576 cases sufficiently definite in character to warrant a record. As to the actual investigations, recorded and unrecorded, they would without question bring up the total of northern New Jersey cases above 30,000. They were from every point of the compass and of every color of the rainbow.

CHAPTER V

THE STORY OF PITTSBURGH

Another Storm Center — Greatest Concentration of War Work in the United States — The Tower of Babel and How it was Held Safe — No I. W. W. Need Apply.

Pittsburgh also was expected to be an alien storm center when the United States declared war upon Germany. This uneasiness was natural and to be expected. Most of our great iron and steel plants were located there, and numerous other important industries as well. These plants were vital to our success in the war, as were the great coal mines in the adjacent districts. It was felt on every side that the enemy would strike here if he struck at all. But the main cause for apprehension lay in the fact that Pittsburgh had an enormous foreign population, especially from countries of the central allies, and the presence of this element in its industries was feared as a source of dynamite, sabotage and labor troubles. The fact that Pittsburgh and Western Pennsylvania throughout the war remained practically free from labor disturbances and war munition destruction, so troublesome in other sections, was due to the splendid intelligence service rendered by the American Protective League, in close coöperation with the United States Department of Justice and Naval and Military Intelligence Bureaus. The Smoky City sends in a very clean report.

Pittsburgh operated the highest percentage on war work of any district in the United States. It filled over sixty-five per cent of all the steel contracts placed by the Ordnance Department, in addition to the tremendous output of munitions and other war materials for the Entente Allies. It was estimated that the district was running from sixty to seventy per cent on war work at the time of the Armistice, that at least 5,000 plants, many of them mammoth in size, were filling Government orders, and over one million employees were engaged in large part in helping win the war. During the latter part of hostilities the daily labor shortage was over 16,000. It was vital to the United States and to the Entente Allies that the Pittsburgh District should be permitted to conduct unmolested its great industries of the war, and that this was possible was due in a large measure to the American Protective League.

A few days after the war was declared, John W. Weibley, a well known Pittsburgh business man, was asked to organize a Division of the American Protective League in the twenty-seven counties of Western Pennsylvania, comprising the United States Western Judicial District. Mr. Weibley conferred with Mr. Robert S. Judge, Special Agent in Charge of the Bureau of Investigation, Department of Justice, to learn if the Government was in need of such an organization. When assured that it was, Mr. Weibley began the formation of a branch for this district.

Representatives of the railroads and other important corporations were called into conference and were asked to coöperate, and within an amazingly short time the American Protective League had active agents in every county, township, city, town and village in the entire district. In the case of Pittsburgh, the operating headquarters, this plan of organization was worked out so minutely that an active agent representing the League, and in constant communication with it, was located in every voting precinct, and where there were concentrations of the foreign element, these agents were to be found in practically every city block.

Mr. Weibley personally perfected and maintained from Pittsburgh this network throughout the District. Mr. Ralph B. Montgomery directed the work in Pittsburgh, each ward being placed in charge of a captain who reported to him, and each captain having his separate lieutenants with agents in every election precinct. Mr. Raymond H. Allen, assisted by Mr. William S. Masten, directed the operation of the intelligence activities in the outlying counties.

Frequent meetings of ward captains and district lieutenants were held to hear suggestions from representatives of the Government. They were thus kept familiar with the latest happenings and knew what precautions to take to make their work effective.

The story of the Pittsburgh Division, as it is related in these pages by its Chief, is the story of a program of action, thoughtfully conceived, carefully and efficiently executed, and successful beyond all expectations. Mr. Weibley says in his report:

> A splendid *esprit de corps* was maintained, as the organization in Pittsburgh was limited to the least possible number in membership, and all members were kept busy. Great care was used in the selection of the men enrolled, and each applicant was subjected to a rigid investigation. If he did not meet the requirements, his application was rejected or placed on file to provide material for future replacements when urgency demanded it. As a result, the highest interest in the work was maintained throughout the war period.
>
> The Pittsburgh district being the most important manufacturing, munition, fuel and chemical center in the country, was largely dependent for its labor upon foreigners, many of whom came from countries at war with us. It therefore was imperative that many of our operatives should be of diverse nationalities and able to speak many tongues. As an illustration, it was estimated that at the beginning of the war fully fifty per cent of the Austrians in the United States were at work in vital coal mines, coke works, steel mills and other industrial plants within a radius of 50 miles of Pittsburgh. This naturally made the alien menace a grave one, but so intensive was the organization of the League that not an important industrial operation in the great district was without one or more of the League agents as active employes. In fact, intimate connection was maintained with every alien gathering or meeting place, and nothing of moment was planned that the League officials were not soon familiar with. In fact, in one of the largest industrial concerns, the principal official was chief of a league unit, and many of his trusted employes were his active associates.
>
> Pittsburgh industrial concerns, vitally interested in meeting the Government's demands for constantly increasing output of war material, quickly solved the question of finances, and the League had ample funds to meet every requirement. This made possible a highly efficient office organization and a suite of offices on the fourth floor of the St. Nicholas Building,

which permitted the Department of Justice and Army and Navy Intelligence Bureaus also to locate quarters there, giving a compact working organization reaching every branch of the service and promoting that intimate contact and close coöperation which assured success. This reciprocal arrangement was especially effective in the case of the Department of Justice, which, under the operation of Mr. Judge, rendered and was rendered assistance on all occasions.

Director Charles B. Prichard, of the Pittsburgh Department of Public Safety, recognized the possibilities of effective cooperation at the beginning, and there was not a moment when the patrolmen and municipal detectives did not do everything possible to promote the success of the League's activities. This spirit of patriotic coöperation on the part of the municipal authorities was constantly maintained through the friendliness and enthusiasm of Robert J. Alderdice, superintendent of police; Magistrate Walter J. Lloyd and Commissioners of Police Dye, Kane, Johnson and Calhoun. Pittsburgh certainly was well policed. In all, the League maintained constantly throughout the trying period over 2,000 active operatives.

The effectiveness of this far-reaching organization was revealed in the complete absence of those disturbances which had been feared. At the outbreak of war, troops had been located at bridges and important public works, but the thorough manner in which the League ferreted out those who were willing to foment trouble soon rendered unnecessary the guarding of industrial plants by soldiers or police. There were no interruptions to the enormous output of munitions and manufactured material, nor were there any accidents, explosions or labor troubles traced to agents of the enemy. In the Pittsburgh division alone, over 25,000 cases were investigated, and every person upon whom the least suspicion had been cast was soon rendered powerless to do harm. Every effort was made to eliminate troubles by preventing alien sympathizers from perfecting their plans. No meetings where incendiary talk could be fostered were permitted to continue, and it was not long before those who had trouble in mind realized that to continue their purpose would only lead to their own downfall and also that of their followers. The record of the League is a tribute to the wisdom of this preventive policy.

It was feared that because of the large proportion of foreigners in the Pittsburgh district, the wide diversity of languages spoken, and the great illiteracy among certain of the nationalities, there would be great difficulty in securing proper observance of the Selective Service registration regulations. During the Civil War, there had been serious draft riots in

Pittsburgh, when the percentage of foreigners and of illiteracy was much less. The American Protective League, in coöperation with Mr. Judge, gave the widest publicity in every possible way to the plans for the registration and the penalty for failure to comply. The result of this work of preparation was that the registration was effected without disorder, and there were no occasions for wholesale arrests to bring evaders or possible evaders to justice. In fact, the League's policy was to prevent trouble by advising those inclined to resent the Government's call, and to make no arrests until other means failed. It was only necessary for an American Protective League operative to appear in open court on one occasion.

I. W. W. propaganda was never permitted to take root. Work to eliminate this menace occupied a large amount of the League's attention. A well organized scheme of the Socialists to evade the Selective Service Law was broken up when a prominent radical and anarchist, a ringleader in the movement, was taken from a meeting he was about to address and compelled to register. The facts that the plans of the scheme were so well known to the League cooled the ardor of the malcontents.

The division had considerable trouble with a Jewish family which used every artifice to protect a lad of selective service age and prevent his being taken into the army. They finally succeeded in spiriting him away, but he was convicted of evading the draft, and by pressure on his family, who were placed under bond to return him, he was brought back to Pittsburgh, sent to jail for six months and then inducted into the army.

A number of Italians, through one of their societies, conceived a plan to make money by filling in questionnaires to enable evasion of selective service. Two ringleaders were arrested, and the chief of the society afterward rendered the League valuable service in preventing labor disturbances. The League also uncovered a scheme of a few unscrupulous lawyers to extort money from men on the ground that their advice would permit them to evade the law. Arrests were not necessary, as the warning of the League of the consequences of any continuance of the practice was sufficient.

The League was able to break the backbone of a dangerous plan of German propaganda through an international organization known as the Geneva Association, whose members were principally alien enemies. The officers were arrested and placed under bond for trial.

One very dangerous draft evader and conscientious objector

was arrested and court-martialed after considerable trouble. He was Walter L. Hirschberg, a student at the University of Pittsburgh. He registered for selective service, but wrote and sent to his draft board his "declaration of rights," as he viewed them, and maintained such an attitude of defiance toward the Government that it was decided to investigate him. In the meantime he disappeared and was traced to New York, where he was placed under observation. He was detained in a locked room in a hotel until sufficient evidence could be obtained against him, but was so shrewd and resourceful that he outwitted his captors and made his escape. It was suspected that he had gone to Chicago, and a Pittsburgh operative went there to find him. The use of commendable strategy secured his arrest and his return to Pittsburgh at the point of a revolver. Although he condemned war as organized murder, he carried a loaded revolver and blackjack for emergencies! The details of his escape and flight read like a trilling story of Sherlock Holmes. As an instance of his resourcefulness and quick wit, he related that when he arrived at the depot in Chicago, he picked up a newspaper to learn quickly the lay of the land. In flaming headlines he discovered that Chicago police that morning were making wholesale arrests of all young men without registration cards. He had none. He espied a woman with a babe and a large traveling case, and politely offered to assist her by carrying the valise. When he was approached by an officer and requested to show his card, he quickly retorted, "Oh, you are too late. You can see that this is my wife and child." He was allowed to leave the depot and go unmolested. He went into hiding until the scare was over. Hirschberg was sent by a court-martial at Camp Lee to the Atlanta prison for twenty years.

"Pittsburgh had some amusing incidents," says the Chief who has been so freely quoted, and he has included several of them in his report:

There was little bootlegging as liquor dealers endeavored to comply with the law forbidding the sale of intoxicants to soldiers in uniform or within restricted areas adjacent to army camps. One negro was suspected, and upon being approached by an operative, readily agreed to sell a quart of "cold tea" for $9.00. The operative bought—and then arrested the negro. When the "cold tea" was tested, it was found to be just what the negro said it was—cold tea!

An alien enemy refused to register and was taken to the League headquarters for intensive examination. The operative was called to the telephone on an urgent message just as he entered headquarters. He hastened to the telephone, leaving his prisoner where he could not escape. When he had finished, he discovered his prisoner missing. It transpired that another operative had come into headquarters, and the prisoner had asked him where aliens registered. The operative asked "Why?" and when he was informed that the man wished to register, he obligingly agreed to accompany him to the United States Marshal's office. He was chagrined to find that he had deprived his fellow operative of a case.

A peculiar case came under the notice of the League. A Russian of draft age, whose father and brothers and sisters were naturalized, claimed exemption on the ground that the father had not taken out his citizenship papers until after he, the subject, had passed his majority, and he had never lost his Russian citizenship. The objector was sent to jail, but the decision was rendered that his point was well taken and he was released.

The League did a wonderful work in reconstructing families, returning wayward sons to sorrowing mothers, and in rehabilitating young men whose patriotism and fidelity to duty were lukewarm. In correcting and preventing trouble the American Protective League performed a splendid service to the Government.

CHAPTER VI

THE STORY OF BOSTON

Massachusetts Somewhat Mixed in Safety Measures—Early Embarrassment of Riches—Brief History of A. P. L.—Organization and Its Success—Stories of the Trail.

After A. P. L. began to reach out into a wide development by reason of the hard work of the National Directors at Washington, D. J. in that town began to cry for more. It sent out to all its special agents and local offices a circular explaining the great assistance which the League was capable of rendering the Government, and asked the assignment of a special agent as an A. P. L. detail in each bureau locality. This circular went out on February 6, 1918, and Boston received a copy duly, as well as the request of the Provost Marshal General to the Governor of Massachusetts for aid in selective service matters. At that time there was no division of A. P. L. organized in Boston. A few days later the Massachusetts Committee of Public Safety, which had been organized and active ever since the beginning of the war, was asked to interest itself to the extent of having some good man start a Boston division of A. P. L. The latter matter was slow in development because of the extent and thoroughness of the earlier state organization. The latter had been taking care of the food, fuel and other administrative work in assistance to the Government. The feeling was that it might be better to enlarge the Committee of Public Safety than to start any new body which might be a source of misunderstanding and friction.

The Department of Justice work in Boston during the early days of the war had not been satisfactory. Boston, so far from being all Puritan, has in reality one of the most mixed populations in the country. There was some feeling against the Department of Justice in Boston, and some feeling also against any new body which proposed to link up closely with that arm of the Government. D. J. had been handling for itself the alien enemy, anti-military and propaganda work. Yet very early in the game D. J. was overworked in Boston, as it had been in every other great city in America, and it really needed help. There were a great many thinking men who believed that it could be much relieved by the well-organized support of the banking, real estate, industrial and commercial activities of the city, as had been the case all over the United States where A. P. L. divisions had been created.

Still another embarrassment, however, slowed up the early activities of A. P. L. in Boston. That city having in its population many French Canadians, Irish, and so forth, of the Catholic faith, had developed a sort of Church problem, and there had become somewhat active the organization known as the "A. P. A."—whose initials are somewhat close to those of A. P. L. Many thought that confusion between the two organizations would result. There had been, moreover, in this state of independent thought, a great many other "Leagues" of this, that and the other sort; so that many felt that Boston had about enough leagues as matters then stood.

At about this time Mr. W. Rodman Peabody of the Committee of Public Safety pointed out to Washington the efficient manner in which Mr. Endicott had organized that committee throughout the State. There was a local committee of safety in every town, and also a state-wide machine organizing the banking, real estate and other important business activities. He suggested that instead of a division of A. P. L., there ought to be a sub-organization "organized by the Committee of Public Safety at the request of the Department of Justice." It was understood that this minor organization should have the general features of A. P. L. and should act as the Massachusetts branch of A. P. L. A list of good names was suggested of persons suitable for the organization as thus outlined.

Mr. Elting of the National Directors, however, made the point that an arrangement of this kind would have a tendency to discredit or to disintegrate the League in other cities. The Attorney-General also was opposed to any organization which did not show the exact status of a purely volunteer body, as had been done in all other parts of the United States.

Mr. Peabody still wanted the Committee of Public Safety to appear as the parent or controlling body, and a lot of valuable time was wasted over this tweedle-dee argument. A compromise was effected, and on April 15, 1918, the National Directors had advice that the Massachusetts organization was hiring offices, and assumed that the work had begun and that Boston would copy as nearly as possible the form of letterhead used by A. P. L., putting the names of the National Directors on the left-hand side and substituting the words "Protective League." Underneath that was to appear the legend: "Organized by the Massachusetts Public Safety Committee under the Direction of the U. S. Department of Justice, Bureau of Investigation." Boston expressed the belief that Washington would not be able to tell the difference between this organization and any other so far as loyalty and efficiency were concerned, although sensible of the Washington feeling that Massachusetts was starting a year late and might be suspected of lack in coöperation.

All concerned having thus been satisfied, Massachusetts began A. P. L. work a trifle late in the game, but none the less proceeded to show that it could produce as effective an organization as any other in the country. Assistant Chief H. E. Trumbull makes his report on the regulation A. P. L. blanks and letterheads, and adds the following data as to the later organization of A. P. L.:

> Mr. Samuel Wolcott was appointed Chief, and we took two offices at 45 Milk Street, in the same building with the Department of Justice. Mr. Trumbull, then a volunteer operative with the Department proper, consented to help with the new organization, and Mr. John B. Hanrahan was appointed by the Department of Justice as a special agent to oversee the work of the new organization.
>
> A few weeks later we found that the work was too great to handle in such small quarters, and about the first of May contracted for half of the eighth floor of the building, the Department of Justice taking the other half. At this time Mr. Trumbull was appointed Assistant Chief.
>
> As a nucleus of the state organization, we took the names of the men who had been doing volunteer work for the United

States Attorney's office, and we proceeded to send out to these men the work that came in their territory, and as they proved satisfactory, appointed them as inspectors of a certain district and gave them directions whereby they organized.

About July first, the League took over from the Department the handling of all draft matters, the Department loaning to the League two special agents to supervise and the League furnishing all the men for the actual work.

We think the strongest recommendation we can give of our loyalty and interest is the approximate number of cases handled from April 11, 1918, to February 1, 1919, which number amounts to about 5,000, with about 4,000 draft cases under the Selective Service Act.

On or about October first, Mr. Wolcott resigned for the purpose of taking up active duties with the Army, and Mr. John W. Hannigan was appointed Chief in his place.

The relations of the League with the Department have been of the closest, and there has never been any friction. Special Agent Kelleher has stated that if it had not been for the activities of the League, it would have been absolutely impossible for his office to handle the great volume of work.

Once in its swing, Boston Division proceeded to do as Boston always does, and to work in thorough and efficient fashion. A detailed statement of the work for Department of Justice covers 525 cases of alien enemy activities, 292 cases under the Espionage act, one case of treason, seven of sabotage, eleven of interference with the draft, 128 cases of propaganda, twenty cases of radicals and socialists, seven naturalization cases, and other investigations amounting to 484.

For reasons above outlined, the division did little in food and fuel, and there was not much to do for the Navy. There were seventy-seven cases of character and loyalty investigations, 331 passport cases, and 262 cases that had to do with war insurance and like matters.

A. P. L. was, as usual, of great use to the War Department. The division conducted 514 investigations for local boards, examined 4,000 slacker raid cases, as well as fifteen gentlemen who did not know whether to work or fight. There were 1,908 applicants for overseas service who were investigated, as well as 510 applicants for commissions. The division deserves compliments for its steady and intelligent administration of the whole range of the complicated problems that rose out of the war situation.

There were all sorts of curious cases which came up in Boston as in other cities, which show alien artlessness or slacker subterfuges much as they appear elsewhere, as well as a certain occasional informality in regard to the observance of the ordinary civil laws. For instance, one does not recall the name of Edward Burkhart as one of the occupants of the Mayflower on its arrival; neither does Mr. Burkhart seem to have been fully possessed of Puritan principles, for it was alleged that he had been dishonorably discharged from the U. S. Navy, was dishonorably living with a woman who was not his wife, and had dishonorably failed to register for the draft. As Mr. Burkhart was hiding out somewhere, an A. P. L. operative was put on his trail. He went to the house where Burkhart was living and told the woman in the case that she was doing wrong in covering up the whereabouts of Burkhart. He added that he believed the man was in the house or would come back to the house, in spite of all she had said. That was at three o'clock in the afternoon, and the operative concluded to sit in the house and wait to see what would happen, all exits being guarded by other operatives. Nothing did happen until 9:15 that night, although the house was searched. At last, up in the attic, a small blind space was found where the electric light wires went up to the roof. A flash light here illuminated the dark interior — and disclosed Mr. Burkhart resting rather uncomfortably on the cross beams, where he had been since early that afternoon — something of a Spartan, if not much of a Puritan. It was found that he was twenty-five years of age and not thirty-seven. It was also found that he had the classification card belonging to another man, whereupon he was accused of failure to file his questionnaire. On December 30, he was brought before the Grand Jury, found guilty and sentenced to East Cambridge jail.

Another gentleman, Mr. Ralph E———, when he filled out his questionnaire, swore that he was a married man and had a wife and child dependent upon him. It was discovered that the woman was not his wife. The man consulted the partner of the A. P. L. inspector — the two being members of the same law firm — in professional capacity. Here, therefore, was a question of ethics involving the privilege of a confession made to an attorney and also the oath taken to the A. P. L. The two law partners called in Mr. E——— and gave him good advice about the crime of perjury. As the man did what he could to square up matters, it was decided to let that part of his case drop. He was not sent to prison.

Mr. Herbert C——— had an ambition to go across as a member of the American Red Cross and had good recommendations. A. P. L., however, discovered that he was an alleged dope fiend. He did not go with the Red Cross.

Peter R———, of a town near Boston, while arguing with two men about the war, made a few such casual statements as " To hell with Liberty Bonds," " To hell with Thrift Stamps," " The Government is no good," " I will not fight for this country," " I will not register," " I am going back to my own country, Russia," and " The whole United States Government be damned." This man was brought before the Assistant United States District Attorney from the police court, but the attorney declined to prosecute and said that Peter was only playful. He did not think that a private trial could be used in a Federal prosecution. Most excellent! Obviously, it is the spirit that killeth, and the letter that giveth life!

A Mr. C——— swore he had a wife and child dependent on him, and so he ought not to be asked to fight. A. P. L. found out that he had spent ten thousand dollars the year before, that his father gave him all he wished, that he was a Boston clubman, that he was not engaged in any productive industry. Held to the grand jury in five thousand dollars bail.

A man by the name of J——— was reported on November 14 to have made disloyal and pro-German remarks. Two days later, three affidavits were before the Assistant District Attorney. In this case the attorney ruled that although the men had a clean cut case against him, there was no need to prosecute him if he had been warned. Indeed, why annoy an alien?

Boston is well known in the matter of tea parties. An A. P. L. officer was taking tea with a navy officer on board ship in Boston harbor, and the latter complained that his men were getting too much cold tea on their shore leave. A. P. L. took it up with the Naval Intelligence, and within a week a man was taken in custody for selling such beverages to men in uniform.

Mr. Charles D. Milkowicz, or some such name, was alleged to dance in happiness at the report of any German victory. It was his custom to fire any employe in the factory where he was foreman, if the employe showed any pro-American tendencies. Once he said regarding the U. S. flag, "Get that damned flag out of the way." He used to wear an iron cross stick pin up to April 6, 1917. He was a member of the German Club, and used to buy silver nails for the Hindenburg statue which they maintained at that club, such nails retailing for a dollar a throw, all for the good of the Kaiser. A. P. L. started an investigation which showed that this man seemed to be uncertain whether he came from Russia or Germany and was equally indefinite as to his age. He was not registered as an alien enemy, and was charged with falsifying his questionnaire as well as violating Section 3 of the Espionage Act. The Assistant U. S. Attorney handling alien enemy matters in Massachusetts refused to act in this case. So far as known, the attorney is still in office, and Mr. Milkowicz is still in Boston.

Mr. Hans D———, a German waiter in Boston, belonged to a German club where considerable advance news of German operations circulated. Mr. D——— said he sent money to Germany; said that Germany would win the war; drank to the health of the Kaiser on hearing that an American ship had been torpedoed. In short, Mr. D——— ran quite true to form in all ways. A photograph was found which looked like him in a German uniform — he must have been a German officer, because they found in his possession a half dozen spoons which he had stolen in New England, in default of better opportunity in Belgium. At least he was prosecuted for larceny and was fined $15.00. Later his reputation was found to be so bad as a propagandist that he was interned on a presidential warrant.

It occurred to the fertile brain of Mr. Julius Bongraber that a varied spelling of his name might prove useful to him in times of draft. Sometimes he wrote his name as Graber, sometimes as Van Graber, and sometimes as Julius V. Gaber.

His classification card named him as G. V. Gaber. When interrogated as to all these matters, he admitted that the initial " G " ought to have been " Y," because that was the way Yulius was pronounced, anyhow, in his country. At the same time he left a card over his door signed J. V. Gaber. He declared that he was a German, also an Austrian, also a neutral, but had sympathies with Russia. To others he said that his name was Von Gaber; that he was an alien, but would go where he liked. He had taken out first citizenship papers, but had registered for return with the Austria-Hungarian Consul. A. P. L. got this multifold party on the carpet, but on his statement that he intended to go to New York, the prosecution seems to have been dropped, although the dossier was forwarded to New York after him.

There was a draft evader in Boston by the name of R———, who did not file his questionnaire. He was found at his home by an agent of A. P. L. and agreed to accompany the latter. It was the intention of the operative to turn over his man to a policeman, but policemen seemed to be rare in Boston, for in two miles not one was sighted. The draft evader then evaded yet more, and was not found for several days thereafter. The man's mother, however, when found, averred she had not seen her son for two months. A plain patriotic talk was made to her with the result that after a while, she found the said son and turned him over to the authorities for service in the army.

Boston Division in one case revoked the credentials which it had issued to an operative. The man's name was Oscar F———, and the position seemed to go to his head. He took to borrowing money right and left, once getting as high as fifty dollars on a touch of one of the special agents. He admitted that he was probably the best secret service agent in the country, and told people he was getting $3,000 a year and expenses. After that he usually touched his listener for $5.00. Oscar was doing well until they let him out. His name ended in " ski."

Boston, being near the Northern seaboard, heard of a good many cases of mysterious light signals. One operative in the Lynn district was sure he had seen dots and dashes coming across the bay at night in the approved fashion of mysterious night signals. They put a telegrapher on the case but he could not make out the message. At one o'clock in the morning four tried men and true of the A. P. L. rowed out with muffled oars to an anchored yacht which seemed to be the place from which the light signals appeared. They found five pairs of feet pointing to the zenith. Calling upon the feet to surrender, they boarded the yacht and explanations followed. It appeared that the five yachtsmen had had a hard day's sail and had decided to remain on board ship over night. The flashes of light which had so aroused the A. P. L. men were nothing more nor less than the reflection of a shore light on the glass of a porthole as the boat rolled and swayed in the ripples of the bay.

Next to mysterious signal lights, wireless stations have produced as many flivvers for the A. P. L. as anything else. Inspector T——— insisted that there was a house in his district which ought to be searched, because he was satisfied it had a wireless plant. As he had no proof, he could not obtain a search warrant. Mr. Endicott, at the office of the Food Administration, gave him a sugar warrant, stating that that would let him into the house, and that he might get some information. Inspector T——— went to the house with a club in one hand and the warrant in the other; searched the house from garret to basement, but found no wireless. While poking around in one of the corners, however, he did discover eighty pounds of sugar, which, being overweight, he promptly confiscated.

Soon after the forming of the A. P. L. in Boston, a man came in with a carrier pigeon which he was sure was a mysterious messenger of some sort. It was a beautiful white bird that had dark dots and dashes all over the inside of both wings. The chief was all wrought up about this and regretted that he had not been taught the Morse code in early life. He therefore took the man and the bird over to the office of Military Intelligence, where they unravel, decipher and decode all sorts of things. The Major in command was very cordial, and he also examined the bird carefully. In his belief the dots and dashes on the wings were of importance, but he could not quite read them all. He sent for the code expert of the Signal Corps. Who shall say that A. P. L. cannot run down any sort of clew? The code expert of the Signal Corps also examined the bird carefully, but at first could not make it out. Then he touched one of the dots with the point of his pencil. It turned out to be a perfectly good cootie, which still possessed powers of locomotion.

Throughout the war, New England was, always, one of the nerve centers of the United States. A great many munition factories were at work there day and night. The atmosphere was tense all the time; war was in the eyes and ears of the people. But let no man believe New England anything but American. Whatever her population to-day, her leadership is American and only American and always will be such. Boston and her environs, the entire state of Massachusetts, the entire section of New England, went into the war from the first word. No part of America is saner or safer; no part was better guided and guarded by local agencies of defense. A. P. L. was accepted as one of these, certainly not to the regret of any man concerned.

CHAPTER VII

THE STORY OF CLEVELAND

Astonishing Figures of A. P. L. Activities in a Great Manufacturing City — Sabotage, Bolshevism and Treason — I. W. W. and Kindred Radical Propaganda — The Saving of a City.

Once more we find occasion to revise the popular estimate of a supposedly well-known American community. No one would think of staid, steady, even-going Cleveland as anything but a place of prosperity and peace. At a rough estimate, before the Cleveland report came in, one would have said that possibly that city might report a total of ten or fifteen thousand cases of A. P. L. investigations. As a matter of fact, the Cleveland total is over sixty thousand! And yet, the Cleveland Chief in his report calls attention to the large amount of war supplies manufactured in his district, and says: "We were a hot-bed of Socialism and pro-Germanism, but not one dollar's worth of material was lost."

Cleveland Division was organized in May, 1917, with a personnel of 1,008 — Mr. Arch C. Klunph, Chief, six Assistant Chiefs, seven Departmental Inspectors, an office staff and eighteen companies. There were also one women's company and about five hundred unattached operatives; a total personnel of 1,551.

As the type of A. P. L. service varied in different cities, it may be interesting to other cities to note the character of work the Cleveland division was called upon to do. The list of investigations covers many heads: Failure to register, failure to entrain, and deserters from service, 5,356; failure to submit questionnaire, 2,100; failure to report for physical examination, 3,100; claims for exemption, 2,500; seditious literature, 50; seditious and treasonable utterances or pro-German cases, 7,113; loyalty investigations for Army, Navy,

Red Cross, Y. M. C. A., etc., 1,746; wireless outfits, 40; enemy agents or spies, 363; I. W. W., Socialist, W. I. I. U. and Bolsheviki, 1,529; industrial sabotage, 318; Liberty Bond slackers, 500. Total number of men apprehended and examined on slacker raids, estimated, 36,000. Total — 60,715.

In addition to the foregoing, the Cleveland division has rendered a large amount of service in investigating cases of violations of food, fuel, electric light and gasless Sunday regulations; cases for the National Council of Defense; registration of male and female enemy aliens (approximately 5,000); work of U. S. Marshal's office; work of Naturalization Bureau by secret investigations of applicants for citizenship; Red Cross overseas work; Socialist cases; details for War Work plants. There also were regular weekly details of volunteer workers with automobiles to assist the Police Department.

As to definite preventive measures, the Chief points out several instances: the stopping of manufacture of a fountain pen which would explode on being opened; the choking off of the establishment of a high-power wireless plant on the shore of Lake Erie; the discharge of countless German workmen in factories producing food for the Army; the confiscation of models and plans of American battleships and submarines, and literature found in the hands of German propagandists.

In May, 1918, an express company notified Cleveland A. P. L. that they were called upon to issue money orders to an unusual number of Germans, who claimed that they were returning to their homes in Russia. The League captured twenty-three men, all claiming to live in Russia, although plainly German in appearance, and speaking that language in talking with one another. Three men left for Chicago, but were apprehended by wire at the railroad terminal in Chicago. This was a concerted movement to get as many Germans as possible back into Russia.

Cleveland, being one of the largest cities of the United States, and having also one of the largest percentages of foreign population, naturally indeed was a hot-bed for Socialism, I. W. W. work and Bolshevism, although such had not been the general reputation of the city. These organizations held regular meetings, often with speeches of the most dangerous character. At most of them, there was an A. P. L. operative noting all that was done and said.

Cleveland Division covered a population of over a million, and that in one of the four largest war working centers in the nation. It is a very proud claim to say that not one dollar was lost to the nation. The Chief points out that this statement is the more astonishing because there were made in Cleveland a long list of military supplies: Air-planes, wings and parts; ammunitions, clothing, trucks, and the hundred other materials for use in the Army and Navy. There were three hundred and eighty-six plants in Cuyhoga County engaged in ordnance work, and there were employed in these plants 1,218 workmen. These ordnance plants had contracts amounting to $175,000,000. Motor transportation plants, making trucks, trailers, axles, forms, etc., had a series of contracts totaling $88,000,000. There were fifty plants engaged in air-craft production, and twenty making clothing, not to mention three large shipyards, all busy practically day and night. That means work! Figures like this are serious. It is no cheap flattery to say to the men who are responsible for the safety of these vast industrial concerns that their record is a more than marvelous one. It is no wonder that there is the best of feeling between Cleveland Division and the Department of Justice, Police Department and all the allied administrations of the law. It is not necessary to print the letters of appreciation from any of these.

The Chief says that the most of the active work covered a period of about fifteen months. The cases handled monthly approximated four thousand. Obviously it is impossible to report sixty thousand, or four thousand, or one thousand cases, but some of the Cleveland specials are too interesting to leave aside. It is regrettable that they must be abbreviated.

On December 1, 1917, Dorothy A———, a nice Cleveland girl, was selling Liberty Bonds for the Y. W. C. A. on a partial payment basis, which did not seem quite right. Dorothy was hard to find, but she admitted, when found, that she was selling these bonds because she needed the money herself. The mortgage on the old home was about to be foreclosed, and she had taken this method of getting what money she could. It was in truth the case of a young girl driven desperate by circumstances. The A. P. L. first got her a good position; second, advanced the money to pay off the mortgage on the home, she to pay them back in monthly installments; and third, found the people to whom she had sold the bonds, and returned the money of which she had fraudulently deprived them. This girl remained clean and straight, and as a culmination of the case she married a young soldier, whom she met through the A. P. L., who later did his bit in France. We do not know of a prettier bit in the history of the A. P. L. than this.

On March 2, 1918, A. P. L. ran down another one of those cruel rumors against the Red Cross which have been started by pro-German women for the most part. This rumor was first circulated by a young woman, and is of a nature which can not be put into print. The girl, when found, confessed that she was guilty. She also confessed that she was hitting the high spots in the city, having left a country home to get acquainted with the bright lights. The A. P. L. did not kick this woman down and out, either, but gave her a hand-up. Two weeks later she came to the Division Office with tears in her eyes, apologized for the false rumors which she had set going, and implored that she might be allowed to do something for the office of the division.

A war plant making areoplane parts kept turning out defective work. The A. P. L. put a woman operative in the factory. She chanced to be a young woman of a wealthy family, accustomed to the luxury of a beautiful home, but she took to the overalls and dirty work as a duck does to water. She was in the factory three weeks, located the trouble, and it was adjusted.

A telephone call reported that a house was being burglarized. An A. P. L. man at the phone remembered that a deserter had been sought for at that number. In thirty minutes the house was surrounded. They did not catch the deserter, but they did get the burglar.

A dangerous type of service was the raiding of I. W. W. headquarters. Sometimes these were boarding houses where thirty or forty of these people would be gathered together. When such a place was surrounded, the suspects would pour out of the windows into the arms of the operatives. This meant occasional fights, and there was danger in the work, but there was no case where loss of life was experienced.

An interesting fact of Cleveland war work was that developed by examination of the draughting rooms in the large plants. In some of these plants the entire draughting force was not only German by descent but pro-German in sentiment. It has often been said that part of German propaganda was to get men in factories where they could get blueprints of all of our machinery. In November, 1917, the League was advised that a draughtsman of a ship-building company was very pro-German, and it was said that the foreman in charge would hire only Germans. Constant surveillance was ordered, but it was as late as June, 1918, before this man was found making derogatory remarks about our Army. He was found to have been an officer in the German Reserves. He was jailed. Many letters were found on him sufficient to warrant his internment.

As though I. W. W.'s were not sufficiently dangerous, operatives were once asked to arrest a colored slacker who worked for a lion-tamer. The latter, a woman, gave the operatives a tip that her assistant ought to be looked into. He was finally caught at the time when he was transferring the lions from the performing ring to their traveling cages, but that did not stop the operatives. After he got the doors locked he was taken to the Federal Building and inducted into the Service, where his courage will be put to good service.

Here are some familiar pro-German statements, this time uttered by one A. C———, who was running an advertising agency. At one time he said that "the war would be ended by January 1, because German training was better than ours — that we should not believe the lies about Germans killing babies — everyone knows that America is going to lose the war — that this is no war for Democracy — that there is no Democracy in America." Indicted. Guilty. Interned. A. P. L.

Cleveland had its own troubles with evaders and slackers, and it took many cleverly laid plans to catch some of them. These are some of the methods. After locating where a suspect lived who was hard to find, a man would appear next day as one of the solicitors of the City Directory whose business it was to get the name of every man in each house.

The solicitor was usually a very old looking man. This usually worked. If it did not, a messenger boy would show up with a message saying that it must be delivered at once. If this failed, there would come a letter from some prominent institution, sent in an unsealed envelope, addressed to the man offering him a job at an unusually high wage. One or the other of these devices would usually establish touch with the man wanted. It was like changing baits in a trap.

An interesting case was that of Harry W———, who was brother of another Mr. W——— sentenced to the workhouse for violation of the Espionage Act. Harry did not register, but was picked up in the City Council Chamber. He desperately tried to convince the A. P. L. men that he was too old, but the operatives got his birth record and proved that he had wilfully evaded registration. Indicted and sentenced to one year in the workhouse.

A deserter from Camp Sherman, in December, 1917, was located wearing civilian clothes as late as September, 1918. He was hidden by a certain woman, who had secreted his uniform and who had supplied him with liquor repeatedly. We learned that this was an illicit relation. The woman had furnished the man with money from time to time. The A. P. L. took her case up with the District Attorney. The woman is awaiting indictment of a charge of furnishing liquor to a soldier and harboring a deserter. Her lover is back in camp.

The division had a good case on certain German sympathizers believed to be sending certain information to the enemy. A dictaphone was installed in a hotel room which they occupied, and the place was watched day and night for a week. Just at the time when it seemed that some information was going to be reported, a parrot which the people had in the room started to chatter and beat them into the dictaphone. Nothing was discovered at that time and the Chief reports, " I regret we cannot print what came over the dictaphone by the parrot."

Adolph R———, a German of the Germans, was within the draft, but resisted in every possible way, and said he would kill any members of the League who came after him. He even called up individual members and told them he was going to shoot them. When an order came he told the A. P. L.

man that he would pay no attention. A detail was sent after him and he was escorted like a little lamb to the barracks. He has been a good German ever since.

The League found that it had in its ranks as an operative a resident of the city of Cleveland, who had been there all his life but was a German alien and not registered. This fellow was arrested and interned for a short period, though soon paroled.

The Cleveland division of A. P. L. took a very prominent part in the Debs case, and furnished abundant men and machines on the Sunday that Debs was arrested in Cleveland. It also helped to assemble the evidence on which Debs was indicted.

Washington was on the hunt for a dangerous enemy alien by the name of Henry H———. Information came that he was working for a photographic concern in Cleveland, but he could not be located. Four months later a complaint of pro-Germanism came in against a man of the same name working for a city directory company. He had changed his occupation but not his nature, and hence was arrested.

The printed page was another form of propaganda in Cleveland. An alien enemy editor of a German paper was allowed at large with restrictions. He abused his privilege and was interned at Fort Oglethorpe. Indictments and convictions were found against members of the staff of a German daily. Yet another editor refused to print articles on food conservation, and he also was indicted and convicted. Sabotage was threatened and planned in many cases. In one instance a tip got out that a big war plant was to be blown up on one of two given nights. The League got on the job and found the plant to be insufficiently guarded. The guard was increased and no damage was done.

Gottlieb K———, an alien enemy, was caught out of his zone without his permit. Operatives went to his home and found two Mauser rifles, a peck of shells, a dagger, a blackjack and several maps of Canada, the United States and Mexico. Gottlieb was thought to be more fit for Fort Oglethorpe than Cleveland.

Mr. A. L. H———, a member of the Cleveland Board of Education, had his own idea about education. In the home of a socialist he remarked that the Liberty Bonds would never be paid, and that the working class for generations would have to work to support these bonds. He stated that the Russian Committee, headed by Elihu Root, who went to Russia to investigate the conditions there, had their report written and signed before they left America. He frequently said that the bonds of the United States were not worth the paper they were written on. Affidavits resulted in the indictment of Mr. H———, and he was sentenced to ten years in the Atlanta Penitentiary, the conviction automatically removing him from the Board of Education.

A mail carrier in Cleveland fell heir to $60,000, but being a socialist, would not subscribe to Liberty Bonds. He was called to the headquarters of the A. P. L. and reasoned with. The next day his son came into headquarters literally running over with Liberty Bonds. He had $10,000 worth, all in $100 denominations! They sent him home with a guard.

The A. P. L. was responsible for obtaining the evidence that secured the conviction of the State Secretary of the Socialist Party and two others. All of these men publicly made speeches against the draft, and were actually instrumental in preventing certain men from complying with the Selective Service Act. All sentenced to one year of peace in the Canton workhouse by the Federal Court.

A gentleman by the name of Joseph Freiheit — Freiheit means "freedom" in German — said that if sent to the army he would not shoot at the Germans. He advised his friends to do the same. He was brought to headquarters and reprimanded. The next day he committed suicide. Case closed.

A man who owned a garage was reported hostile to Liberty Bonds and Thrift Stamps. A certain operative went to talk over with him the question of Thrift Stamps. The question was asked, "How many do you want me to buy?" The solicitor said he thought about a thousand dollars worth. He bought a thousand dollars worth in cash, then and there. Almost persuaded.

A very elusive draft dodger was Geo. F———, who was chased from pillar to post, but not come up with. He was discovered to have an intrigue with a waitress, Jennie M———, who also would change her name once in a while, leave her place of employment and be gone a day or two.

The question was, where did she go? The operatives on the case took Jennie down to the Federal Building, where she told so many conflicting stories that she was locked up. Meantime, the Post Office Department advised that certain letters were sent back from Elyria, Ohio, addressed to "F. J. P———." The return card brought the trail around to one of the original dwelling-places of the suspect. The operative now went to this address and found the owner of the home and threatened to arrest him for abetting a deserter from the United States Army. These letters were opened and it was discovered that the man desired was getting mail at the post office at Monroe, Michigan. So the operative went to Jennie in jail and said, "Well, we have got George over in Michigan." "Is that so?" said the girl; "how did you get him?" The operative declined to tell, and said the only thing he wondered about was what name George was going under in Monroe. The girl finally admitted that his name there was "F. J. P———." It took patience and shrewdness to follow the trail in Monroe. However, a name was found written in two places in a register of a workingmen's hotel there. The initials were the same as for F. J. P———, one of the many alias names. The landlady was found, and a picture of Jennie was shown her. She said it was the same picture that "F. J. P———" had in the back of his watch. The rest was rather simple. The operator hired a taxicab and started out in search of his man, who then was engaged as night watchman on some road work. A steam roller was found in the middle of the road, displaying a red lantern, with a man fast asleep on top. The operative awakened him, and identified him as the much wanted Geo. F———, alias Ed. D———, alias Geo. W———, alias F. J. P———, alias F. J. P———. The man was handcuffed and the party started back for Monroe. In due time, the suspect was taken to the Department of Justice, and on December 14 the long trail ended for him. The details of this pursuit are among the most interesting of those which have been turned in for any case on the Cleveland records.

One operative had what he took to be a regular Conan Doyle novel, all spread out before him. It involved what was known as "The House of Mystery," where all kinds of mysterious goings and comings and every sort of dark, secret midnight interview took place. After a long, long time the house of mystery was closed. The inspector was able from other information to tell the operatives what was the matter with his case — which is not reported in full. The inspector said: "Your elderly woman there is the mother of the younger woman, who is married to a worthless scamp, from whom she is seeking a divorce. They have a beautiful home in the mountains of the West, and that is where they go on the mysterious trips you have been noticing so long. Their trunks are filled with valuable papers, and when they finished discussing these, they put them back in the trunks. The little child is the son of the young woman. The reason they rented this isolated house and made a prisoner out of the child was because the father has been trying to kidnap the child. The mysterious chauffeur is the secretary of the ladies. When he enlisted for the war they found cause to weep on that account." The operative had been working on an ordinary society detective story instead of a plot against the United States.

Perhaps these very few random cases may serve to show the variety of the sixty thousand handled in Cleveland. What did it all mean for the safety and security of the United States? Who can measure it? That is a thing impossible. But that the good citizens of Cleveland appreciated what the A. P. L. has done may be seen from abundant local evidence. Under date of December 24 the Cleveland newspapers came out in open condemnation of the wave of crime then threatening the city. The *Plain Dealer* said very plainly:

> The amazing boldness of bandits, burglars and miscellaneous plug-uglies in Cleveland has finally stirred the city to an insistent demand that something approaching war methods be adopted in dealing with them. It is peculiarly irritating to know that most, if not all, of the criminals are young men of military age. While better men have been giving their lives to free the world of the terror of Germanism, these stealthy enemies have been staging a reign of terror of their own in a modern American community. The American Protective League has wisely placed its services at the disposal of the police. All public spirited citizens should coöperate in every

> possible way. The police are shooting to kill, and the more frequently their aim proves true the better it will be for Cleveland. It is not time for leniency or compromise. The thug of to-day, who has so serious a misapprehension of the privilege of being an American, deserves nothing beyond a snug grave. There have been other epidemics of outlawry in Cleveland, and perhaps the present "crime wave" is no more menacing than some that have gone before. But coming just at this time, when so great a price has been paid to make America and all the world safe and decent, the impudence of the gunman is peculiarly infuriating.

The Cleveland *Press* headed one of its editorials: " Chief, call out the A. P. L.! " In answer, the Chief of the Cleveland Police did call on the A. P. L. once more, although this was six weeks after hostilities had ceased. All of the following Saturday night and Sunday there were A. P. L. men patrolling the streets of Cleveland in motor cars in company with the police.

The disbanding of the A. P. L. was openly deplored in Cleveland. What is going to be the future condition of the United States in these days following the war? One thing is sure, the thinking men of the country are uneasy. There is reason to feel concern, in a city like Cleveland, over bolshevism and labor troubles. There do not lack those who predict for all America the wave of disregard for property and life which quite often ensues at the close of a great war — and this war was the greatest upheavel of human institutions and human values the world has ever seen. But matters in Cleveland might have been worse — much worse.

CHAPTER VIII

THE STORY OF CINCINNATI

Data from a Supposed Citadel of Pro-Germanism—Gratifying Reports from the City Which Boasts a Rhine of its Own — Alien Enemies and How They Were Handled — Americanization of America.

That Cincinnati had a vast population of German descent and of pro-German sympathies was known throughout the United States. It would be folly to say otherwise. Had open riots or armed resistance to the draft, or to the war itself, arisen in Cincinnati, there were many who would not have been surprised. Those, however, did not really know the inherently solid quality of the city on the Ohio River. They may find that from the study of the able report of the Cincinnati Division.

Perhaps a very considerable amount of the quiet on the Rhine at Cincinnati was due to the fact that there was such an organization within its gates as the American Protective League. The members of the League were on the watch all the time for anything dangerous in the way of pro-enemy activity. That the division had a certain amount of work to do may be seen from the summaries.

There were 2,972 investigations for disloyalty and sedition; 4,232 selective service investigations; 3,004 suspects taken in slacker raids. Of propaganda by word of mouth, there were 7,000 examinations. Three hundred and seventy civilian applicants for overseas service were examined. There were eighty-one examinations made into the character of persons identified with the I. W. W., the People's Council, and other pacifist or radical bodies. The Secret Service had fifty examinations made for it and the Post Office three. There were fourteen thousand visits made at homes and places of business of alien enemies, and twenty-eight alien enemies were required to report to the supervisor every week.

Heatless Mondays required three hundred investigations and gasless Sundays one thousand, five hundred and seventeen. In 250 instances the A. P. L. rendered automobile service to various Government departments. These figures show that something was doing in Cincinnati. As to the exact nature of the activities, it is much better to give the sober and just estimate of the local chief, as gratifying as it is admirable:

From its inception the Cincinnati Division of the American Protective League was vibrant with possibilities. Cincinnati was known from coast to coast as a city settled by Germans. It was presumed, of course, to be very largely pro-German as a result of this reputation. "Over-the-Rhine" meant Cincinnati to many who lived outside of its confines. The reputation of the city was at stake. Those who knew Cincinnati, however, felt that this reputation which came to us from abroad was unjustified, and that although there was no gainsaying that German blood flowed in the veins of a very large number of its people, it was still ninety-nine per cent loyal; and the record of the war has demonstrated the truth of this statement.

Under the direction and supervision of Calvin S. Weakley, Special Agent in charge of the Department of Justice, work was carried on with quietness and despatch. He approached every matter with an open mind, and it is to his excellent judgment and his avoidance of brass-band methods that the record of the Cincinnati office of the Bureau of Investigation and its auxiliary, the Cincinnati Division of the American Protective League, has been clean of criticism. In the burglar-proof steel cabinets, however, repose documents and reports which would create a sensation in the community, and perhaps the day of reckoning is not far. While the fact that many of these acts occurred before the United States became an active participant in the world war may mean legal immunity, yet the record is made, and in many cases public opinion has been the sternest prosecutor of those individuals (many of whom enjoy the rights of American citizenship), whose sympathies as well as activities will always brand them as having been unfit for the privileges which they still continue to enjoy. It has brought to many of those individuals social isolation—a punishment incomparable with anything that can be meted out by judge or jury—and they cannot help but feel the ignominy of their unpatriotic actions. Loyalty to the country and a fine patriotism for the cause was the keynote which seemed to animate the membership.

Hardly had the ink dried upon the President's signature to the document which made operative the original Selective Service Act, when word filtered through to the office of the Cincinnati Division American Protective League that there was an undercurrent of opposition developing which would culminate on Registration Day, June 5th, 1917. So-called Socialists, who were in fact German propagandists, were the most active in their criticism. Venomous advice was being offered to young men, who, upon that historic day, would enter their names upon the rolls of the prospective great National Army.

The preliminary information which was gathered left no doubt in the mind of Special Agent Weakley, at Cincinnati, that unless an example was made of these so-called pacifists, there was danger of an incomplete registration, and it became very apparent from the preliminary investigations made that the opposition to registration centered in a local unit of a Socialist organization known as the Eleventh Ward.

Out of four operatives who entered into this particular case, three were dropped, and one became a member of the inner circle. The open meetings of the club divulged nothing, but the secret sessions of the inner circle developed the plan which would make as ineffective as possible registration in Cincinnati and which undoubtedly would have succeeded. Circulars and posters were secretly printed, and on the night of June 1 they were to be distributed broadcast throughout the northwestern section of Cincinnati. This literature not only was seditious in character, but in the opinion of the District Attorney, treasonable.

The League plan was so carefully and thoroughly developed that not a guilty man escaped. There was quite a scene at several police stations when operatives of the League, detailed with local police detectives, brought in their men, each with his pile of circulars. A. P. L. had direct evidence of where these circulars had been placed—in letter boxes, on door-steps, or handed to individuals on the street—and thus made each case complete in itself; and when, the next day, the newspapers told in detail the story of how this plan had been nipped in the bud, anti-conscriptionists became enthusiastic registrants. Even men who were arrested asked for the privilege of registration. Cincinnati not only gave the quota estimated for it, but a percentage so much higher as to elicit surprise.

After the investigation had developed the real culprits, the printing shop also was located, the form from which the circulars had been printed confiscated, and the complete chain of evidence was sufficient to bring a unanimous report from the Grand Jury, charging everyone involved with conspiracy against the Government.

This was the first real big work successfully undertaken by Cincinnati Division of the American Protective League. It was carried out with thoroughness and dispatch, and nothing was left undone that was necessary to make the cases complete. It was wonderful training for the men who had come from their business to the work of the League, and it developed some of Cincinnati Division's best operatives, who from that time on approached every assignment with enthusiasm and understanding.

Cincinnati Division supervised the parole of enemy aliens from Fort Oglethorpe and the Federal jail in this district. These paroled men, being released from prison, were ordered to report at the office of Cincinnati Division once each week. The day selected for them to report was Saturday morning. Failure on the part of a paroled man to report on the date set resulted in a prompt investigation. So thorough was this supervision that Cincinnati Division could at any time put its hands on these paroled men, whose ranks included actors, draughtsmen, electrical engineers, art glass designers, chefs, waiters, barbers, bakers, auto experts, laborers, machinists, farmers, and merchants.

Only one man refused to mend his ways and live up to the regulations. He is now at Fort Oglethorpe. When he first was released, he tried to induce the Federal authorities to give him permission to talk pro-German so he could "find others who were against this country," as he put it. He was informed by the Special Agent in charge of the Cincinnati office, Department of Justice, that he could do better work by telling all his former associates how foolish they were, trying to work for the Kaiser in this country. He had claimed that his prison term had changed his opinion and that now he was "for the United States." He was instructed to tell this to his friends as he would thereby be doing more good. His term of freedom did not last long, for he was soon at his old tricks again. He was interned for the "duration of the war."

After the German campaign against conscription in this country had fallen flat, the active propagandists looked for new fields for their malicious and insidious work. The notorious German propaganda alliance known as "The People's Council," newly formed in New York, was in its infancy when word of its activities was brought to Cincinnati by an advocate of the single tax, who up to that time had been considered an extremist, but honest in intention. He became associated with a certain Cincinnatian, American born of German descent, an attorney of some reputation. These two men contemplated organizing in Cincinnati a branch of The People's Council.

From the beginning, the League was represented at both the private and secret meetings of the Council, which, for a time, were held in the attorney's office, where four or five gathered; but as new recruits were enrolled by the Council and larger quarters were required, they were transferred to an office in Odd Fellow's Temple occupied by a former minister, a Socialist radical, a man whose career marked him as an advocate of extreme measures, and who carried with him a considerable following which he had organized several years before. Pacifism was the big keynote of its original platform. Without interference, however, the speakers became bold. The intellectuals who enlisted under its banner included a leading Sinn Feiner, a professor of a well-known college of Cincinnati, who was chairman, a pastor of the Lutheran Church, and, of course, the attorney and organizer.

It was the day of the original Espionage Act, and it was difficult under this unamended Act to find violations; but some of the speeches rang with treasonable utterances. After months of this sort of thing, the Bureau of Investigation, Department of Justice, decided it was time to act. A meeting had been called for Friday night, at the office of the former pastor, at which many things were expected to happen, and on that night it was decided to make a search, not only of the meeting place, but of the homes of the leaders. The District Attorney asked every man present — League operatives, agents of the Department of Justice, deputy United States Marshals, and local police detectives who had been assigned to the work, to set their watches with his. At 8:30 o'clock prompt, the search, under due warrant of law, was made in all parts of the city, and the papers and documents which were brought to the office of the United States Attorney made it impossible forever after for The People's Council to carry on its nefarious activities.

From that day Cincinnati was rid of openly organized anti-government activities. Some of the papers found, proved of great value to the Government. A special solicitor from the office of the Attorney General at Washington was assigned to Cincinnati to go over these papers, and the information which he gathered was of great use in many other cities. As a result of this search, the professor who had taken such an important part in the work of The People's Council was censured by his Board, and eliminated from the local theatre of activities.

The case of The People's Council was one of the high spots in the work of Cincinnati Division, American Protective League, and the record in this case is one of which it can well be proud. Later, the former pastor, much to the regret of Cincinnati Division, was taken in hand by citizens of Kentucky for special treatment. His experience on that dark night in the foot-hills of Kentucky evidently broke his spirit enough to dishearten him. He is no longer a factor in Bolshevism in Cincinnati.

After the reorganization of Cincinnati Division had been effected, to conform to the new plan of the National Directors, Chief Gerson J. Brown decided that it would be good policy to keep in close touch with the fifteen hundred male enemy aliens in Hamilton County. Accordingly, after fully considering the matter, he organized the Enemy Alien Bureau. The operatives were instructed as to all regulations governing these aliens, so that they could give advice whenever called upon by their charges, who did not know just what the Government expected of them. All delinquents were taken to the office of the Marshal by American Protective League members and made to complete their registration. Following out their instructions, American Protective League members fully explained to the aliens the object of their visit and just what their privileges were under the regulations. In a majority of the cases, it was found that the alien really had never fully understood what the Government regulations were.

Many peculiar situations were found. In several cases it developed that aliens, who had passes issued by the Marshal permitting them to go to their places of employment and return by the most direct route, lived above the store in which they worked. Arrangements were made with the Marshal whereby these men, when found worthy, were given permits entitling them to enjoy more privileges. Others were found who went direct to their work, and on returning in the evening, feared to go out of the house. Others would not go to church, fearful that they would be arrested and interned.

There were also cases of men who were in business which made it necessary to go into zones not mentioned in their permits. Many other odd cases, too numerous to mention, were found. All were taken up separately with the Marshal, and where the League records showed that the alien was trying to obey the regulations, necessary permits were issued.

There were found by American Protective League operatives aliens who wanted to become citizens but who did not know what to do. Others had tried to pass examinations in court, but failed. All these were sent to citizenship schools and now are on the road to becoming desirable citizens. The work of the Bureau has been such that many aliens now have a different opinion of what it means to live in a country where all men who behave themselves have an equal chance. In one day, after citizenship schools were opened in Cincinnati, the Enemy Alien Bureau issued over two hundred permits to aliens who desired to gain knowledge which would permit them to apply for the necessary papers.

This close supervision also forestalled attempts by agents of the Kaiser to induce aliens to commit acts against this Government, if they were so inclined. No meetings could be held without an American Protective League member hearing of it, as they visited the alien at his home and place of employment at irregular intervals, and never less than once a month.

After the war, there will be many, now classed as enemy aliens, who will thank Cincinnati Division for having helped them at a critical time when they were floundering about under regulations which they did not understand, and feared to ask anyone how to become loyal citizens of this country. Of the many curious cases Cincinnati handled, we may report at least one, which shows how well the A. P. L. sometimes took care of a man who didn't deserve it.

An emergency telephone call came to the office of the American Protective League from an official of one of the largest trust companies in the city, to send an operative to the bank as quickly as possible. The two men who answered the call found they had what appeared to be a German agent in prospect.

During the afternoon a telegram came to the bank from the Empire Trust Company, New York, authorizing it to place $25,000 to the credit of Frank K———. K———, on his arrival at the bank, seemed to be a man about fifty-five years of age, typically German, with all the Hindenburg ear-marks. An over-anxiety to display his naturalization papers in proving his identity led the bank officials to put him off until they had been able to communicate with the League. He had given his room number at the Gibson Hotel, and with this information in hand and a code message to the New York Division to investigate at that end, the scene shifted to the hotel.

His room was searched but absolutely nothing was found that could possibly throw light on the use he intended to make of the money, or the purpose of his visit to Cincinnati. He was "covered" that night by operatives of the League, and on the following day was taken to the office of the Special Agent in charge, and there questioned for two hours, without his disclosing anything of importance. K——— finally told his story, and from this point on the plot quickly unravels.

He was born near Hanover, Germany, emigrated to America at the age of sixteen, settled in New York, married, and was naturalized at the age of twenty-two. Three children blessed his union. He was a stone-mason by trade for ten years after his marriage; then he entered the contracting line and continued in it for some eighteen years, later removing to East Orange, N. J., where for some five years he operated a saloon and road house, later retiring from business and removing to West Hoboken, N. J.

After a severe siege of rheumatism, he was ordered by his physician to Mount Clemens, Michigan, early in the spring of 1918. At that resort he came in contact with two very affable gentlemen, "Fred B. Grant" and "Jack Connel." They made a lavish display of wealth and finally were successful in getting him to ask where these large amounts came from, whereupon Grant, who was the spokesman of the two, told K——— he was a wealthy coal operator of West Virginia and that he had a special system of playing the races. After taking K——— behind one of the buildings at Mount Clemens, he swore him to secrecy, and "let him in" on his get-rich-quick plan.

The party left Mount Clemens and went to the Vendome Hotel, Newport, Ky. They took K——— to a supposed pool-room and in less than a week he had won upwards of twenty-five thousand dollars in bets, whereupon the proprietor of the pool-room told him that he could not withdraw this money, under the laws of the State of Kentucky, unless he had an equal amount on deposit in the State. K——— told his daughter in Hoboken that he must have twenty-five thousand dollars to complete a business deal. He put up some of the money himself, and she secured the rest by a loan from the Empire Trust Co. Again the shuttle moved back to Cincinnati, where he arrived on Monday, August 5, 1918, and the League came to his rescue. K——— was now convinced that he was marked for a victim, and he did all he could to help land his supposed friends. All these were taken and the prisoners were held in $15,000 bond. They were notorious confidence men!

The pool-room was found with its complete telephone and telegraph outfit, which was not connected with any outside line. The money which Kaiser saw in this pool-room was paper cut from a New York Telephone directory to the size of a dollar bill. This paper was placed in stacks of probably four or five inches thick, with a hundred dollar bill placed on top and a hundred dollar bill on the bottom. The "money" lay around in great profusion. K——— stated with bulging eyes that he saw "at least a million dollars in this room." At least, the A. P. L. saved him $25,000 by taking him for a Cincinnati German spy!

CHAPTER IX

THE STORY OF DAYTON

Aircraft-Center Well Cared For—Midnight and All's Well—Some Stories of the A. P. L. and the Melting Pot—Possible and Impossible Citizens.

The thriving city of Dayton, Ohio, is one of the best known towns of the size in the Union. In some way the idea has gone abroad that Dayton is up-to-date, modern and advanced alike in industrial, civic and social ways. There surely is no reason to alter that belief from the story of the A. P. L. turned in from Dayton. An additional interest attaches to the report from this industrial capital because of the fact that it has always been a sort of a capital of industrial enterprise, and has been known as one of the points of manufacture of Government aeroplane material.

The large foreign element gave rise to 661 disloyalty cases and made necessary 269 instances of persuasiveness in Liberty Bond matters. For the War Department there were handled 1,681 slacker cases and 1,078 other cases under the Selective Service Act, with 387 cases of deserters and 241 character and loyalty examinations. The total number of investigations was 6,118. Many of the local " case stories " show that Ohio still has her claim to be called a center of pro-German sentiment, but the A. P. L. did fine work in the reclamation of such citizen material as was worth reclaiming — some of it was not worth while. The American Protective League has been the best and almost the first real Immigration Board this country ever knew, and the one great need of America to-day is a wise and wholly fearless combing out of the aliens.

Mr. George S. Blanchard was first Chief of the Dayton Division. In the early days of April, 1917, he was talking with a friend from St. Louis and during the conversation asked him what he was doing toward the progress of the big war. His friend replied that he had gone into the American Protective League, which had just been organized in St. Louis. The remark set him to thinking that probably an organization of this kind could be effected in Dayton. The League at that time was in a very primitive state. That is to say, the desire to assist the Department of Justice was there, but neither the League nor the Department of Justice had yet been able to work out the best method by which inexperienced citizens could assist in Federal investigations. Mr. Blanchard visited the divisions of the League at Columbus, Ohio, Chicago, San Francisco, New York City and other places, and called a number of times for conferences at National Headquarters. The mode of conducting operations as determined by experience and observation of the work carried out by other divisions and as directed by National Headquarters was as follows: Alien Enemy; Pro-German; Draft Board Matters; Vice and Liquor; Military Coöperation; Food and Fuel; Suburban; War Risk Allotments; Headquarters; Flying Squadron; Character Investigations.

The general direction of the work was made by the Chief. The work was then carried out by ten different divisions, each governed by a Captain with as many Lieutenants and operatives as his work demanded. Later came the general division of all workers into two classes — Investigation and Information. The captains, lieutenants and active members were taken from the investigators. In October, 1918, Mr. Blanchard resigned as Chief of the Dayton Division to enlist in the Motor Transport Corps of the United States Army, being succeeded by Mr. Frank Schwilk, who carried on the work very successfully.

During a war drive, an operative, No. 161, called on a Mr. B———, who had refused absolutely to give a cent, although financially able to contribute. Operative reports: I questioned him as to why he would not give, and he replied:

"Why should I give? I don't live here anyhow. My body belongs to God and He told me not to give."

"That's all right," replied the operative, "but you have citizenship here, have you not?"

"No. I vote in Heaven. You can take me and place me in jail, but Christ will take care of me."

"If the Germans came down the street and were about

to strike down your children and take away your wife, what would you do, — sit down and allow it?"

"I could not raise a hand against them because God tells me not to strike my enemies, so the Germans could do as they saw fit."

"Religious crank — what's the use?" asks the operative.

An old man and his wife, both German, were reported to the A. P. L. one day last summer as being pro-German and Lieutenant No. 177 was assigned to the case. He called on the old couple and found them very German indeed — so much so, in fact, that their niece was produced to act as interpreter. The old man, when he realized the object of the visit, became greatly agitated, and trembling like an aspen leaf, he hurriedly produced his naturalization papers and protested that three times had he foresworn the Kaiser. At last, as final proof of loyalty to his adopted land, the old man displayed some sheets of manuscript — gospel songs, which he himself had written in his mother tongue! At this point his wife, who had been as distressed as her husband over the interview, could restrain herself no longer.

"Ach no!" she spluttered. "No! Ve are not Chermans. Ve are not Chermans! Ve are Christians! Ve are Christians!"

Operative No. 113 reports the details of a case which has in it endless possibilities of mischief:

> There was held in Dayton, Ohio, during the summer of 1918, the national meeting of Automotive Engineers, and at the A. P. L. luncheon that day it was reported that a German from a nearby city, who was an associate member of the Automotive Engineers, was registered in Dayton and would attend the meetings of the convention. From the history we had of this gentleman from the files of the A. P. L., he was undoubtedly a dangerous citizen and one who should not have the opportunity of inspecting and carefully examining the Liberty Motors and many other new ideas which were being shown at the convention. I offered to investigate the situation, took the information which was in our hands, got in touch with the head of the Aircraft Production Board here and was immediately sent to the convention, where I conferred with the Secretary, explaining to him in detail the facts. We found that our man was not registered at the convention, and we made arrangements with the registrar that as soon

as he made his appearance, some one should shadow him and see that he did not have access to any information or special displays, and that he should be kept under surveillance during his entire time in our city. I knew where he was stopping and kept him under surveillance. We frustrated any plan he might have had to gain confidential information. All this was done without his having any idea that anyone knew his history or his reason for coming to the convention.

One of the most interesting cases investigated was that of two families, Mr. A. and Mr. B., who lived on the same street. Mr. A. died, leaving one son of draft age, the main support of his mother. He filed no exemption claim, was inducted into the United States Army, and is now serving in France. In the family of Mr. B., father and mother were both living, both born in Germany. They had a son of draft age, who was inducted into the United States Army and sent to Camp Sherman, where he stayed for three months and was then discharged because of flat feet. He came home and went to work at his trade as a plumber. Mr. B., Sr., owned the house wherein the widow of A. lived, and immediately upon the return of B., Jr., proceeded to raise the widow's rent and put her out of the house. The Red Cross had been paying the widow's rent, but finally legal notice was served allowing her ten days in which to vacate the house.

An A. P. L. operative took the matter up with a local attorney and arranged for the protection of the widow in case force should be used to eject her; he then called on Mr. B., Sr., again and began praising him regarding his success in life, his unusual ability, and so on. He finally asked him this question:

"Mr. B., if you were in America and your mother in Germany, and some one were annoying and abusing her and trying to force her out in the street, what would you do?"

"I would fight," he said.

Then the operative reversed the question and cited the other young man who was fighting for his country, and some one trying to put his mother out into the street. Mr. B. silently looked down at his feet and then said:

"You have proven to me my great mistake. I have done

wrong and am going to make everything right." He dismissed his case in court, apologized to the widow, and from all recent observation, is trying to be a truly American citizen.

Another operative reports:

During the spring of 1918 there were rumors in the city of Dayton that Mr. B———, a hardware merchant, American born but of German parentage, was very pro-German in his talk and attitude, and as I had known the man for some years, I made it a point to get his viewpoint as to the war and his opinion regarding the United States entering the war. Mr. B——— was very guarded in everything he said, but would always intimate just enough to arouse the anger of a good American citizen, and while he would not make any statements that could be considered as absolutely unpatriotic or dangerous, yet it was evident that at heart he was pro-German and was quietly spreading propaganda in favor of Germany. I talked to him until I found that I was getting a little too warm around the collar and would have to move on. One morning I was quite interested when B——— advised me that he was going to enter a certain Officers' Training Camp and would leave on a certain fixed date, two weeks later. I pumped him as well as I could to get all the facts, which within an hour's time I communicated to headquarters. The information was communicated to headquarters of the Officers' Training Camp and B——— was advised by the proper officer that he need not report. What reason they gave him I did not know!

I called on B——— about a week later and expressed to him my surprise that he was still here and asked why he had not gone to camp. He replied that he was too busy to get away and would wait until a later period. This excuse, of course, was all right with me, but he did not know that some one had been on his trail and kept him from becoming well acquainted with the inside workings of training camp activities, and removed the possibility of his slipping across his German propaganda.

Dayton sends in another story, worth pondering and remembering by every American. This book is written for Americans. The story will show what other races we sometimes harbor. The man's name is given.

Captains No. 145 and No. 245 were given an assignment

entitled "Frank Weiss, alien enemy; Refusal to Register." The story, as told by them, is as follows:

Having been informed that Weiss was a dangerous character, we proceeded to his place of employment and asked for an interview, which was granted by the superintendent of the concern. We found Weiss busily engaged at his work, told him our business and were informed that we could "go to" so far as he was concerned, that he had not registered and did not intend to do so, although he had been given seven days in which to make up his mind or go to jail. We did not argue the question with him but immediately took him before the Special Agent in charge of the Department of Justice, Harold L. Scott. Mr. Scott asked him what his objection was to registering with his Local Board, as the law required, to which Weiss answered:

"I have registered with the police and that is sufficient. I'm not a citizen of this country. I'm a subject of the Kaiser, and there's one thing sure—after this war is over, I'm sure going to leave this country. I've thought it all over and that's what I'm going to do."

U. S. Marshal Devanney happened to be present and explained to Weiss that the best thing for him to do was to register, telling him that he did not blame him for maintaining his allegiance to his own country; that he admired a man always for doing what he thought was right, but that he must conform to the laws of this country governing alien enemies.

All through the interview, Weiss's attitude was one of defiance, but he thought the matter over for a few minutes and then stated that he was willing to register with the Local Board. He was escorted to the Board by No. 145 and the Chairman asked:

"Mr. Weiss, where do you work and what salary do you earn?"

"I work at B——— Machine Company and get eighty-five cents an hour; with overtime I make $100.00 per week."

"Making such a salary as that, Mr. Weiss, don't you think you owe this country something? You could not possibly earn that much money in one week in Germany, could you?"

"No," replied Weiss, "but I'm a skilled mechanic and that's what they pay in this country, and I'm entitled to it."

"Yes," replied the Chairman, "but in view of the fact that this country affords you such good wages and allows you to send your children to the public schools, don't you think it your duty to at least comply with all the laws governing alien enemies such as you?"

To this Weiss made no reply, but by constant questioning the questionnaire was finally filled out and Weiss was asked to "swear" to it, to which he replied:

"I will take no oath. I do not believe in a God, and refuse to recognize him in any way whatsoever."

His convictions in this matter were respected. He was allowed to affirm, and was then taken to the Miami County jail. After his incarceration it developed that two of Weiss's children were living with a Mrs. Smith in Dayton, Ohio—two bright little girls—and that there would have to be some provision made for them, as Mrs. Smith was simply boarding the children and was unable to keep them unless their board was paid. Mrs. Smith wrote a letter to Weiss setting forth the facts, to which he replied that she should "take the children to the office of the United States Marshal and leave them there."

Mrs. Smith brought the children to the office of the United States Marshal, who made arrangements with the Juvenile Court to place the children in the Orphans' Home, where they were to be cared for until Weiss was released. Weiss was arrested on October 24, 1918, and on account of good behavior, was granted a parole on November 14 and was released from the Miami County jail on December 5, 1918. Immediately upon being granted his freedom, after having complied with all the rules and regulations governing his parole, he went to the Juvenile Court and obtained release papers for his two children, who were confined in the Orphans' Home, the Judge of the Juvenile Court having been notified that Weiss's behavior since his incarceration had been first-class and it was thought that he really had a change of heart. But it was the same old story of "Kamerad! Kamerad!" As soon as Weiss had obtained the release papers for his two children he presented himself at the institution where they were being cared for and demanded them immediately.

"They are in school now," replied Mrs. Hartrum, Matron of the Home, "but will be dismissed in about twenty minutes. Won't you be seated and wait for them?"

"No," he replied, "I'm tired of this damned dirty red tape. I want them right now."

Pauline, the office girl, hearing Weiss's remark and fearing trouble for the teacher, ran to the school and related what she had heard, so that in case Weiss came to the school to demand the children, the teacher would be prepared for him. Pauline was right, as Weiss refused to wait for the coming of his children and left Mrs. Hartrum, going to the school and demanding that the children be turned over to him immediately. He was told that school was just being dismissed and that he should wait at the door for the children and could get them as they came out. When he at last obtained possession of the children he took them toward the Home and was met at the gate by Pauline, who told him that Mrs. Hartrum had requested that he bring the children in that she might change their clothes, as they were wearing the uniform of the Home. Weiss struck at Pauline, saying: "I'll knock you down and slap your face if you don't keep still."

Pauline rushed into the house to tell Mrs. Hartrum and Weiss followed closely behind her.

"I want my children and I want them now," said Weiss.

"You can have them as soon as I take them to their room and change their clothes," replied Mrs. Hartrum.

"You will not take them from this room. I'm G—— d——d tired of this red tape business, I'm not going to wait, and don't you dare to take these children from this office."

Mrs. Hartrum replied that she would take them to their room and change their clothes and then bring them back. Whereupon Weiss pushed Mrs. Hartrum backwards and she fell into a chair, her head striking a table nearby, and he then struck her as she lay on the floor, took his children and hurried down the street to a Fifth Street car.

Mrs. Hartrum screamed. Her cries were heard by an attendant in the yard, who came to her assistance, but Weiss had fled. The attendant got into an automobile and followed the street car, and when Weiss alighted uptown with his children, he was arrested by the traffic policeman, the story of Weiss having been previously related to him by the attendant.

Weiss was taken to police headquarters, the proper authorities were notified, and after a thorough investigation his parole was annulled and he was again committed to the Federal jail. Investigation showed that Weiss was really an anarchist at heart, and on the same day the assault was committed upon Mrs. Hartrum, the following advertisement appeared in the Dayton Journal:

> WANTED—Dayton men and women out of work to send names and addresses to FRANK WEISS, Post Office Box 387, to form a union to get Justice to make the American workman's home a decent place to live in.

A few days later the good word came to us that Weiss had been interned at Fort Oglethorpe until after the war, and will be deported at that time.

If a few hundred thousand more went with Herr Weiss, this country would be yet better off. His attitude is not unusual — America is simply a place for making easy money, but Germany is the real place for a man! How should we feel about letting in a few hundred thousands of the recently demobilized German army? It is reported in the European despatches that many of them are planning to come to America as soon as possible. The ablest publicists of the day agree that American immigration must be sharply restricted. Some extremists believe that practically all immigration should be stopped for a term of ten years.

CHAPTER X

THE STORY OF DETROIT

History of the Great Munition City—Clock-Like Mechanism of A. P. L.—How the War Plants were Protected—Guarding the Neck of the Great Lakes Bottle.

It often has been said that the shipping of the Great Lakes, all of which passes through the Detroit River, is greater in annual tonnage than that which goes through the Suez Canal or the Panama Canal. A continual procession of ore ships and carriers of other freight passes by the water front of Detroit, going and coming on the clear, blue, rapid flood of the river which may be called the "neck of the bottle" of the Great Lakes.

Obviously, such a situation, collecting the riches of an empire, is one offering its own purely geographical menace. An unwatched enemy could sit on Detroit River front and destroy untold billions in property in the course of a month. But no such enemy did any such thing in this war.

Speaking of Detroit itself, without reference to its geographical situation, it is to be said that it had as many munition contracts as any city in the United States — Detroit contracts for war material and munitions ran over $400,000,000. These great war plants attracted the attention of men hostile to this country. No one can tell how much harm was wished against such enterprises by aliens who only awaited their opportunity. The point is that this twenty miles of water front of Detroit, these miles of railroad tracks for switching facilities, these many great buildings where manufacturing went on, were kept free from any destructive enemy activity. That is a great story of itself, and far greater than it would have been had it to record some great disaster — interesting and thrilling, but none the less a disaster. Detroit had no disasters. Instead, it had the A. P. L.

Detroit division began operations in the Spring of 1917,

and at first was financed by the payment of a one dollar initiation fee by each member. This continued until December, 1917, when it was seen that this division could not go on unless better financed. A meeting of officers of prominent manufacturers of Detroit was held, and these assured the division better quarters and competent finances. A committee went to Washington to see the Attorney General, with the result that the offices of the Department of Justice and those of the League were established close together.

Mr. Fred M. Randall, the first Chief, resigned in May, 1918, and was replaced by Mr. Frank H. Croul, former Commissioner of Police, who took the oath of Chief not only for Detroit but also for the County of Wayne. He started in by reorganizing the work.

Since the Detroit contracts for war material were so enormous — Detroit claims they were greater in volume than for any other city in the country — a division was organized under the name "Plants Protection Department." A thorough covering of each plant was made and a captain of the A. P. L. was stationed in each factory, where he had entire supervision and reported direct to the Plants Protection Department at the League's main office. That this system worked well may be shown by the records. Detroit was practically free of any destruction of war material. Several attempts to blow up plants were frustrated. It was not unusual for a man to be brought in from the plants for an interview, and many such cases were turned over to the Department of Justice and District Attorney's office. The dynamiter and other alien enemies were held down hitless.

A Pro-German Department was organized with captains, lieutenants and operatives under charge of an Inspector. The Inspector assigned all complaints, took all reports and returned them to the Record Department where the original papers were attached, and then forwarded them to the Pro-German Committee room where they were examined and passed upon.

A third department was called the Selective Service, its work being to attend to the local boards of Detroit, of which there were twenty-seven, exclusive of those in the district and Wayne County. A unique manner of handling delinquents was inaugurated — and why all states did not adopt the same system is a mystery. This bureau was kept open to receive delinquents twenty-four hours a day and handled thousands of draft cases.

Department No. 4 handled all personal cases, such as applicants for war service or for commissions. Department No. 5 had the soldiers' allotment cases. The last of the departments was the Emergency. This department held a group of experienced and reliable operatives who held themselves in readiness to obey any call, whether during business hours or in the cold, gray dawn. Four shifts were worked by squads, six hours each, so that no matter what time a telephone rang there was someone on the desk. Emergency Department was of great service to the local draft boards, from whose shoulders A. P. L. took all the responsibility. It very often apprehended men who were ready to make a quick getaway.

In connection with Plants Protection work, there was a system whereby the plant sent to the main office each day a personnel card saying that such and such a man had applied for employment, that he had registered in such and such a town and that his classification was as shown on the card. Then the central office would write to the man's local board asking about him. If he was wanted, a complaint was made out against him and the Emergency squad was ordered to locate him and take him at once to the Bureau of Delinquents. The number of daily notices sent in by different boards all through the United States several times ran into three figures.

Often the Department of Justice would want emergency help to cover a suspect who was on his way to Detroit under charge of some D. J. agent. Detroit operatives would meet the train and keep surveillance until the party left the city. In the matter of raids on dance halls and theatres for evaders and slackers, the Emergency Division also gave great assistance to the police. It often took to the central headquarters hundreds of men who could not show proper credentials.

A. P. L. Detroit Division took under charge also the tremendous tonnage of the Detroit River. Operators boarded every boat going up or down the river, and each man on that boat was examined as to his credentials and citizenship. A man might be allowed to go on his trip under guarantee of the captain, but in the meantime if there was any doubt the wires were kept hot further along the Lakes to see if the man was wanted. Several were apprehended in this way at ports of call on information furnished by Detroit.

Another A. P. L. custom was to investigate each actor's card as he appeared at any theatre, and if there was any doubt, wire his board giving his description and asking for his status. Several alien actors were landed in that way — who were bad actors. They could not get away because they were booked. A. P. L. never waited, but always was on hand at the first performance of a company. These investigations furnished several theatrical men for Uncle Sam's Army.

The division worked to protect the Government and to protect the people also. There were a number of cases where a man and wife were reconciled; where a man and woman had been living together without marriage and where a marriage was performed; where a soldier's dependents were in destitute circumstances and did not get the allotment. Domestic tragedies such as these ran into hundreds, and quite often the division was able to straighten them out. Many a man was considered a slacker who had tried every means of getting into the Army. Many a man looked healthy, though the Army regulations disqualified him. Such men were, as a rule, sensitive as to their physical condition. The division made things clearer and made them easier in many cases.

There were many ways in which the division proved itself useful on a common-sense and practical business basis. For instance, a soldier, gone to France, left his home in charge of a friend who had agreed to rent it, keep up the improvements, and so on. A. P. L. found that the friend had collected the rent for months, but did not keep up the improvements and did not pay the taxes. It was found he had collected several hundred dollars and had not paid out anything. He happened to own a house of his own, so he mortgaged that and paid over the money he had collected. A. P. L. arranged with one of the banks to act as trustee for the soldier. The taxes were paid and the rents are now being placed to the credit of the soldier. If it had not been for the A. P. L., the soldier would have found his property badly depreciated on his return.

This gives the barest, and, indeed, a most vague idea of the many and well-organized activities of this division. As a machine of protection it was deadly efficient. No place in the country had more to lose than had Detroit. It was a vulnerable point. It was the armor and weapons, offensive and defensive, of the A. P. L. which guarded it. The manufacturers of Detroit furnished cash for the A. P. L. The individual citizens of Detroit did not pay a cent, nor did the United States Government. Recognizing this unselfish work of thousands of its citizens, the Detroit Patriotic Fund Committee in July, 1918, made an unsolicited grant of sufficient funds to keep the division going for another year.

Detroit Division had a total of 30,056 complaints entered on the files. Of members there were enrolled in all 3,903. To each of these in good standing there was given an engraved testimonial, his sole pay for months of time given free to his country:

> THE WAYNE COUNTY DIVISION presents this testimonial to .... in appreciation of your volunteer enlistment, as a member without remuneration, for the assignment to any duties that might arise in connection with the requirements of the Government for the duration of the Great War. We especially desire to thank you for your patriotic services in making this Division so valuable an adjunct to the general success attained by the Organization during the strenuous period just passed.
>
> FRANK H. CROUL, Chief.

The total of 30,056 investigations were distributed as follows:

Department of Justice cases: Alien enemy activities, male 500, female 400, total 900; Espionage Act, disloyalties and sedition, 2,000; sabotage, 1,000; anti-military, etc., 250; propaganda, (a) word of mouth, 5,000, (b) printed matter, 25, total, 5,025; radical organizations, I. W. W., People's Council, etc., 100; bribery, 150; naturalization applicants, 550; impersonating officers, 25; other investigations, 1,000, total, 1,575; total Department of Justice cases, 11,000.

War Department cases: Counter-espionage for Military Intelligence, 800; Selective Service Regulations, 15,756; work or fight order, 300; character and loyalty, (a) civilian applicants for overseas, 500, (b) applicants for commissions, 400, total 900; camp desertions and absent without leave, 600; total, 18,356.

Other branches of the Government: Food and Fuel Administrations, 200; Treasury Department, War Risk insurance allotments, etc., 500. Grand total of investigations listed January 1, 1919, 30,056.

Detroit Division assisted the Bureau of Delinquents and the Police Department in several raids for slackers at which about 5,000 or 6,000 men were examined for registration cards. Those who had registered and qualified are not included above. They would number about 5,000 more. The division also gave material assistance to the police and fire departments, especially during the armistice days, when from four hundred to five hundred operatives were on special duty.

It would be rather bootless to delve deep into the individual records of a city where the totals are so large, but a few of the Detroit cases might be given in passing. One of these had to do with an alleged attempt of a draft board official to obtain money from a registrant for keeping him out of the service. That complaint came in at noon. By four o'clock of the same afternoon Lieutenant No. 610 had the facts. That was Saturday, and Monday was Armistice Day. Tuesday morning the matter came up before a judge of the Federal Court. A thirteen months' sentence at Leavenworth penitentiary was imposed the third day after the complaint came in.

This accuation was that a clerk, S. W——— (the name is unpronounceable) of Board No. 6 had told a registrant, G———, apparently of the same nationality as himself, that for a certain sum he would keep him out of the draft. He was to appear between noon and one o'clock on November 9 and make the payment. Operative says he told G———'s employers to pay him the nine dollars due him, and he took the numbers of the bills. "I told G——— to come with me to Local Board No. 6," he says, "and see this clerk whose name I did not know, and if he took the money to report to me on the first floor of the building. In the meantime I informed one of the members of our Delinquent Board of my intentions, with a view to forestalling any later accusation that the money had been 'planted' by the clerk. In a little while G——— appeared and said he had paid the money to the clerk, who demanded that he bring in some more money the following Monday, as that was not enough. I then went to Local Board No. 6 with G———, who pointed out this clerk as the one who had taken the money. I took this clerk into a side room, accompanied by the others. He acknowledged he had the money and that it had been given him by G———. I told him to turn it over to a member of the Board of Delinquents, and we verified the bills with the description and numbers on the list already made out. I then took the suspect to the Special Agent's office, where we obtained a signed confession from him. He was taken before the District Attorney and held for the grand jury. The grand jury met November 11 at 2:00 P. M. and returned an indictment. On Tuesday morning he was arraigned before the judge, pleaded guilty, and was sentenced to Leavenworth penitentiary."

Detroit had an interesting alien enemy case in that of Fred G———, escaped petty officer of the Germany Navy who had been working in Detroit for six months under the name of Walter B———. He was an attendant in a sanitarium and somehow seemed a little worth suspicion, although nothing he said could be looked on as much out of the way. The man who reported the case was used as a stool pigeon. At length they met in a hotel under the pretense of an invention which would be useful to any one of the nations in the war. A dictaphone was put in the room where they were to meet, and four A. P. L. operatives were in the next room at the other end of the instrument. There were three such meetings, and finally sufficient evidence was secured to warrant D. J. in arresting the man. The final play was made the next Saturday night, when he was arrested at the hotel and locked up until Monday. This man had first papers issued to him under the name of Walter B———, as a Hollander, and when brought before D. J. on Monday, he maintained that he was a Hollander and had left home at an early age owing to brutal treatment from his father. After one and a half hours' work he finally broke down and gave up his story. He admitted that his real name was Fred

G———, that he was in the German Navy and had been on the commerce raider *Emden* when that ship was driven with several others into Guam by the Japanese fleet. He was taken sick and transferred to Mare Island, California, after internment. After his recovery in California he escaped, he said, by swimming the channel to the mainland. He began to beat his way on freight trains to various parts of the country. He was employed in New York for a time as messenger in a bank. Then he drifted to Detroit, worked at various occupations in automobile factories, etc., and was a motorman on the street cars. This man finally opened up and gave the Department of Justice a line of information which, had the war continued longer, would have proved of the greatest importance. He was ordered interned by the United States Government. In this case the division was able to see the actual results of its work. There have been many other cases which might have turned out as well in the dénouement, but this one seemed to begin with nothing and ended with good and visible results.

CHAPTER XI

THE STORY OF ST. LOUIS

How the Pro-German Was Kept Mild—Sober and Well-Considered Methods—A Big Secret Code Puzzle—Business As Usual.

The summaries for St. Louis tell the same story of patient and indefatigable loyalty, resolved to hold America strictly American. The St. Louis story is modest, straightforward and convincing. It is given in substance as written by the Chief, Mr. G. H. Walker.

The St. Louis division was organized on April 3, 1917. The initial organization was composed of sixteen companies, organized each under a captain and lieutenants, divided into professional, commercial and industrial groups, so as to embrace all fields of activity. Only dependable and loyal men were taken into these companies, which ranged in size numerically from fifty to one hundred and twenty-five each. The business and financial interests of St. Louis responded generously to the plan and made possible the marked success that always attended the division.

Captains, lieutenants and operatives from the outset were required only to use their eyes and ears and to send in their reports, through their appropriate superiors, to Mr. G. H. Walker, the Chief of the division, who in turn submitted such reports to the Special Agent in Charge, Department of Justice, at St. Louis. It became evident in the summer months of 1917, from the increasing number and variety of reports sent in, that the facilities of the Bureau of Investigation were wholly inadequate, and that the investigating forces of the Bureau would require enlargement unless the St. Louis Division of the American Protective League itself undertook active investigation of its reports, thus relieving the Bureau to that extent. It was the same old story of the breaking down of a most important branch of the Government, and the prompt, patriotic rallying of our American citizens in support.

The decision was made, involving the opening of a suite of offices and the enrollment of a number of competent volunteers who could give their time to this work. Concurrently with making this decision, which meant so much more work, the St. Louis division undertook the formation of a geographic organization distinct from the company organizations, members of which were not only required to report all matters of interest through immediate superiors, but were also called upon from time to time for auxiliary investigation work in their respective neighborhoods. The district organization embraced twenty geographical divisions within St. Louis proper, there being from twenty-five to fifty operatives in each division, all of them responsible to a deputy inspector, who in turn was responsible to an inspector presiding over four districts. Four districts constituted a zone. St. Louis County, on the west, was similarly organized, as were East St. Louis and adjoining towns and villages in Illinois. In the summer of 1918, East St. Louis and considerable adjacent territory were separated from the St. Louis division and created into a distinct division, continuing, however, in close coöperation with the St. Louis division.

The increasing volume of work out of St. Louis headquarters required the active services of approximately fifty operatives, most of whom had abandoned their personal pursuits and were giving their entire time to the work of the League. In addition, two hundred and fifty men in the district organization were being called upon, more or less regularly, to undertake active investigations with respect to matters arising in their respective neighborhoods. The personnel of the organization was made up of loyal and self-sacrificing citizens in all walks of life. Much excellent service was rendered in investigations made at night by those who were unable to devote other time to the work. Each man did what he could.

Cases of intense and varying interest were arising daily to sustain the zeal of this large body of volunteers. One of the most interesting involved a letter, mailed in St. Louis March 17, 1917, to "Mr. W. Bernkong, Berlin, Germany," which found its way into the St. Louis headquarters and which appeared to be a code letter written in Greek characters and words. An inspection of this, and a close following through of the case in all the hands it reached, will give a reader some idea of the uncanny sureness of the United States government experts in deciphering any sort of blind communication that may come before them.

The average unskilled person could make little out of the original letter, which was worse than Greek. Interest in this puzzle deepened when it was discovered that, although written in Greek characters, Greek scholars to whom it was submitted were unable to translate it. It was ultimately sent to the War College in Washington, that House of Mystery, which in due time returned a German translation, revealing the fact that Greek letters had been adapted to the formation of German words. It might still have remained possible for the real secret of the letter to have been concealed in an unknown code — as one may learn by reference to the brief mention of ciphers and codes in an earlier chapter (See "Arts of the Operatives"). Therefore, a first-class mystery story, indeed the best detective story of all those the League chiefs have sent in, still remains for any wise doctor who can solve it. It is easier to write a "detective story" than it is to read a cipher and double code, because a story-writer knows his own answer, whereas in the other case, no one knows the real answer.

This letter had been stopped in transit in France a few days after the entrance of the United States into the Great War. There seemed to be some small hope of finding a clue to the author through advertising it as an undelivered letter. While this plan was under contemplation, however, a report reached headquarters, from an operative, to the effect that while soliciting Y. M. C. A. subscriptions in a St. Louis office building late at night, he had surprised a citizen of German origin, alone in his office, who appeared to be attempting to decipher a letter with the aid of two books, seemingly code books.

The letter was then advertised and two operatives were assigned to watch the appropriate window at the General Post Office. After a week's vigil, the clerk in charge beckoned to the operatives and pointed to the retreating figure of a woman of small stature, almost wholly enveloped in a black shawl, and informed them that she had inquired for the Bernkong letter. She had said that she was not the author but would be glad to pay any additional postage necessary to send it on its way. In the course of this explanation the woman had left the building and was lost in the crowd on the street. It therefore became necessary to continue the surveillance at the Post Office in the hope of the woman's return. Within a week she did reappear, late in the afternoon, and inquired for mail under the name of a Catholic Sister. It was learned that she had been receiving mail under this name for a considerable length of time. She was followed for a number of blocks and was seen to enter a large institution conducted as a girls' rooming house.

A woman operative of the St. Louis Division, American Protective League, that night, carrying a suit case, applied at the institution for a room, explaining that she had just arrived from a nearby city. She had a detailed description of the woman, but for a period of more than three weeks she was unable to find anybody in the place fitting the description. This woman operative was then also assigned to the Post Office, where, in due time, the woman reappeared.

The operative followed her to the institution, entering the door only a few moments behind her, and saw her enter a room on the second floor. A few minutes later the woman operative was surprised to see the suspect leave her room, wholly changed in appearance, the black shawl having been replaced by a dark sack suit and a black sailor hat. As the woman had that afternoon received a letter at the Post Office, it was suspected that, as a go-between, she would deliver this letter to some one. She left the building and boarded a street car. The woman operative entered a waiting automobile and followed. Again the mystery woman proved too elusive. The next morning the woman operative was up and on guard before daybreak and was enabled to trail the woman to a business establishment, where, it was learned, she was employed in clerical work. She was again dressed in the sack suit and black sailor hat, and apparently assumed the habit of a nun only upon inquiring at the Post Office for mail.

The most thorough inquiries failed to reveal any additional evidence indicating this woman's connection with enemy activities, or solve the dual character she was impersonating. It was ultimately determined to take her to the Bureau, where she might be thoroughly interrogated, which was done. Her explanations were simple but unsatisfying. However, there was no violation of the law with which she could be charged, and it was necessary to permit her to go. She moved to another hotel where the St. Louis division continued to keep her under surveillance, without, however, throwing any further light upon the mysterious letter. Other apparent clues were likewise run down in vain.

The letter bears every evidence of having been a serious attempt to communicate information of more or less value to the enemy and appears to permit of further decoding through the use of some additional cipher. It is by no means sure that the ultimate code for it will not be found by some expert government man in Washington. The world little knows what marvels of unraveling secrets is done in the Intelligence work of the Government. Always the battle goes on between those trying to make codes that cannot be read by an outsider and those who say they can master any code if given time. In any case, here is a fine detective story.

Little or no successful attempt was made by St. Louis Division to keep the organization's work a secret, and in a center so large, that always is a moot question. In the first place, any large operations, like raids and drives cannot be kept secret, and in the second place, the fear created by the thought of hidden regulators has proved a valuable deterrent, as has been shown countless times. In any case, months ago the local press was "playing up" the League in many stories that named it very frankly. Since that is true, some of the anecdotes collected may be given here.

A St. Louis German, with the boastfulness which fortunately offsets much of the cunning and industry of his species, bragged to his sweetheart that he was a member of the Imperial German Secret Service. Perhaps he showed her the card which German spies are not supposed to show. She, very proud, confided to a friend her lover's distinction. The friend went to one of the local officials of the American Protective League. She had four brothers in the service, three in the Army and one in the Navy, and said that if there was a German spy in the city the authorities should know it. Unfortunately, she had forgotten the man's name. The man's room was raided, and evidence was unearthed that he was not only an unregistered enemy alien, but indeed a German spy. In his trunk were found firearms of the German army. He was promptly interned. Perhaps no sweetheart should have a spy, and certainly no spy should have a sweetheart.

A German who predicted the defeat of the Allies before the United States entered the war, persisted in his harangues afterwards, until a League operative went to the bank where he worked. The man's dismissal resulted. He continued at times to return to the bank, assailing some of the young women clerks with abuse and threats because of their loyalty to America. He was arrested for violating his zone permit, which the United States Marshal had revoked when the bank's notice of his dismissal was filed. Later he was interned.

One night a party from the Naval recruiting office in St. Louis was seeking enlistments at a West End theater. Moving pictures were thrown on a screen and an officer made a speech, in which he declared: "The Germans went through Belgium and France like barbarians." A stout, well-dressed man in the audience exploded: "That's a damned lie!" Two sailors with revolvers sprang for him over the footlights, but the first to reach him were two members of the League, who, although they had gone to the theater only for amusement, had not forgotten their duties. After a sharp tussle the disturber was overpowered. He protested indignantly that he was an American citizen, but refused stubbornly to give any other information about himself. Borrowing an automobile, the League operatives and sailors took him to a police station and notified the Federal authorities. Search of the prisoner's effects showed that he was an unnaturalized German subject, though he had lived in the United States for fourteen years. He was interned for the duration of the war. Of such is the glorious Kingdom of Deutschland.

A client went to the office of his attorney, and after their business was concluded, tarried for a chat, in which he dropped the information that he had heard a pro-German say: "Every American child should have its neck wrung as soon as it is born. The German army could rule the United States better than Wilson — and it will, too." The lawyer obtained from him the name and address of the offender, and the names of witnesses who heard his remarks. After the client had gone, the attorney, being a member of the League, made out a report on a blank form supplied by the Department of Justice, and sent it to the Captain of his company, signing it with his number. The lawyer's duty ended here, for he belonged to one of the occupational units and was pledged to give information but not to investigate. The Captain took the report to League headquarters, where the officials approved it and sent it to the local office of the Department of Justice, Bureau of Information. It was O. K.'d there as a matter worth looking into, whereupon the League called upon its other arm, the investigators. They went out to obtain affidavits to corroborate the hearsay information first turned in by the lawyer. In this roundabout way was secured evidence to be placed before the Attorney General. You can never tell, even if you are a pro-German and have to spill over, when you are also going to spill, upset or overturn the legumes known in common parlance as the beans.

A naturalization department was organized on the initiative of the St. Louis office, which was followed in other divisions. On May 18, Congress repealed the law prohibiting the naturalization of aliens if they had filed declarations of intention not less than two or more than seven years before the United States entered the war. That is, citizenship was possible under these conditions, providing the applicant established his good moral character, his attachment to the Constitution, his belief in organized government, his ability to speak English and the genuineness of his wish to become a citizen and renounce forever all allegiance to any foreign Power. About eight hundred persons in the St. Louis district, according to local press data, sought to avail themselves of the opportunity provided by the new law. Their applications called for a thorough investigation in each case. This work the League volunteered to take off the shoulders of the Bureau of Naturalization. The inquiries put in the questionnaire are interesting as official tests of loyalty. The most important of them are as follows:

> Has applicant affiliated himself directly or indirectly with any organization or propaganda in any way opposed to the position taken by the United States in regard to the war, or with known or suspected agents of the enemy?
>
> Has applicant at any time expressed his approval of (a) the invasion of France and Belgium? (b) the sinking of the Lusitania? and (c) the general conduct of the war by Germany? If so, when, where and in whose hearing?
>
> Has applicant been opposed to (a) the United States' entry into the war? (b) acts of the United States in conducting the war (c) shipping munitions to France and England? (d) the draft? (e) Liberty loans?

Can all the foreign-born or foreign-descended citizens of the United States swear before God that they are fit to gain or to retain their citizenship under a test like that?

A St. Louis journal, in commenting on the work of the American Protective League in that city, gave a rather interesting summary of the growth of the espionage idea in the United States, for which place not inappropriately may be found here.

> The dangers that hung upon the flanks of the nation, the adroit moves of detective forces which set at naught the plotters, and the manner and means adopted to nip in the bud the creeping plans of Pan-Germanism, is one of the most fascinating and in many respects one of the most thrilling chapters in the recital of America's first months in the great war.
>
> Previous to the Civil War, the United States had no secret service. It came into being when reports were brought to Samuel H. Felton, president of the Philadelphia, Wilmington and Baltimore Railroad, that President Lincoln would be assassinated while traveling by special train from the West to his inaugural at Washington. Felton sent for Allan Pinkerton, who was then conducting a small detective agency in Chicago. It is interesting to note that Pinkerton, in taking the task of protecting Lincoln's life, outlined the method which is the keynote of the secret service system. In describing the work he wrote: "I resolved to locate my men at the various towns along the road where it was believed dissatisfaction existed. I sent the men to their posts with instructions to

become acquainted with such men as they might, on observation, consider suspicious, and endeavor to obtain from them, by association, a knowledge of their intentions." Later, Pinkerton, under the name of "Maj. E. J. Allen," directed the intelligence department of Gen. McClellan's Ohio army.

Brig. Gen. Lafayette C. Baker was the organizer of the military secret service that performed the detective duty of the Civil War. At the outbreak of hostilities, a national detective bureau was an idea entirely new, and was regarded as contrary to republican institutions. The service went out of existence with the close of the war.

The present day Secret Service, proper, is a division of the Treasury Department. It was created at the time "shin plasters" were in existence and counterfeiting thereof had become general. Its duty at the outset was to run down counterfeiters, but later its duties were somewhat broadened, and in recent years it has been intrusted with the safety of the President.

In April of this year, the United States had at its command (besides M. I. D. and Naval Intelligence) the Secret Service, the investigators of the Department of Justice, the Immigration Bureau inspectors and the inspectors of the Post Office Department. These organizations for the detention of criminals are now working in close harmony against the common enemy.

With these agencies also worked the American Protective League, regarding which this comment was printed and should be reprinted:

It is no exaggeration to say that the American business men who conceived the plan and who to-day constitute the myriad meshes in the spy net cast over America, have accomplished a feat which, for efficiency, for secrecy, for loyalty and patriotism has never been equaled or approached by the men of any nation since time began.

The St. Louis division embraced a membership of 3,000 operatives, the large majority of whom made up the listening and reporting organization. The number and variety of cases developed and investigated are as follows: Alien enemy activities, 225; Espionage Act cases, 1,142; sabotage, 11; anti-military activities, 15; printed propaganda, 1,741; I. W. W., including pacifism, 48; bribery, graft, etc., 45; impersonation, 2; naturalization, 600; counter-espionage, 53;

draft cases, 7,075; character and loyalty investigations, 589; liquor cases, 49; vice, 26; wireless cases, 52; profiteering, 80; miscellaneous, 256.

The credit for the patient and self-sacrificing labors required in this large volume of work is due not only to the patriotism and fidelity of the listening and reporting force and to those operatives who devoted their time to work of investigation, but also to conscientious coöperation of the district organizations and their deputies and inspectors. Sharing with these must be remembered, on the silent roll of honor, all those deputy chiefs in charge of the respective departments at headquarters under the immediate direction of their Chief, who must stand for all.

CHAPTER XII

THE STORY OF KANSAS CITY

The Gate City of the Great West in the War—If K. C. Ever was Wild and Woolly, That was Long Ago—Let Us Have Peace, if We Have to Get It With a Gun—All Quiet Along the Missouri.

Kansas City claims and has claimed for a long time the title of Gate City to the Great West. This is hers by legitimate right and has been ever since wheel-power first went west of the Missouri River. Independence, Missouri, which we may call the mother of the modern Kansas City, was for years, early in the last century, the jumping-off place for all the great western transcontinental trails. That way lay Oregon, on the upper fork. The left fork of the main traveled road led to Santa Fé. The men bound for the Arkansas Valley passed by here, and the old fur hunters said good-bye to civilization at this point even before the wagon had replaced the pack saddle on the Santa Fé trail. Here began the wagon-road that later was railroad, and all the time, from the wildest to the tamest days, whether in staid 1842, or in wild 1882, Kansas City was the Gate of the West, letting in and passing out a wild and tempestuous life in the days of the Homeric West.

Time was when Kansas City was bad, and had her man for breakfast with the best of them. But always the worst was farther West, and Kansas City sat tight. She did not care for the movies of the future, but quickly went in for law, order and business. So she has grown up, by very virtue of her geography, her situation, and her history, into an immense commercial center, solid, law-abiding and prosperous.

There was no reason to expect any great outbreaks of violence in Kansas City at this date of her history, nor do we find any; but the A. P. L. was there as it has been in every other great city of the Union throughout the war. That it was active may be seen by a glance at the totals. In D. J. work, forty-five cases of alien enemy activities, 1,237 cases of disloyalty and sedition, and eight cases of propaganda cover the list. The War Department offered more work, the selective draft alone involving under its several heads 3,182 cases. There were 410 investigations connected with character and loyalty; 227 cases of investigation of civilian applicants for overseas service. Raids to obtain evidence for illegal sale of liquor to soldiers brought visits to fifty-three doubtful saloons, and twenty-five convictions of violators. Kansas City is dry, so far as the Army is concerned, as may be witnessed by an editorial of September 17, 1918, in the Kansas City *Star* — which also shows why it is dry:

> The sale of liquor to soldiers has been going on in Kansas City for months. Officers at Leavenworth and Funston have complained of it. The consequences have been apparent to everybody. Yet the police—Governor Gardner's police—did nothing. It took a voluntary organization to get the evidence and force the arrests. The law-breakers whom the police—Governor Gardner's police—could not find, were run down by the volunteers of the American Protective League. They discovered the most open and flagrant violation of the law. It was no trick for amateurs to get evidence and find the people who deserved arrest.

A tough North-end colored saloon was visited by A. P. L. operatives late one Saturday evening. A large crowd was encountered. Most of them had been drinking heavily and were in rather a noisy condition. The A. P. L. men first encountered a large colored fellow. He explained that he was past the age, but that he had served in the 21st Kansas (colored) in the Spanish War, and produced his papers to prove his assertion. A colored fellow was encountered who refused to show his card. He said he had one, but stated he would not go to headquarters and that it would take a fight to get him there. Whereupon this ex-colored soldier stepped up and informed him that if there was to be any threshing done, he asked the first opportunity, and that no. 2 would show his card or he would take it off him. He was supported by two or three other colored men, with the result that every man in the crowd brought out his card. This story is given to illustrate one fact — no matter how tough and disorderly the crowd, eighty-five percent at least still had manhood enough left to be loyal.

In another saloon a big fellow was leaning on the bar. He was notified that operatives outside were looking at the cards, and he said: "I have my little old card right here," slapping his breast, "but the man who sees it will first have to walk over my dead body." Operative B———, who had entered the saloon a few minutes before, was leaning on the bar facing the fellow and when he finished his tirade, he said quietly and very low: "Let me see your card, please; I am from the American Protective League"— and he showed his star. Instantly the fellow replied: "Oh, certainly, here it is "— accompanied by a roar of laughter from everybody in the saloon.

A man was reported by neighbors as having taken down a flag that was put on his house. It was said that he read the reports of German victories in the early part of the war on the front porch to the neighbors and gloated over them. He also said he knew how far to go, what to say and when to quit. A. P. L. operatives had a quiet interview with this party. He was well educated, held a good position, and was desirous of arguing the question. At that moment he was reinforced by his wife, who immediately ordered the operatives out of the house, with the statement that no one could accuse her husband of being disloyal. She was very determined and unusually long of wind. His change was immediate. He took his wife to a back room. Evidently he runs the house, for she did not reappear. He assured us he had made a mistake, and, in fact, termed himself a plain d——d fool. He promised to be loyal and said that he invited checking up.

It was the experience of the Eastern District of Kansas City that about twenty percent were American-born citizens of German descent, or naturalized Germans who looked upon the war as simply a question of taking sides, instead of a question of loyalty. A. P. L. pointed out to these the need of being loyal, what they owed this country, why they should be subservient to the law — and what was going to happen to them if they were not. This twenty percent either was made into good citizens or it remained a class of people who said nothing and did no harm. The five percent of bad stuff represented the actual Germans who were interested in the success of the Germans, and the slackers, deserters and men who had violated the law and had to be apprehended.

A typical Kansas City case was commented on in the "Spy Glass," the national A. P. L. paper:

> Fred W. S——— was born on March 29, 1888, entered military service in Crefeld, Germany, October 15, 1909, in the 53rd Infantry Regiment of the 5th Westphalian Division, Co. 6, and received his discharge on September 25, 1911. His military book in addition to giving his record as first-class marksman, shows that he was recommended for corporal. In April, 1913, he secured a furlough to North America, but was subject to call in March, 1915. Claims he came to this country to visit his brother. Interviewed, S——— was frank. He stated that he made it a rule never to talk, but that prior to the United States entering the war, he had let some remarks slip to his fellow workmen, which he had regretted, as these remarks had caused him a great deal of trouble since then. He showed us his registration card. He stated that he had applied for his first papers and that he was ready and willing to take out his last papers the moment he was permitted, and that he wanted to become an American citizen. He had four brothers in the German Army, and has not heard from them for three years. This was given as an explanation for his mistake in making a few remarks at the beginning of the war. He asserted that he would live up faithfully to every rule, would attend strictly to his business and would report whenever desired. He declared that he had bought First, Second and Third Liberty Loan Bonds. He also stated that he had given to the Red Cross. Conclusion: He has violated no law and do not believe he intends to violate any. Kept under observation.

Here is another story which illustrates that curious psychological bluntness and one-sidedness of the German intellect. The widow of Fred E———, deceased, who had a drug store, was asked for a subscription to the hospital fund. She said: "I won't give any money to the Research Hospital, but maybe, if you take the old name back, I will give to the German Hospital, but not to the Research Hospital."

The manner in which she said this and the spirit demonstrated by her attitude showed that she was thoroughly pro-German. Operative No. 60 called on the party, and says in his report:

> We charged her with disloyal talking. She stated that she had done no disloyal talking, and in fact had taken good care not to talk against the Government in any way; furthermore, that she had a son in France and if she was against the Government she certainly would not have allowed him to go. We then asked her about her statements regarding the Research Hospital. She stated she had spoken to her lawyer about it and he had told her it was not so necessary to change the name of the Hospital as it would be to change the name of a business. She thought the name should remain "German" because the Germans had in the beginning founded the Hospital. We stated that there were no Germans over here to found it. "Well," she said, "I mean German-Americans." We then stated there were no German-Americans here, either, but all Americans. She began crying and said that no one could understand her position, that she had sisters in Germany and nephews fighting in that Army, while her own son was in the American Army fighting against them. She stated that the dirty stories about the German army were all lies. We told her that it was our duty to demand that she should not do any talking. We were convinced that she is very pro-German and that the only way to prevent her from talking would be to put her where there are no other people except Germans.

This is a very fair statement of one of the greatest problems of America today. What shall be done with the hyphen? It must go, else this war will be fought again.

While the war was yet young, a tip was received from the draft board that a certain young man had failed to appear when called. Investigation showed that he had deserted his wife, leaving her in a destitute condition. He had three sisters in the city, consequently A. P. L. assumed he would at some time communicate with one of them. By certain means, operatives established a watch on the mail as it was delivered, locating him at different times in Oklahoma, Colorado, Arizona and other western points. One day a telephone call was received stating that one of the sisters had been heard to converse with him over the 'phone; that he had arrived in town at 2:30, and at 4:00 would be at a certain place to visit a sister. A. P. L. men arrived at that place. In a few minutes a man of the draft-evader's description, wearing a cowboy hat and typical cowboy attire, came swaggering up the steps. When taken, he put up a somewhat original and unique story:

> You see, I am hard of hearing and have a bad heart. I am not at all yellow. I am ready to fight at any time, and have always been ready, but it occurred to me that as I could not fight on account of my hearing and bad heart, I ought not put the officials to the trouble of examining me. You see, it would take a lot of time to examine me, so I thought the best plan was just to save them that trouble, and as I was going west anyway, etc.

Operatives then locked the cowboy up for the night, and the next morning took him before the Department of Justice. He was very repentant, and while adhering to the same story, was anxious that something should be done to keep him out of the Army. This matter was explained quietly to the Department man who met him, and upon being advised by the cowboy that he was hard of hearing, had a bad heart, etc., the latter said: "I feel awfully sorry for you, but you see, you are delinquent. You have laid yourself liable to the law and a penitentiary offense. Now, we usually are considerate and give a man a chance of going to war, but you tell me you are hard of hearing and have a bad heart, and of course, under those circumstances, we cannot send you to the Army. That is too bad, and I suppose the decision of the court will be that it is the penitentiary for you."

A very pale, excited listener immediately said: "Mister, now I think you misunderstand me. A man who goes through what I went through yesterday, being arrested and being locked up with a lot of bedbugs all night, has a fairly good heart. In fact, I believe I have entirely recovered my hearing, and am all over the heart trouble. If you will only let me go to the Army, I will waive all examination." He went.

In one day A. P. L. received three different complaints that a spy was working in the north-eastern part of the city. He was supposed to be German through and through, though he had never said anything pro-German. He was generally considered to be a wise fellow who worked and did not talk. Every Saturday night he met a bunch of spies in his basement, one tall and one short, both dangerous looking. They always carried a secret basket of mysterious contents. Neighbors were very much aroused. Insisted that the Department do something, quick. A. P. L. placed operatives on a Saturday night, the night on which these mysterious meetings all occurred, and watched the long and short men come with their deadly baskets. Shortly after, a light appeared in the basement. Curtains were at the windows and the windows were up, so the operatives crawled up closely and quietly and listened to the conversation, which was about as follows, in mixed German: "I played the ace." "No, you didn't, you led with a king!" "You don't know anything about playing pinochle." And so forth. S'nuf, Mawruss. The mysterious basket contained beer bottles!

CHAPTER XIII

THE STORY OF MINNEAPOLIS

Clean-Cut Work of One of the North-West's Capitals—Straightaway Story of a Good Division—Many Anecdotes Showing How Operatives Worked—The Dignified and Sober Side of Saving the State and Making Over Citizens—A Model Report.

The great city of Minneapolis is one of the foci of the agricultural and industrial realm of the vast Northwestern country for which the Twin Cities make the gateway. It was not to be supposed that its staid and sober population would cause any great amount of trouble. None the less, trouble did develop in Minneapolis as elsewhere, and A. P. L. cases and figures mounted steadily upward, just as they did in other large centers of industry the country over.

Alien enemy cases for the Department of Justice ran 127; disloyalty and sedition, 1,222; sabotage, 17; interference with draft, 44; propaganda, 392; I. W. W. and other radicals, 70. War Department cases had 5,725 investigations under the selective draft: 997 slackers; 507 work-or-fight cases; character and loyalty, 337 cases; liquor, vice and prostitution, 593 cases. The Treasury Department had 1,129 cases on war risk and allowance grounds. The Fuel Administration turned over 2,356 cases for investigation; the gasoline work, 427. The grand total of cases handled by Minneapolis division men, November 26, 1917, to December 16, 1918, was 15,415.

Minneapolis had a very thorough organization, and has reported the results in so thorough and explicit a fashion as to leave small option in matter of handling the report. It could not well be amended or improved upon, and is given in substance in the following pages.

Entries on the case cards include every conceivable

offense against the wartime laws and orders of the Federal Government. Each card contains the condensed history of an investigation important in the prosecution of the war, and, collectively, the 15,415 cards represent uncountable hours, days and nights of devoted service to the Government during a period of thirteen months. They record adventures as thrilling as any of the detective stories of Monsieur Lecocq or Sherlock Holmes, although these form a minority of the experiences encountered.

The Minneapolis Division of the American Protective League entered upon active service November 27, 1917. An organization with a limited membership had been effected in Minneapolis previously, but its members served principally as observers, and it was not until Charles G. Davis, a Minneapolis contractor, had been induced by H. M. Gardner, Vice-President of the Civic & Commerce Association, in charge of war activities, to accept the position as Chief of the Minneapolis Division, that the American Protective League became an active local agent for the apprehension of anti-war activities. Mr. Davis entirely abandoned his private business to enter upon this important Government service. After having established relations with Mr. T. E. Campbell, Chief Special Agent in charge of the Bureau of Investigation U. S. Department of Justice in the Northwest, he opened headquarters and immediately began recruiting a force of operatives. He continued in this position through the thirteen months without salary.

Under the plan of organization, a captain was appointed in each district and operatives assigned in the numbers required to meet the conditions encountered. Lieutenants also were provided, each having charge of groups of operatives up to ten men. Headquarters held each captain responsible for all operations in his district.

The jurisdiction of the Minneapolis Division extended throughout Hennepin County. In the principal county centers outside of Minneapolis, special operatives were appointed to take instruction direct from headquarters. Another group of picked operatives composed a headquarters squad operated directly under the chief and handling emergency cases.

Because of the importance and confidential nature of the business entrusted to the League, extreme care was exercised in the selection of the operatives. They were men of proved loyalty as well as of ability and influence. As the work of the division increased, the personnel was enlarged until a total of more than four hundred operatives from all lines of business, trades and professions had finally been called to service. All served without pay or expense allowances. Some of them gave practically their entire time to the work of the League. Most of them definitely pledged and gave from six to twenty hours of service every week.

The total members sworn in numbered 491 on November 30, 1918. The active list at that date included 326 officers and operatives and sixty members of the so-called "Eye and Ear" division, consisting of men not able to render continuous service, but so situated that they were in a position to communicate to headquarters reports of anti-American activities and other Federal offenses. Among the active members were scores who had tried in vain to enter the Army or Navy, and who, failing to find any other essential war service open to them, found an outlet for their patriotic energy in the ranks of the American Protective League. Notwithstanding this, the League report shows that twenty-four members resigned during the thirteen months to go into the army; five to enter the overseas service of the Y. M. C. A. or Red Cross; and eighteen to accept other Government service.

In the pursuit of their duties, operatives and officials of the Minneapolis Division, A. P. L., arrested several well-known criminals, and encountered scores of desperate offenders of various kinds. It is a tribute to their courage and efficiency that there was not a single case of extreme violence. Men who were recognized everywhere as dangerous were apprehended as easily as persons who had offended unwittingly. In its work, the League employed all of the scientific as well as the ordinary devices utilized in the detection and conviction of violators and evaders of the law. Dictaphones and disguises were used, and miles were covered and hours spent in skillful "shadowing."

While the files of the Minneapolis Division contain records of many cases of extreme importance, including participation in two investigations which led to the internment of alien enemies, the conviction of eleven offenders against the espionage laws, the capture and conviction of numerous deserters and the successful prosecution of other offenders, Chief Davis and his associates take greater pride in the results of constructive work of another type. This included the re-establishment with their boards of 4,479 delinquents under the selective service regulations, and the apologies and promises to mend their ways obtained from men and women who, in some cases, had deliberately, but in most instances unwittingly, extended aid and comfort to the enemy. It is estimated that at least two hundred men and women, who had been guilty of spreading false reports or of other conduct of an unfriendly nature, were shown the fallacy of their actions in such a manner that they voluntarily surrendered their previous ideas and embraced Americanism with more — or less — zeal.

For the protection of active members, who frequently encountered emergencies requiring authoritative action, and often were obliged to make immediate arrests to insure the detention of persons guilty of serious offenses, an arrangement was made whereby a large percentage of the operatives were formally deputized as special officers of the Minnesota Public Safety Commission. This gave them sufficient police authority to cope with any situation which arose. But for this, it would not have been possible for the organization to make its record of important arrests. This authority permitted the carrying of arms for protection, and although instances where "gun play" was required were few, the U. S. Department of Justice and the Minnesota Public Safety Commission had no occasion to regret the authority and responsibility conferred upon these men. They were enabled, by virtue of this authority, to enter many places, which otherwise might have been closed to them, in time to correct conditions which, if neglected, would have given rise to serious difficulties.

The Minneapolis Division American Protective League was the first local division to attempt a large-scale slacker round-up. The results and experience of the Minneapolis raids were responsible for similar activities in other cities, which put into the Army hundreds of men who otherwise might have evaded military service. The first organized slacker " raid " in Minneapolis took place on March 26, 1917. One hundred and twenty operatives were employed in hauling the drag-net through the cheaper hotels in the Gateway lodging house district. Approximately one hundred men were taken to the temporary detention place, and twenty-one men — deserters, unregistered enemy aliens and men whose draft status could not be determined — were sent to the county jail.

On April 6, two hundred and fifty operatives, with two hundred National Guard escorts, visited saloons, cafés, pool rooms and dance halls, starting at 8:00 p. m. and continuing until 10:00 p. m., and picked up 1,150 men in various places. The Chief and a corps of assistants conducted the questioning throughout the night. There were still two hundred men in custody when breakfast was served Sunday morning. Long distance telephone and the telegraph were employed to determine the status of the non-residents. Twenty-seven men were locked up. Other less extensive raids were conducted through the spring and summer of 1918 and at different periods, squads of operatives being stationed at the various railroad stations to search for draft evaders. As many as twenty prisoners were taken in these stations in a single day, and it was seldom that a day passed which did not yield two or more deserters or delinquents.

One morning a dapper individual who arrived at one station was asked if he had his draft card.

" Certainly," he replied, reaching confidently into his pocket. The smile gradually disappeared from his face and he delved into pocket after pocket without finding the necessary credentials. Finally he gave up in despair and admitted he did not have his card. He was an exception to the rule, however, and did not become indignant. He said, " Take me along — I deserve it." At headquarters he proved to be " Chick " Evans of Chicago, national open golf champion of the United States. He had come to Minneapolis to participate in a golf foursome for the benefit of the Red Cross! He waited fully two hours until a telegram was received from his Board in Chicago stating that he was in good standing.

Another spectacular raid conducted by the Minneapolis Division was on the show lot of the Ringling Circus. Thirty men were taken into custody on charges of draft irregularities, and nearly all of these were inducted into the army. It was reported that resistance might be offered, and precautions had been taken in the arrangements for the raid. No difficulty was encountered, however, and later in the day the proprietor of the circus complimented us on the manner in which the round-up had been conducted.

A different type of raid was undertaken at the request of commandants of the various Army detachments in and near Minneapolis. They complained that a number of imposters in army uniforms were bringing discredit to the soldiery and requested that these be apprehended. There were so many soldiers on leave in Minneapolis at all hours that it had been found extremely difficult to identify the imposters, and so it was decided that with the coöperation of the various commandants a literal drag-net process should be resorted to on a given evening. Forces of operatives were stationed at opposite extremes of the central business district. More than two hundred men participated, squads being formed, and one squad being stationed at each end of each street. The operatives stopped every uniformed man who was encountered and demanded his pass. An even dozen uniformed men who did not have passes were picked up and turned over to Army and Navy authorities, who attended in automobiles. For a long time there was an entire absence of reports of offenses on the part of imposters in service uniforms.

Early in the summer a system of nightly A. P. L. patrols was established in the down-town section of Minneapolis. Operatives worked in squads of two or three men, some of them giving attention to draft evaders, others to the work-or-fight order, and others to bootleggers. Scarcely a night passed without a record of one or more important arrests, and the entire personnel of the League became intimately acquainted with the down-town business and social structures.

In the conduct of these nightly patrols a special headquarters was established in a down-town public building. The captain in charge directed operations from this place. Not only was he able to keep the railroad stations, hotels, cafés, saloons and other public places under continuous surveillance for slackers, but he also had forces constantly available to meet any emergencies which arose during the evenings. Squads frequently were dispatched from this headquarters to various points of the city to give attention to special cases.

One of the first draft evasion cases investigated by the Minneapolis Division is a great short story ready-made. It concerned a young man prominent in labor circles. He had been an avowed opponent of all the national war measures, and was particularly bitter in his condemnation of the Selective Service Act. It was reported on good authority that although he was within the draft age he had declined to register and intended to resort to any device necessary to evade service.

The first inquiry was made at the Board of Health, where it was ascertained that no record of his birth was on file. Attention was next called to the poll books, and it was found that the age he had given when registering as a voter placed him safely within the provisions of the draft act. His school enrollment record was investigated and it was found that the ages given in the various grades made him amenable to the draft. He had three insurance policies, and the original applications which he had signed showed him to have been less than thirty-one years old on June 5, 1917. The last step was to search for the marriage record of his father and mother. They were found to have been married in a small town near Minneapolis in November, 1885.

When the young man was summoned to headquarters he admitted the authenticity of all these records, but insisted that he knew he was past thirty-one on June 5, 1917. He refused to state on what information he based this assertion, and was held for prosecution. One final attempt was made to clear his status, and with considerable effort his mother, who had divorced his father more than twenty-five years before, was located. At the end of an unsatisfactory interview lasting nearly an hour she finally broke down and in tears admitted the boy had been born out of wedlock and that she had been responsible for the falsification of the records in order to indicate his legitimacy. She said that she had withheld this secret even from the subject, not divulging to him until a few days before the day of registration and then only because he seemed so bitter over the fact that he must register. Her appearance was so venerable and her determination to assist him so emphatic that there appeared little chance of successful prosecution, so the man was released. Headquarters never received any further reports of un-American activities on his part.

A later case of interest involved an admitted deserter, both from the German and the United States Army. Whether he is guilty of other offenses has not yet been determined. On September 12, 1918, the day of registration for men up to forty-six years of age, two operatives on duty were struck by the peculiar actions of a man who appeared to register. They managed to get near him without attracting suspicion. In stating his occupation he said he was an iron moulder. They noticed that his hands were soft and white. When he left the registration place, one of the operatives followed him. The other telephoned to the plant where the man had said he was employed and learned that he was not known there. The individual was " shadowed " to a lodging house, but had departed while the first operative was telephoning. The house was put under surveillance, and after a period of five days the operative gained entrance and searched his room. Among his effects were blank checks from banks in various cities, photographs in German army uniforms of a man recognizable as the subject, and various letters and pamphlets in German, some of which were suspicious. Under the carpet in the room was an official United States Army discharge blank.

The fact that this paper had been so carefully hidden caused further suspicion, and the watch was maintained for another five days, when a man appeared at the house seeking to rent the room which had been occupied by the subject. He described the particular room. On instructions from the operatives, the landlady let him have it. When he entered the room he started packing the effects of the subject, and shortly afterwards left the house with the subject's two suitcases. He was stopped outside and questioned. He said a man had given him $5.00 to go to that lodging house, to rent that particular room, to get his belongings and to meet him at a certain place the following morning, where he agreed to give him $50. This man was held over night and was sent out the next day to make the appointment arranged by the subject. The subject was there and was taken into custody. After a gruelling examination he admitted being a deserter from the United States Army. He later confessed that he was a German alien and said he also had deserted from the army in Germany. He would not account for his activities in the months which had elapsed between his desertion from the Army and his capture in Minneapolis. He had a considerable sum of money, but could not prove he had done any work. He was turned over to the military authorities.

Topping all other humorous experiences was that encountered by one of the most efficient of the Minneapolis District A. P. L. Captains. He had orders to arrest a deserter who bore a Polish name ending in "-ski." After a long search he was informed that this man lived in one of the slum sections, working all day and arriving at his lodging place generally about 1:00 a. m. He could not learn where the man worked and so was compelled to locate him at his room. Going there to make inquiries one night, he was told that the man was there. Having been informed that the fellow was dangerous and fearing that he would become alarmed and flee if he was not taken into custody immediately, the captain went into his room. Asking if he were "So-and-so-ski," the man said he was. He was told to get up and dress and come along. Although he was surly he showed no resistance and accompanied the captain outside. The captain felt, however, that this docility might be assumed, and thought he would take no chances. The place was about a mile from the jail. The captain had an automobile, but did not feel it would be safe to take the prisoner in the seat with him. He therefore compelled him to straddle the hood on the car, and on this ungainly perch, with the temperature 20° below, the unfortunate suspect was driven to the court house. Arriving there, the prisoner scratched his head and asked:

"What yuh bringin' me down here for?"

"Why, because you didn't register for the draft. You know what."

"Didn't register for the draft? I guess I did! Here is my blue card and my classification card."

Explanation followed. This man's name ended with the Polish "-ski" and was otherwise almost identical to the name of the culprit who was sought. When he was asked if he was "So-and-so-ski," it sounded so much like his own name that he admitted it. He was taken back to his lodgings in the seat beside the captain and proper apologies were made.

In most cases where humor existed, there was sometimes a mixture of tragedy. There was one man, a motor truck driver, who had made himself exceedingly popular with a number of women by wearing a uniform of an infantryman without having gone through the formality of enlistment. He was captured one day while paying a call on one of his admirers. Operatives burst in upon the imposter and told him he must straightway doff the uniform.

"But this is the only suit of clothes I have," he protested. One operative went to his truck and found an oil-stained suit of overalls. He was taken behind the screen and forced to get into these and give up his military raiment.

Another incident of this kind involved a young man who was subject to draft and who said he was ready to respond when called. He could not wait the Government issue of clothes, however. He went to a tailor and equipped himself with a suit of khaki which fitted perfectly and further adorned himself with the insignia of the Artillery Service and an officer's sleeve braid. When he was summoned to headquarters, he explained that he intended to take this uniform to camp to wear when "he went to town." His readiness to wear the uniform was communicated to his draft board by telephone and brought orders for immediate induction. Although he had sold all of his civilian clothes, one suit was recovered from the second-hand dealer who had purchased them, and he went to camp in it.

One Saturday night a young man of stentorian voice, wearing classical shell-rimmed glasses, appeared at a prominent down-town corner, mounted a soap-box and shouted, "Step closer, gentlemen. I have no bombs, no T. N. T., no lyddite, no dynamite or powder explosives of any kind. Step closer though and I'll treat you to some talk-bombs." In the vanguard of those who stepped closer were two A. P. L. operatives. Five minutes later the orator, Herbert Blank, alias Herbert C——, deserter from the British army, was registered at the county jail. The shell-rimmed glasses and his predilection to Bolsheviki oratory had proved his downfall. They had been mentioned in a bulletin asking his apprehension, sent out from Chicago headquarters of the Department of Justice and received that morning in Minneapolis headquarters.

The leading man of the theatrical company which scored the biggest hit of any troupe playing Minneapolis last winter applied his cold cream and other theatrical embellishments for his Saturday matinee performance under the eyes of an A. P. L. operative whilst he confessed to the operative that it was quite possible that he should have registered for the draft, although he had not. At the request of the New York A. P. L. headquarters, this man was examined, and although he carried with him a sworn statement from his father to the effect that he had been born prior to June 5, 1886, coöperation with the Toledo A. P. L. had developed evidence that this was not true. Before the interview was concluded, ample evidence was secured to warrant the arrest of the actor, but his role was so prominent and there was such a certainty that the company would be compelled to cancel all of its engagements with distinct losses to all its members, that mercy was shown and he was allowed to continue the performance until such a time as his draft status could be adjusted. For several weeks, during the travels of the company, he was compelled to report daily at the offices of the U. S. Department of Justice in the various cities visited.

One night a squad of operatives, led by the Chief, visited

an apartment in a down-town building to investigate a report that liquor was being served to soldiers and sailors. When they gained entrance they found no uniformed men upon the premises, but one of the operatives who had lived in San Francisco recognized the unmistakable odor of opium smoke. He said, "Hop, Chief!" A search was made and a large quantity of opium was found secreted in various nooks of the apartment. Further search revealed twenty-three sticks of dynamite, a complete kit of burglar's tools, a supply of saws and other devices used by crooks. A bolt of silk and other new merchandise, afterwards identified as property stolen from stores, also was uncovered. Five men and a woman were taken to jail.

One of the most interesting cases was that of a German who left Germany fifty-six years ago, at the age of six years. He went to South Dakota, where he prospered greatly, and moved to Minneapolis about fifteen years ago. At the outbreak of the war his remarks were such that his business associates and social acquaintances practically ostracized him, and the members of his lodge preferred charges of disloyalty against him. The man was brought to headquarters. Members of his lodge were invited to be present, and he was given twenty minutes seeing himself as others saw him. His attitude at first was stubborn and defiant. The Chief then began to dwell on the suffering of his children; said they were refused admittance to fraternities, were not invited to parties and that his boy departed for the mobilization camp brokenhearted and in tears over the fact that none of his family were at the station to bid him good-bye at the most important milestone in his career. This line of talk seemed to soften the subject. He broke down and said, with tears: "I never was talked to like this before in my life, but I never had anything said to me that did me so much good. Will you please shake hands with me?" After that his fellow lodge members affected a reconciliation on the spot. This man's future conduct was above reproach after this incident, and he became one of the most active workers for the Red Cross and Liberty Loan.

A well known clairvoyant and spiritualist medium of Minneapolis was brought into the office by one of the District Captains. She was told that she had been talking sedition, and waxed indignant at the idea of anybody accusing her of sedition when she was a woman so far removed from ordinary planes, who could see into vast rounds of space. Her complacency was seriously jarred when informed that one of our operatives had crawled into her basement through the coal chute and listened to her seditious talk. Her inability to see into the basement caused her to have renewed faith in the long arm of Uncle Sam.

A bond salesman earning $10,000 a year was only two weeks under thirty-one years of age on the 5th of June, 1917. A report came in from a former sweetheart who had been jilted. Operatives found where the subject had made application for two insurance policies, taken out two or three years previous, in another city, which gave his age and place of birth. When brought into the office, the man stated that no authentic birth record was in existence, and that his birth was recorded in the family Bible in a Southern city, in the custody of his mother. Not having the address of his mother, that angle not having been covered, we anticipated that he would attempt to communicate with his mother. The wires were covered and a message was picked up about thirty minutes after subject had left the office instructing the mother to destroy the family birth record page in the Bible and to send him an affidavit that he was born a year earlier than he was. Needless to say, the local operatives in that district where his mother lived secured the necessary legal data. We hope that this young man has done more for his country during the months he has been in France than he did previously as far as being a patriotic American is concerned. Incidentally, he felt so secure in his position that during the spring months of 1918 he had married.

A man and woman occupying a small cottage in the outskirts of the city were reported as acting in a very suspicious manner, keeping the windows carefully covered, not allowing anyone to come into the house, and not even allowing the meter readers to get in until after considerable delay. Boxes of glass of a small size were delivered very often, and investigation at the glass house showed that they always paid cash, would not give any name, and always received the supplies at the front porch, and that the same practice was indulged in about the delivery of hardware, small orders of lumber, and other materials. The house was carefully watched for a couple of weeks, and many attempts were made to get in. The sound of machinery could be heard and one of the operatives who finally got in as a meter reader reported a small electric motor in the basement which seemed to be some sort of a work shop. The man and woman who lived there kept so close to his heels that he was not able to do much without exciting suspicion. At regular intervals the couple visited the post office, where they shipped packages to different addresses throughout the Northwest. These packages were registered, and they seemed to be very careful in their handling of them. It was decided that we had best pick them up on the street and bring the couple to the office when they had these packages in their possession, and the operative would follow. Examination of the packages in the office disclosed the fact that there were small framed pictures which this man and woman were manufacturing and sending to the woman's husband, who was on the road selling them. This satisfactorily explained the mysterious packages which were thought to be infernal machines. The queerness of this woman in always carrying a small leather traveling bag prompted us to examine the contents of the bag, which proved to be a large amount of money which this woman was carrying openly through the street of Minneapolis, part of it in coins. When reprimanded for this matter of taking the money around with her, she explained that they were Danish and did not understand American customs very well. While living in Chicago they had deposited the savings of several years in a private bank which failed, and ever since that time they had kept their savings constantly on their persons. We explained the banking system to them and sent them to a fellow countryman, who is the vice-president of one of our large banks. They left their money in his custody, except a considerable portion which they invested in Liberty Bonds.

CHAPTER XIV

THE STORY OF NEW ORLEANS

The A. P. L. in the Sunny South—Strong Division of the Crescent City—How the League was Organized—Rapid Growth and Wide Activities—Curbing of Vice—Cleaning Up a City.

There is not in all the United States a more lovable city than that founded by Iberville, in an earlier century, above the Delta of the Mississippi. At first French, then part Spanish, part American, all Southern and yet all cosmopolitan, New Orleans has what we may call a personality not approached by any other community on this continent. Up to the time when, a decade or so ago, the once self-contented South began to reach out for a commercial future, so-called, New Orleans was the true Mecca on this continent of the Northern tourists. No need to go to Europe if one wanted different scenes. Here existed always the glamour of old-world customs, an atmosphere as foreign as it was wholly delightful. As the home of easy living and good cooking, as the place of kindly climate and gentle manners, all flavored with a wholesome carelessness as to life and its problems, New Orleans was, to use a very trite expression, in a class quite by herself. She never has had a rival, and more is the pity that the old New Orleans has succumbed to the modern tendency towards utilization and change which has marked all America.

Of such a community it might be expected that none too rigid a view of life and law would obtain. This would not be true of the better elements of New Orleans, yet it was in part true of all the life along the old Gulf Coast, where Lafitte and all his roisterers once lived, and where all the gentleness and ease of nature tended toward what we might call loose living — or at least *joie de vivre.* The soul of New Orleans came out annually in her Mardi Gras — the exuberant flowering of a spirit perennially young and riante.

And yet to New Orleans came the sobering days of the war, as to all the rest of America. The conscription fell upon her as upon every other city in America; and she also was asked to open her purse for the furtherance of the war and its purposes. How she responded need not be asked, and need not really be recorded, for New Orleans has always maintained beneath her laughing exterior as stern a sense of duty as may be found anywhere in all the world. To be French is to smile — but to be firm. Indeed, New Orleans showed one of the strange phenomena of American life which is not always known in the North — the truth that the South is more Puritan than ever New England was. Texas, supposed to be a bad border state, to-day has stronger laws regarding vice and liquor than New England ever has had since the time of the Blue Laws, and more strictly enforced. Louisiana also, gentle and kindly, has a stiffer code of morals than any commonwealth of the stern and rockbound coast. She smiles — but stands firm.

These reflections become the more obvious as one reads the main story of the activities of A. P. L. in New Orleans. The division does not pride itself ever so much upon its promptness with Liberty Loans, its activity in slacker drives, its firmness as to sabotage and propaganda, as it does upon other phases of work which at first were incidental to the prosecution of the Government war activities. The great boast of the New Orleans division is that it has kept young soldiers away from bad women, and kept women, once evil, away from themselves and gave them a chance to reform and to live a different life. So, therefore, one who shall study all the manifold activities of the American Protective League in this country will see that it had many ways in which it rendered service to the people. Perhaps, long after the League shall have been dissolved, in part forgotten, the New Orleans rehabilitation home, ten miles out from the city, will remain as a monument to the activities of that singular organization which, like King Rex himself, ruler of the Carnival, came from some mysterious region and vanished thence again, leaving behind only good memories.

On January 29, in 1918, the New Orleans division of A. P. L. had only thirty-eight members. At that time Mr. Charles Weinberger became manager, there being associated with him as assistant chief Mr. Arthur G. Newmyer. There were at first but limited office quarters, but in a very short time new headquarters were established and the plant installed covering approximately ten thousand square feet of space. This was on April 1, 1918. On February 1, 1919, the total membership was 2,097.

League operations were distributed under a Bureau of Investigation and a Bureau of Information, each in charge of an assistant chief. The investigation work was divided by Special D. J. Agent Beckham as follows: Headquarters bureau, handling enemy alien activities, disloyalty, sedition, propaganda, etc., had two units, a staff of eighty-three headquarters lieutenants, and also a ward organization. In each of the seventeen wards of New Orleans there was a lieutenant who had enough operatives under him to cover his neighborhood thoroughly.

The second bureau, that of Information, took up on its part the trades classification rather than that which we may call the geographical classification into city districts. There was a captain in each of the seventy-eight commercial lines of the city, and each captain had lieutenants and operatives in his particular line of business. In this way there was what might be called a double covering of the city, both as to information and investigation. For instance, in each hotel there would be a captain, lieutenant and operatives. The Bureau of Information had entire charge of the financial end of the League, and it supplied men to the Investigation Division for the purpose of raids, or for whatever matter required special assistance.

In the War Department work, the selective service bureau was in charge of a captain with proper assistants, who handled all violations under Section 6 of the Act. A member of this bureau was detailed with each exemption board, and this division handled all the draft investigations. It made a great many searches of this sort, prevented a great many evasions, and corrected many incorrect classifications. In the slacker raids which New Orleans had in common with practically every other big city of the country there were sometimes as many as three hundred operatives employed, and it is estimated that more than 20,000 slacker investigations were made in all.

New Orleans was a "wet town," in close proximity to two Naval stations, three aviation fields, and two cantonments. It is easily seen what this meant in the way of activities for the A. P. L. There was a special liquor bureau put in charge of a captain and assistants. The division Chief and his aids made an agreement with all the local breweries and all the wholesale and retail liquor dealers that no intoxicating liquor should be sold in bottles after 7:00 p. m. This cut off a great deal of bootlegging and much of the heavier drinking which could not be controlled by the local police. This bureau was most efficient, as is demonstrated by the fact that Colonel Charles B. Hatch, U. S. Marines, who was in charge of the police forces of Philadelphia, was sent down to New Orleans by Secretary Daniels of the Navy to make an investigation of the New Orleans situation, and reported that so long as the A. P. L. was on the job there was no need for the establishment of a military police in New Orleans, or of extending any other law-enforcing organization. A. P. L. has rarely had a better compliment than this.

This bureau had chemists making analyses of several alleged soft drinks, and caused a cessation in their sale when they were of a suspicious character. In general, it locked up the town in a manner entirely satisfactory to the military and naval authorities. Anyone going to New Orleans in war times would have found it anything but a wide-open place.

Yet, but lately, New Orleans was called rather an "open town" in other ways: hence the vice bureau, established under the constant personal supervision of the division Chief. There were squads kept out all the time in control of the "district" and uptown sections of the city, this patrol being kept up day and night. It was not in the least infrequent that A. P. L. men would be out many nights on service of this sort.

In order that the operations of this vice bureau might

be facilitated, Chief Weinberger was named U. S. Commissioner by Federal Judge Foster. Women apprehended under Section 13 of the Conscription Act were brought before Commissioner Weinberger, their cases investigated and affidavits made. When necessary, they were sent to the isolation hospital for investigation as to their physical status.

In order to prevent sending these unfortunate women to jail with criminals, the American Protective League at New Orleans engaged in the enterprise earlier referred to — its "Amproleague Farm." Here there were ample dormitories, fully equipped, and a garden was maintained. There was a matron in charge. The place was kindly and helpful in every way, and every attempt was made to change the women spiritually as well as physically during their stay. Thus the League went a step further than acting simply as a merciless police force. It took care of young men who ought to have taken better care of themselves, but it did more. It took care not of one sex alone, but of both sexes, and in the truer and more lofty sense of the word.

In this operation of the liquor and vice bureaus, local Army and Navy camps detailed men to help the A. P. L. The local organization of the Home Guard, to the number of about a hundred, were admitted to membership in the League also. This organization, which was under military discipline, could be quickly assembled for night service. Transport of the League was cared for by the automobile division of the Bureau of Information. The latter men rendered special service to prevent the shipment of liquor into dry territory, whether in violation of the Reed Amendment or in violation of Section 12 of the Conscription Act. The New Orleans district had one neighboring cantonment which was in dry territory.

In brief, New Orleans showed what all the divisions of A. P. L. did throughout the country — good judgment and common sense. It did the thing necessary to be done, the most obvious and most useful thing. That duty was the caring for the personnel of the soldiers and sailors grouped in such numbers in or close to New Orleans. Human nature was accepted as human nature, and dealt with as such. These are the conditions which perforce colored the work of A. P. L. in New Orleans. They do not reflect the average community life of that city in any ordinary sense of the word, although many of the cases most valued by the Division itself have had to do with that manner of work.

For instance, the vice bureau apprehended two young women under Section 13 of the Conscription Act. Brought before the U. S. Commissioner, they were released upon their personal recognizance, but failed to appear on the next morning. Later they were located in Houston, Texas, and brought back to New Orleans. They were not kicked down. They found homes at the "Amproleague Farm."

Matters did not go so gently in the vice operations so far as they had to do with the older and more persistent offenders. There were raids on some of the more notorious resorts, and several of them closed their doors entirely. There was a general cleaning up in New Orleans which was good for the city whether or not it remained a center of military activities.

A common practice of New Orleans taxicab drivers was to meet all trains coming in from the cantonments and to offer the sights of the city, liquor and taxicab included, to any enlisted man for a net sum varying from five to ten dollars. The League practically wiped out this pernicious practice by putting on the trains A. P. L. men in uniform as soldiers. When they got off the train and were thus accosted by taxicab drivers, they had all the evidence which was necessary. The taxicab practice was seriously interfered with.

A neighboring city was alleged to have examined incorrectly before its draft board a certain young man, giving him a classification to which he was not entitled. Investigation was set on foot by the A. P. L., who uncovered the fact that the man's father conducted a sanitarium patronized by drug and liquor patients. He had treated several members of the board in his sanitarium, and had likewise had the Federal district judge as a patient, as well as several other influential citizens of the community. Thus, having rather confidential information, A. P. L. had very little difficulty in framing up its case.

It will perhaps not be necessary to go into the usual series of narratives of interesting cases in the instance of the Crescent City. The report, as outlined above, is so different in its general phases from that of the average division that it may be allowed to stand, with the addition of its tabulated totals, which cover all the forms of assistance to the Government in which A. P. L. has participated throughout the United States.

Alien enemy activities	292
Citizen disloyalty and sedition	1,626
Sabotage, bombs, dynamite, defective manufacture	24
Anti-military activity, interference with draft	34
Propaganda—word of mouth and printed	1,326
Radical organizations—I. W. W., etc	43
Bribery, graft, theft and embezzlement	82
Naturalization, impersonation, etc	827
Counter-espionage for military intelligence	2
Selective Service Regulations under boards	2,194
In slacker raids, estimated	20,000
Of local and district board members	4
Work or fight order	254
Character and loyalty—civilian applicants	103
Applicants for commissions	57
Training camp activities—Section 12	2,919
Training camp activities—Section 13	2,843
Camp desertions	140
Collection of foreign maps, etc	3,500
Counter-espionage for Naval Intelligence	206
Collection of binoculars, etc	8
Food Administration—hoarding, destruction, etc	453
Fuel Administration—hoarding, destruction, etc	964
Department of State—Miscellaneous	7
Treasury Department—War Risk Insurance, etc	625
United States Shipping Board	15
Alien Property Custodian—Miscellaneous	7
Red Cross loyalty investigations	409

The decision to demobilize the American Protective League was arrived at somewhat suddenly, for reasons more or less obvious to all members of the League. As recently as November 13, 1918, Mr. Bielaski, Chief of the Bureau of Investigation of the U. S. Department of Justice, wrote to Chief Weinberger, expressing the assurance that the American Protective League by no means ought to disband, since peace was not yet declared, and since need for the League's services still existed. He said, "I am entirely satisfied that the need for this organization will continue for some time to come, entirely without regard to the progress of peace negotiations. The tremendous machines which have been organized by the Government for the prosecution of this war cannot be stopped abruptly, and must continue to operate for many months under any circumstances. The American Protective League has a large share of the work in this country which has made possible the united support and the full success of our arms abroad, and I am sure that your organization will continue to play its full part until the Department is willing to say that it has no further need for its services."

Now, a few months after these expressions, the League is dissolved and its work declared ended. Is it ended? New Orleans thinks not, and points at least to one instance of civic betterment which has not yet demobilized — its "Amproleague Farm." The officials found there an old sugar plantation which dated back to 1857. The old residence was built over as a modern home, equipped with forty windows, a dormitory with fifty beds, a room with six sewing machines, also ample galleries and well-fitted kitchens. Here the League has built a little community home which it is not yet ready to see die. It is a home where an erring person is given a chance to begin over again. And after all, has not that been a part of all the work of A. P. L. in all the country? From time to time in other reports we have seen it stated: "We tried to show this or that pro-German where he was wrong"; "We tried to change rather than to punish"; "We endeavored to improve our citizenship rather than penalize those who had made mistakes." So, therefore, we may say that New Orleans has added a good chapter to the good history of this body of thoughtful citizens — it has helped make the world and the country better than it was before.

CHAPTER XV

THE STORY OF CALIFORNIA

A Series of Graphic Case Stories from All Over the Golden State—Stirring Romances from the Capital of Romance—The A. P. L. in San Francisco, Los Angeles, Santa Barbara, San Diego, and Everywhere Between—the Pacific Coast in War Times.

Time was when there were just two really cosmopolitan towns in the United States. Merely being mixed in population does not mean cosmopolitanism; but San Francisco and New Orleans were two towns which could offer any American something to see. The fire changed San Francisco to a certain extent, and the North has ruined New Orleans all it could; but the soul of each of these two towns still goes marching on, incapable of destruction. If sudden wealth could not make San Francisco avaricious, nor solid prosperity leave her sordid; if earthquake, fire and famine could not daunt her unquenchably buoyant heart — what reason have we to believe that a small matter like a world war would much disturb her poise?

'Frisco by the Golden Gate — that last viewpoint where America faces the Orient and her own future as well — took her war philosophically, allowed her Hindu conspiracies to run their course, and viewed with none too great agitation the flood of disloyalty which inevitably was caught by the western shore, just as once a better sort of material was caught in the sluices of her old Long Toms. San Francisco knows she is here to stay, and believes that this Republic also is here to stay.

The A. P. L. in San Francisco

That there would be an A. P. L. organization in San Francisco admitted of no doubt. The city was ably organized and certainly took able care of Fritz and his Boche-loving friends. But all California is divided into three parts: Northern California, Southern California — and all California! An offense to one means a fight for all, although each allows a certain amount of thumb-biting on the part of a native son. The A. P. L. in California followed precisely this ancient line of cleavage, so that there was established a Northern Division, a Southern Division — and a State Inspectorship! The State Inspector was Mr. Douglas White, who himself is a traveling man, and therefore cannot be accounted as belonging to either North or South. Mr. A. J. DeLamare had the division office in San Francisco, where the organization so closely followed the general lines already described in other cities that it perhaps is not needful to go into details here.

That California's polyglot population meant potential trouble may be seen in the heads of the Frisco reports: a total of 1,612 cases of disloyalty and sedition, 277 cases of propaganda, and 105 of radicalism, such as that of I. W. W., etc. The work for the war boards — slackers, desertion, character and loyalty, etc. — footed up 2,415 cases in all, the grand total carried on the records as actual "cases" amounting to 5,691.

The Department of Justice labors, as usual in all the great cities, meant a vast amount of time and energy expended on the part of A. P. L. men, with the usual percent of win, lose, and draw — all offered in the infinite variety afforded by the California climate. Some of the cases were odd, some mysterious, and a good many of them big. Perhaps a few from the many turned in by Frisco may be found interesting, though chosen practically by chance. One of these is a wireless case. It should not be dismissed as another "mysterious signal" flivver until read quite through to its close.

Mrs. B——— and her mother had moved into a flat on Williard street. The persons who occupied the flat before them came back to get some plates and other material, which looked so strange that Mrs. B——— thought there had been a wireless plant there, so she reported it. They refused to give up the fixture material then in their possession. The place was on a high hill overlooking the bay and would have been an ideal locality for a wireless plant which might have given information to the enemy.

Operative No. 440 took over this case. He found that the house stood at the edge of a wood on a rocky hill. The two women explained that the place had been occupied by a man named G——— who seemed very mysterious. He would hang around the house all day and come home at different hours. He moved away suddenly. He used to make trips in the woods with people not known about there. Operative found in the house several base plates for electric light plugs, also electric wires grounded on the water and gas pipes, and also a hole cut in the side of the house, as is done when a high tension wire is passed through.

Mrs. B——— stated that at night sounds similar to those made by a wireless sending outfit often were heard, also that a sound representing rapping signals occurred at the rear of the house. The operative, making all allowances for a woman's nervousness, returned that evening. Sure enough, he heard the sounds persistently as described. They did come from the rear of the house, and, although examination was made there at once and next day by daylight, he was unable to tell what made the sounds.

The case now looked promising, so the operative again went over the premises. He could not find any trace of wireless apparatus. He did find a pipe starting at the edge of the woods and tried to follow this. It led to the brink of a high bluff. Just at the edge of the bluff the operative almost stepped on a rattlesnake, and in attempting to escape he rolled to the bottom of the bank, carrying the pipe with him! When he came to, he was free of the snake. He looked at his pipe, but found it clogged with dirt. It therefore could not have been used lately as a wire conduit.

Nothing could be learned of the former occupant, G———, except that he was a musician. Inquiry among musical societies and unions finally located him as a player in a place called the "Hoffbrau"—since very patriotically changed to the "States Café." Reports were that he had been born in the city of New York and served honorably in the United States Navy. His wife's father had fought in the Civil War. After G——— had been found, the operative had a talk with him. Soon thereafter, light was offered on a very mysterious situation. G——— explained that he had to move very quickly as his wife had rented a new house without notifying him. When he moved he had forgotten those base plates — which were intended only for household use, percolators, etc. But when he went away the dog was not taken. He had come back a number of times to the old place trying to locate the dog. At last he had remembered these base plates and tried to secure them, as he had put them in himself. It looked like a clean bill of health for G———; but how about the mysterious noises?

The operative once more secreted himself at the edge of the woods at about ten o'clock that night and began to watch the house. At eleven o'clock he again heard the mysterious sounds at the rear of the house. He slipped up quietly and there found the solution of his really wireless mystery. The "signals" were made by the home-sick dog, which was trying to locate its former owner! He would come to the house in the night and scratch on the screen door, making sounds like a wireless discharge. His tail knocking on the boards made the rapping nose. When a strange person would open the door he would disappear in the darkness of the woods, so no cause for the sounds could be traced. So there you were — a perfectly beautiful mystery! It is told in the report in a very unagitated style, but really it is a pretty good case of A. P. L. work.

All sorts and conditions of men were enlisted and carried on the A. P. L. rolls; but did you ever hear of an anthropologist A. P. L.? There was one at San Francisco. It was reported that a man living in Alameda, a geologist and mining engineer employed by an oil company, was fitting out a launch to go to Mexico and purchase supplies. His trip was alleged to be for the purpose of oil prospecting. He appeared to tell a straight story, and said he had bought surveying instruments and food and intended to clear duly.

Two days later another A. P. L. operative heard that this man had left for Washington, stating that he must get some passports, although he was known to have passports already. As a third man from the San Francisco A. P. L. office was going on to Washington, these facts were given him and he was asked to give the man the once-over in Washington. He did this and found that the boat-owner was getting passports to England. He found also that this person was associated with Professor M———, who claimed to be looking up oil conditions in this country and studying anthropology on the side.

As this operative also was interested in anthropology, he and Professor M——— got on very well, although the San Franciscan was not very much impressed by the learned man's fundamental knowledge in a scientific way. There was nothing, however, to show that the professor was engaged in any enemy activities. But the San Franciscan operative gathered the notion that the visiting passport-seeker might possibly be engaged in spreading German propaganda among the many negroes about the city of Washington. He finally discovered in his possession a lot of pictures of a very undesirable sort, intended for German distribution among negro troops in France, with the intention of creating dissatisfaction among such troops. These pictures carried the legend, "See what is happening to your wives and families while you are in France." Copies of these pictures were obtained. The operative made the further discovery that Professor M——— was in the employ of this pseudo-mining-engineer, who now stood revealed as an active German propagandist. It was also learned where this latter Kultur-spreader got his pictures.

Arrangements were made with one of the professor's photographic subjects so that the operatives might listen in on certain flashlight performances by night. To cut all that unprintable sort of thing short, it may be said that the operatives, while seated on the porch, heard and saw all they liked of the German color-blindness.

The learned professor, however, having his suspicions aroused by the fact that the door kept opening and would not stay shut as it ought to have done, came to the door, poked his head out and saw the operatives sitting on the porch. One operative sat there with a camera in his lap and a flash gun in his right hand, intending to make pictures of the picture maker himself, so that evidence of the reprehensible nature of his own pictures might be discovered. The professor, however, sprang back into the room and presently came out armed with a gun and a bayonet. The operatives at once fell off the back of the porch. Lunging at the first man, the professor missed; but he caught the second operative with the bayonet in the wrist and ripped up his forearm. The men closed in upon him and there was a warm fight for quite a while. Details are not desirable and need not be given. It is sufficient to say that the nature of the photographs was disclosed and details turned in to the proper quarters. The anthropological German professor later was arrested and turned over to the Department of Justice. At last accounts he was in jail at Washington awaiting trial. Regarding his performance, it is only fair to say that his anthropological tendencies seemed to run true to German scientific form.

The A. P. L. in Sausalito

Not so far from San Francisco by way øf the crow's flight is the Marin County Division of the A. P. L. at Sausalito. This division also had a case of mysterious light flashes —from Belvidere Island. Signals came from several different directions and several different sources, but no one could ever be located as receiving them. Across the bay from Belvidere is Angel Island, a large internment camp, and in either direction lies a neighborhood which is very pro-German. There might have been signals, but no one seemed to be able to trace the code or get anything intelligible. Investigation of this thing lasted for over a year, and finally the division concluded it was the action of someone trying to intimidate the residents of that vicinity. It was not run down.

Located in the hills was an organization knowns as the " German Tourists' Club," which had been incorporated in Vienna, Austria. Prior to our entering the war it was visited by many alien enemies and many German-Americans, so that it was under constant surveillance of the Intelligence services of the United States and also by the A. P. L. of Marin County. Considerable information was furnished to the authorities, and one alien enemy was interned. Another alien enemy was apprehended who had $2,500 cash on his person and was trying to get to South America, whence he intended to return to Germany. The same club turned out yet another man who, on a railroad train, was heard abusing this country. An A. P. L. man heard him and asked a constable to arrest him at once. He was taken to the county jail, where his remarks were so abusive that the Department of Justice immediately took him into custody for internment.

The hilly, wooded and mountainous character of Marin County, bordering on the ocean, made it a favorite resort for hikers, hunters, fishermen and the like, and it has many locations which would afford excellent rendezvous. It kept the A. P. L. operatives busy in all their spare time walking and driving through the country. On one such trip along the sea shore, in a very remote place, a Navy torpedo was found. It proved to be only a practice one, having no war head, but it might have been worse.

The A. P. L. in Los Angeles

The sun-kissed Southwest handled its A. P. L. work in a wholly modern way, as perhaps some of the sidelights will show. How quaint and curious some of these chuckle-making anecdotes — and how grave some of the serious ones — will seem fifty years from now, when California will be looking back on another generation of her large and swift history!

The report from the city of Los Angeles is one entirely consistent with the reputation of that busy community, and as usual the totals ran large. Los Angeles handled 2,136 cases of alien enemy activity; 5,275 selctive service investigations; 1,494 examinations for disloyalty and sedition; 289 cases of propaganda by word of mouth and 61 by means of the printed page. There were 289 investigations of radicals and pacifists, and 648 of all other natures, not mentioning those which had to do with food hoarding, waste, etc., which made a formidable total of themselves. There are not many sections which report a wider or more interesting range of experiences.

As in the case of practically all our cities, at the time the war broke out, the Deparment of Justice for Los Angeles was inadequately equipped with men, motor cars and data-chasers to deal with the numerous alien enemies, German sympathizers and non-patriotic citizens. Los Angeles frankly says that this species of the human fauna seem to be peculiar to Southern California, and certainly the totals of Los Angeles would indicate as much. The Chief says:

> Some of regretted that we could not do more for the Government, for the work of the A. P. L. appealed very strongly to us. When we saw the local Government situation, a number of us at once offered to help. The outstanding feature of all this work was the absolute cowardliness of the pro-German individual. In all our cases I cannot recall one where anything like courage was displayed on the part of the subject. The moment they realized they were confronted by anything like authority their fear and their efforts at self-protection were, to say the least, extreme. Individuals were brought to the attention of the various departments who did not understand and cannot to this day realize how the intimation was received. They did realize, however, that there was authority back of us. In many cases, the Military Intelligence Department called us to their assistance where information could not be secured in any other way. We also were able to help the Food Administration.

There is distinct food for thought in the closing remarks of the all too modest Los Angeles chief, made before the dissolution date of the A. P. L. was announced:

> In conclusion, I will say that a great deal of good could be done by some form of permanent organization of the A. P. L., or at least the retention of a nucleus for a continuation of this work if it becomes necessary. From time to time certain conditions are certain to occur in this country, brought about either by war measures or discontent among a certain class, which will require drastic handling. The American Protective League can secure more valuable information and better assist in bringing the attention of the authorities to such facts than any other similar body of citizens in the country.

These are words of gold and show the heart of Los Angeles to be certainly in the right place. It is a new and troubled America that we have all got to face now, with or without an A. P. L.

As to the odd and interesting stories noted by the Los Angeles operatives, the latter as usual seem to take more delight in telling of their fiascos than they do of their successes, but saving grace was usually there. For instance a woman and her husband living in Glendale were very rabid about the war, and hence received a visit. The informants turned out to be church members and apparently desirable citizens. The female suspected fell into hysterics, cursed the Frenchman who lived next door and the Englishman who lived several houses beyond, and declared she had bought Liberty Bonds and had up flags enough to be left alone. The German himself demanded to know by what authority he was visited. The League man told him there was plenty of authority all right, and that he did not need to specify. The suspect took a good hint, and from that time neither the man nor his wife was guilty of any public utterance of any sort whatever on war matters.

One Herman F. H——— claimed that he was a " secret service man " and showed a badge and some handcuffs, but still talked very pro-German. He said among other things that the American people would wake up — that the Kaiser would show them something — that we could not win the war. His nearest friend was an army sergeant by the name of Paul S——— of Fort McArthur. These two would talk together in German. The doughty U. S. sergeant was also of the belief that our army had no chance and said the soldiers were all dissatisfied. They were both investigated. The sergeant was put in jail at Los Angeles. Military Intelligence took over the rest of the case — and M. I. D. has never been noted for its mercifulness.

An over-zealous woman in one instance reported suspicious activity on the part of a family which had a great many mysterious packages delivered at their address. She said they had quantities of large pipe which they would fill with guns and ammunition, also boxes of rifle cartridges. Investigation proved that some of the mysterious packages were only lunch baskets; that the trucks were hauling large pieces of well-casing and sometimes small articles of grocery or hardware were slipped into the pipes to save space. They had no packages of ammunition at all, and the packages of cartridges were only pasteboard boxes containing shelled walnuts. Jumpy times.

A man by the name of M——— came from Chicago, and closely following him came a report that he was wanted by the Chicago police. Operatives located the man and thought he would look well in the uniform of the United

States Army, but the recruiting office, inquiring into the reason for the Chicago telegram, found that the man had served a term in the penitentiary. He was not, therefore, classified even as a slacker and he did not get into the Army, which will not receive anyone who has served a prison sentence.

Los Angeles had considerable to do with the stoppage of propaganda by means of motion pictures, that city being the capital of filmdom. Newspaper reports of the cases of the film " Patria " and of " The Spirit of 1776 " are familiar to the reading public. A. P. L. was always on hand for film censorship purposes.

A case which attracted considerable attention was known as the von H——— case. The subject was a native of Germany, fifty-three years of age, a resident in the United States for thirty-two years. He never had become a citizen, although once employed in the California post office. Von H——— was a movie actor who did spy parts. He fraternized with the soldiers and sailors *in propria persona,* and liked to ask them to his room for conversations over the war. At length he was arrested. His rooms turned out a mass of evidence, including four hundred snap shots and some forty letters of the vilest nature. He had intended to send this material over to Germany to show the lack of morale of the American soldiers and sailors. He had an oil painting of the Kaiser, a picture of von Hindenburg and one of the German flag. He was sentenced to five years, but it is not thought that he will live out his sentence. Perhaps we can struggle along without him.

There is no character in whom the public more naturally reposes confidence than in the tried and true negro Pullman porter, but this is the story of one such porter accused of draft evasion. He was confined in jail but was offered release if he would go into the Army. He told the operative that he would go all right, but that his check for forty dollars was not on hand and that he needed about five dollars to " float himself." The operative loaned him the five dollars and the Pullman porter is still floating. Neither Army nor anyone else has heard of him since.

Most of the more groundless suspicions and imaginings of Americans regarding German spies arose among the women of the country. Their apprehensions at times would lead them to report almost anything. One small demure little woman once applied to the headquarters of the A. P. L. in Los Angeles and said that she knew parties — German spies — who received money from Germany and who had no resources other than the funds of the German Government. The chief asked her upon what she based her information. The little lady looked carefully around the room, under the table and out of the window, and then came close up to the chief before she gave him the real basis of her charge. She said that the parties referred to were the possessors of a cuckoo clock which she was sure was made in Germany; hence they must be pro-Germans, and therefore spies!

The German ministers, it seems, infest the Pacific slope as well as the northwestern part of the United States. Herewith the case of Emile K———, minister of a German Methodist church. An operative went into his church and took his seat in the last pew. He reports:

> A broad shouldered man in a frock coat sat down beside me, introduced himself as Rev. K——— and asked me if I was one of the Liberty Bond salesmen. I denied any such impeachment, saying this to him in German. This seemed to please him very much, and Mr. K——— thawed out. He told me after a while that he was born in Wisconsin but that his heart was in the right place, like most people that were born there in "Little Germany." He said he had been in Mexico, where he had spent four years "very profitably." He smiled at me—rather meaningly, I thought. He wanted to know how the Irish were behaving toward our people in New York. He also said that it was too bad the Americans did not want to fight. He thought that if the Japanese were to come over, it might arouse our manhood. He asked me to be sure and call again, as he enjoyed my company very much. There was something cold-blooded about this man that made me think he would look better in a German uniform than in a preacher's coat. What worries me about him—and I hope the A. P. L. will square it—is that I had to put a quarter in the collection plate to keep up appearances. I demand that two bits back if the A. P. L. ever puts him in the jug!

An operative was sent out to get a deserter who seemed to be rather of an inventive turn of mind. He found his man in a barn, and when the suspect came out, the operative ran up and called him by name. The suspect turned and asked him if he was arrested. When the operative asked him, " Arrested for what? " he replied, " You know, all right." He then admitted that he was a deserter from the Navy at San Francisco. He wanted to go into the house after some letter paper, but the operative would not let him. Afterwards he said he wanted to go in to get a gun, and would have shot the operative rather than go with him. Returned to San Francisco from Los Angeles jail.

A carload of A. P. L. men went out to a deserted spot in the San Fernando Valley near the Los Angeles aqueduct. A mysterious German had been seen about, possibly with evil intent. Operatives surrounded a small cabin which was occupied by a very arrogant German and two women. The man on the case reports: " I noticed a big revolver on the dresser, secured it and put it in my pocket before we went on with the investigation. We went through all his letters, mostly in German, but discovered nothing in the way of evidence. We told him why we had come and warned him to keep away from the aqueduct. He took it all very submissively, so I thought it would be all right to leave the revolver which I had captured. When I took it out of my pocket to look it over, I found that it was empty, the hammer had been knocked off and it could not have been fired. But " you will note," writes the operative with an exultant note, " that I responded fully to the demands of the occasion in the way of bravery! "

A case came down from Seattle to Los Angeles, having to do with an itinerant slacker who came from Pennsylvania and who, since then, had lived in Idaho, Washington, and California. The suspect's physical description was that of a man six feet tall, weight about 220 pounds, health apparently the best, appearance very shabby, an additional circumstance being that he had a pronounced aversion to the use of water which was very evident at close range. It was stated that the man owned at least nine different properties, and although indolent, was apparently well to do. He was found in possession of Socialist literature, and declared that he would not buy bonds or assist the Government or have anything to do with the Red Cross. He was asked how he would like to join the Army. Since he did not like the proposition, he was arrested for violation of the Selective Service Act, found within the age, and indicted September 20, 1918, by the Federal Grand Jury for failure to register for the draft.

Los Angeles had a practicing physician who fled from Germany to escape the rigors of its military laws. When war broke out between this country and Germany, this suspect — for he very soon became a suspect and was placed under the espionage of A. P. L.— planned to turn a pretty penny by the practice of sabotage, not upon property, but on personnel. There were some cowards in this country of so yellow a type that they were willing even to have their eyesight tampered with that they might escape the draft. This monster in human guise assisted such depraved beings, sometimes perhaps to the permanent loss of their eye-sight — they took their own chances. This man got a sentence of ten years in the penitentiary and a fine of $5,000. A woman accomplice was sentenced to eleven years penal servitude.

A German, von B———, was a close friend of R. B———, the two rooming together. The latter was with the National Guard of California in the Mexican trouble, was mustered out, but registered for the draft, being exempted on the grounds of having a dependent wife and child. After he had received his exemption, B——— was told by von B——— to get into the Aviation Corps at San Diego, and that he would show him how. The exempted man was admitted to the Aviation Corps in the United States Army, went to Berkeley for three months' training, and then was transferred to San Diego. He is a German and his wife is also. These two men were reported to have made a great many mysterious trips together. Subject was interned on presidential warrant, it being obvious that neither he nor his room-mate meant well towards the United States.

Can a leopard change his spots? The answer would appear to be that he cannot — if he is a German leopard. For instance, one William S———, a German small grocer in Los Angeles, was doing a good business and living very well. He had a son enlisted in the Aviation Corps of the United States Army at the outbreak of the war. There was no reason why he, himself, should not have remained loyal to this country, which had been kind to him. But although he had been away from Germany for a score of years, he was foolish enough to retain all the German spots. He said that Wilson was a Kaiser and that the people ought to kill him; and he uttered a good many additional sentiments of like sort against this country and its Government. He was so bitter in his pro-German attitude that he lost practically all of his customers. As a result he began to worry, not only for the Imperial German Government, but for himself. And then one night he died — which closed the case for A. P. L. and opened it for a Higher Court. Since it has been shown in many instances that the River Jordan has not been able to wash out the German spots, the query is whether the River Styx is any more able to do so? That is the question in which all admirers of German *Kultur* and its practices are interested.

The A. P. L. in Santa Barbara

There is an unsettled rivalry between the two types of beauty, blonde and brunette, which never will be concluded so long as women live and men admire them. So also, one supposes, time will not last long enough to determine which is the more beautiful and lovable spot—Monterey in Northern California, or Santa Barbara in the South. You can start a riot over that question on any railway train on the Pacific slope. One man will be ready to shoot anybody who does not agree that the Seventeen Mile Drive out of Monterey is the most beautiful region in all the world, bar none. It is — it is! Who can deny it? But who, also, can deny even at the point of a gun that the Santa Barbara coast is also the most beautiful spot in all the world? Besides, the latter community has scientific records as ground for the assertion that Santa Barbara has the finest mean temperature on the North American continent, and hence is the one ideal dwelling spot for human beings. It is — it is!

But, very naturally, so fair a region as that of the California slope must have attracted all sorts and conditions of men, evil men as well as good, designing transients as well as those calling California home. For this reason Santa Barbara also had her organization of the A. P. L.

One of the colony of wealthy men who had built palatial homes in and around Santa Barbara was a certain millionaire who had what might be called advanced ideas or free thinking tendencies. Early in the year 1917, Mr. H——— associated himself actively with the pacifist movement. He had, as a co-agitator, a reverend doctor who was pastor in a church at Santa Barbara. They both printed pamphlets in opposition to the war, and finally came out with a book which was a very violent denunciation of war in general. The two gentlemen divided the authorship of this book, H——— doing the first part and G——— the second. Reverend G——— had the advantage of also being able to deliver sermons from the pulpit. He denounced the United States Government and referred to the American flag as a "worthless rag." After we had declared war with Germany these men kept on with their activities, hence A. P. L. took their cases under advisement with instructions from the Los Angeles Department of Justice. There were hundreds of operative reports turned in on these two men.

After a time another book, published by H———, came out — a very violent arraignment of the Government for its stand in the war, and very hot anti-draft literature. These publications attracted to H——— and G——— a large number of the weak-minded people who affiliated themselves with the "Fellowship of Reconcilation" — a society which ought to go strong in Berlin, now that the war is over.

Reverend G——— was expelled as the pastor of his church, following a very seditious letter which he wrote, saying that he had relegated the American flag to the flames, expressing sympathy with I. W. W., and opposition to the draft. It has always been understood that the climate of California attracted a great many people, and the state has always seemed to be prolific of great differences of opinion among those people, but when it comes to a minister of the gospel uttering such things as these, it is going a little strong even for the most free-thinking country in the world.

The H——— case kept on attaining proportions, and heavy shipments of literature were made into Santa Barbara and distributed out of that city to various points. All of these shipments were followed and full reports were made. In the latter part of 1917, another reverend doctor, F.

H———, and one C. H. B———, became active associates with the foregoing. Pacifist meetings in Los Angeles were raided, and all these parties managed to get themselves arrested on a charge of disturbing the peace.

In April, 1918, a letter addressed to a man in Santa Barbara, California, who had a name quite similar to the first man above mentioned, fell into the hands of A. P. L., because the wrong recipient had opened it. It was found to be a letter from the secretary of the I. W. W. organization at Los Angeles, setting a definite date for a meeting at Los Angeles where Mr. H——— was to be present and address the assembled multitude. The Chief of A. P. L. at Santa Barbara notified D. J. in Los Angeles. At the same time, Santa Barbara was requested to locate the new reverend, Mr. F. H———, whose whereabouts now were unknown.

There now came into the case a Miss E———, a prominent young woman who had been a canteen worker and Red Cross nurse in France. Her family were friends of the H——— family, but Miss E——— was a friend of the United States Army above all things. She learned that the second reverend was at Modesto, California, and that Mr. H——— would leave Santa Barbara on Sunday, April 7, for Los Angeles; that he would stop at the Alexandria Hotel, and would address the meeting on April 8.

This information was turned over to D. J. at Los Angeles.

It was decided to arrest all the foregoing alphabetical gentlemen. About twenty members were assigned to the work and these arrests were duly made at 9:00 P. M. on the night of April 8. Certain residences of the above parties were searched and an immense amount of literature and pamphlets on pacifism and radical Socialism were discovered. Most of the books were seized.

The first mentioned Mr. H——— was hard to catch, the deputy marshal being obliged to chase him through the streets of Los Angeles for several blocks. H——— had to spend his night in the county jail. The next morning he telephoned to his mother that he had "spent the night with some friends of his, the Marshalls." At least, he had a sense of humor, because the only "Marshals" he knew were the deputy United States marshals at that time, and he had indeed been their guest temporarily.

All the defendants, excepting two incidentally connected with the case, were convicted of violation of the Espionage Act. The wealthy pacifist millionaire was fined $27,000. The vitriolic clergyman first mentioned, and his ally, the clergyman of the second part, were fined $5,000 apiece. Two lesser fines of $500 and $100 were imposed also. The second reverend doctor was arrested on information furnished by Santa Barbara A. P. L. to the Los Angeles office. Other persons of ultra-pacifist tendencies in Santa Barbara have been kept constantly under surveillance. So it would seem that in peaceful Santa Barbara all is not always peace — unless it is the right sort of peace.

Santa Barbara made twenty-three arrests and secured fifteen convictions. Fines were collected by the Government through A. P. L. investigations amounting to $37,100. Santa Barbara had the usual percentage of flivver cases, especially as to mysterious signal lights. One of these proved to be nothing more dangerous than a night watchman on a railroad track, signalling with his lantern. The operatives uncovered one rather tragic case. A Franciscan monk wrote to the draft board that his own brother claimed exemption falsely, that he was living with another man's wife, and had been guilty of forgery. The couple were found making their confession. They confessed further before the draft board that they both were married but had separated from their respective mates. They fell in love and began living together within two weeks after they had met, and they had lived together as man and wife for some time. The woman was released; the man was inducted into the service and sent to camp.

A Santa Barbara operative evinced a certain sleuthing ability in a case which reached its climax when someone blew up an old barn at the rear of the place belonging to the complaining couple. There was a box containing a setting hen, malignantly maternal over thirteen eggs. This box was within six feet of the place where the explosion occurred — but there was not a mark on the box, although the barn door had been blown to bits. It seemed that something was wrong. Matters simmered down to a spite case of a middle aged couple against some neighbors, who finally had determined to get their kind of justice by blowing up their own barn — but they did not wish to blow up their valuable hen, so they removed her before touching off the charge.

Santa Barbara County — not the town — reported 94 cases of disloyalty and sedition, 24 male alien activities and 20 female alien enemies, besides the 34 I. W. W. cases. The man does not live who can predict the end of all the vast social problems which will have to be worked out eventually on this beautiful Pacific slope.

The A. P. L. in San Diego

We have on our southern borders the Mexican situation, not yet settled, but one day to be settled. Germany did all she could to set Mexico on our heels, and her atrocious Zimmerman note was one more instance of her venomous but blundering diplomacy. Perhaps she wonders still how we got that note when it first was despatched from Mexico; and how we sat tight so long with knowledge of it in our possession. This is by way of saying that the old Spanish city of San Diego is an important naval base, located close to the edge of the intriguing border of the Southwest — and a borderland is always a zone of espionage.

It is, therefore, not surprising to say that San Diego had 65 cases of alien enemy activities and 842 cases of disloyalty and sedition, 286 instances of propaganda and 32 I. W. W. cases. For the War Department, there were 554 investigations, 98 of these being character and loyalty investigations. So that, on the whole, it may be seen that this once indolent city of the Southwest, now a busy center of affairs, also had an A. P. L. during the war.

There is a curious range of cases reported from one and another corner of the country to the National Directors of A. P. L. Sometimes an extraordinarily troublesome case has had very little at bottom; and again a simple case often turned out big. Yet again, a case might have all the earmarks of simplicity and prove full of trouble. For instance, if you were sent to arrest a woman, you customarily would not expect her to disclose herself to be a walking arsenal of offensive weapons — a woman's portative appliances, lacking pockets as they do, not seeming to give her natural facilities for heeling herself in any way practical for quick action. Such, however, proved to be a wrong estimate of a certain young lady whom we may call Miss M. E———, reported in connection with certain alleged "German activity." She certainly turned out to be active.

An operative found Miss M. E——— living in a garage about six feet square. The room was in much disorder, showing trunks, boxes, tin cans and literature all about. Some ammunition was found, which the operative left in place. He did not open the trunk. Suspect was reported sometimes around a print shop, which next was visited. The proprietor said that the suspect sometimes did some printing herself in his little shop. Neighbors seemed to be afraid of suspect, and said she had been seen with a revolver in her coat pocket.

Operative interviewed the suspect herself and asked her how about the literature she had been printing. She admitted she had distributed about one hundred copies of a circular. We may at this point allow the operative to tell his simple and uneventful story in his own words.

> I then told her we had a search warrant, but she had better come down to the Federal Agent. She refused, saying she had work to do and must get it out. I told her we had a car outside and would bring her back to her print shop, but she still refused. I then told her I would walk down with her to the print shop and then we could talk over the 'phone and get more instructions. When we arrived at the print shop, which is about eight feet square, I told Operative No. 9 to go into the house and call up Mr. W———, Federal Agent, and ask for instructions. Being warned by the neighbors that subject carried a gun, I went into the printing shop and asked her if she did carry a gun. She immediately became enraged and rushed for her leather grip and pulled out a .38-Colt, fully loaded. I made a grab at her, and after a tussle obtained possession of the weapon. While putting this gun in my pocket, she obtained a hammer and was endeavoring to hit me over the head, and also at the same time calling for assistance. I now called Operative No. 9 from the house, and between us, we obtained the hammer. But in some manner she pulled from her clothes a .32-automatic revolver and then endeavored to shoot us if possible. Operative No. 9 and myself overpowered her and took this gun from her.
>
> We proceeded to take subject to the car, which was about

> half a block away. She continually screamed, "Help! Help! Won't someone help a good Protestant?" We finally got her in the car, and then I sent Operative No. 9 back after my hat, her bag, and the search warrant, which we had dropped. I stood outside the car, holding subject by one arm, when she drew a knife from her bosom and slashed at my hand. I got in the car and we tussled again, and I finally got the knife away from her. I had just thrown the knife over into the front seat of the automobile when she drew a small dirk from her bosom. Between Operative No. 9, who had come back, and myself, we got this dirk away from her, slightly cutting her hand. We then thought it would be best to have a witness as to what was going on, and seeing a man standing looking at us, we called him. Upon noticing some women standing at the corner watching us, I thought it would be better to have them come and search her, and upon calling them they came over. I told them what I wanted them to do and they asked if it would be safe, and told them yes—by this time. I explained who we were and what we were doing, and asked them to search subject and they agreed to do so. During their search they found a pocket containing ten bullets, sewed on to her petticoat, an 8-inch Bowie knife, and also another revolver, a Colt .41, fully loaded.

Nothing much further seemed to disturb the calm of the scene, so the operators took the lady to the county jail, where she was later turned over for examination to the Department of Justice. The two operatives then went back to the subject's room and found in every conceivable place ammunition of every description. It was sewed in the mattress, stuffed in tin cans, concealed in her trunk. There were also found a Winchester repeating rifle and a Remington repeating rifle, and ammunition in all amounting to about 1,000 rounds. When her hand-grip was searched at the office, it was found to contain four tobacco pouches of bullets, sixty-six in all, and a full clip of .32-caliber bullets. In the garage where the lady lived, some bottles were found and some cans containing powder, which were taken away for analysis.

The District Attorney recognized in Miss M. E——— a woman who had been tried twice for insanity, having been sent once to an asylum. She was committed to the State Asylum at Patton, and the authorities there were notified that in case of her future release she should be kept under surveillance. Thus endeth the first lesson, about Miss M. E———. If she had had more money, probably she would have bought more guns. A pleasant day's work for men not on anybody's pay roll.

San Diego had another case which kept the local division going for a time. Among its operatives was a crippled newsboy who once belonged to the Army. This lad had both his legs cut off in a railroad accident as he was changing from one train to another, on his way to a new army post. To make a livelihood, he took up a newsboy's occupation and became a familiar figure on the sidewalks. He had a board to which he fastened a pair of roller skates, and by means of a small block of wood he learned to push himself along the sidewalks at a very good rate of speed. It came to the attention of the division that this newsboy was a very keen observer and it was known he had a knowledge of six languages. He was enrolled and became very useful — indeed he was at the bottom of one of the biggest and most dangerous cases San Diego ever had; which shows that no crippled soldiers ought ever to despair.

The crippled newsboy ate in a certain restaurant, and there by chance he overheard a conversation between some Mexicans. He got a mass of information and turned it into the office, where a report was made to the Navy Department, which later ferreted out a plot that was laid in Mexico. With no more than this passing mention of the A. P. L. operative who, like so many others, gets small glory beyond the reward of his own conscience, some mention may be made of this plot, which really involved the extensive machinations of Germans in Mexico against the United States. It ended in the capture by the United States vessels of the Hun raider *Alexander Agassiz.*

A young woman owned the *Agassiz,* but had not been able to make much money out of it, and so sold it to one Fritz B———, once a German naval reservist and for a time chief officer on a German ship interned at Santa Rosalia. At another period in his career he had been interned at Angel Island as an alien enemy. At any rate, he made his way to Santa Rosalia, and thence to Matzatlan, where he got in touch with the German Consul. B——— was sent to Mexico

City for a conference with the German Ambassador there. There were Germans from all parts of Mexico who appeared at that meeting. When B——— came back, he sought out the acquaintance of the young woman who owned the boat and induced her to sell it to him. The boat then was hauled out and thoroughly overhauled by German sailors who had arrived from the fleet of German ships at Santa Rosalia. The hull was calked, new sails were bent on, the machinery was overhauled, and in general the boat was made ready for her career as a raider.

In the meantime B——— obtained full armament and instruments for his ship. He had some of his arms on an island seven miles northwest of Matzatlan, but he rest of the equipment was taken aboard the *Agassiz*. This was carried on openly and the news got out to the American Patrol Fleet. A cruiser put in an appearance off the mouth of Matzatlan Harbor. Hence, instead of sailing out with a crew of twenty Germans, only five Germans were put aboard the *Agassiz,* with two American women and six Mexicans. B——— figured that the boat would be taken as a harmless trader and allowed to go out. He guessed wrong. The *Agassiz* made a dash for the open sea. But by this time wireless had brought up two other American warships. They closed in on the incipient raider and signaled her to heave to. Not being obeyed, they planted a shell in front of the raider's bow, which brought her up.

Before the naval men could get aboard the *Agassiz,* her crew worked as hard as they could to throw overboard everything of an incriminating nature. They also tried to wreck the engine and destroy the bearings in the magneto. The blue-jackets found some rifles and revolvers, some German flags and a secret cipher. From the papers it was learned that B——— was in hiding at Venados Island. This was on Mexican soil, so he could not be seized.

It was learned that the German Consul at Matzatlan had forced all the crew to take the oath of allegiance to the Kaiser. He had instructed B——— to capture speedier boats, and after raiding Pacific shipping to work the Southern Pacific, thence to go by the west coast of Africa and north on a dash for some German port, so that he might send to Wilhelmstrasse — Germany's Scotland Yard — the package of papers entrusted to him by the Mexican German ambassador.

Had this raider gotten into the open seas and taken captive a faster and better equipped ship, it might have done a very considerable damage to shipping, just as did the several German raiders which for a time harrassed the Allied commerce. That her career was stopped at the outset was due to the keenness of a legless newsboy, anxious to do his bit for the country whose uniform he once had worn. There is enough, let us repeat, in this very story to give hope to every crippled soldier coming back from France — for this, taken in all its bearings, was about as important a piece of work as this busy division had, and is one of the biggest of all the A. P. L. cases.

The A. P. L. did not disband at the signing of the Armistice, and it is well that it did not. San Diego, like many another city, has had more than its share of bootlegging and vice investigations to carry on, owing to the fact that the growing feeling of license, which had developed since the Armistice, had spread among our troops. Among those quartered near San Diego, there were, of course, some not above reproach, and the bootlegger was known here as elsewhere. This pleasant and peaceful town in the sun-kissed South also had its share of the German-born. It would take a Luther Burbank, perhaps, to change them, and even Luther "would need time."

There was one man of great wealth naturalized in California in 1898, who held a prominent position in San Diego business life. He was known to have been in close touch with all the famous Germans, and had a pretty good insight into affairs American and Mexican. When we went into the war, this suspect became distinctly pro-German and was one of the most active propagandists along the border, apparently entirely forgetful of the fact that he owed allegiance to the United States. Being well acquainted with the German population in Mexico, he and others are alleged to have aided in the establishment of a wireless plant in Mexico, and to have financed people who ought not to have been financed, in view of their past records. It was charged against him by fellow-citizens that he worked to some extent with German money; that he was connected, at least indirectly, with the

Hindu plot case, and that he knew more than he should about the illicit shipment of arms in the *Annie Larson* steamship case. In fact, he was charged rather openly with having been interested in the German efforts to give aid to the ship *Maverick* in the Pacific Ocean. The wireless plant in Mexico was located and wrecked, which spoiled the attempts of an enemy clique to establish wireless communication between Mexico and German ships in Honolulu.

This same man was linked with the scheme of buying arms in New York and shipping them via San Diego into Mexico. British Military Intelligence also charged this man with being head and front of the most complete pro-German organization in that part of the world. He was charged with delivering coal from San Diego to a German steamship. The British Government and that of the United States joined hands in following out this pro-German citizen of America. He was traced to Europe and found to have gone to Berlin instead of to Paris. He was alleged to be guilty of fraudulent transactions at an Army post, and a man connected with him in his operations has been convicted. He succeeded in getting his son and son-in-law exempted from the draft, and attempted to get his son a commission in the Quartermaster Department. For months United States agents from various departments have been after this man, recording every move he made. Finally a joint meeting of the several agents of the United States, gathered in San Diego, decided that the time was ripe to get out a search warrant and go through his place of business, his safety deposit box, and his residence. Just then there came a change in the personnel of D. J. — and after this adjustment the Armistice ended it all! The investigation, therefore, is not closed at this writing, and the Department of Justice is still on the trail of this disloyal "American." He is one of a great many of his type claiming citizenship in this country.

It would seem that after a native of Germany had passed forty-two years in the United States, he would learn to feel a certain pride and appreciation of the benefits he had enjoyed here. That was not always the case — certainly it was not true in the instance of the gentleman who is filed away as Case No. 392. This worthy had abused the Allies in language too foul to print, and seemed to think that no one in this country would resent anything he said. When called down by a loyal citizen, he dared anybody to make him stop talking. He said that England started the war and had an agreement with Belgium whereby England could go through Belgium in order to strike at Germany. He said England sunk a great many boats and then blamed it on the German submarines. He said that England sent one hundred and fifty newspaper men here to write up stories against the Germans; that he hoped the submarines would blow up every damned American boat on the ocean, and sink all the transports and ships carrying munitions; that the men the Yankees had in France in March, 1918, did not amount to anything; that the United States couldn't make him fight; that this —— —— Government was rotten to the core. He made other remarks of like violent nature, and his remarks against the President of the United States were coupled with such language that swift hanging would really have been about the only just punishment for him. He was arrested and undertook to deny the remarks reported against him. The jury found him guilty. He was sent to prison for three years. He ought by all means to be deported when he gets out of jail, and so ought any German in this country who has been found at any time to be guilty of any such talk. We do not need that sort of "citizens" in America, and we are not going to have them here.

There was another case, No. 300, in peaceful San Diego, in which the suspect seemed anxious to spread broadcast every manner of pro-German propaganda. He had been a naturalized citizen of this country for twenty years, and through his position in one of the city banks, he had been closely associated with many of San Diego's leading business men. Yet, still deep in his heart was that love for the Fatherland which made him willing to fight this free country where he claimed citizenship and where he had all the benefits of our too weakly-lenient Government. It finally dawned on the minds of some of the customers of the bank that this man was not right. A. P. L. was called on to investigate him and worked on the case for months. The man was finally taken into custody, and the issue was joined between the United States Government on the one hand and this suspect and his influential friends on the other. A long trial was had and the jury disagreed. A second trial came off and A. P. L. had fifty witnesses ready to testify. The result was a conviction and a sentence of four years at McNeill's Island. Truly, anyone reading the San Diego cases must agree that that division did not lack in energy and diligence.

The A. P. L. in Pasadena

Life is so idyllic in Pasadena — roses — oranges — that sort of thing that you would not suspect that anything evil could happen there, or that anyone ever could suspect anyone else in those select surroundings. But Pasadena had her A. P. L., and they were not in the least above suspecting the right people once in a while, as a brief tale or so may prove. In short, Pasadena had more than 100 cases of alien enemy activities, 321 cases of disloyalty and sedition, of which thirty-six were concerned with persons not citizens of the United States. These totals show distinctly the amount of investigation required of transients, for the War Department cases, having to do with the Selective Service Act, came to only 155 investigations.

The B——— family of Pasadena were known as prominent pacifists. They held some very pleasant pacifist meetings in their houses until the Home Guards and the A. P. L. got after them. After that their meetings were neither so pacifistic nor so pleasant. There was a professor of languages at Throop College, who was always a German sympathizer and who always was very outspoken for Germany. He was reported a number of times to the Pasadena A. P. L. Throop was made over into a military training school, and that was about all for Professor B———. He did not last.

Mrs. Jack C———, a society woman of the Maryland Hotel, was gay and liberal with officers and soldiers — would even give them a drink without the formality of their removing their uniforms. Reported to the authorities. No action could be taken under the law at that time.

Miss Helen F——— was a very arden pacifist and a very ardent Socialist as well, and a great friend of some of the Socialists who write books and have a national reputation.

She was investigated by the Department of Justice at Pasadena, and when she went east to New York last summer, the Navy Intelligence had her under its watchful eye all the time. Perhaps she does not know that.

Dr. H——— of Pasadena was arrested by Federal authorities, it having been alleged that he " doctored " the eyes of boys who were subject to the draft.

" Friends of Irish Freedom "— a branch of the Sinn Fein organization — contributed to the defense of leaders of the latter organization who were on trial in New York. Their meetings were attended by two A. P. L. operatives who reported to Department of Justice. Meetings discontinued.

M. J———, a prominent Russian, staying at a prominent hotel with a prominent count and countess, was kept under very prominent surveillance for some time and reported daily to the Department of Justice.

Ben and Robert L——— were not so prominent, but were content with evading the draft, so it was charged. They and their mother fled the country and went to San Salvador in South America. Pasadena Division, A. P. L., greatly assisted D. J. in Los Angeles in locating these parties. The case was of international interest.

Then there was the case of Madam P———, reported to be the wife of a Russian count who is now a citizen of Germany and an officer in the German army. Subject arrived in America by way of Scandinavia, by way of Germany. She pronounced herself as frankly pro-German in a talk with the A. P. L. operative, who speaks very good German and who claimed to be in sympathy with Germany. In public, Madam is more guarded. She confided to the operative that she is getting mail from her daughter in Munich through the president of the Norwegian-American Steamship Line, who arranged with the captain for the forwarding and receiving of letters. The Department of Justice got all of this as well, as did the Postmaster General in Washington.

In Pasadena you might run against a count or countess or baroness almost any way you looked. There was the Baroness P———, wife of a Philadelphia man, who spends her winters in a Pasadena hotel. Very pro-German before we went to war, but more quiet since then. She is watched whenever she is in Pasadena. It's getting so a lady can do hardly anything at all without those vulgar, dreadful people knowing all about it!

The A. P. L. in Whittier

This division had thirty-three sedition cases, in spite of the glorious climate of California. For instance, information came that one Jack H——— and his wife were pro-Germans. They were running a fake jewelry business in Los Angeles. An A. P. L. investigation discovered that the gentleman had two names; that he left the Pacific Coast in 1910 with another gentleman and that they conducted a fur business in New York, where they failed handsomely and went into elegant bankruptcy. Suspect was alleged to have been convicted of perjury and sentenced to two or three years in the Federal prison at Atlanta, Georgia. It was developed further that he was given a stay of execution under bond of $10,000. The bond was forfeited and subject came to Los Angeles, where he resided with his purported wife and did business under the name of Jack H———. Upon said information, duly secured, the gentleman with the alias was arrested, returned to New York, and re-sentenced to three years in the penitentiary. His wife is still trying to find out where A. P. L. learned all about these things. Tut, tut! Cannot an honest jeweler be allowed to get away from his past in the wilds of the Far West?

Whittier is reported to be a quiet Quaker community. It has a population of approximately 25,000, being, in effect, a suburb of Los Angeles. The local division had forty-three men. Whittier always has boasted that it is a place where crooks do not congregate. There are Whittier oil fields, which are the second best on the Pacific slope, but there were no I. W. W.'s in this territory, and no pro-Germans of any very outspoken sort, no depredations, but for the most part calm, as becomes a Quaker capital.

The A. P. L. in Orleans

Perhaps you do not know where Orleans, California, is located? And perhaps you did not know that a branch of the A. P. L. was located in Orleans? That, however, is the case. There were just three members of the Orleans A. P. L., and, since there were but three, why not break the more or less inexorable rule about names and just give them in this case? J. A. Hunter was Chief at Orleans; C. W. Baker was Secretary; and P. L. Young was the third member.

The Chief reports:

> In this small and isolated community, this seemed to be all the organization necessary. These men were selected as the best representatives of the community, and all subscribed to the A. P. L. oath. The local headquarters are at Orleans, with no further executive and office force necessary. Expenses were nominal and were defrayed by individual members. Orleans is an isolated point, 102 miles from a railroad, communication with the outside being by auto stages. It was easy to watch all travel through the district, and the few aliens, only two, who were resident were easy to keep track of. There is no telegraphic or telephone communication with the outside, so all reports had to be made by mail. We looked after the work necessary in our district, rendering such assistance as we were able and were asked to do. We had no trouble at any time with the local authorities.
>
> [Signed] J. A. HUNTER, Chief.

We may be content to close the story of California, ragged and incomplete as it has been, with this report from a little mountain community of California. It is what the author is disposed to call incontestably the best report that has been found in all the great Golden State, if not, indeed, in all the United States.

Only three men, away out in the hills — but all of them Americans and all of them ready to work for America — that is why this League was great; because it had men such as these ready to do its work, as best they could, in whatever form it came to hand for the doing. One fancies that in all the stories of the many different towns reported in these pages, there will not be one better received by the great brotherhood of the A. P. L. than this one from Orleans, 102 miles from the nearest rails, with no telegraph and no telephone. The author of this book hopes to see Orleans some time. He believes it may be American.

BOOK III

THE FOUR WINDS

How Manufactures, Munitions and Agriculture were Protected — Briefs of Cases from All Over the Country — Chips from the Little Fellow's Axe — Odds and Ends from the Files — The Far-Flung Work of the A. P. L.

CHAPTER I

THE STORY OF THE EAST

In deplorably skeletonized fashion, we have offered a brief story of the League's growth, its purposes and its methods, and the stories of some of its great centers. But how about the country-wide achievements of the League, its field story? How can it be told? It is matter of regret that in no possible way can that ever be put within the compass of book publication. The records of these millions of cases, as has been said, runs into tons.

If you should visit the division offices, for instance, of New York, Philadelphia, San Francisco, Chicago, or any other large A. P. L. center, you would see in each city a room full of filing cabinets, with indexed drawers, carrying in permanent form the story of the League's work in that given locality. Mass all these from the hundreds of cities engaged in the work, and you would have a pile of filing cabinets as high as a tall building. Go to the National Headquarters and you would find more rooms full of cabinets, covering the national work — an enormous total, painstaking, exact, correct. Go over to the Military Intelligence and you see more of the League's work there. Go to the Department of Justice and look at the vast accumulations there at hand from the reports of this auxiliary.

Now, in imagination, pile all this uncomprehended assemblage of records into the middle of some park or square and have a glance at it in mass. In that mountain-pile of written and printed material, thousands of brains have recorded their soberest and most just conclusions, and have told why they concluded thus or thus. Thousands of stenographers have worked long days and nights on these tons of millions of pages. Be sure, in this mass of a nation's story in counter-espionage, there is to be found, ticketed and tabulated, filed and cross-indexed under name and number, as part of the archives of the United States, the life and actions, the birth, derivation, antecedents, convictions, assertions and beliefs of practically every man and woman of German name in America. But close to the foot of this mass of the archives, lay down upon the ground a book, a volume of ordinary size; let us say, this book now in your hand. How small it seems! It is small. It is no more than a fraction, a mite. It is not enough. Some man's loyal, unpaid, patient labor went into every one of these records.

There came, curiously, cumulatively, the feeling that this was not merely a mass of quasi-public documents, but an assemblage of the most valuable human documents ever collected in America. This was massed proof, not of work, but of patriotism. Then we did have, we do have, a country; there *is* a real America? Yes, and let no man doubt it ever again. It is a great and splendid country. These hundreds of thousands of pages which have been read — and every report sent in has been read — make the greatest reflex of America it ever has been the privilege of any man to know. Talk no more of a merely material America — it is not true. The real America at least is a noble, a splendid, a patriotic country, eager to do its share, determined to take its place.

The bewildering amount of material from all over the United States made condensation and classification alike difficult. It was therefore decided to separate the country into four loosely divided sections, the North, the East, the West, the South, and to throw into each division just so many condensed reports, taken at random from the whole as might be possible within the existing space limitations.

In the East and Northeast were located many or most of the great munition works and embarkation points as well as many centers of war work, manufacturing and shipping. This meant one form of work for the A. P. L. In the great middle section of the country — the semi-industrial, semi-agricultural central and north-central states — the activities of the League were slightly more varied. This cluster of inland states we have grouped as North. The South is known almost traditionally; and the West may arbitrarily be made to cover the far lands to the Pacific Coast itself, the state of California, with its great cities, alone being given subclassification in another section of this volume. Into these several hoppers the grist was thrown.

Would you like a real history of the war, a story which does convey a comprehensible picture? The simplest way is the best way. Read the *Atlantic Monthly* for January, 1919. Does it give a great pen picture by some artist in words? No. But it gives verbatim translations of bits of conversation heard by a nurse in a hospital full of wounded Russian soldiers; detached, disconnected comments, points of view, records of personal experiences. That is great reporting — the greatest reporting in the world. Had our more famous correspondents kept away from the routine of the alleged " front " and gone into the hospitals for a half million personal statements of wounded men of every nation, they would not have failed to show us the war. They would have written a great story of the war — a real history of the war. Now the astonishing thing about the record of the A. P. L. is that its reports came in precisely that way. The story of the League becomes a history of the country served by the League.

NEW YORK

Once in a while an operative landed a big case on a small clue. A New York operative was sent out to look up one R. R. A———, an employe of a shirtwaist factory, who was alleged to have said that he knew how to beat the draft. The same suspect was heard to say that he knew of four men, the knowledge of whom would be worth $10,000 to the United States. When interviewed by an A. P. L. operative, he denied most of the allegations made against him, but he did give the name of an Austrian army officer named L——— who had plans of submarines and battleships of the United States. This latter gentleman was followed, his baggage searched, and the plans confiscated.

Chautauqua County, New York, includes the cities of Jamestown and Dunkirk, each of which had an A. P. L. branch, the former being the first to organize, June 26, 1918. The Chautauqua County division proper was organized as late as October 28, 1919, an assistant chief being appointed for Jamestown and for Dunkirk. The entire county covers an area of about 1,000 square miles and has a population of more than 100,000.

The League was of great service in rounding up delinquents who failed to return questionnaires. Local Board No. 1 of the Jamestown District on November 20, 1918, had ninety-eight delinquents. By December 10, the A. P. L. had reduced that number to twenty-one, and since then fifteen more have reported, leaving only six delinquents out of a total registration of 2,135.

The community was carefully organized with regard to each of the financial war drives. In the war stamps campaign one E——— was discovered selling stamps without having been authorized to do so. Investigations showed that he had been secretary of the local branch of the German-American Alliance and was in constant association with alien enemies. An associate of his, who may be called R———, said that the German Club was pretty much run by a man named F———, an Austrian enemy alien who belonged to some lower order of German nobility but had moved to Austria. He became an "Austrian" when the United States declared war on Germany, but was willing to claim citizenship in any country now that diplomatic relations were severed with Austria, since he could speak several languages. The A. P. L. found means to inspect the living rooms of F———, discovering great quantities of German papers and an Austrian flag. The remainder of the story, told in the words of the Chief's report, shows how a mighty small fire sometimes can generate an enormous volume of smoke:

> We learned that F——— had admitted himself to be engaged in getting German subjects out of the United States and into the German army. Operative on the case, R———, was confidentially informed by him that six thousand men had left this country the preceding month and were to be carried by the large trans-Atlantic submarines. F——— himself was going to sail October 4.
>
> The operative invented a German cousin whose wife was in Germany, and told L——— that this cousin was very eager to get across. The cordial clubman instructed him to write a letter to "Freiherr Hans von Ungelter," former German Consul in New York, and enclose it in another envelope, which should be addressed to (name given), care of General Delivery, New York. The addressee's name, operative was in-

formed, changed week by week. Further, it was learned that the system followed by L———'s New York friends was to give men physical examinations, and if found fit, to furnish free transportation through the channels mentioned above. The sole requirements were loyalty to Germany and a sound physique. Operative stated that he showed surprise when L——— gave him this information, and said: "Then the report that a German captain was seen in New York was true?" F——— replied: "Certainly, they stay there a week at a time, taking in the theatres and waiting for their cargoes to be delivered at various ports, where they pick them up on their way to Germany."

R——— furnished the name of the New York man for the current week, and a good operative went to New York to confer with the Special Agent of D. J. there and with the New York Division A. P. L. General Delivery was covered, but nothing showed. A second week was tried with the same result. Operative was then asked to arrange an interview with F——— for his supposed cousin, but F———, according to operative, refused to talk or to see this cousin.

R——— came back to us declaring that F——— knew he was being watched and suspected him, and might kill him. Tension was high at local headquarters. Then we started in to investigate R——— who had been our informant right along. We learned that his record was none too good, for he had offered to procure releases for drafted men for amounts ranging from $15 to $30 a head. We then traced R——— back to Buffalo and got this report: "Great talker and fine salesman, but always away over his head." In other words there was no case and never had been one. By this time we had almost forgotten E———, the thrift stamp man. We were younger in detective work then than we were later.

A report comes from Jamestown, New York, regarding one whom we will call Henry D———, described as follows: "Known to many in this town as strongly pro-German; a radical socialist; believed to be an anarchist; has been very active going from one town to another. He left Jamestown for Rockford, Illinois; he went thence to Chicago, thence to Grand Rapids. From the latter city he came back to Jamestown. He has now gone to New York. We understand he is contemplating a trip to the old country. Has been very secretive about his movements. Seems to spend a great deal of money in travel, although he is only a workman; has boasted that he had strikes called in every shop to which he was sent.'' This man was put under surveillance by the New York office of the American Protective League under charge of being a dangerous alien enemy, and was properly dealt with.

There were no instances of violence in Chautauqua County arising out of the war situation. The community was at all times right side up. Those who have sought to belittle or impede any war activity were effectively stilled.

Schenectady, New York, organized its division on March 1, 1918, with one chief, two captains, four lieutenants, and eighteen operatives. The division conducted sixty-seven investigations for character and loyalty; forty-two under the Espionage Act; twenty-six cases of propaganda, and fifteen of draft evasion. The division was commended by the War Department for showing a high standard of efficiency; also by the Federal Reserve Bank at Albany. Schenectady has a large foreign population, among whom may be found quite a good proportion of radical Socialists. These people were expected to make trouble when we went to war, especially as two of the largest local industrial concerns, the General Electric Company and the American Locomotive Company, were engaged on munitions and other war work. There was no overt act, however, but on the contrary, the people of the city proved intensely patriotic, over-subscribing every loan.

Rochester, New York, reports routine work for its division, but had a good many operatives ready for any emergency that might arise. The record-cases do not represent the amount of work actually done, but yield the following figures: Character and loyalty reports, 190; selective service, 4; training camp activities, 2; liquor and vice, none; war risk insurance, 1; sedition and disloyalty investigations, 25. Rochester would seem to have been much more pacific — not pacifistic — than at first would be expected.

Albany, New York, offers an instance of a phenomenon more or less frequently recurrent during the war — namely, the apprehensiveness of the feminine mind as regards mysterious flashlights in the stilly night. The informant stated that for some time she and her neighbors had been watching flashes which came from a certain house at night and kept up for a long time. She was very much excited. Two operatives visited the vicinity shortly after dark. A light did appear which might have been that of a lantern. It would dim and come on again. The informant stated that sometimes the light would grow as bright as an automobile light, and sometimes it would seem to be red. The next morning the operatives found a farmer plowing near the suspicious house. He admitted that he owned the house. He said he and his wife were American born, of British grandparents. The operatives asked him about the mysterious lights. Smilingly he asked them to go through the house. It then was clearly evident that the light they had seen came from a lamp in the middle of a room. The mysterious intermittent flashes were only due to persons passing between the lamp and the window. The farmer also said he often worked nights bundling up beets, carrots, radishes, etc., which he had pulled during the afternoon and expected to take to early market the next morning. He usually did this work just outside the house on a bench. On inquiry as to what he used, he showed a large carriage lantern with a reflector, in the back of which was a piece of red glass. So the women had been right after all. He would move this lantern from one end of the bench to the other as he worked, and this made the changes in the color of the light. The intermittent flashes were due to his passing back and forth in front of it.

A big chemical poison scare was nipped in the bud by the investigation of a German woman who was found putting up capsules of a white powder in her house. Of course, nothing less than poison for our soldiers and sailors could be predicted. Investigation proved that though the woman was of German descent, she was entirely loyal to this country. She made a little extra money at home filling capsules for a drug house in the city. These capsules contained bicarbonate of soda, tartaric acid, etc., and the woman took a few of them in the presence of the operatives to show that they were harmless. Thus, another case proved to be a "dud."

An alien enemy was wanted at Albany, reported by D. J. to be traveling on a motor-cycle. It was known that he had a girl not far away and called on her or wrote to her occasionally. The mails in this case, as in many others, were used for decoy purposes. A registered special delivery letter, marked for personal delivery only, was mailed to him at the girl's address, with the idea that she would give forwarding directions to the messenger who delivered the letter. The result was better than expected. When the messenger arrived at the house, he saw a man just about to leave on a motor-cycle, and thinking that this might be the man, he hailed him and presented the letter. The suspect signed for the letter and was at once arrested and turned over to the Department of Justice.

Syracuse, New York, had a man at the head of its division who, before he came an A. P. L. chief, had made four hundred investigations, and since that time has directed one hundred and fifty more. A very close liaison was maintained with the Department of Justice and the local police department.

Just as valuable as though it recorded some great crime is the report from Hudson Falls, New York: "Our community is made up of loyal, patriotic citizens, who responded to each and every call to duty. We have been active in local, state and national matters throughout the war."

PENNSYLVANIA

It is hard to tell what is going to become of all the military fakes and pseudo-heroes now that the war is over. Take, for instance, the case of one Captain Robert H———, ostensibly in the United States Navy, who fancied Philadelphia as his residence. This worthy captain was also known by other names. Sometimes he wore a uniform of an ordinary seaman with overseas service wound stripes, although he never saw service abroad. He wrote to his wife that he had been wounded and told her to hang out a service flag with a silver star, which she dutifully did. The star had not hurt Captain H———, so why not put it in the window? This gentleman spoke of a great many flag-raisings and elaborated on the seventy-two days he had spent in the trenches. He told all about German atrocities, and quite often took up collections for sick and wounded soldiers and sailors in the name of this or that hospital. There never yet has been found a hospital to which he has turned over a dollar. Naturally a good organizer, this young officer invented a good Navy of his own, the "Naval Home Defense," and at one time had enlisted one hundred and fifty-six members, including one lady and her two young sons. The project came to grief because of a generous order for some uniforms, costing something like $1,000, which was placed with a local clothing firm and had to be paid for. It is too bad, because the organization also had a ladies' auxiliary, his wife being president thereof. This is only one of a very great number of cases of imposters parading as officers of this or that country.

Bradford, Pennsylvania, is in the heart of the big oil country, and it had its own troubles by reason of its necessarily motley population. A very interesting report on local conditions, submitted by the Chief of McKean County Division, says:

> At the outset we were confronted with a situation fast becoming serious, as so many industrial claims had been allowed by the district board. Only one or two young men of social prominence had been inducted into the service, and charges were frequently made that the Government did not intend taking men of wealth or prominence and that it was the laboring men who would have to do the fighting. The Socialist element was quick to take advantage of this situation, and men who left here for the service went away feeling that they had been discriminated against.
>
> We took up this situation with the Department of Justice, who sent us a Special Agent. A contingent of boys leaving for the front did some printing reflecting very seriously on the methods of the draft board and scoring the local slackers. They had planned to put a banner on their train with such inscriptions as, "My father owns an oil well, but I didn't claim exemption"; "We have a garden in our back yard, but I am not a farmer"; etc. We headed off this plan, but the worst thing about it was that many of the names upon the slacker list referred to were of men who had legitimate reasons for exemption. At the same time, there were some men named who clearly ought to have been inducted into the service. To silence criticism, we had a district draft board man come to Bradford, and with him we went over a lot of cases which had caused trouble. As a result, many of these cases were reclassified, and many men inducted into the service. This caused an entire change of opinion here, and since then we have had no trouble of that nature.
>
> We had one exemption claimer, a young Jewish merchant, who told a very pathetic story about dependents — among

others, a blind father and an invalid brother. This young Hebrew was of the belief that he could do so much more for his country if left at home to take care of these unhappy relatives of his. Investigation did not seem to bear out his point of view. He was not, however, turned over to the authorities for action in regard to his statements, as he was wanted for the army more than for the courts; and yet, when he was turned over to the medical men for examination, it was found that he had something which he did not know he had — serious heart trouble which actually exempted him! There are some people you can't beat any way of the game.

A Bradford pro-German, born in Germany but naturalized before the war, has always been socialistic. Put under observation, he was heard to say in the presence of many, at a meeting in honor of a man who was going to join the colors: "Here is your —— —— capitalistic system taking the best men we have and leaving men like——" His remarks were resented and caused a row. Investigated and reported to Department of Justice at Pittsburgh, this pro-German was arrested and placed under indictment.

At one of the plants the loyal workingmen had fixed it all up to paint a man a nice yellow color because he did not subscribe to any Liberty loans. A. P. L. operatives arrived just in time to prevent the frescoing above mentioned. The suspect himself was taken aside and argued with by the A. P. L., with the result that he presently disclaimed his disloyal remarks, said he was sorry, and wanted to buy some bonds with the other boys.

The Chief goes on to say that Bradford operated under cover as much as possible. A good many townsfolk, he says, could not identify A. P. L. at all, although there were very few who did not know that there had been some sort of checking up of pretty much the entire population in matters of interest to the Government. This impression aided in suppresing a great deal of radical and seditious talk, and served as a warning to others not to begin that sort of thing.

Reading, Pennsylvania, reports 170 cases of alien enemy activities, 226 cases of disloyal and seditious talk, 38 cases of investigation of radical organizations, such as the I. W. W. Among other interesting stories contained in the Reading report is one which has to do with a professional labor agitator, a wrong telephone number and an alert A. P. L. operative. A workman called up a man whom he supposed to be his friend, and stated that there was going to be a strike pretty soon at a certain factory. The recipient of the message happened to be an A. P. L. operator, who at once took up the trail and located his man in the shop where he was employed. Witnesses soon were found who proved that this was the man who had started the strike agitation. He had been there only two weeks. He had been in three other plants where they were doing Government work and had made trouble in each plant. He knew the percentage of Government work in each factory where he had been employed. He was sent to Philadelphia for full handling. It seemed that he was trying to get in touch with an official of a Socialist organization and pulled the wrong telephone number by mistake! You could never tell in war times when you were talking to an A. P. L. man.

Wilkesbarre, Pennsylvania, had sixty-six members enrolled. Considerable character and loyalty investigation work was done, and a great deal of seditious talk was stopped which otherwise might have caused trouble. The Chief adds: "The mere fact that such an organization as ours existed and that we were working in secret had a wonderful moral effect on the entire community. I regret exceedingly that this organization has to be dissolved, and am of the opinion that it will play an important part in the readjustment which is now taking place."

Meadville, Pennsylvania, had the usual routine work on deserters, delinquents, etc., and fourteen operatives were kept busy throughout the community. The Chief modestly says: "We did everything we could for our country."

Bristol, Pennsylvania, did not turn anything in to the Federal courts, but weeded out a number of undesirable alien enemies from the shipbuilding plants in that locality. The League gave very material assistance to the State Constabulary and Borough Police Officers in making investigations.

NEW JERSEY

The Trenton, New Jersey, district was one of busy environments, and it offers a number of three-star cases. Let us consider one Graboski, who had a friend, Grabinski, who tipped off the A. P. L. that Graboski was not a carpenter, but a chemist with a doctor's degree from a foreign university. This amiable masquerader was believed to have been instrumental in blowing up the plant of the General Electric Company at Schenectady, New York. In view of his information, Grabinski was dealt with leniently, but Graboski was followed to his boarding-place and was there found in bed listening to the conversation of the occupants down stairs. He was taken before the United States District Attorney as a preliminary to his internment in a southern detention camp.

Much more proper than contrary is the conduct of a German bearing the homely name of Schmidt, living near Trenton, New Jersey. Investigation was made on report of a neighbor. By the time the operative called, Schmidt had a service flag in his window. Many different subjects were discussed, including music. Old man Schmidt had no more investigations after he declared himself:

> Yah, ve Chermans ist fond of musik. I like musik, und mine vife, she like it to. I haf der old violin vot I brot mit me from Chermany. I blay him a liddle alvays — old Cherman tunes — vot ist all I know. Maybe you hear me sometimes — last year, vot? No? Vell, I blay him not any more now. You see, der boy — mine son — you don't know him — he never live mit us here — he vork in Chicago — he ist in American Army already. Und I luf to blay, but all vot I know ist shust Cherman tunes — dat's all — so I don't blay any more. I hav der old viddle avay put.

Trenton, New Jersey, staged a draft raid with two hundred A. P. L. men and a detachment from Philadelphia under the leadership of the Assistant Chief of that city. At the Trenton Fair there was a crowd of 75,000 people. The raiders set out in fifty automobiles and broke up into small parties. At four o'clock in the afternoon the dragnet went to work, and no one was allowed to leave the grounds without credentials. Even the fences were watched. All operatives, whether from the Department of Justice or the A. P. L., worked with courtesy, and there was no more difficulty in getting out of the grounds than there would be in getting into a theatre if provided with a ticket. Many of the men apprehended were farmers from out of the way places and had their wives and children with them. Those being evidently not of the slacker variety were released with the understanding that they report to their local boards. No one was delayed unnecessarily. After this, all the side shows and amusements were combed out, and several men were picked up in this way. About 300 were apprehended and taken to the armory, where their cases were passed on. Four deserters from our Army were taken, and the British Military Police apprehended a man, thought to be a pickpocket, who was masquerading in a Canadian uniform. This raid was conducted after the much criticised New York slacker drive, and the contrast was commented upon by the local press.

CONNECTICUT.

New Haven, Connecticut, might very well have been a seat of trouble, but appears to have pursued the usually even tenor of her way, sending her young men out in hundreds to fight the country's battles, and making very little fuss about it. The division took part in five minor slacker raids, in which the men gave satisfactory account of themselves, working closely in touch with the Department of Justice and the Military Intelligence, especially in the matter of protection of the large munition factories against sabotage. New Haven is one of the great American centers for the making of firearms, and that there has been no serious trouble there is a matter of congratulation. There were 226 investigations made for the War Department, each investigation necessitating interviews with at least three persons. The organization at New Haven was quiet, even tempered, and strictly efficient, a fine example in a state which was very strong in its A. P. L. organizations.

New London, Connecticut, besides routine activities, had one case which involved the trailing of a count, a princess, a Russian banker, a Greek candy manufacturer, and a prize-fighter, besides a person described as a " male," but who proved to be a young lady in a well-known local family. With these ingredients as preliminary, it might almost be sufficient to tell any reader to write his own ticket — and indeed the case is not yet closed. It will probably turn out to be one of American Bolshevism. The Chief says there is enough in this for a good movie scenario. As much might be said for another pro-German case in which the beautiful and accomplished suspect was followed by D. J. men, who installed a dictograph in her hotel apartments. This case also had to do with a draft of $14,000 traced from Montreal to a New York bank, through which British Secret Service men discovered a paymaster of German spies in this country. This woman met several Army and Navy officers in the course of her travels along three-fourths of the Atlantic Coast. It is most disappointing to have the Chief add: "We are unable to disclose for publication any further facts at this date."

New London had a number of special investigations, some of them interesting, others ludicrous. One of the latter was Case No. 245, Subject "Mysterious Flashes." A woman residing on the shore reported mysterious flashlights, intermittent, but long continued. She was sure of nothing less than a German invasion. An operative was put on the case and worked five hours one night. He found a mysterious man walking up and down the beach. He had an electric torch which he flashed here and there, muttering to himself the while, and now and then putting something in his pocket. Summoning all his nerve, the operative cried: "Halt! Who goes there?" Inquiry proved that the man was in sailor garb. When questioned as to the nature of his mysterious actions, he replied: "I am catching night-crawlers for fishing. I want to get some eels for my breakfast."

Mystic Village, Connecticut, furnished another scare of the same variety. Near the village is a hill, known as Lantern Hill since Colonial days, because it is a convenient signal post. Stories got out about mysterious lights on Lantern Hill. On one clear night the investigators saw what seemed to be unmistakable signalling. The light was brilliant and changed in color from green to red. State and Naval authorities resolved to look into the matter, and it was arranged that on a given night patrols of naval reservists from the submarine base and detachments of the Home Guard should surround the hill, while forces of the Guard were to patrol the shores of the sound to catch sight of any answering signals from the sea. The patrols were duly set, and, sure enough, the light began to show as brilliant and mysterious as could be asked. It seemed to swing at an altitude of about two hundred feet above the woods. It occurred to one of the naval officers on watch that with the aid of his powerful night glass and a convenient perpendicular presented by the side of the barn, he might triangulate the position of the light. He had not been at this very long when he broke out into laughter and announced that what they had taken to be a mysterious light was only a star rendered abnormally brilliant by the refractive effect of the damp night air. Its later disappearances were accounted for by the later rise in altitude, when of course the light would cease to be distinguishable from others of like altitude. Taking it all in all, this about finished the cases of the many mystic lights which were reported from time to time.

Litchfield, Connecticut, up near the stern and rockbound coast, offers a good example of sober-going loyalty. There were only fifty-one cases of seditious talk and twenty of propaganda, whereas the selective service regulation involved 734 cases.

Ansonia, Connecticut, was honored by the presence of a Russian Soviet Society called the "Society Lunch," which had regular meetings and was organizing other societies in nearby towns. Sometimes this society would get a speaker from the outside, such as the editor of the *Russian Voice,* published in New York. The city of Ansonia did not like these things, inasmuch as they tended to promote anarchy and foster revolution. The division had one of its operatives among the membership, he having joined the society for the purpose of reporting on its activities. What the society did became henceforth a matter of interest not only to its membership, but also to the local body of A. P. L. vigilantes.

The Chief of Norwalk, Connecticut, worked in close touch with the police of his city and was on the lookout for the various alien enemies reported from headquarters. He says: "No alien enemy actually apprehended in my district. The only way we can account for it is that they were afraid to come here."

Essex, Connecticut, says something which will meet general agreement: "We firmly believe that the A. P. L. has done an inestimable work in the protection of our country. Every man in this division is glad of the opportunity afforded to be enrolled as an A. P. L. member."

MASSACHUSETTS

Springfield, Mass., had only nineteen members in its division. That we may know the nature of the League membership as a whole, let us look at the qualifications of these nineteen men. They included a lawyer, a physician, a broker, a private secretary, a social service worker, an advertising manager, a college president, a bank president, a furniture buyer, a merchant, a superintendent of the Bradstreet Company, a traveling salesman, a life insurance agent, a masseur, a surgeon, a musician, a shipping foreman, a bank teller and a high school teacher. The work of the Springfield division had to do largely with character and loyalty investigations, which ran all the way from nobody at all to a bishop in the Episcopal Church. Some male and female applicants for Y. M. C. A., K. of C. and Red Cross were found unfit "either because of immoralities or bad habits." Once in a while a case of disloyalty and sedition came up which would cause a smile. An applicant for a commission whose father was a Belgian and whose mother was a German was investigated and was found to be a loyal American. When questioned, he said he was for the United States of America, but that "father would never forgive mother for the invasion of Belgium."

A more spectacular Springfield case hung on a letter sent by the War Department to the A. P. L. reading as follows:

> Will you please have your agents investigate a man living at 71 Catherine Street, Springfield, Massachusetts, known as August X———, and report the result of their investigation to me?

The final result of this investigation was that the subject was interned, having been proved to have been a former soldier in von Kluck's army of invasion in 1914, who had been taken prisoner by the French, had escaped from France to the United States and drifted to Springfield, where he got employment in a machine shop. " I have always wondered," says the Chief, " from whom the War Department received the first information regarding August X———, and wonder if again we have a case of *cherchez la femme.*"

DELAWARE

This state is not one of the largest in the Union, and its report is not one of the largest in the world, but it foreshadows a very satisfactory state of affairs, both past and future.

Mr. Robert Pennington was State Inspector for Delaware. He worked by means of three county associates and a full set of captains, one for each representative district of the State. A great deal of routine work was handled, much of which had to do with applications for commissions, overseas service, etc., as well as a certain number of sedition and disloyalty cases. Some Red Cross rumors were run down, and at least one important investigation was made of a man who was putting out machinery better adapted for mixing explosives than for grinding alleged dental powder. These machines were to be shipped to Switzerland to a point near the German border. Some draft evaders, deserters and slackers were rounded up duly. Many investigations were made by the various chiefs and reported direct to Washington. The State Inspector had almost daily requests from the Department of Justice in Washington in the matter of draft deserters.

RHODE ISLAND

Providence, R. I., had a good active organization of 275 members, all loyal and hard-working Americans. They did yeoman service in assisting the local branch of the Department of Justice, whose offices were so crowded with work at times that the help of the League was sorely needed.

The A. P. L. in Wakefield, R. I., was small but busy, like all the rest of that great little State. Much of the League's activity in this district had to do with covering the rough and broken seashore, a region largely occupied by well-to-do Germans. Some of these alien inhabitants were found to be out-and-out disloyalists, over sixty such cases being investigated.

NEW HAMPSHIRE

The lack of any extended reports from this state would indicate an absence of many of the tortuous problems that assailed her larger New England neighbors. Manchester, N. H., reports that the local division coöperated with almost every governmental activity in the State, including the Department of Justice, draft boards, Red Cross, Four Minute Men, and other branches too numerous to mention. We may write almost identically the same comment for Maine and Vermont.

CHAPTER II

THE STORY OF THE NORTH

Nature has not put upon the face of the globe any region more fit or more inviting for human occupancy than the temperate zone of North America. The soil is fertile, producing with fair tillage all the forms of food needful for the full development of the human species. The climate is precisely that which calls for sufficient human exertion in the unescapable battle of life, but not enough to debar men from a rich surplus of things beyond the mere living, which in the tropics is all a man asks, or in the Arctics is all a man may hope. Lastly, its natural transportation is easy and abundant. The rugged, virile, enterprising and successful population of that region is Nature's offering to the problems of the world's future, and it is safe prophecy that in this region of America always will be produced many of the world's greatest thinkers and greatest doers; because here, surely, is a splendid human environment.

But man, like other species, is a product of two forces, environment and heredity. What was the heredity of the temperate zone? Of the best, the strongest, the most enterprising. The Colonies, New England and the upper South, sent their strongest sons west in the early days. Later, the restless populations of Europe, of Irish, Teutonic and Scandinavian stock, began to swarm into that favored region, a good part of which, then known as our West, lay unoccupied. The Civil War prevented what we might call the Americanization of the Northwest, which attracted heavy immigration of North-European stocks. But all the men moving out along the forty-second parallel as a meridian line of latitude were of strong, well selected human stock. That was the original ancestry of what we might call our "North."

We rudely may group this region as that lying along the Mississippi, the Missouri and their upper tributaries. Here lies one of the great future countries, one of the anchoring grounds of humanity. Beyond doubt it will eventually offer support to a vast population. The great population-centers, the great civilizations of the world, always have been along the great river valleys.

In the North, then, we see a rich region, rich in soil, in forests, in minerals. Consider what ore Minnesota and Michigan, by means of natural transportation, have sent to Ohio and Pennsylvania for manufacturing! Consider what millions of feet of rich pine Michigan, Wisconsin, Minnesota have given the world! And consider, if you can, the wealth which has come out of the soil of Ohio, Indiana, Illinois, Iowa, Minnesota, the Dakotas and all the rest of what we call the North! The earth has known nothing like it. Here was won the great war of the world, in which Peace overthrew Militarism, let us hope, for all time. Here grew the sinew which America put into this war, and it is in great part because of her rich river valleys that America to-day is the hope of all the world in the day of peace.

Naturally, if we should consider all these things, consider the persistence of racial types, consider the natural contest of all these strong men for the wealth of a rich new region, we could in advance predict that here in the North, there would be presented bitter phases of that combat which the enemy fought on this side of the Atlantic.

OHIO

Typical among the thriving industrial cities of the Middle West is Akron, Ohio, a city of 150,000 inhabitants, well known for its prominence in the rubber industry and other lines of manufactory of great use to the Government. The A. P. L. division in such a city might naturally be expected to have something to do. The Akron division began in the brain of a somewhat solitary agent of the Department of Justice, W. A. Garrigan, who was sent to Akron to serve his country all alone, equipped with one perfectly good aegis of the law, but not much else. There were men all about who were more or less actively engaged in helping Germany — men who were spreading Socialistic propaganda hindering the draft; men failing to qualify, knocking the

Liberty Loan, and doing everything else they ought not to do and leaving undone the things they ought to do. Mr. Garrigan found that the Government had not appropriated money enough for his office rent, much less enough to employ men to keep in touch with the Akron conditions. He needed men. Then overnight the Akron division of the A. P. L., beginning with two hundred men, sprang into existence, as it did so magically and mysteriously all over America. Mr. Elihu Harpham, manager of a local manufacturing concern, took the position of Chief. He had able assistants, and always these men worked in close touch with the Department of Justice, even in its most delicate and dangerous enterprises.

Akron, according to all reports, had an exceptionally large number of draft slackers — men who had registered here and disappeared before the numbers were drawn. It was estimated at one time that 3,000 men had registered in Akron and never been heard of again. It was indeed a Port of Missing Men. Akron Division took this matter up, and in its first year's work rounded up 6,856 men. The word passed among all the employees of Akron's great factories that it was not a good thing for a man to be around without his draft card in his pocket. Many hundreds of men who were delinquent came in voluntarily to their draft boards. Perhaps the figures will tell the tale as well as words:

Slackers	6,856
Alleged false questionnaires	255
Interned alien enemies	17
Pro-Germanism	245
Socialistic propaganda	98
Sedition	124
Food regulations	94
Liberty Bonds and Stamps	86
Soldiers absent without leave	51
Alien enemy investigations	159
Character investigations: War Department, Red Cross, Y. M. C. A., etc	34
Miscellaneous	4,847
Total cases handled first year	11,866
Delinquents and deserters sent to Camp Sherman, Chillicothe, Ohio, by this office	870

In the comprehensive report submitted by the Akron division, Chief Harpham says:

> We started out in a small way to assist the Akron office of the Bureau of Investigation, but expanded rapidly and soon had thoroughly equipped offices, complete card filing systems, and a sufficient force to keep our records and carry on our work in an efficient way. We now have a membership of two hundred and eighty-three, enrolled from the ranks of representative citizens who have given untiring efforts to the work. I know of no single case that has not been handled to the entire satisfaction of the Department of Justice, and without any display of officiousness. It is very gratifying to those who have performed service to receive these expressions of appreciation. I shall never be able to convey to our members the keen appreciation of their loyal support which has made our success possible. It has been a pleasure for me to serve as Chief and to know that we have been a part of the powerful organization which has contributed so much toward the winning of the war.

Of these men who did the work — and it is work to handle nearly 12,000 cases — all were unpaid volunteers. Other members of the business community contributed money, although classified as inactive members. Such laborers in the ranks must be content to go unsung and unhonored, although they truly helped to win the war.

Columbus, Ohio, is another solid, steady-going town which may be depended upon to do the sensible thing and the loyal thing — albeit at times in rather violent fashion. A Lutheran minister of Columbus was reported for pro-German talk and was found to be of German parentage, although himself American born. He acknowledged he had never allowed an American flag in his church, and had never uttered a prayer for this country or its army. An operative told him to be careful about his praying for "our country," lest he should be understood as meaning Germany and not the United States. The community forced him to leave his charge — none too soon, for the sentiment toward him was rapidly becoming dangerous.

A Columbus restaurant employed a German-looking cook who seemed to have considerable money, and who acted rather suspiciously. A. P. L. traced his history, covering two or three positions which he had held, and at length called him in to headquarters for a general going over of the third-degree sort. He was found to have acted as cook in the army cantonments at Chillicothe, and was discovered to be a German alien without permit or any papers allowing him in this country. Among his papers there was found a photograph of himself in the uniform of a lieutenant in the German army, also his order for mobilization in the German army in 1913. He is now interned.

That the Columbus division of A. P. L. was at all times busily engaged in winning the war on this side is amply proved by its report:

Slackers	135
Delinquents and deserters	366
Alleged false questionnaires	83
Bootlegging	107
Pro-German	375
Socialistic propaganda	83
Vice complaints	235
Soldiers absent without leave	8
Alien enemies	48
Character investigations	192

Toledo, Ohio, had 162 cases of disloyalty and sedition to investigate, and 600 cases of word-of-mouth propaganda. Many of the reports turned in by zealous operatives are worth reprinting.

A slacker was brought into Toledo headquarters minus his card, but he protested that he had registered. He declared himself to be drunk, said that the registrar was drunk, that it was funny they couldn't find his card, but if they would go to Detroit and find his friend Heine So-and-so — street address unknown — Heine would tell them he had registered. Not considered conclusive.

Another operative in Toledo fancied himself very much in the rôle of Sherlock Holmes. In one case assigned him, he was trailing a subject who turned and started toward the operative. The latter stated in his report: "When I noticed the subject coming toward me, I immediately jumped over a hedge and hid behind some bushes."

Toledo did some business in the slacker raids, having examined some 2,000 men in one drive.

Youngstown, Ohio, reflects a very sensitive social condition which existed during the war in every community which owned a considerable foreign born population. The Chief comments on this quite frankly:

> A feature of our work was the demand, made by people in all stations, that the Federal Government, of which we were supposed to be a direct agency, should look after the enforcement of laws concerning health, morals and even family relations. A remarkable fact in connection with these investigations was the utter inability of a certain class of German origin to forget their German ties and to live up to their oath of allegiance to America, which they took, many of them, fifteen or twenty years ago. In one case it was frankly admitted by the subject that he had never thought about Germany going into a war with America when he applied for naturalization papers. We have developed the fact that many households in America have been, are and always will be nothing but a part of Germany in our midst.

Youngstown turns in 157 cases of alien enemy activities, and 459 of disloyalty and sedition. There were 213 cases of anti-military activity and 674 cases of propaganda, not mentioning 183 cases of I. W. W. and other radicalism. In the report of this division, the Department of Justice work quite overshadows the War Department activities, because there are only 213 investigations under the Selective Service Act and 67 for character and loyalty, although there were 141 investigations of desertions and absences without leave.

There was a certain man in the vicinity of Napoleon, Ohio, who put up a really stubborn fight against Americanism. The Chief of the division says:

> I got a telephone message that one hundred Germans, armed with guns, were gathered in an alien enemy's house and wanted to fight. As county president of the League of American Patriots, I called out five hundred members, and with fifteen A. P. L. members, we started for the place after nightfall. We traveled the eighteen miles in cars, but as we were approaching, the Germans saw our headlights and dispersed, except for a few who didn't get away. We got three men, and found some ammunition and one gun in a wheat field. We were shot at, but none of us were hurt, although the report

got noised about that we had fifteen killed. A carnival was being held in a little town nearby, and when we got back at 2:00 A. M., the ladies were waiting with hot coffee and sandwiches for us, so we didn't call it a bad night's work. We nailed an American flag to the house of that enemy alien, and it is still waving there. The next day the Department of Justice was on hand. We traveled into three counties to get a man who said that some Germans had guns and would use them. It was said that these guns were to aid Germany in case she could effect a landing in this country.

About seventy per cent of the inhabitants of Henry County are of German descent, and many remained in sympathy with Germany even after we went into the war. We could do little with them. Our League of Patriots tried nineteen cases in Henry County, relieved a bank cashier of his position, got a State road superintendent dismissed and brought a good many other pro-Germans out into the open. The A. P. L. assisted in getting much of the evidence against the road superintendent, who was heard to say: "If this country goes into the war with Germany, one million Germans will rebel, and I will be one of them." Thus far, the million Germans seem less disposed to rebel since the eleventh of last November.

Yellow Springs, Ohio, is another instance of simple, honest, heel and toe hard work. The division assisted in all the war activties, and helped out the Department of Justice in divers instances in collecting testimony.

Wooster, Ohio, says: "Our principal activities had to do with conscientious objectors. We tried to deal with these people in accordance with the law, and also in accordance with the regulations promulgated by the President. We had some amusing cases with members of the Ammish church, including their Bishop, who was accused of advising men not to comply with the draft order. This man caused the county boards a great deal of trouble. He would not come in and talk with the military authorities, but the A. P. L. brought him in. You have to know these people to appreciate the obstructions they will put around all draft matters."

Coshocton, Ohio, had fifteen citizens who were suspected of being disloyal, and thirty who talked too much. Members worked when the thermometer was twenty below zero, trying to catch parties who were tearing down and mutilating Liberty Loan posters.

A quite usual form of report comes from Washington Courthouse, Ohio — and it is one of the best sorts of reports: "Assisted in the sale of Liberty Bonds and Stamps to the amount of $150,000; rounded up slackers, and did investigation work for the Red Cross. We had much automobile travel. In the eight hundred cases that we investigated, our men traveled more than twenty-five thousand miles by auto, half of this mileage being covered by one man."

INDIANA

Indianapolis, Indiana, attributes much of its success to the care with which its membership was selected. All new members were brought in by other members who were acquainted with them, and were in a position to know of their loyalty. The Chief says: "Our men conducted themselves with dignity, tact and discretion, bearing in mind at all times that they were representing the Government and the League. We believe that much of our success in keeping down propaganda, sabotage and other Hun depredations was due to the secrecy which guarded the identity of our officers. Indianapolis had a total of 209 cases of disloyalty and sedition."

Indianapolis caught one deserter 1,200 miles from home. He deserted from the Rainbow Division at the port of embarkation and headed west. He was found, working under an alias, in a camp forty miles from Casper, Wyoming. This case was started within fifty feet of the Indianapolis headquarters, through overhearing a chance conversation in which a woman said that a friend of hers was corresponding with a man she thought to be a deserter. The suspect at first denied he was the man wanted, but finally confessed, and was delivered to the proper authorities. The whole case was finished inside of two hours, the order for the man's arrest going by wire to Casper from the Department of Justice. Another man deserted from Camp Sherman, Ohio, and without coming back home to Indianapolis, went to Hastings, Michigan. Here, through a woman who passed as his wife, he had gotten a novelty concession at the County Fair. Indianapolis A. P. L. got in touch with M. I. D. of Washington. Everything was waiting for the gentleman on his arrival at Hastings. He is again in the Army — or was at the time of the Armistice.

Though wireless scares are most frequent on the seaboard, almost every city can boast several of them. An Indianapolis operative thought he had discovered certain wireless antennae on the property of a family with a German name. A pole was found fastened to the roof of a shed, wires being used to connect it with the attic of the house. It was noticed that the attic had close-drawn blinds, whence lights were occasionally seen. The whole thing simmered down to an outfit put up by some young men to practice telegraphy.

Indianapolis also became interested in a man who claimed exemption on account of heart trouble. He weighed 225 pounds, and stood six feet and one-half inch, though he was only twenty-five years old. It was arranged to have this man examined by an out-of-town physician. This resulted in his being brought before the medical board in Cleveland, where he was found fit for military service. There was no direct evidence that he had been taking any depressant for his heart, although the facts were thought to point that way. It was said that some doctors gave slackers medicine to give them temporary "heart disease."

Michigan City, Indiana, had a very busy A. P. L. division whose activities were sometimes curious. For instance, the town boasts a somewhat well advertised mayor, Fred C. Miller, who has made Michigan City famous as being the proud possessor of the only alien mayor in the United States. Miller openly violated the President's proclamation barring alien enemies from Washington, D. C. He was held until a thorough investigation could be completed, and during this investigation A. P. L. furnished D. J. with a report showing that twenty-one of the city officials and employees of Michigan City also were alien enemies! It would seem that America has not yet been discovered at the foot of Lake Michigan. The loyal minority of the population, during the mayoralty campaign, turned over information to A. P. L. to the effect that one hundred and forty-four alien enemies had failed to comply with the President's proclamation obliging them to register. A number of these were placed under bonds. Indeed, with the assistance of the League, the U. S. Marshal's office registered a total of 2,200 male and female alien enemies. A. P. L. developed the evidence on which one Herman Kauffman was interned at Fort Oglethorpe. This division also caused something over one hundred and fifty draft evaders to be taken before the local board as the result of a three months' drive under cover, which combed all the factories and railroad yards.

At Peru, Indiana, A. P. L. worked in combination with the "Loyal Citizens' Vigilance Committee of Miami County," an earlier organization of loyalty lovers which embraced about three thousand members of the hundred percent-loyal class. Mr. F. D. Butler was chief, and Mr. W. F. Schrader, head of the Vigilance Committee, assistant chief of A. P. L. The two organizations appear to have had amiable and efficient relations. There is something in the character of the Peru Vigilance Committee which seems to be reminiscent of the old "Know Nothing" party which had existence before the Civil War, and whose general platform was that of America for Americans. Does this Indiana Vigilance Committee, indeed, foreshadow a revival of some such political movement at a later date? It seems to have retained some of the tenets of the old Know Nothing party, which also worked in absolute secrecy, and had its grips, pass words and countersigns.

One may recall that it was an Indiana poet who wrote the line, "The Booger man will get you if you don't watch out." At least, between A. P. L. and the Vigilantes, a good and sufficient scare seems to have been thrown into the disloyal element around Peru.

There is grit, shrewdness and loyalty all combined in the report of the Chief of Rensselaer, Indiana, division. It is too good to change and the cases cited are given in the Chief's own words:

> I am also sending you a few sketches of our work; if you can use them in the history of the League it will be appreciated. I am very much interested in the history.
>
> *First Case:* There were numerous complaints and rumors of pro-Germanism and disloyalty in Northern Jasper County. Our operatives got a great many affidavits against a certain Lutheran minister, and an enemy alien named Herman S———, who had been bragging that no one could make him register. Accompanied by an operative, I took my car one Sunday and

we went out to S———'s house and the following conversation took place·

Q. Herman, why haven't you registered as the law requires you to?

A. Well, I supposed that my father had taken out his papers and I did not need to register.

Q. Well, how did it come that your brother Paul registered; he must have understood the law?

A. S——— flushed up, but did not answer.

Q. Well, Herman, you had better come in to-morrow and register.

A. But I have some oats that have to be harrowed, and I can't come in.

Q. Well, all right, if you would rather harrow your oats and not register and spend the remainder of the time of the war in a Federal prison, you harrow the oats.

He registered. Monday.

On this same expedition we stopped to see the Lutheran minister as private citizens, and told him that the people of Jasper County wanted no more German preaching and no more German teaching in the schools; also they would like to see Old Glory floating from the mast-head. We told him also that this was the last time that he would be notified. In about three hours we returned that way and stopped again. Old Glory was floating at the mast-head; the German school books had disappeared, and there has been no more German teaching nor preaching.

Second Case: The Local Board gave the name of Harrison L———, who had registered in Carrolton, Green County, Illinois, but had not reported for physical examination at Rensselaer. He was living with his parents nine miles south of this city, and he should have reported to the Local Board of Rensselaer for physical examination. I went out as a deputy sheriff to find out the reason why. I first called at the post office at McCoysburt, where they got their mail, and found that he had received his card calling him for examination. I then drove out to the farm and found the young man, and he claimed that he had not received the card. I finally told him that he would have to go with me. He replied that he would have to see his father. We went out into the cornfield where Mr. L——— was picking corn, and when I told him my business, he exploded. He called Mr. Wilson a Czar, and the United States Government almost everything he could lay his tongue to, and then I asked: "Mr. L———, what are you, a German? About five more words of your talk and I will take you along, too." He had no more to say of a violent nature, but evidently felt very hostile.

I brought the boy in. He passed the physical examination and was placed in Class I. I told him that probably he would be called to entrain in June. I tried to get him to tell me whether or not he would be here to entrain, and he said: "Yes, sure, I have learned my lesson and will be in."

In the meantime, Mr. L———, Sr., had been talking wildly and saying that he would rather see his son dead than in the Army of the United States. He also said that if anybody came out to get his son and make him go over there and fight the rich man's battles, they would have to take him over his dead body.

I finally got in touch with Mr. P———, whose son married L———'s daughter. He went over to see L——— and told him that if the boy was not in by nine o'clock on the day of entrainment, the officers would have to come after him. L——— replied that if they did come out there, he had a double-barreled shot-gun loaded with buck-shot and would let the first man that stepped on the place have it.

Nine o'clock the next morning I took one of my operatives and a good 30-30 rifle and went out there; drove in the gate as fast as I could make it, and caught the old gentleman in the barn.

L——— had mislaid his shot-gun, but his wife found it, and was approaching him with it. After quite a tussle, we convinced Mrs. L——— that she had no use for a gun, and I took it away from her.

In the meantime their loyal, patriotic son had started for Monon, about six miles from the farm, to get some mower repairs. I left my operative on the premises, and started after young L——— in the car. I found him about three miles from the farm, jogging along with his thoughts dwelling on the hardships of war. I stopped him and told him he would have to go with me, and he said: "Well, what will I do with the horse and buggy." I replied that that was not worrying me, that I wanted him. He tied the horse to the fence, and I took him in the car and went back to the farm. I told him that if he would go like a man, I would give him five minutes to change his clothes and get in the car and go with me to entrain.

He was ready in three minutes and thirty-five seconds. I took him to Fort Benjamin Harrison and turned him over to the Provost Marshal. This man was inducted into the Army, and has been in France shooting Huns.

These cases do not exhaust the files of Rensselaer. There are more of the same sort, but these give a good idea of the sort of problems which tested the courage, ability and resourcefulness of A. P. L. operatives and chiefs throughout the war.

Elkhart, Indiana, is present or accounted for in almost every branch of the service. The Chief says: "We found most of our cases pro-German, with some spite work. Elkhart Division handled a total of 600 cases of all sorts, of which 117 were concerned with alien enemy activities. A number of reports were investigated which charged certain German sympathizers with offering up prayers in church for the Kaiser and the success of the German arms. There would seem to be no use in praying for the Kaiser now."

One of the most American parts of Indiana is good old Brown County, long famous because there is no railroad within its confines. The Chief reports: "This has been a quiet sector. Our people are native stock, absolutely loyal and patriotic. A few late-comers of German origin began to talk too much, but when they found they were being watched, they stopped. It is good to live in an old-fashioned American community such as we usually read about in books."

MICHIGAN

Perhaps not many people in the United States have heard of Midland, Michigan — it is one of the many new names on the war map. But the Midland report — in many ways the best report turned in by any A. P. L. chief in the entire country — bulked large and was very thorough indeed; in short, it was a day-by-day record and report of activities in a town engaged in making deadly gases and other chemicals for use in the war. Midland is the site of the Dow Chemical Company's chief plant, a concern which manufactured acetone for airplane dope, mustard gas, T. N. T. and a number of other special products for the Government. As a consequence it seems to have been a magnet for alien enemy workmen and American laborers with pro-German sympathies. Something broke loose almost every day; on some days, two, three or even four cases came up. Altogether the Midland report is an extraordinary document — indeed the most veritable and illuminating day-to-day record of all which the League has produced. This blotter form of report supplies a remarkable narrative of the chances and near-casualties which the presence of a munitions plant brought to a normal American community. It is too bad such a report cannot be given in full, but it runs to 12,000 words, spans ten months of time and covers one hundred and fifty-seven cases of investigation. This splendid report came out of a wholly unexpected quarter. We hear much of the romance of big business. Perhaps when the reader shall have discovered how many men were waiting day-by-day to wreck and ruin one big business, it will not always seem to have been so romantic after all. We may make at least a brief resumé of things which happened in and around Midland. Names cannot be given, but it may be stated in advance that practically every case investigated was that of a man who had a German, Russian or European name.

Carl L——— was a German Lutheran minister at Midland, and seems to have been much like his brethren of the cloth in that denomination. He remarked to a friend, "Why, you do not seem to realize that Germany will soon control the world." When the Lusitania was sunk, he said, "The people who went on that ship should have been blown sky-high." Preacher L——— is still preaching at Midland.

Alex B——— is a retired citizen of Midland. He was born in Germany, came to this country penniless, yet acquired sufficient wealth upon which to retire. This country is full of Germans of similar description, who have remained just as German as they ever were. This was the case of Mr. B———. In discussing the war, he said, "You can't get your troops over there because our submarines will sink them." By "your" he meant American troops, and by "our" he meant German submarines. He was of the belief that the German was a far superior race to ours. Natürlich! Gewiss! Das versteht sich!

S. F. S———, another employe, was found taking pictures of one of the buildings devoted to the making of sulphuric acid, including the railroad approaches. United States asked him please not to take any more such pictures.

A can containing a pint of giant powder was found in a car of coal which was being hoisted into the boilers at the power house of the Dow Chemical Company. Two Germans, J. O. M——— and Carl S———, were heard talking of prospective trouble at the Dow Company. The former said, "I have a bottle planted near the gate that they will hear from." Both men were watched, and their plot seems to have been aborted.

John S——— once claimed he was German, then claimed he was Russian. He could not speak nor write Russian, but was familiar with the German language and associated only with Germans of the hostile type. He attended the German-Lutheran church and was very insolent toward Americans. Whether German or Russian, he was discharged by the Dow Chemical Company. He found his solace in conversation at the German store, run by two Germans, all enjoying themselves very much, conversing and settling the war.

Ernest W———, reported as an alien enemy in the pay of the German Government, a sailor on the Great Lakes in the summer time. Reported to the steamship company of Cleveland which used to employ him.

C. B——— works for the Dow Chemical Company. Operative reports he said United States was to blame for the war and that Germany had told the people of the United States not to board English ships. All of which sounds familiar — if not convincing — to an American. Ja wohl!

John W———, reported pro-German, had expressed himself as opposed to the United States in the war. Since we declared war, has been more discreet. A common case.

H. S———, in the army cantonment, but reported to have stated he would desert as quickly as he got to France. His officers duly notified.

E. L. K———, a foreman in the wood shop of the Dow Chemical Company, reported to be willing to bet $100 that the United States would never whip Germany. Too bad someone did not take him up several times! Ach! das thut uns leid!

A. B. B———, reported by some patent attorneys to have appeared at their office desiring the Russian patent for a dinner pail which would be capable of containing several sticks of dynamite hidden in coils. A compartment for a clock was also called for. This would be a fine thing for a workman to take into a building such as this Government enterprise. The attorneys did not care for confidential relations with such a client. Close watch was kept for three weeks, but the client did not come back.

John G——— said when the Lusitania was sunk, "What in hell were the ——— ——— on that boat for, anyway—were they not warned to keep off?" Which again sounds familiar. Indeed, that was the attitude of practically every German or pro-German in America, no matter whether naturalized or not.

Alma, Michigan, is a pleasant and quiet city, but you can't tell where a big story will break. Drama is no respecter of geography. Which is by way of saying that one Herman R——— is reported by Gratiot County Division to have been raised on a farm in this locality. During the war he went to Spokane, Washington, and joined the I. W. W. He was indicted among others in the Haywood trial and disappeared while waiting for trial. Gratiot County Division was directed to look him up.

A visit was made to the sister of R———, who herself appeared as much an I. W. W. as need be. Through persistence, however, they learned where Herman was approximately. It was concluded that the brother and sister might correspond, so the mails were watched. Sure enough, on the third day there came a letter from Spokane addressed to another sister, and bearing the Spokane postmark. Then a brother of Herman was visited, and from him and from his unmarrried sister a snapshot was obtained of Herman and his pal, each holding an I. W. W. paper facing toward the camera, which sufficiently well identified them and their tendencies.

Later on both Herman and his pal were located, apprehended, tried, convicted, and sentenced in the Chicago trial.

Ottawa County, Michigan, has in its population a large percentage of people of Dutch descent. There are also many immigrants from Holland, some naturalized, others not. Most of these people have an inborn hatred for England, which was mistakenly called pro-Germanism. A correct understanding of the psychology of these people was no easy matter to arrive at, but the A. P. L. handled most of them in such a way as to convert them into patriots rather than malcontents. The Chief adds, however: " It should not be gathered from this that our population as a whole was not heart and soul for America. We rarely met anything vicious in the way of disloyalty. Hollanders are ultra-Calvinistic, unemotional and not easily stirred to enthusiasm, and it was sometimes difficult to reach their hearts with feelings of patriotism and love for the land of their adoption."

Washtenaw County, Michigan, had the reputation of being the worst pro-German community in the Eastern Division of Michigan. Fully four percent of the people were pro-German. Large districts are nothing but old German settlements, " infested with that worst brand of citizen — the second or third generation German." The Chief instituted a series of Star Chamber courts which put a wet blanket on this gentry and changed Washtenaw County into one of the quietest communities in the State. The A. P. L. men were not known to one another, but they were in all strata of society. They uncovered several rampant cases of Bolshevism and conducted a good many character and loyalty investigations. They investigated also 144 alien enemies who applied for naturalization. The total number of alien enemies investigated ran above 700, so it may be seen that this organization was kept pretty busy.

Ludington, Michigan, looked into fifty cases of disloyalty and sedition, and investigated six hundred cases of oral propaganda. The Chief says: "We investigated about two thousand cases; delivered upwards of two hundred speeches for the Red Cross; nullified three strikes of workmen — one on the railroad, and the other two in plants doing government work. Over seven hundred men were involved." Ludington also reports the case of a German reservist who was traced from this point to France, from there to Winnipeg, thence to Seattle, thence to Chicago. The suspect was finally apprehended in Chicago and interned. Real sleuthing!

Benton Harbor, Michigan, is adjacent to strongly German neighborhoods. There were 1,000 men who signed up for League work, each man contributing one dollar to the common fund. The county was split up into five districts, each manned by a lieutenant and several operatives under him. A general secrecy obtained as to the membership, and the division was very active and efficient.

Grand Rapids, Michigan, was a busy center of activity, and one of the best-handled divisions in the United States, 3,907 cases being investigated, exclusive of about 500 minor cases in regard to German language, Liberty Loan, War Savings Stamps and other miscellaneous cases. Of the grand total, 2,357 cases were investigated under the "work or fight" order. A. P. L. at Grand Rapids had a busy season, and did its work well. It deserves as many pages as it is given lines.

Iron River, Michigan, had the usual routine. One case, slightly unusual, had to do with one Victor F———, a Swede fifty-eight years old, naturalized in America. He reluctantly admitted a pro-German tendency, but as he had a large family, the local chief was disposed to leniency. The Chief says: "I had previously learned that this man, with his family, was worth about $8,000. I had him agree to purchase $2,000 worth of Liberty Bonds at once and to leave them in the custody of the local bank until the end of the war. He also contributed $300 to the local war chest, and agreed to aid soliciting committees among his neighbors. He has kept his promise in these respects, and has kept silent about the war."

Manistee, Michigan, is in one of the most pro-German counties of the State. A number of German agents had a sort of representative at Manistee. There were seventy-eight residents who swore fealty to Germany, although only twenty-one of these remained loyal during the closing days of the war. Not infrequently times became a trifle heated at Manistee. German sympathizers once shot at the Chief of the A. P. L., who had just apprehended several German suspects who were accused of making blue-prints of pumps going into United States battleships. The organization was active throughout the war, and was on its toes at all times.

Mount Clemens, Michigan, is in Macomb County, a large proportion of whose inhabitants are of German origin. A flying field is located near Mount Clemens. Hence a special officer of the Department of Justice was in charge. Most of the work had to do with pro-Germanism, ninety-seven of such cases being investigated. There were seven cases of alien enemy activities, two of sabotage, fifty-six connected with selective service matters, thirty of character and loyalty, and seven of food-hoarding. No grass grew under the feet of this division.

ILLINOIS

There ought to be at least one good stiff report from some town located near a big Army cantonment. Rockford, Illinois, entry point for Camp Grant, has submitted a report which meets every specification. It must be understood that from 30,000 to 75,000 troops came under the jurisdiction of Rockford Division each couple of months or so throughout the war. Rockford is a great manufacturing point and for some time has been a center of I. W. W. activities, a considerable number of I. W. W. clan being found among the laboring classes there. The League watched these people very closely, secured stenographic reports of their club speeches, etc., and thus got some strong Government evidence.

After war was declared, these agitators became very violent, and carried on an active compaign against the Selective Service Act. On one occasion they conducted an all-day meeting and picnic at Black Hawk Park, which was nothing but an organization meeting so timed as to interfere with the draft registration. We locked up three men, at which the other members of the two local unions thronged the streets to the jail and demanded the release of the men. We put an additional one hundred and thirty-five members of the I. W. W. in jail, and standing room only was available. Special interurban cars were chartered, eighty persons being removed to adjacent counties. The jail was pretty badly wrecked. The leader of these men got two years imprisonment, it being proved also that he was an alien and subject to deportation. The Immigration Bureau has secured a warrant for his deportation, and he will go abroad permanently at the expiration of his sentence. Federal Judge Landis sentenced one hundred and eleven of these men to one year in the Bridewell at Chicago. This case has been referred to in the report of Mr. Colby, D. J. agent at Chicago, as one of the most important in the Western country. A special agent was sent out by the Department of Justice to Rockford, with the result that an office was established there to carry on the joint work more efficiently.

After Camp Grant was located at Rockford, the A. P. L. had much more work to do. While the buildings were going up, about 50,000 men passed through the employment bureau, from 7,000 to 10,000 being employed in the work. All classes of men were attracted to Rockford, and the local division was busy in keeping watch over them. Thirty-five I. W. W. members were taken from the camp laborers and handled in different ways — always with encouragement to go away and stay away. Two alien enemies were found among the laboring men at Rockford. They had come to America surreptitiously after the war began in Europe and had worked at various cantonments. They finally admitted they were German subjects, and were interned for the war. After the cantonment was completed and the troops began to arrive, the divisional activities of the A. P. L. centered largely in the detection of violations having to do with the morale of the troops. Five operatives were put to work on liquor cases, all working together under cover. Twenty-six men were sentenced for supplying soldiers with liquor, getting an average of ten months' imprisonment each.

The most notable case handled in Camp Grant, or in any other camp, was that which resulted in the court-martial of twenty-one negro soldiers. Louise S———, a white woman visiting a white soldier at Camp Grant, was set upon and assaulted by fifteen to twenty-one negro soldiers on the night of May 19, the crime being committed on the reservation at Camp Grant. At nine o'clock that evening Major General Charles H. Martin, in command at Camp Grant, telephoned to the local chief to meet him in town. He said his officers had been unable to make any headway on the case, and asked that it be taken up by the Department of Justice. The League put men on the case, and in three days had twenty of the culprits in custody, ultimately securing confessions implicating all the others who were held. All of these men were tried by court-martial; fifteen were convicted and dealt with, five were let go, and one was declared insane. The assistance of the civilian authorities and auxiliaries to the military arm was so distinct in this case that General Martin wrote a frank letter of thanks, in which he said: "I am free to confess that until your entrance into the game, we had not progressed very far, and I wish to make it of record that it was principally due to your able and efficient service that we finally succeeded."

The nature and extent of the activities of the Rockford division may be seen from the following summary: alien enemy activities, 95; citizens' disloyalty and sedition, 50; sabotage, 5; anti-military activities, 13; propaganda, 13; miscellaneous cases, 211. The Navy Department asked assistance in 55 cases. Investigations made by the War Department covered 21 for Military Intelligence; 242 under the selective service regulations; 164 slackers; 45 character and loyalty applications; 90 liquor cases; 44 cases of vice and prostitution; 25 cases of desertions, and the collection of over 200 maps and photographs for M. I. D. The Department of State also reaches out as far as Rockford, and the quietly efficient League handled forty-six passport cases alone. The Treasury Department had ten cases under War Risk, and the United States Shipping Board asked for two investigations on character and loyalty.

In the nature of things, the activities of A. P. L. being so wide, so impartial, and at times so energetic and aggressive, friction of social or business sort was sure now and then to arise. The only wonder is that there was not a great deal more of it. Sometimes this grew out of spite work and personal jealousy, and again resulted in clashes of a wider and more distinct sort, resulting in something like community cliques.

Mattoon, Illinois, had this sort of a tempest in a teapot from some such causes. That town has a Merchants' Association, and this association, for reasons into which it is not necessary to go here, but which perhaps had a personal basis in some measure, saw fit to fine certain members of its body who had contributed money for the organization of A. P. L. This caused considerable hard feeling. The Chief, P. A. Erlach, asked permission to explain the purposes of the League to the Merchants' Association. This permission was not granted. The Chief held a conference with Judge MacIntyre, who suggested that the members who had been fined by the Merchants' Association might be subpoenaed and brought to the court room, not for trial, but for the purpose of clearing the situation, which did not seem to be good for the community or the government. The Merchants' Association hired a lawyer to represent them, and a very warm session was held, out of which, of course, nothing was derivable except hard feeling. In the mutual recriminations, one member of the Merchants' Association was alleged to have remarked at a certain time: "After this war is over, the Germans will be the aristocrats of the world"—a belief which seems to have lacked confirmation. All these matters, however, did not succeed in destroying the usefulness of the A. P. L. in Mattoon, where it did a great deal of hard and conscientious work.

Probably the most interesting Mattoon investigation is that of one O'H———, son of a wealthy farmer, who claimed exemption on account of agricultural occupation. He was alleged to be living in town and engaged in keeping books. The League went into the history of the family and produced proof that certain other paternal ancestors of O'H——— had been engaged in the so-called Charleston Riots during the civil war, when a band of men known as "Copperheads," among whom was an ancestor of O'H———, had fired upon several Union soldiers with fatal results in several instances. The Mattoon Chief of A. P. L. submitted to the Adjutant General at Springfield, Illinois, a full brief of the investigation of the case of young O'H———, also transcripts from Government records covering the Charleston riots. Young O'H——— was sent to Camp Zachariah for training.

Pastor Russell had certain followers in Mattoon, religious fanatics of the sect known as Truth-Believers. They did not believe in anything but the Truth, certainly not in Liberty Loans, War Savings Stamps, or any war funds or activities. Two members of the sect were arraigned, but the Federal grand jury did not indict them because one was a woman and the other concluded to go into the employment of the Government at Washington.

Near Mattoon is a settlement of the peculiar sect known as Ammish, whose religion tells them not to bear arms. They opposed the selective draft, and although it was determined to exempt their young men from actual drill, the community preaching became so bad that a stiff investigation was made, after which there was no more trouble.

The secret of the Mattoon fashion of investigation is not

told, but a number of case-reports close with the words: "There has been no further complaint from the party." This covers the case of several citizens who did not buy as many Liberty Bonds as they might, or were too free in their talk about Germany as compared with this country.

Joliet, Illinois, has certain mills which harbor a large foreign element, Austrians and others. Several arrests and one internment put a quietus on German propaganda work among these people. "We worked through local foreign priests in whom they have confidence," says the local chief, and he adds: "We feel now that this hotbed of Austrianism is a fertile field for the so-called Bolshevist movement, as the sort of people most frequently dealt with are very susceptible to this propaganda. They feel that they can express themselves freely, now that the war is over, and they are pleased at this opportunity. We believe that there is still much work ahead before the Bolshevist movement ceases to be a menace in these parts."

Bloomington, Illinois, cites as its stand-out case the capture of a German sailor, who was interned with the *Princess Irene,* the German boat at Hoboken, and had broken parole. The Chief says: "We had considerable other work to do in conducting investigations and in stopping the propaganda of loud-mouthed Germans."

Rock Island, Illinois, is one of the most famous arsenal towns in the country, the Ordnance Department having erected large works there many years ago. All such posts were danger foci during the war. Rock Island Division investigated 382 disloyalty and sedition cases, and 138 cases of propaganda. The selective service regulations required 548 investigations. There were also the usual number of cases taken on for the Housing Committee (it was a big problem to house Rock Island's war population), the Red Cross, the U. S. Commissioner, the U. S. Marshal, the County Sheriff, the Liberty Loan committees and war charities. Certainly a very satisfactory record for a place where something might have blown loose had enemy wishes come true!

Epworth, Illinois, worked in close touch with the State Council of Defense. The Chief reports: "Our community was loyal during the Civil War, and when this work came on, we gladly put our shoulder to the wheel again. A few said things quite out of place, but you can believe we were never Germanized here. Our worst enemies were those who would rather part with their sons than with their coin — though they did neither willingly. We examined some applicants for overseas service."

Alton, Illinois, just across the river from St. Louis, had some investigations for Military Intelligence, and some overseas investigations. The division had occasion to assist the Special Agent of the Department of Justice in St. Louis a number of times when quick action was needed.

WISCONSIN

Justly or not, Milwaukee, Wisconsin, had the reputation of being about the most German community in the most nearly German state of the Union. No sweeping conclusions need be advanced as to either side of this proposition herein, for evidently, all said and done, Milwaukee is Milwaukee, and is well known throughout the country. There was a time, even previous to our entering the war against Germany, when salesmen traveling out of Milwaukee were unable to sell their goods to the retail trade throughout the Middle West. They were obliged to go back to their houses and to say that the city which they represented was in bad repute. Just or not, these were the facts, and in time the better-class business men of Milwaukee, most of whom have not lacked in loyalty, began to see that some remedy must be found for this prejudice existing against their city.

During the Civil War the Germans of Wisconsin, descendents of the heavy German immigration of 1848 and the years immediately following, had a splendid representation in the Northern army. The sons of these men are among the most prominent business men in Wisconsin and of Milwaukee to-day, and it were worse than wrong loosely to accuse them all of disloyalty to this country. Upon the other hand, Milwaukee, being a heavy German settlement, did not lack in wrong-headed persons who retained their allegiance to a flag other than our own. These did the usual amount of talking — perhaps more than the usual amount. For them the Milwaukee Division of the American Protective League had the same remedy that has been found efficient in other communities comprising a large foreign element or an element with foreign sympathies. It went to work quietly and steadily, showing good judgment and good sense, as well as good patriotism. Mr. B. K. Miller was Chief of the Milwaukee Division. The membership was made up of substantial men of proven loyalty. The following table tells the story of their work:

Alien enemy cases	10,000
Sedition and disloyalty investigations, and violations of the Espionage Act	2,400
Character and loyalty reports	700
Liquor and vice cases	75
Internments	40
Selective Service cases	6,500
War Risk Insurance cases	68

Sparta, Wisconsin, from the spelling of the suspect names in the report, appears to be located in the heart of darkest Germany. One Mr. H——— of that vicinity declared that a letter written to his father in anything but the German language would be an insult. He was interviewed, and it is believed that he has changed his idea by this time. Another local pro-German volubly declared that the Y. M. C. A. was a "damn fraud." He is also thinking it over. Gus L——— would not allow a card with the admonition, "Speak English," to be placed in his store. It may affect his application for his second papers. Carl B——— was called on for a subscription to the Red Cross, but turned down the callers flat. He said he had never sworn obedience to the United States and never would, adding: "They can take me back to Germany or any place they like, and I don't care a damn how quick." Such a man, it would seem, ought to be obliged in the matter of such preferences. A preacher, Rev. E———, seemed to talk German propaganda rather than the Holy Scriptures. He was indicted. August Y——— made seditious remarks in the open, and was reported to the Department of Justice. Henry B——— was reported for threats he made against his neighbor for taking part in the War Work campaign. Several alien enemies who were applying for citizenship were held while their records were looked up. Joe M——— believed the Y. M. C. A. to be a "graft," and thought our boys were sent to France to be butchered. Duly interviewed about it. O. W. S———, cashier of a bank, wrote a letter in which he stated his bank would not take any Government certificates. He gave as his reason that he was short of help, as one of his men was being held in the army against his will and "against the wishes of the community." He was spoken to.

Neillsville, Wisconsin, apparently, was up on its toes. It reports the investigation of an alien German Lutheran minister; utterances against the President and the Government, and the discovery of socialistic campaign literature for evidence in the Socialist trial at Chicago. It searched the community for the Socialist paper called "The Voice of the People"; investigated the Russellite sect and looked up the record of 118 petitioners for naturalization; investigated juries in the trial of a murder case growing out of an attempt to evade the draft, in which several people were wounded and two killed, and investigated a Socialist candidate for sheriff who made contributions to a fund for printing radical literature. The foregoing civil activities were done in the interest of the Department of Justice. Neillsville, for the War Department, investigated a woman who was trying to get information about the Edgewood Arsenals; assisted the U. S. Marshals in arresting draft dodgers, and investigated civilian applicants for overseas service and applicants for commissions. The Chief apologizes for not having done more!

Oshkosh, Wisconsin, had one hundred and eleven men — lawyers, doctors, bankers, manufacturers and workmen — on her A. P. L. rolls. The investigations throughout the war period totalled 343. There was much outspoken Germanism in this district before the United States went into the war, but after that, it died down. One old German, when confronted by the operatives, said: "Vel, I dell you vat I dink; it is so; I dink vat I dink. How can I helb id? But I *say* not von dam vord — nefer!" A safe rule. "Since the war ended," says the Chief, "known sympathizers with Germany have been as quiet as oysters here. When Germany has been a republic for twenty years or so, I hope some of these imported old bigots will soften."

Racine, Wisconsin, has a population of 50,000. In a slacker raid it gathered in 3,000, including a number of real dodgers and deserters. Two companies of State guards and Spanish war veterans, organized into thirty-five squads, carried out the League's orders to perfection.

Berlin, Wisconsin, reports: "Berger carried this county for Congress. We had some German propagandists who said that America could not win the war. We quieted them. Most of our work had to do with Liberty Bond campaigns, Red Cross, exemption claims, and Food Administration matters."

Eau Claire, Wisconsin, makes a clean-cut report on the activities of that division, being in touch constantly with the Agents of the Department of Justice and ready to act at once at all times. D. J. complimented this division on its compilation of evidence. The Chief says: "Among our cases are several which proved vexatious. We succeeded in silencing such disloyalists as we had. Notwithstanding the fact that the war is over, we know there yet lies ahead of all good citizens an enormous work of education in righting and keeping right the obligation of the individual to the Government."

MINNESOTA

The City of Duluth, at the head of the Great Lakes, lies close to the edge of the great Northern wilderness whose fastnesses might well beckon the evader as well as the explorer or the discoverer. Her geographical situation makes Duluth a sort of Mecca for dodgers, drifters and deserters, and a good part of the A. P. L. work at that point — and hard work it often was — consisted in running down these unwilling patriots who preferred the seclusiveness of a logging camp, trapper's shack, or even a logging drive, to bearing arms under their country's flag.

Olsen is a name somewhat indefinite in the upper Minnesota country, but it was claimed by a deserter from Camp Dodge who originally registered from Ely, Minnesota. The entire Olsen genealogical tree was combed over, and many shacks housing Olsens here and there in the woods were examined, but the right Olsen was not found. At last an operative hit upon the expedient of spreading word that this particular Olsen was wanted to sign a receipt for some property that had been left to him. The proper Olsen came into town, was arrested at once, and sent to Fort Snelling — the victim of several kinds of misplaced confidence.

There came into Duluth a rather pitiful story of a young girl of East Texas engaged to a U. S. soldier who was taken prisoner and sent to the interior of Germany. The prisoner sent out a letter to his sweetheart which stated that he was well treated. He also said that he was sending her his watch as a souvenir, lest she might never see him again. The girl took the watch to a jeweler. Inside of the works there was a note which said that everything the prisoner had written in the letter was not true, that his nose and ears had been cut off by the Germans, so that he felt himself unfit even to be seen by her again. The girl herself lived at Nacogdoches and had met her Northern sweetheart in a Southern camp.

From Ashland, Wisconsin, there was reported to the Duluth office the name of one J———, a deserter. He was traced out into the woods, found in the garret of a shack whose owner disclaimed all knowledge of him, hauled down and out and sent to Fort Snelling, all in jig time.

From Erie, Pennsylvania, there came to Duluth warning that there probably would be on a steamer due to land at that point a deserter from the service. The boat was met, the deserter was found, and within thirty-six hours he was on his way to Fort Snelling to repent at his leisure.

One O———, an Austrian or Russian, a mill hand, was found in bed when an operative went after him as a draft evader. He was so indiscreet as to say, "To hell with America." At that time the operative landed on him with a stiff right, and O——— went down for the count. The short and simple annals of Mr. O———'s case read: "He was dragged to jail with his toes up, put in a cell with his toes still up, and left alone with his toes up. The next day he was sent to Fort Snelling as a deserter."

All the way from Great Falls, Montana, came a deserter who thought he could hide himself in the North woods around Duluth. As a matter of fact, he succeeded in doing so for more than a month although he was traced here and there in the forest. He located on a river-drive where he worked for a time. This Mr. C——— always went armed and was reported as dangerous, but this did not act as any deterrent for A. P. L. men. The evader was classified as having strong I. W. W. affiliations. He was chased far in the woods, but will have to come out some time. When he does, he will find the Duluth A. P. L. ready to welcome him.

The totals for Duluth might be expected to run high. Accordingly we need not be surprised to find that Duluth reports 1,293 investigations of disloyalty and sedition; 3,287 men taken in slacker raids; 41 investigations for propaganda, and 186 naturalization investigations.

Freeborn County, Minnesota, submitted a very optimistic report: "The loyal folks were so plentiful that if any pessimist happened to say the wrong thing about the Red Cross or the Liberty Loans, he was promptly reported. A few fines of $500 each in the district court soon stopped all disloyalty talk. The Non-Partisan League was watched closely but we got nothing disloyal at their meetings and could find no openly disloyal acts. They have an unusual proportion of persons of German extraction in their membership. At the beginning of the war a good many farmers tried to keep their sons at home, often using strongly colored affidavits. Some honestly felt that the duty to furnish food was greater than the duty to fight, which attitude sometimes led to unfounded accusations against them."

Wilkin County, Minnesota, watched Non-Partisan League activities closely. Members of this none too loyal organization talked less freely when they learned that they were being watched. The community had some clergymen with strong German tendencies, but these also experienced a change of heart. One German alien, registered at Omaha, Nebraska, who had left without permission, was arrested until the Department of Justice at St. Paul could take him over. The fact of his arrest created a large silence among the pro-Germans of the region.

Grant County, Minnesota, has a little report. "A few minor investigations of false statements about deferred classifications were made. We got the facts. Our County is small, no large settlements, and everyone knows practically everybody else, so there was little for us to do."

Winona, Minnesota, sends in the best kind of a report — with few or no figures under most lettered heads. Winona has about 20,000 inhabitants, and is a small farming community with a floating population. Much of the work of the division was in stopping local gossip and loose talking. The League did, however, locate one deserter, who was duly turned over.

MISSOURI

The tracing of a deserter may take a hundred pages in a file. A certain man registered in St. Louis, but never turned in his questionnaire. He was classified by the Adjutant General of Missouri as a deserter, and A. P. L. was requested to find him. Search revealed him in James City, Pennsylvania. The chief of police of a nearby town found the man in bed. The deserter, whose name may be called Bates, resisted fiercely. It was stated of him that he was the first man the chief of police ever arrested who succeeded in breaking a pair of handcuffs. He fought all the time until he was put in jail. Mr. Bates, it is to be hoped, fought equally well in the army. He certainly got his chance to do so.

D. W. B———, from St. Louis, was once in the 108th Infantry, but vanished therefrom, leaving his uniform in New York with a friend. One paragraph, the last page in the file, will cover the case of Mr. B———: "As subject was apprehended in Buffalo, the commanding officer at Fort Niagara was communicated with, and he detailed a sergeant to come to Buffalo on December 17. The sergeant took B——— into custody and conveyed him to Fort Niagara, where he is at present."

Kansas City, among other cases, turned in a love letter written by a local young lady to a Japanese, Heroshirmo, at present living in Japan. The letter begins: "Dear Heroshirmo: How I want to write to you pages and pages of something, I am not sure what. I want to tell you first about the beautiful summer that has just passed, how beautiful the trees and flowers were, how infinite and blue the sky"— but perhaps that will be enough.

The A. P. L. noticed the post-mark and thought that this sort of correspondence ought to be looked into. It should. The Japanese had once stopped in Kansas City as a member of a Commission on its way to Washington, and had visited local friends. No international plot was unveiled in this case. Just the trees and flowers were discovered to be beautiful and the sky very blue. To be sure, the writer being a woman, the letter had a postscript: "Just because I have been sick, would you like to send me a genuine Japanese kimona? I must tell you that all of the first page of your last letter except the first few lines were cut out by the censor. D——n the war."

Jefferson City, Missouri, has jurisdiction over several counties but the division consisted of only twenty-one members. These men were of great value to the Department of Justice at Kansas City. The sparsely settled nature of the country around Jefferson City meant a great deal of automobile travel. The Chief says he has traveled as high as ninety-five miles in his own car on one case. This meant a vast amount of work for the small membership of the League at that point. It acquitted itself admirably.

Clinton, Missouri, faithfully performed a large volume of routine work such as comes to most of the divisions — some three hundred cases in all, under various headings. The Chief concludes: "Our activities have been abundant. We mean to continue our organization here until there is no further need for it. Our personnel is made up of the best men in this county. Our system of warning by red-white-and-blue cards has been adopted in many States and by the National Council of Defense."

Monett, Missouri, had some trouble from the fact that drafted men were at first able to obtain alcoholic beverages there. This was stopped by the local League. There was considerable propaganda by word of mouth in this locality which was choked off. One deserter defied all local officers to capture him and take him back to camp. Nevertheless he was taken, returned to camp, court-martialed and sentenced to a term in the federal prison. As a whole, the people of this community are law abiding 100-percent Americans. Hence the League's work was light.

Fayette, Missouri: "Thirty investigations resulted in reclassifying twenty-five men. We arrested three camp deserters and two men for disloyal acts. Found three men hoarding sugar and made them take it back. In some cases we just warned parties that their conduct had been reported to be reprehensible, and evidence was produced by them to prove their later love and loyalty to the United States."

IOWA

Des Moines, Iowa, the very prosperous capital of the prosperous state of Iowa, had an A. P. L. man attached to the Intelligence Service of the Army. He spoke German fluently and in order to investigate conditions inside a neighboring camp, he pretended to be a conscientious objector, thus being confined to barracks with other conscientous objectors, some real and some camouflage. A picked War Department Committee, including the Governor of the State, was combing out these objectors and ran across the A. P. L. man. The latter was unable to explain, and had to go through as a conscientious objector and listen to a good lecture to boot!

Des Moines had another case of a fine looking young man who weighed about 175 pounds and who sported a clever little military mustache. He was caught in a slacker drive and on the following morning hesitatingly handed the agent a telegram sent by his father, which read: "I have told you that damned eye-brow on your upper lip would get you into trouble. Tell the Government I say you are only twenty — you look older, but act younger. If you wish to please your father, enlist in the Navy." The son enlisted.

Iowa City, Iowa, is a university town, a good, peaceful and thrifty community and one of the most useful in the West. The foreign element in that district has been rather Bohemian than German, but the population has the usual admixture. There are two precincts populated by Mennonites, whose religion is work and not war. One of these good folk refused to buy Liberty Bonds but sold enough walnut logs from his farm to make several thousand gun stocks. This man was finally persuaded to buy as many dollars in bonds as his logs made gun stocks. Some conscientious objectors from Camp Dodge were sent out to farm among these Mennonite brothers and thus escaped the draft, whereas local loyal farmers' sons had to go to the front. This created bitter feeling. Most of these dodgers were recalled.

Oskaloosa, Iowa, had its own share of local wrangles over

League war activities. One suspect was brought up under charges of disloyalty by reason of many reports coming in against him. He was indicted and the local Chief says: "I have no doubt of his conviction had he not died since."

Hardin County, Iowa, had an organization which kept this community decent and orderly and up to the front in all of the war activities. The chief was a member of the Bureau of Military Affairs for Hardin County, which had charge of all the war work. He was also on the County Committee of Four on Military Instruction, whose duty it was to instruct and train drafted men. Other members of the A. P. L. were on the Legal Advisory Board and also were of assistance to the drafted men. A steady-going and firm-stepping community.

Corning, Iowa, worked in the usual unostentatious way with the Food and Fuel administrations, etc. Two indictments were brought against a man who blocked war activities, the fines going to the Red Cross.

Green County reports: "All quiet in this section. Very few Germans in our county. None showed disloyalty except one old German woman who wrote to her son, a missionary in China. Her family promised to keep her loyal. We examined into the German Lutheran schools and German language assemblages. Nothing of much consequence."

Decorah, Iowa, is another peaceful community in a peaceful State. Little or no trouble was met here. "The A. P. L. was organized rather late." says the report, "owing to the fact that we had a most thorough and efficient Defense Council at work."

Indianola, Iowa, is also a place of peace. The League had been organized only a short time when the Armistice broke, and there were but few activities. "Indianola has a rural population," says the Chief, "with a very small percentage of foreign born. No trouble of any consequence."

SOUTH DAKOTA

Aberdeen, South Dakota, must have been a good talking point for German propagandists, because it reports 122 cases of propaganda by word of mouth, and 128 cases of propaganda by printed matter. The division was called on to take active part in the I. W. W. labor troubles, and this part of its work is described at some length in the Chief's report:

> Thousands of I. W. W.'s drift here at harvest time. Their jungles sometimes contain as many as one thousand men. They take charge of whole trains, and force railroads to carry them wherever they wish. They have forced the city authorities in small communities to send them a specified amount of food, and have defied the authorities of larger cities to control them. By their methods of sabotage, murder and arson they have terrorized certain sections of this state and destroyed millions of dollars' worth of property. In the summer of 1917 the annual influx started. The A. P. L. was called on for assistance, and decidedly effective measures were adopted. Home Guards and citizens were organized — later called by a D. J. officer "the Klu Klux Klan of the Prairies." Anyhow, this section of the prairies was soon clear. In consequence, a strike was declared by the Minneapolis branch of the I. W. W. and some of their gunmen were sent out. The property of the Chief of Police at Aberdeen was burnt. In less than two weeks four of these men were under arrest and two of them are now serving sentences in the Federal Penitentiary at Leavenworth. The methods adopted by this branch of the A. P. L. have proved efficacious. Thousands of dollars' worth of property have been saved.

As Aberdeen is located in one of the Non-Partisan League districts, and as reports have come from nearby towns denoting a large percentage of pro-Germanism, it may be well to quote further from the report of this division. The Chief says that one family living in Hecla, strongly pro-German, declared they would never be taken alive. The A. P. L. took over the case. One man was shot resisting arrest. Five members of the family were arrested and two were convicted, while one remains to be tried. "This stopped pro-German utterances in that community," says the Chief, "and materially aided in the sale of bonds."

In December, 1917, Fred H——— of Aberdeen was interned for pro-German utterances. His wife turned state's evidence on members of the local German club where members had been fined for speaking the English language. Four of the leading spirits of this club were taken into custody, one of them the publisher of three German language newspapers of wide circulation which were openly pro-German. This man had sent to von Bernstorff $10,000, ostensibly to be used for the German Red Cross — all of it raised from readers of his publication through the sale of the "iron ring." This man was sentenced and fined $500. An associate editor of the same string of papers was interned also. One of the parties was president of the South Dakota German-American Alliance, and published a German language paper at Sioux Falls. He was charged with writing a letter which reads as follows:

> I have never given any declaration of loyalty and never will do it, nor subscribe to any Liberty Loan. The name is to me already an emetic because hypocritical and misleading. That a man perhaps buys bonds for business considerations, I can understand, but I myself couldn't do it without thinking that my $50 or $100 might perhaps buy the explosive which American accomplices of the allied plunderbund might throw on the house of my mother.

The writer of the above, as head of the German-American Alliance, raffled a picture of the crew of the *Deutschland* after our declaration of war, and sold souvenirs from the boat, remitting the funds to New York German centers. He was sentenced to ten years in the Federal penitentiary.

The active Chief of Aberdeen also caught H. M. H———, a former lieutenant in the German Navy and an ex-instructor in the Naval School at Hamburg, who was also active in the German-American Alliance. He got five years in the Federal penitentiary for urging young men of draft age not to enlist. Another alien enemy whose papers show that he once had wealthy connections in Germany, although he was engaged in making a scanty living at baling hay, was reported as a Prussian and believed to be dangerous. Yet another, William B———, was picked up in Aberdeen and told a tale that sounded like one by Deadwood Dick. He said he lived in the mountains of California with his uncle, who was a smuggler. He was found to be communicating with the I. W. W., and was sent to a detention camp. Another arrest was made, of Ed. R———, a wealthy farmer who stated he would rather see his daughter in a house of prostitution than a member of the Red Cross. He was sentenced to five years in the penitentiary, and this has discouraged the expression of such sentiments near Aberdeen.

Now, if there were nothing else whatever printed in these pages, the foregoing would show the necessity for such an organization as the American Protective League, even in communities far away from manufacturing centers and not supposed to be governed by the foreign element. The report of the Chief of the Aberdeen Division affords grave reading and matter for grave consideration. In that one little community, which does not turn in memoranda of all its cases, there were 312 Department of Justice cases, 156 War Department cases, and three Navy Department cases. Seventeen persons were arrested or interned. Perhaps the most noteworthy of the recommendations made by the local Chief is this: "It has been the experience of this branch that the communities reached by the German language publications have been decidedly disloyal. It is our opinion that action should be urged upon Congress to discontinue the foreign language press in America." These last are words of gold. They ought to be remembered by every man holding office in the United States and by every man seeking the suffrages of real American citizens. The time for mincing matters with these gentry has gone by.

NORTH DAKOTA

Fargo, North Dakota, hands in a report which varies in one important particular from those received from neighboring districts. The division was not making trouble enough for the rampant pro-Germans in Fargo, so the League turned around and investigated some of its own officers. None the less, the report tells of a story of accomplishment, there being 101 disloyalty and sedition cases, 109 cases under the Selective Service Act, and eight cases of enemy sympathizers who threatened the life of the President.

KANSAS

It will be no surprise to those who know Kansas to learn that this ultra-progressive, prosperous, energetic State was unswervingly loyal throughout the war, and had few cases of any kind to report. A few sentences quoted from the reports of several representative little towns will serve to show the Kansas war temperature varied from normal but slightly, if at all.

Oswego, Kansas, reports succinctly: "One hundred percent patriotism — no aliens."

White City, Kansas, says: "Ours is a community of loyal citizens. We spoke to a few about talking too much. Nothing serious."

Council Grove, Kansas, proved to be a great deal quieter than it used to be in the days of the Santa Fé trail. The Chief says: "We had a few pro-German sympathizers whose cases we turned over to the Department of Justice to investigate."

NEBRASKA

The A. P. L. Division at Omaha, Nebraska, was organized at a rather late date, July 1, 1918. The Armistice shattered the activities at a time when there were three hundred members of the League, each man ready to do what was asked of him. The Omaha Chief reports sixty cases of disloyalty and sedition, and several thousand investigations made in conjunction with D. J. as a result of the slacker raids, as well as 700 in connection with the Department of Labor.

The Chief at Hastings, Nebraska, says: "I did not know the work would be so extensive, or that there would be so much to do. We have investigated some cases for Omaha, and have done a great deal of work on draft cases for the state and county boards. We have been glad to do this work, and I am thankful that I could help my country this much."

Callaway, Nebraska, has a grievance: "I had one genuine case of seditious utterance, but we did not get the evidence. This man was elected State Senator by the Non-Partisan League. He worked against the Liberty Bond drive. Fortunately, this year our Senator is not of his sort politically."

David City, Nebraska, reports the usual routine work. One pro-German was taken into custody for making seditious remarks, and was bound over to the grand jury for trial. The local Chief reports that his organization is being held intact against any future emergency.

CHAPTER III

THE STORY OF THE SOUTH

The South is, in its percentage as to population, the finest, cleanest, truest and most loyal part of the United States to-day. It holds more of the native born Americans, fewer oı the foreign born, and fewer alien enemies than any like extent of our National possessions. The only pure-bred American population, sufficiently so to entitle it to a distinct origin-color of its own on the government census maps, lies along the crest of the southern Appalachians. There, in parts of Kentucky, Tennessee, North Carolina, Georgia, Alabama, lower Virginia, there are Americans who for generations have known no admixture of any foreign blood. You will find illiteracy there, poverty, small industrial development. That has come about by reason of a topography which has left transportation undeveloped. The people have been held back from the westbound progress of the nation almost as though caught by the cleats of the great flume through which poured our early Scotch-Irish, Indian-fighting, wilderness-conquering ancestry. But it is the finest of gold that those cleats have caught—a clean-bred, persistent type, of the highest honor, the highest courage, the highest intellectual quality, the highest physical qualities. Here and here alone you will find a true American type, come down with little change from our Colonial days. Would God that every state in the North and West had these men as the real inheritors of America, and not the snarling mob of foreigners who in the last few decades have come to be called American citizens. We have seen in some part how loyal these last have been, how much they cared for the flag of America.

The stock of our Highlands has furnished us many strong men, many of our greatest leaders, our greatest statesmen. Above all, it is fierce fighting stock. It has been held back by lack of education. These stark mountaineers are far more illiterate than were their grand-parents. To-day, in a Cumberland cabin, you may find a Latin grammar, or a tragedy in the original Greek, of which the owner will say, "I kaint read none of hit. Grandpap fotched it across the mountings when he come." "Across the mountains" lay the Carolinas and Old Virginia, seats of the most cultured and aristocratic life this country ever knew, and equal to the best of any land. When we lost that, we lost the flower of the American civilization. We never shall replace it. There is no America to-day. There never can be, unless the seed of the old American stock — never lacking in leaders — one day shall raise its voice as of old in councils where it will find hearkening.

The South is a wide country, covering a certain diversity of nature, but it remains singularly like throughout its borders. Politically it is still the slave of the color question, whose end no man can see. That same question restricts the South largely to agriculture. Of late, Northern money and methods have been reaching out for the raw wealth of Southern mines and forests, even farming lands. It is in respect of these later slight changes in the character of the southern life that the A. P. L. has found its main function there. Had it not been for imported labor, the A. P. L. would have had no alien and seditious cases, no propaganda and no disloyalty to report, because it is absolutely true that our Southern States, which once thought themselves constitutionally justified in secession, to-day are more loyal to the American flag man for man, town for town, state for state, than any or all the remaining states in this Union.

This is true; and yet it is also altogether true that a few Southern States furnished more cases of desertion or draft evasion than thrice that number of states in any other portion of the Union, even though with heavy foreign-born population. How can these two statements be reconciled?

It is easy, and the level-headed A. P. L. chiefs time and again have made it plain in their reports. A large percent of the selective service work had to do with brave young fighting men to whom liberty and personal freedom made the breath of their nostrils. Many of them were ignorant —more is the pity. While we have coddled the treacherous European immigrant, we have forgotten our own children.

Better had we thrown the maudlin Statue of Liberty into the sea, or turned its face about the other way!

The young Southerner who could not read grandpap's Latin book, or any other book, who saw no daily paper and knew nothing of the outside world, knew only that he did not want to fight in a war of which he knew nothing and in which he did not think he or his had any stake. Nobody had threatened him, no men had stolen anything of his, he did not know where Germany was, and he had never seen a German to learn to hate him. Why should he fight? He concluded he would not fight. He would just hide till this war was over, because it was none of his war.

Very much of the A. P. L. work in the South had to do with getting into the young man's comprehension that our Flag was in danger; that our women and children had been killed by men that did not fight like men but like brutes. Once that got into the mountain man's mind, the day for desertion was past and gone. There are no braver or more skilled fighting men in the world than in these Southern hills. There are none more loyal. They did their part and were ready to do it wherever called. They helped win the war for America as well as those from richer states. Now that the war is over, let America forget Europe's sordid sycophants, the grinning reservists of the "unbeaten" German Army, and turn attention to these, her own children — no cuckoo product without an ancestry to claim, who have no love for this country beyond their love for this country's easy money.

MARYLAND

Largely Southern in its population, traditions and political sympathies, yet Northern in its aggressive spirit and industrial enterprise, the city of Baltimore perhaps is entitled to be called "American" more than any other big city on the Atlantic seaboard. It has always been American, and in this war has only proven anew what has always been known by those who knew Baltimore. A hundred years or so ago, in the War of 1812, its citizens fought and fell gloriously in defense of their city before the British. A beautiful monument commemorates their heroism. In this war, there was no city in the country more loyal to our Government and our Allies.

Let it not be thought, however, that the enemy was inactive in Baltimore. Trouble, active and potential, was present at all times. That it did not flare up into open destruction was no fault of the trouble-makers. Like all ports of entry, Baltimore has a considerable foreign element. Thousands of foreigners were employed in its shipbuilding plants, on its docks, and in the Bessemer steel works located near the city. Of pro-Germans and alien enemies there was a plenty. Many of them, indeed, remembering the landing of the *Deutschland* at Baltimore before the war, would have welcomed and aided a wholesale submarine raid by the enemy—were this possible.

However, this did not come to pass, nor did many other things come to pass that were justifiably feared. The pro-German, the alien enemy, the agitator, the Bolshevist were held safe at all times. Baltimore's many industries were guarded well. Happily, that industry which has given her world-wide fame—the oyster industry—required no protection, and it is a pleasure to record that the nation's supply of sea-food was uninterrupted during the war.

A prolific source of trouble for the Baltimore Division lay in the city's proximity to the national capital. The overcrowded condition of Washington during the war forced a huge overflow of population into Baltimore, and thus doubled the amount of work that otherwise would probably have been required. This work was tackled with energy and efficiency by the Baltimore Division, which was one of the very largest for a city of its size in the country. When the Armistice came, there were 2,500 operatives engaged in the multifold activities of the League. The following report does not begin to tell the full story of their achievement:

Alien enemy cases	110
Sedition and disloyalty	685
Character and loyalty	309
Draft evasion	546
Deserters	225
Liquor and vice	100
Food Administration	3
Miscellaneous	110

Baltimore Division organized and was on the job during the very first month of the war. Its first Chief was Mr. Edmund Leigh, who solved the many knotty problems of organization and finance which arose in the early stages of the League's growth. Mr. Leigh was succeeded by Mr. William J. Neale in August, 1918, who acted as head of the division until November, 1918, when Mr. Tilghman G. Pitts became Chief.

VIRGINIA

Norfolk, Virginia, was fortunate in having as its chief a gentleman very prominent in all the war charities, and also of such generosity of nature that he paid all the expenses of the League out of his own pocket.

Conditions might have been much worse at this seaport locality, for only eight cases of alien enemy activity are listed, and five cases of disloyalty and sedition. This division, however, was able to do a great deal of work for the War Department, and among other matters found one illicit still and made four I. W. W. investigations. Another phase of the work was supplying the M. I. D. officer at the Army Supply Base — Quartermaster's Terminal — near Norfolk, with many photographs of alien enemies and slackers. The Division had operatives in Army and Navy headquarters, among workmen, etc., and had such men included in its personnel as bookkeepers, timekeepers and others whose work was much appreciated by Military Intelligence. The chief had twenty-one assistants, all good men.

White Sulphur Springs, Virginia, had one typical pro-German case. Adolph S———, a baker of this town, held certain opinions which would not strictly classify as American. When asked to purchase War Savings Stamps, he expressed himself as follows: "To hell with your War Savings Stamps. If Uncle Sam didn't have money enough to finance the war, why did he go into it? When the American soldiers get to France, you'll find they won't do anything but run like hell."

He said a great deal more in similar vein, which "was hardly suitable," says the Chief's report, "for polite ears." In the U. S. District Court, at Charleston, S——— confessed to a violation of the Espionage Act, was fined $100 and sentenced to two years in the penitentiary.

Lynchburg, Virginia, reports that it was rather quiet. One thing it did was to draw the fangs of an organization which was formed to punish such pro-Germans and war obstructionists as the law did not touch. The A. P. L. has always done its work hand in hand with the law, and throughout the war has resolutely set its face against anything savoring of lynch law.

Considerable local trouble arose from returned negro soldiers, discharged from service, who stated that they had saved the world from Hun oppression and were entitled to recognition. These statements had effect on the ignorant population, and it is firmly believed by the Chief that the "South has a problem on its hands in this connection which will require considerable time, effort and patience, if not bloodshed, to solve." Any one acquainted in the least degree with the great problem of the South will realize the gravity and sincerity of this comment.

WEST VIRGINIA

There were "hot times in the old town" of Hinton, West Virginia, in good part by reason of the activities of one man, the local Chief, who, for some time was cook, captain and mate of the Nancy brig. Local disloyalty induced him to go to Washington and ask government help, and the League organization followed. One pro-German in Hinton had the Kaiser's picture on the wall. It is not there now. The head of this family was a locomotive engineer. The Chief notified railroad officials not to allow him to handle any troop trains. Another engineer expressed the belief that a troop train was carrying "some more fish bait." He was also relieved of any future work on troop trains. Two school teachers, after talking with the Chief, hung up four United States flags and began to sing all the latest war songs as well as take an active part in Loan drives, Red Cross work, etc. The largest hotel in the town did not speak well of the war, and the Chief notified the officers in charge of troop trains to get their meals somewhere else. A local newspaper printed an article reflecting on the Red Cross canteen. "I had all the papers publish an article over my signature," says the Chief, "that any criticism of the Red Cross should be addressed to the Bureau of Investigation at Washington. For this I have been commended by the Red Cross membership." It appears that he ought to be commended for his own record, which, on the face of it, is in the blue-ribbon class.

NORTH CAROLINA

Lexington, N. C., is in the southern mountains. The Chief says: "Owing to the peculiar reaction of the mountaineer's philosophy to the draft laws, many of them 'stepped back' into the 'brush' to wait until the war was over. We spent much time in traveling around among the lumber jacks and sent out word to many delinquents. It was a simple thing to reach most of these men through the medium of some trusted friend — much simpler than sending armed men into the laurel thickets after the fugitives. I don't believe there is one case out of ten in western North Carolina where any of our men avoided the draft through a malicious motive. Whenever a friendly adviser could reach them to explain the situation, the majority of them gladly came out. We often made trips of from thirty to fifty miles into the isolated sections. At one point thirty miles from a railroad we got information which was sent across the sea to France and stopped an undesirable appointee to Y. M. C. A. work there. Some humorous things came up in our mountain travels. One day our road dwindled to an almost obliterated trail with grass growing all over it. We sighted an old woman, the first human being seen for several hours, and asked her if that was the right way to Doeville. The old woman looked at us with great contempt, and remarked: "Lord bless us, you-all is right *in* Doeville dis minute!"

The Chief of Lexington says that not everyone understands the mountain boys and that they certainly make excellent fighters when in the army. "One of them in my district," reports the Chief, "had to be run down and captured by his own father, who delivered him over to the authorities for military service. This boy was the first of his company to distinguish himself in France."

The Chief of Salisbury, North Carolina, Division sends in his final report in homely and convincing phrases, a mark of the good common sense employed in his work. One pro-German was called into the office and the Chief said to him: "Mr. ———, I hear that the next time you and your family come to town over the public road, you are going to be blown up without any warning." The man struck the table with his fist and said: "I'd like to know how! The public road is mine and I'm going to travel on it." The Chief said: "So our ships had a public highway to Europe. The Germans have destroyed vessels, women and children without warning. What do you think of it?" The pro-German thought this over a minute and exclaimed: "Why hasn't some one talked to me like that before? I never saw it that way before."

Hickory, N. C., says: "Our work was largely educational. We had no aliens — all native born American citizens. Thirty of our leading citizens constituted the membership of the League. When we went to work, all the 'aginners' who were against the war got on the right side. Especially was this true after the amended espionage act went into effect. In my judgment," says the Chief, "the psychological effect of an organization that could be felt but not seen helped wonderfully in bringing to their right senses the small minority that were not in right at the start."

Durham, N. C., pulled off one raid on a circus crowd and got ten slackers. "Our community has a foreign element," says the Chief, "and is above the average in respect to law and order. Our members were prominent in the war activities."

SOUTH CAROLINA

Anderson, S. C., says: "Our organization has been anxious to answer every call. There are practically no foreigners in this section, so violations of the war measures have been almost negligible. Most of our work has been making reports for overseas service. The men all consider it a great honor to have been members of the League."

A man whom we may call Benny Vogel deserted from the 105th Infantry at Camp Wadsworth, South Carolina. In some way, he found his way to Schenectady, New York, where he proceeded casually to marry a young lady of that city, under date of April 19, 1918. The wife was watched. The deserter was caught and returned for punishment.

St. Matthews, S. C., reports: " On the whole there was little enemy activity. We unearthed six cases of discharged soldiers drawing government money who were not entitled to it, and eight cases of parties receiving allotments from soldiers for incorrect amounts. We changed such undesirable sentiment as existed in our community, and with tact and judgment rather than by drastic measures. We think our community is among the most loyal of any in America and doubt seriously if there is one per cent disloyalty here. Some who at first were lukewarm changed, and we knew it was due to the policy adopted by our organization. We worked on the Sunday law and the fuel laws, the food regulations, etc., all in a quiet way, but, we think, with good results throughout our county."

GEORGIA

All sorts of stories show in the League files. One regarding submarine bases along the Georgia and Carolina coast was traced down to the purchase of a piece of land by a former grocery clerk, a naturalized German, who resided in Savannah for many years. He was outspoken in his sympathy with Germany before the United States entered the war. A report made by the Navy Department to the National Directors of the League states:

On January 6, 1918, this man was tried in the city court of Savannah and found guilty of violating the prohibition laws. He was fined $400 and sentenced to six months on the chain gang. Before he had fully served his sentence he was re-arrested by the United States Marshal on a presidential warrant and subsequently interned." The brief phrase " presidential warrant " covered many and many a case of naturalized Germans who became too loquacious in this country before and after we entered the war.

Atlanta, Georgia, had a nice scare about the report that a German U-boat captain had landed and was on his way to Atlanta, dressed in an American officer's uniform. Operatives were out and trailed every military or quasi-military looking man on the streets or anywhere else. Their first haul included a major from the Judge Advocate General's office and a Judge from the Federal Court. The next alarm came from two operatives who trailed an officer just off the train, who turned out to be a colonel of the Quartermaster's Corps, U. S. A. The latter was able to make his escape. The Chief adds: "Just how many suspects were held up that night it would be difficult to state. Operative No. 3 turned in a report of his activities the next morning. It seemed he had held up the following personnel: One Lieutenant-Colonel, sixteen Majors, twenty-three Captains, forty-two Lieutenants, one Lieutenant-Commander, three Ensigns, and seven Sergeants — a total of ninety-two suspects. He closed his report with the following heartfelt remarks: "Well, I didn't know what kind of uniform the German had. Besides, every man I stopped was a blond. I didn't stop any other sort." D. J. reported it was satisfied that no German submarine officer had visited Atlanta.

ALABAMA

Birmingham, Alabama, was one of the most active and interesting divisions of the League. It took on 1,849 cases under the Selective Service Act, 76 investigations of pro-Germans, 123 cases of deserters, and 153 Red Cross loyalty reports, besides a large list of general war activities. Some of the star cases of deserter hunting at Birmingham are reported in another chapter.

Like many another community, Birmingham also had its wireless case, and like most cases of the sort throughout the country, it created much excitement in the division while it lasted. Certain mysterious light flashes, supposed to be signals, were reported along the top of a high hill on the outskirts of the city. Operatives detailed on the case could learn nothing, but still reports kept coming in. Finally, one astute visiting chief followed a high-powered transmission line along the mountain and found that the limb of a tree at a certain spot would touch the wire when swayed by the wind. The repeated rubbing had worn away the insulation, exposing the bare wire. When the limb came in contact with the wire, especially during a rainy night, a spark would be made when the limb and wire separated: The Chief adds: "When the limb was cut off, we received no further reports of mysterious signals." There has been bluish-white lights which some thought indicated a wireless outfit in operation.

Montgomery, Alabama, reports one of those curious cases which were sometimes met with in the course of the League's investigations. This was a straight-goods, dyed-in-the-wool, bona-fide conscientious objector. His name was W. A. P———, a farmer who had a son in the draft, but who needed him on the farm. He accompanied the boy to the examination board, after the young man had been arrested by the sheriff. He brought his Bible to the board and tried to prove that he was justified in his objections; that he was responsible for the care of this boy; that the Lord had given him that duty and no one else. The old man was violently opposed to bloodshed and quoted the scriptural words, "Thou shalt not kill," and "Children, obey your parents." The Chief had a long talk with him at his farm. He admitted that he told his son not to answer questions, and that he had another son who had attained his eighteenth birthday and had not registered. The Chief told him to be careful or he would get into trouble. He said, "I am not getting into any trouble; it is you people who are provoking the wrath of God." All the agent could do was to tell him that he must come before the United States Commissioners. P——— was brought in to the Committee, and bound over to the grand jury. Before the trial, he stood up and remarked, "Let us have a word of prayer," and prayed fervently for several minutes. He carried his Bible with him at all times. P——— seemed to be generous. "He came to Montgomery and brought a couple of gallons of nice syrup for the Deputy and Commissioners," says the Chief. One would think that the A. P. L. would be glad to have peace at any price in such surroundings, even without syrup.

Selma, Alabama, is another one of the loyal Southern communities. "We kept down seditious utterances," says the Chief. "Without doubt we have had a most wholesome effect on our citizenry by letting every one know that this was not a time for anything that was not one hundred per cent American. I do not believe there was a greater force for good in the State of Alabama than the American Protective League."

FLORIDA

Cocoa, Florida, is not far from one of the Government shipyards, and so had had some contact with persons inclined to be pro-German. By way of explaining the additional activities sometimes taken on by the League, the Chief says: "This office worked with the Special Agents at Jacksonville, and with officers of the Seventh Naval District. We have also given information to the Collector of Internal Revenue concerning those who should pay income tax. Our division consisted of twenty-four members — all high-class men who could be relied upon in any emergency that might arise. We were taking steps to enlarge the organization when the German balloon burst."

Eustis, Florida, was more especially concerned with war cases. Forty-one cases of draft delinquency were handled; two slacker raids were conducted, and there was a little "work or fight" activity. Eustis is in a county which had the reputation of harboring a good many slackers and deserters, who sought peace and quiet in some of the out-of-the-way places. Through the activities of the local A. P. L. division, this situation was cleared up distinctly. The Chief says: "We believe we have been instrumental in protecting many people from their own follies, and have brought to justice men who were engaged in obstructing the Government's war activities in one part of the country or another. It has been a pleasurable though arduous service that some of us have rendered in this work."

Kissimmee, Florida, reports: "All quiet along the Kissimmee. Our community was singularly free of annoyance of any character. Two or three persons were indiscreet in their language, but we found that a small reminder was sufficient to stop the talk."

KENTUCKY

Louisville, Kentucky, is a busy and famous old town with a reputation for being engaged in the manufacture of trouble-making products, but there seems to have been very little trouble. Only eighty-nine cases of disloyalty and sedition are reported, and 308 under the selective service regulations.

Mr. George T. Ragsdale, the first Chief of Louisville Division, instructed his men to keep under cover, so that the personnel of the division was very little known. More than 700 reports were made in all, and nine men were sent to the penitentiary. Local business men furnished most of the working capital. Upon Mr. Ragsdale's resignation, Mr. J. V. Norman was appointed Chief, taking over about 400 members. The city was divided into nine districts and the County in three, with the usual subdivisions of captains and lieutenants as operatives. The membership was up to about 700 at the time of the signing of the Armistice.

Most of the investigations handled by the Louisville Division were on requests coming from local draft boards, although the several branches of the government's legal organization frequently asked for aid. Several thousand men were questioned in the slacker raid of August 3. Thirty-five men were taken to jail and fourteen inducted; among these, several deserters. Sometimes at a race track a quiet investigation would be put on without any open raid.

Among the list of delinquents turned in was a man named Lyle D. B———. An intercepted letter resulted in an examination of the man's mother, who refused to tell where he was. Portland, Oregon, was suspected as his present residence. The case came to an end when it was found that the delinquent had been committed to the Federal penitentiary at McNeil Island, Washington. His questionnaire was forwarded by the local board to the penitentiary and returned properly filled in. The man had a fairly good alibi. The usual cases of religious fanatics, loud talkers and bearers of false witness were uncovered in the League's work. Many of the best citizens of Louisville were engaged in these somewhat undignified and often thankless tasks of ferreting out such matters.

Lexington, Kentucky, as might easily be expected, reports in American fashion: "The sentiment of our entire population is hard against the Germans and their allies. Our people are almost unanimous in their opposition to showing

Germany any consideration, even with furnishing them food after their defeat. The one sentiment is that Germany could feed herself while in war; now let her feed herself since she is out of war."

The work of the Lexington Division was mostly concerned with the local and district boards. It handled 405 cases of this sort. There were only thirty cases of disloyalty and sedition investigated, and forty cases of word-of-mouth propaganda.

Marion, Kentucky, says: "We are glad to report that our county has been so patriotic that little of any importance required to be done. We had to caution a few of our citizens as to the bad results of opposition to the United States in the war. We have no foreign element. Our citizens come from Virginia, Tennessee and North Carolina, and are of old families. We rarely see anyone of foreign descent in this section except traveling men who make trips through the county."

Somerset, Kentucky, had a bad man — a deserter who escaped from Fort Oglethorpe once or twice, the last time taking along his rifle and pistol. He barricaded himself in an old house at Helenwood, Tennessee. The A. P. L. took him all right, in spite of his threats. He is in Fort Leavenworth for twenty years. From far off Livingston, Montana, came a request to Somerset Division to arrest one Willie McK———, a professional evader. He was found attending church. The Chief says: "We walked in and gave him a tap on the shoulder, and told him to come out. Just as we started for the door, the choir began to sing, 'God be with you till we meet again.' It is going to be some time." Somerset concludes: "We did not stop when the Armistice was signed, but kept watching everything and giving the Government the best that was in us!" Isn't that fine?

TENNESSEE

The A. P. L. work in the beautiful and historic old city of Nashville was somewhat circumscribed because of the activities of other agencies already in existence. The division did its share in the routine work of war activities, apprehending evaders, conducting numerous investigations, and vigilantly keeping tab on the comings and goings in the Old Hickory Powder Plant.

Chattanooga, Tennessee, did its bit and did it well. Ten prisoners who escaped from the local War Prison were apprehended by division operatives, and brought back for reinternment. One member of the division discovered an extensive system of graft in connection with the Government construction work on the Nitrate Plant at Sheffield, Ala. Report of this was furnished to a Special Agent, who was detailed by the Government to conduct an investigation. The Chief comments: "Just what can be proven in this case remains to be seen."

Some of the most amusing Chattanooga investigations were those of the religious sect known as the "Holy Rollers." Several of these preachers had preached sermons in which they condemned the Red Cross and the Government generally. These men were apprehended, and members of their congregations testified at local headquarters. Some of these preachers were moved by the "spirit" in their testimony, but after they remained in jail a short time, they saw the Scriptures in a different light, and very few of them offended a second time.

Another Chattanooga case had in it the possibilities of great mischief. A large amount of mail to an illiterate mountaineer caused an A. P. L. operative and a Special Agent of the Department of Justice to go to the top of Sand Mountain, and in a dirty log cabin they found a wagon load of I. W. W. literature and correspondence in which were letters from Emma Goldman and other leading lights of socialistic faith. The man himself was working in a foundry turning out Government orders; he was organizing a strike at the time he was taken into custody.

Clarksville, Tennessee, is in the loyal Southern country, and is very free from alien population. There were only twenty-five investigations for disloyalty and sedition, and propaganda was almost negligible. As this is the tobacco producing section, there was considerable property investigated under the Trading with the Enemy Act, and some helpful reports were made to the Alien Property Custodian. The League members were active in all the war work.

Hopkinsville, Tennessee, had a great deal of trouble over

illegal transportation of whiskey, a great deal of which went to workers in government powder plants in an adjoining city. "We arrested so many that no record was kept," says the Chief. Things became quieter later on.

Huntingdon, Tennessee, is another disgustingly quiet and satisfied community. "People nearly all natives," says the report, "and mighty few expressions of disloyalty. We have watched for violations, but nothing has developed worthy of report."

TEXAS

San Antonio, Texas, is in a strongly pro-German neighborhood and has a large citizenry of German descent. It is refreshing nevertheless to see that in this good old Texas town, once distinctly Spanish, the language of the United States prevails to-day and only one flag floats over the Alamo. There were thirty-four investigations for sedition, and twenty-four cases of propaganda. The usual number of overseas examinations were held. On the whole, San Antonio seems to have been quiet and peaceful and distinctly loyal in every way, in spite of her location so close to New Braunfels.

The San Antonio Chief concludes his too brief report with a little story:

> The telephone at my elbow rang insistently. The man at the other end of the wire was incoherent, and I could not understand what he wanted.
>
> "Hold on a minute!" I finally interrupted. "Who is this speaking?"
>
> He would not tell me; he merely said that he was a friend of mine. I did not like to give information over the 'phone when I was not sure as to whom I was talking. I again insisted that he give me his name; once more he refused to do so, reiterating that he was a good friend of mine. I could not recognize the voice. But what he said was startling.
>
> Recently I had been appointed Chief of the American Protective League for this District, and how my informant had learned, or guessed, that I was engaged in it, I could not tell. I did not like to undertake a wild goose chase; at the same time, if I should refuse to follow up the clue he gave me, the lives of many might be endangered.

Anything could happen in San Antonio. It is one of the oldest cities in the United States, and ever since the day the Spaniard founded it, has been a hotbed of intrigue. Just at this time there were fully twenty thousand troops stationed in the various Camps about the City, and in order to impress the Mexicans with the idea that we were not altogether helpless, it had been suggested that a patriotic military parade be given. This was to take place the following day, and I had spent many hours helping to arrange the details. And now, my mysterious "friend" had told me over the 'phone that he knew certain parties were plotting to throw a bomb into the parade; that if I would go to the certain house named by him, I would find a meeting of the plotters in progress!

There was no time to be wasted. I got in touch with one of my lieutenants, M———, and asked him to meet me in half an hour, and to come armed. Before leaving the office I sent for a couple of suits of overalls, one of which I donned, and when I met M———, I gave him the other.

I told him all that I knew, and he realized that it was serious. We parked our car about two blocks from the house designated by my informant, and approached it afoot. The neighborhood was questionable. The house to which I had been directed stood a few feet back from the street in a neglected tangle of shrubbery. There was a fence about the property, but no gate. It was a small frame shack with two rooms in front and a third forming an ell. We walked around it cautiously several times, and finally discovered a light in the ell. The blinds were all tightly closed, and it was but a faint glimmer through a crack that we saw. We crawled carefully to the gallery and each looked through the crack.

We could barely distinguish the forms of five men huddled over an oil stove in the middle of the room. Three were in overalls and had the appearance of laborers; one wore a shabby old suit of civilian clothes, and the fifth appeared to be in uniform. Their heads were close together and they seemed to be talking in low tones, but neither M——— nor I could distinguish a word that was said.

There was a door a few feet from where we were, and I noticed another one on the opposite side of the room. I told M——— to go around to the other door and I would remain where I was. If either of us was able to distinguish any suspicious words, or if we found any reason to suspect that the five men were actually plotting, a low whistle was to be the signal to the other, and simultaneously we were to break in the door and rush them.

While the whole thing had the appearance of a conspiracy, and I was inclined to take the bull by the horns and give M——— the agreed signal, I was also suspicious that someone might be playing a practical joke on me. While I hesitated, M——— suddenly sneezed!

I have lived in the Southwest the greater part of my life and have been in some pretty tight places, and always have prided myself on my ability to take care of myself in an emergency; but the next thing I knew after M———'s sneeze, he was bending over me trying to staunch the blood that was flowing from a wound over my right eye, at the same time reading the riot act to me in choice language.

"What happened?" I asked, feebly.

"Why, the whole darned shooting-match jumped your way, walked over you and beat it!" he explained in exasperation. "What I've been trying to find out is why in hell you didn't shoot?"

I could not answer in words, but mutely I showed him that in my haste I carefully had put on the overalls over my clothes with my gun in the usual place in my hip pocket. It would have taken me five minutes to get it out.

"It's a good thing you had it so well hid," he remarked. "They might have taken it away from you!"

We searched the deserted house. Except for the stove it was devoid of furniture, and we found nothing in the way of a clue.

We arranged for a strict patrol of the route of the parade. Each man was given a "beat." If any man saw anything suspicious, and particularly a suspicious package, he was to investigate and report at once.

The parade was crossing the Houston Street bridge, where I happened to be, when I saw a negro man elbowing his way to the front of the crowd along the curb. In his right hand, held high over the heads of those about him, was a package wrapped in newspaper! He seemed in the act of hurling it into the street when I sprang forward and grabbed the upraised arm, dragging the negro back to the railing of the bridge.

"What have you got in that package?" I demanded.

"My Gawd, boss, you'se the fou'th man to ast me about ma lunch in the last five minutes. If it's worrying you white folks so much, guess I'd better git shet of it!"

Before I could prevent him, he threw it into the river, and turned to view the parade with a muttered opinion on my interference with his personal liberties. All we succeeded in accomplishing was scaring a poor negro out of his lunch, but whether or not we thwarted others in a worse plot, we never knew.

But that was much our story in San Antonio. We did the best we knew. Had we not been there, and were it not known that we were there, matters might have been worse. The makings of trouble were around us all the time.

Laredo, Texas, on the Mexican border, was organized for business. The Chief says: "We have very few alien enemies resident here. Before we organized, there was some talk of a disloyal nature, but this situation changed at once when it got out that we had seventy-five or eighty members whose identity was unknown to the public but who would be pretty sure to be out for business. For the six or eight months before the Armistice we heard scarcely a word unfavorable to the United States or her Allies. We think we did something in the way of prevention if not of cure."

Yoakum, Texas, has ten cases of disloyalty and a like number of word-of-mouth propaganda. A good local chief of a fighting family says: "We were ready at all times to meet any emergency regardless of distance or difficulty."

Beaumont, Texas, is in the oil country, and such centers quite often attract alien population. The Beaumont report covers sixty-three cases of alien enemy activities, eighteen cases of disloyalty, and ninety cases under the selective service regulations.

ARKANSAS

Cotter, Arkansas, reports that it is a community with very few foreigners, the population being American for generations back. The Chief says: "We had two deserters who lived for two weeks in an inaccessible camp in the mountains. They finally got hungry, came in and surrendered. We also had one draft-dodging case of a peculiar sort. This young man, according to his marriage license, should have registered in June, 1917. He did not. We traced him to Oklahoma, and from there to Springfield, Missouri. He was taken into custody by the Chief of Police at that point on our order. We sent a certified copy of his marriage license, but he had enough of his relatives on hand to swear to his true age, to secure his release."

Helena, Arkansas, also comes into court with very clean hands. Its report shows a membership of 127, which proved to be none too large, as all hands found work to do. Investigations were handled all over Arkansas, Mississippi and Louisiana.

Fort Smith, Arkansas, found its slacker raids more interesting than anything else. It conducted two of them, a slacker or two being apprehended each time. One stranger, who was sufficiently indiscreet as to fail to register, was unceremoniously hauled out of bed and turned over to the local war board. No alien enemy activities came to the attention of this division.

OKLAHOMA

The State of Oklahoma does not submit a wealth of material for this history of the A. P. L., and indeed the evidence seems to indicate that there was comparatively little material to submit. Chickasha, Oklahoma, sends in a little report, covering three alien enemy investigations; four cases of disloyalty and sedition; one case of sabotage; five cases of word-of-mouth propaganda; two deserter cases, and seven character and loyalty investigations.

There are numerous reports at hand, which are made in the form of figures only, but it is impossible to print these in detail.

CHAPTER IV

THE STORY OF THE WEST

Under the caption of The West, we arbitrarily are grouping all of the states lying west of a line running north and south from the western borders of the Dakotas to the eastern edge of New Mexico. This excludes part of that great region long known in America as the Great West, — a country that is no more, and never again can be on the face of this earth, unless war and pestilence one day shall quite remove our present human population. What we retain as the West for A. P. L. classification purposes still has some distinct characteristics. It still is largely unknown land to Eastern citizens, still holds the flavor of a romantic past, as well as that of a great and unknown future.

The region thus set off comprises more than a third of the acreage of the United States. It is the most thinly settled portion of the United States and, made up as it is in large part of arid lands or mountainous regions, no doubt on the average it always will remain so. Yet here lie the richest remaining forests of America, and no one may know how much of additional mineral wealth. Here also, our country halts at the shore of the Pacific and looks westward at the future. In the march of King Charles, his knights paused at Rockfish Gap, and those merry gentlemen carelessly claimed possession of all those unknown lands that lay to the westward, "as far as the South Sea." Well, we have made the crossing of the continent. We are at the South Sea now.

Who and what are we, however, who stand at the edge of the Pacific and look westward? Are we Americans? Who could call us such? We are not the same Homeric breed now that we were when the first rails went west. Taking our arbitrary section herein, west of the Dakotas, and studying the statistical census map of the United States made in 1914 — the first year of the war — we find that the population of Montana is more than fifty percent foreign-born, or of foreign-born parentage. The same is true of Utah, Wyoming, Colorado, Arizona, Nevada, Idaho, California, Oregon and Washington; all have population thirty-five to fifty percent foreign of birth or parentage! This, in what we have thought was the American West!

There is no American West. There is no America. But for the Grace of God, we are gone. This is no mere rant. Study the census maps yourself — you can have no more thrilling, no more fascinating and no more saddening reading, search how you may. The trouble with most of us Americans was that we did not know our America. For America, this war is not over. It is just beginning. The more we set aside preconceived notions or biased and unctuous conclusions based on suppositions and not facts for premises, and the more we learn the actual facts regarding this country's problems to-day, the more we shall be obliged to that sobering and wholly distasteful thought that America is at the threshhold of her real war. That man does not live who can with any color of authority predict the end of that irrepressible conflict. No Statue of Liberty can avert it; no jaunty melting pot doctrine can conjure it away.

But the great West, which with the great South remains in larger percent American than do the North or the East, was zealously on guard throughout this war. Few of our far-flung marches but had an A. P. L. outpost of Americans, and these were eyes of the same sort that long ago looked down the brown barrels of long rifles in the frontier days. If we had a frontier now, here it would lie, between the Prairies and the Pacific; and the frontier always has been loyal. It was loyal in this war. The next great American will come from the land of the old Frontier. What, think you, will be his message? Will it be of melting-pots?

COLORADO

Denver, Colorado, must have a rather thrifty population, for there were 140 cases of food hoarding reported from that division. Operatives of the League investigated 789 cases of disloyalty and sedition under the Espionage Act, and the division as a whole worked in close coöperation with the local draft boards. The Chief says: "We looked into the German language situation; also vice, liquor, bootlegging, and general lawlessness in coal mining camps. We investigated the loyalty of many individuals who were under consideration for membership in patriotic associations or for City or State positions."

Delta County, Colorado, had one simple and kindly pro-German section foreman who left spikes sticking up in the wagon road crossing, so that they might possibly destroy some American tires. Very thoughtful, but not very damaging. Apropos of one of the more lurid happenings in this division, the Chief says: "We got a riot call to a small settlement six miles out, and I responded with three details of A. P. L. members. We arrived on the scene at 11:00 p. m. and found thirty armed Americans who were just starting in to clean up a settlement of eleven German families. We quieted things until we could make an investigation, and then found that a poison scare was at the root of the trouble. A German administered a pint bottle of bluing to one of his sick horses. The horse very promptly died. Heated imagiation did the rest. The A. P. L. certainly prevented bloodshed in this instance.

Mancos, Colorado, gives a pleasant little touch of local color: "Just a few days before war was declared with Germany, one G. B. B———, a resident of Mancos, Colorado, made some very derogatory remarks to the effect that the war, if it was declared, would be a rich man's war, for the benefit of the wealthy class, and that the United States had no business in war with Germany; that the American flag would soon be dragged in the dust, and by the Germans, if war were declared. His wife also stated that the Germans had done nothing worse than the soldiers did in our late civil war. Many remarks were made showing sympathy with the German cause. When the news of the first big victory of the Allied armies was received here, an impromptu celebration was held on the streets of the town, and all of doubtful sympathies were asked to mount a box and wave an American flag. Some half a dozen did so, and did it gracefully and with seeming willingness, but Mr. B——— refused to come out. Later, at another celebration, he was made to come out and wave the flag, though he did it with bad grace and only upon being strenuously urged to do so. He made a long talk trying to tell how loyal he was, but he would not submit to waving the flag until really made to do so, and then in a very insulting way. He made no more violent utterances after the time mentioned.''

Red Cliff, Colorado, had at least one hectic moment: ''On October 14, 1918, the County Treasurer's deputy, Mrs. F———, deliberately tore down the Fourth Liberty Loan poster, remarking that 'That has been up there long enough; it has almost ruined our flowers in the window.' It was developed that our County Treasurer, Mr. C———, was a hoarder of food, and the local Food Administrator arrested him and fined him $25 for the benefit of the Red Cross. The County Treasurer called me into his office, caught me by the throat and tried to scare me, saying: 'I understand you are showing a paper around here trying to ruin my character; that you are saying that I am a dirty slacker. Aren't you ashamed of yourself to circulate such dirty lies about me?' Then the fun began. I struck him and told him that if he was guilty of hoarding 2,000 pounds of flour in his brother's attic, he certainly was a dirty, low-down slacker and traitor. He weighs about 225 pounds; I weigh 143. He threw me down and sat on me for fifteen minutes, trying to make me apologize. I didn't, and never will for any man of pro-German type.''

For a man weighing only 143 pounds, the Red Cliff chief seems to have been active. He sent back three Canadian subjects and caused a decided change of heart in a pro-German who was the son-in-law of a local banker. The suspect got wind of the fact that he was being investigated, and his conversion was very prompt, he making no attempt to sit down on the local Chief.

Prowers County, Colorado, investigated fifty cases of mouth-to-mouth propaganda, a notable case in its annals being that of a German Lutheran minister who refused to answer the question as to which side he wished to win the war. It did not take him long, however, to realize that he had made a blunder. He asked for time. The next day he declared very promptly that he wanted the United States to win. He was instructed to prove this by preaching and praying it in private as well as in public, which he agreed to do.

MONTANA

Billings, Montana, organized its A. P. L. division only three months before the signing of the Armistice. The Chief says: "It was a privilege to serve. We are grateful for the opportunity that came to us. Our field was small, and our time of service was short, but if we contributed in some small way to the success of the League's work, we feel amply repaid."

Red Lodge, Montana, is a coal mining town with a considerable foreign element, so it early organized a "Liberty Committee" of two hundred citizens. This committee worked in with the A. P. L. The fact that a division of the latter body was organized was not definitely known, but the belief got out that the Government had a secret agency working at Red Lodge and that it was in working order; "which it was," says the Chief.

NEW MEXICO

An instance of shrewd detective work comes from Albuquerque, New Mexico, whose Chief reports:

We received a copy of a letter mailed from this point several months previous, illegibly signed, but clearly addressed to a man named H——— in Holland. The letter, intercepted by censors, contained disloyal statements about Liberty Bonds, and referred to "our bank." We assumed from this that the writer of this letter was a banker. The use of blank paper instead of a business letterhead suggested that he was a transient. Albuquerque being quite a health resort, we surmised that the banker was probably a well-to-do health seeker. Accordingly, we combed the higher class resorts frequented by visitors of this type. Going through the list of patrons at one of these places, we found the name of A. H———, resident of an Arkansas town. By referring to the bank directory, we discovered that this man was a director and officer in the bank at that town. We sent this information to the National Directors in Washington.

It was sufficient. The investigation of the whole case consumed thirty minutes. We admit it was a little different from the usual routine that we usually had to follow.

UTAH

Green River, Utah, had a couple of cases which made some trouble. One was that of William F. A———, and Callie A———, his wife. Evidence was secured showing that this man was not a citizen, although he had voted as such. It was alleged that he was handling high explosives in violation of the law and that he expressed disloyal sentiments. Military Intelligence in Salt Lake confiscated the arms and ammunition, and had A——— registered as a German alien enemy. His wife was very bitter in her denunciation of the United States and the Red Cross. The son of the two was charged with being a draft evader. Another man, James H———, was alleged never to have registered for the draft, although within the age limit. He was arrested, admitted his guilt, and was turned over to the County Board.

Hiawatha, Utah, seems to have been for the most part quiet during the war. This division says: "Due to the loyal spirit of our people, our report is short. We are in a thinly settled locality. We got only one fine imposed, a violator of the food regulations, who pleaded guilty."

Richfield, Utah, is a farming community off the railroad, having no large labor organizations to make trouble. The Chief says: "A few pro-Germans were quietly warned, and that was all that was necessary. All our members were organized and watchful, and there was not much to do. Any service we could render we gladly gave."

Santaquin, Utah, sends the best and most satisfactory kind of a report: "I am proud to state that this little town has been loyal to the core. We have not found a single slacker or disloyal case. Investigated one or two cases of men asking for military service and found them O. K. In all the drives for bonds and thrift stamps, we have 'gone over the top,' and we hope to continue with the same good spirit and loyalty."

Moab, Utah, has a local chief of a calm turn of mind. He says that most of the talk he heard was just that of some ignorant people who didn't know the difference between war and peace times. The Chief adds that he saw only three or four parties who refused to buy bonds. "I had a talk with them, and they bought willingly," he adds!

From Fillmore, Utah, the Chief reports: "Not much to do in this out-of-the-way place. We watched every person who came into town. No telling when we might not have been of service in apprehending some person badly needed."

Smithfield, Utah, reports: "We had only twelve in our organization. Our community is only two thousand — a farming community of good quiet citizens. We support the constitution; over-subscribed for Liberty Bonds, Red Cross, and War Savings Stamps. If you realize what a rural community like this is, you know there is not much to do. We have done what we could with the local boards in draft matters."

ARIZONA

Tucson, Arizona, is the land of sunshine and appears to have been very peaceful. The Chief reports that there were plenty of war activities going on all the time, but none of these were of a nefarious sort. There apparently was nothing wild or woolly about an A. P. L. job in Tucson during war times.

Cochise County, Arizona, was once somewhat famous for loading up a railroad train with undesirable citizens and then telling the engineer to steam ahead. None the less, this last year or so Cochise has had absolute peace and quiet. Ever so often, of course, a dissatisfied citizen would go over to Mexico, subsist on red beans for a while, and then try to get back. He would usually find the getting back a trifle more difficult than the going over. About 1,000 investigations were made, most of them referred to the Department of Justice at Bisbee and Douglas. About forty-five or fifty men of the live-wire type did the work. There was always an element of danger present, though nothing ever broke.

Naco is directly on the border between Mexico and the United States. Douglas, not far distanct, is a busy town of which smelting is the big industry. The historic town of Tombstone is the county seat. Bisbee is one of the largest copper camps in the world. There were good men and true with the A. P. L. in all of these towns, and they did fine, loyal service for the flag.

WYOMING

An artless report comes from Weston County, Wyoming: "We had a number of people here who were pro-German, but all such cases were quieted with a little assistance. One man said that he was in hopes that he could eat another good meal in his own country, Germany. When he got through talking to all the people who waited upon him, he went home and committed suicide."

Moran, Wyoming, is hardly a place where you would look for a Russian countess. None the less, Moran contained one for a while, and A. P. L. found her there and made certain investigations. One I. W. W. leader was also discovered by alert operatives.

Sundance, Wyoming, is in the short grass country, and reports but little German activity. Most of the work of this division had to do with draft board matters. The ranch country of the west was in a very large measure strictly loyal, as the reports show.

IDAHO

Idaho Falls, Idaho, had one case which again shows the pronounced anti-Americanism of the German Lutheran church in America during the war. C. C. M———, a minister of this denomination located at Blackfoot, Idaho, applied for the position of chaplain in the United States Army. The local chief of the A. P. L. investigated him and found him to be violently pro-German. It was known that he had threatened to blow up the town of Blackfoot with dynamite, and had also made threats to poison the source of the water supply of the town. Did Rev. Mr. M——— get his chaplaincy? He did not. A local applicant for the position of Captain in the United States Army, as Inspector of Arms, was also investigated, and was turned down on account of his strong pro-German tendencies.

Almo, Idaho, reports: "Our locality is wholly a stock

raising section and is sparsely settled, so there has been no disloyalty or trouble whatsoever. There is nothing to report except that the people of this section are absolutely O. K. in their loyalty to Uncle Sam."

CALIFORNIA

Long Beach, California, sends in a two-page report which is entirely too modest, because it covers 8,590 investigations. Out of this number, ninety were held in the Federal courts. Twenty were convicted, and three were found not guilty. Forty slackers and deserters were arrested, and three alien enemies, who were taken in the shipyards, were interned. Some 3,000 persons who had made indiscreet remarks against the country were warned to good effect.

In the Long Beach district were four shipbuilding plants. It was learned that several I. W. W.'s were numbered among the employees. They were taken from the shpyards for cause. The Long Beach chief was reluctant to disband, and when the time came to do so, he made arrangements by which the division will be held as a sort of reserve. " If at any future time you need our assistance," says the Chief. " you will find us waiting."

Oakland, California, looked into the color of the hair and eyes of 387 persons under the heading of disloyalty and sedition. There were 356 investigations under the draft act. Oakland Division dealt out its punishments to the enemy drastically. Seventeen well-known local Germans, business and professional men, drank a toast to the Kaiser in the Faust Café, a German restaurant. The A. P. L. got the necessary evidence, and ten of these men were convicted of disloyalty. The court put the punishment at three months in the chain gang, and a fine of $250 each. They do not now know any such phrase as " Hoch der Kaiser."

Crescent City, California, had at least one high light. The Chief reports that an enemy alien, a baker, learned in some way that his loyalty had been questioned, and immediately started to gather all the rifles and pistols that he could, declaring that with a dozen guns he could hold the whole town at bay. Officers searched his place of business during his absence, and found several of the guns loaded.

The man claimed to be a naturalized citizen, but could not show his papers. His case was cared for.

OREGON

The far Northwest bordering on the sea caught flotsam and jetsam, caught problems, as seaboard regions always have and always will. The city of Portland, Oregon, shares in these matters, though it is old, settled, and much disposed to quiet. Portland's main concern in life is the growing of roses; but early in the war Portland had already thrown away her rose-growers' club and set her hand to the ax rather than to the garden trowel. As a city, it is a good place for roses, but a poor place for alien enemies.

A certain man of many aliases, whom we may indicate as D———, was arrested for being found within half a mile of the Armory without an enemy permit. He was found to be the owner of a great deal of I. W. W. literature. Investigation proved him to be a man of vitrolic temper, and one possessed of considerable means. He was very well investigated and jolly well interned.

A man by the name of F——— was arrested as a German alien, traveling without a pass. Very naturally, he claimed to be a Swiss, as do all German waiters. Investigation of his case proved he was in the habit of signing as a seaman, on ships about to sail, and then refusing to go on board at sailing time. His peculiar conduct got him in wrong with the Sailors' Union. A close examination developed that he was a former German naval officer, and pictures of him were found in the German uniform. He was interned as a dangerous alien.

If Portland's A. P. L. could not get a man one way, there were always other ways available. One J. B———, placed under suspicion by the angry accusation of a woman whom he claimed to be his wife, was discovered to be a draft evader from Chicago. It was found also that he had a real wife living in Oklahoma. The pretending wife forged the wife's name to the man's questionnaire, thus securing for him a deferred classification. He was indicted for violation of the Mann Act and Conscription Act, and got eleven months in jail.

The first slacker convicted and sentenced for violation of the Conscription Act in the State of Oregon was C. B——— of Portland, who was discovered to have failed to register. He was arrested the 10th of July, 1917, tried and convicted and served thereafter as an example.

The hundreds of cases in Portland were of much the same sort as those arising in other cities. The law of averages held good. Once in a while a man was reformed, and once in a while a flivver was found. E. B———, of California, registered at Fairfield, California, June 5, 1918, was posted as a deserter and arrested by an operative of the A. P. L. at Portland, Oregon. He was of Swedish descent, and the hearing of his case developed that many of his friends had told him that he could get out of the Army by claiming exemption as an alien subject to deportation. It was explained to him that if he went back to Sweden under deportation, he could never again return to the U. S. as a citizen. This cleared up his mind distinctly, and he resolved to go into the Army and will probably make a good citizen.

Canyon City, Oregon, says: " We had one man who was constantly spilling over in favor of Germany. Our members took him over the jumps and made him subside. He could have been convicted, but neighbors promised to be responsible for him, and they kept their word. Our people as a whole were very loyal, and we had only a small number of cases to handle."

WASHINGTON

Yakima, Washington, tabulates its activities as 93 cases of disloyalty and sedition, ten cases of word-of-mouth propaganda and sixteen I. W. W. cases, besides the usual routine work.

Snohomish, Washington, sends in a report indicative of an unexpected amount of activity. There were 302 cases of disloyalty and sedition, nineteen of sabotage, twenty-four of anti-military activity, fifteen of propaganda, as well as 116 cases under the selective service regulations, and 124 under the " work or fight " order. The Chief closes his modest summary with the statement that the work was largely connected with I. W. W. and Socialistic activities such as were noted in the Northwest during the war. He says: "We had the state secretary of the Socialists in the penitentiary. Many I. W. W.'s were jailed, and many more were inducted into the Army. Some of the latter tribe have been court-martialed since entering the Army." As it were, and so to speak, Atta Boy!

ALASKA

And now let us give, as the very last tribute of The Four Winds, the report of a town which may seem a long way from home to many readers, but which, out of all the many hereinbefore mentioned, will show best of all the far-flung activities of the American Protective League. This report comes from Anchorage, Alaska. Leopold David is Chief at this far off station, and every word that he has written shall go to the readers of the League:

> Members of the League have been active in Red Cross work here, in food conservation, and in the sale of Liberty Bonds and War Savings Stamps. From the moment the Anchorage branch was first organized, I impressed upon the members the necessity of counter-propaganda to refute any insinuations or charges that they might hear against the causes leading the U. S. into war, and the conduct thereof. Everything in connection therewith which was derogatory to the interests of the U. S. was immediately traced to its source, if possible, and the false impression corrected. We have a large foreign element here employed in railroad construction, and members of the League made it a point in their trips up and down the line to explain the reasons for all restrictions.
>
> When a strike was threatened on the Government railroad last year, members of the League explained to the men the necessity of staying at work until their case could be decided, so as not to interfere with the development of the coal fields to which the road was being built, as coal was a war necessity. I believe that such action by the League was in large measure responsible for avoiding a strike.
>
> Members of the League were on all committees in connection with war work activities, as well as on the Territorial Council of Defense, of which the Chief of the Anchorage branch acted as Chairman. During the time the League was organized, every member did his best for the interests of the country, and no need arose for disciplining any member. The

work of the League was carried on in such an unostentatious manner that very few people knew of its existence except the members.

It has a safe and significant sound — the A. P. L. at Anchorage. Not a large place, indeed, but there were seven cases of alien enemy activity, twenty-eight of disloyalty and sedition, five of anti-military activities and thirty-two of propaganda, beside two I. W. W. investigations. Anchorage seems to have been uncertain whether to work or fight in some instances; 206 cases came up of this sort. In addition to these, 143 draft cases came before the local boards, as well as 62 slacker cases. Twenty-two cases under the head of liquor, vice and prostitution were disposed of. The Food Administration had only four cases. It is gratifying to note that every head and sub-head of the report is filled out conscientiously and carefully.

We may now cease the reading of further reports from the four points of the compass in America, and rest with this one from Anchorage, submitting once more the conviction that these many varying reports, covering multifold lines of investigation, make the best and truest reflex of America ever gotten together in printed form. The reading and summarizing of the reports made an extraordinary experience, such as can hardly have come to many individuals, probably to none outside of the Department of Justice; and it is not known whether a similar enterprise ever has been undertaken even in that great office. By no means is it to be supposed that all the reports sent in have been mentioned in these pages — only a small fraction have had even the briefest mention. Many hundreds remain unnamed in public as do hundreds of thousands of men who made them up, not asking recognition for their work. It would be cheap to thank such men, or to apologize to them. In A. P. L., each of us has done the best he knew. For that, there is higher and better approval than that of any printed page.

BOOK IV

AMERICA

"IN FLANDERS FIELDS"

Challenge of the Dead in Battle

In Flanders Fields the poppies blow
Between the crosses, row on row,
That mark our place; and in the sky
That larks still bravely singing fly,
Scarce heard amid the guns below.
We are the dead. Short days ago
We lived, felt dawn, saw sunset glow,
Loved and were loved, and now we lie
In Flanders Fields.

Take up our quarrel with the foe!
To you from falling hands we throw
The Torch — be yours to hold it high!
If ye break faith with us who die,
We shall not sleep though poppies grow
In Flanders Fields.

— *Col. John McCrae.*

CHAPTER I

THE RECKONING

Our Duty to the Soldier — Our Lasting Quarrel With the Foe — The Story of the Census — No More Traitors — Shutting the Gates Against the Huns — The New Patriotism for All Americans.

Vox populi, vox dei is a fine phrase. But fine phrases often half-state or mis-state facts for sake of the half-idea's sound. Many popular conceptions are wide of the truth.

The world had come to call the French people light, fickle, inconstant, volatile, incapable of grave and deep emotions. That was the popular American idea of France up to 1914. The man who would voice that idea now would be treated with anger or silent contempt by all the world. Now we know the silent, modest, simple, enduring faith, the unfaltering courage, the undying flame of heart which made the real France.

We thought Great Britain cold, phlegmatic, emotionless. Who would say that to-day of a brave and strong people trying their best to ask us not to mention their battles against odds, their steadfast courage in holding the line, but to feel and understand the real admiration and love Britain really feels for us in these days.

We Americans thought ourselves above fickleness and lightness always, boasted always of our common sense and steady practical point of view. We called France hysterical. Was it so? No. Once again popular counsel is wrong. It is we Americans who are the most hysterical people in the world. We make a purpose and forget it. We erect a hero and forget him. We believe, boast, acclaim, hurrah — and forget. We are easily excited — it is we who most easily grow "high headed," as the French say. It is we, of all nations, who most quickly forget.

In that fact regarding the American character lies the

great hope of Germany to-day. It is the great fear of our gallant friends in arms, who held the line from which we so long were absent. It is the great danger of America. Lest we forget! Lest we forget! The danger is that we shall forget. And if we do, the great victory of this war is lost.

Our Army is turned back toward home again. We greet our soldiers with much blare of trumpets. We mention large plans of industry for to-morrow. We slap each man in uniform on the back and say: "Fine! Noble! You are a hero! You have saved the world!"

But to-morrow — To-morrow! And once more, what of to-morrow!

The soldier comes back to his old world shyly glad that he still lives, hoping for the renewed touch of hands he knew, seeking the place in life that once was his. But, in spite of our protestations, that place is no longer his. It is as though he really were dead. The waters have closed over his place and he is no more. To-morrow he is forgotten — and he may listen to stay-at-home stories of how the war was fought and won — the "history" of this war, which, like all other history, will not be the truth but what we all accept as the truth because that is the easiest thing to do.

But if the soldiers of this country are to come back only to the old America, the hurrying, scrambling, hectic, hysterical America — and those are our deserved adjectives more than any other people's — then we have not won this war but have lost it.

Our quarrel with yonder foe is not done. We shall have been faithless to our own blood and kin if now we forget. The war begins now; not ends. It must yet be fought out here at home in America. It will require all our courage to win it; if indeed it can still be won.

There have been some great editorials struck off in the white heat of American conviction in these tremendous days following the Armistice and before the conclusion of the Peace Conference. Here is one from a Chicago journal which ought to be read and remembered by every statesman and every citizen in America.

Those sentimental souls who think Lloyd George and Clemenceau are "too severe" in insisting that Germany must pay to

> the limit of her capacity for the damage she has wrought, should consider the speech in which Herr Ebert, temporary dictator in Berlin, welcomed the returning Prussian troops, especially the following paragraph of that speech:
>
> *You protected the homeland from invasion, sheltered your wives, children and parents from flames and slaughter and preserved the nation's workshops and fields from devastation.*
>
> This to the soldiers whose bestiality has made the very name of Prussia a stench in the nostrils of a decent world.
>
> There is not in Ebert's speech a hint of repentance for the atrocious crimes which Germany has committed. There is no recognition that Germany has committed crimes. Instead, there is a boasting glorification of the returning armies, and a reminder to the nation that German lands have been kept inviolate. It is one in sentiment with the kaiser's speech six months or so ago, in which he commanded his subjects who complained of their sacrifices to look at the devastated fields and cities of France, and see what war on their own ground would mean.
>
> The victorious allies are civilized. Therefore, they can not repay German crimes in kind. They can not reduce Frankfort to the present condition of Lens, or desolate the Rheingau as von Hindenburg desolated Picardy. But in some way, they must bring home to the German people both the villainy and the failure of the German spring at the throat of Europe, and there seem to be but two methods of doing this. One is to inflict personal punishment on the men responsible for the grosser outrages, and the other is to make the German people pay, and pay, and pay for the ruin which they wrought.

Germany is not dead or defeated in America. She will raise her head again. Again we shall hear the stirring in the leaves, and see arise once more the fanged front which has so long menaced the world. The time to scotch that snake is now, to-day; and this is no time, when our maimed men are coming home, when our young boys are growing up, to be faithless to those men who — their eyes still on us as they fling to us the torch of civilization — lie not yet content nor quiet in Flanders Fields.

The great debt of the world is by no means yet paid. Whether or not Germany pays to the material limit, is not so much. Whether or not we get back a tenth of our war money, is not so much — that is not the way the great debt of the world is going to be paid. We cannot pay it by oratory or by fine phrases, or by resolutions and conferences and leagues of nations. We cannot pay it with eulogies of the dead nor monuments to the living heroes. We cannot pay it by advancing our breasts again against shot and shell.

The debt of the world must be paid by America. We can pay it only by making a new and better democracy in America. We can pay it only by renewed individual sacrifices and a renewed individual courage.

We must remake America. We must purify the source of America's population and keep it pure. We must rebuild our whole theory of citizenship in America. We must care more for the safety of America's homes and the safety of the American ideal. We must insist that there shall be an American loyalty, brooking no amendment or qualification.

That is to say, we must unify the American populace — or we must fail; and the great debt of the world must remain unpaid; and the war must have been fought in vain.

The old polyglot, hubbub, hurdy-gurdy days of America are gone. We are no longer a mining camp, but a country, or should be that. Happy-go-lucky times are done for us. We must become a nation, mature, of one purpose, resolved at heart. Now we shall see how brave we really are, how much men we are.

What is America to-day? What undiscovered soul was there lying under the paint and the high heels and the tambourine and the bubbling glass in the fool's paradise of our excited lives? What was there of sober and resolved citizenship under the American Protective League — a force so soon developed, so silently disbanded? Very much was there. All that a nation needs was there — if that nation shall not forget.

It is one thing if a quarter million men go back to business and forget their two years of sacrifice; if three million soldiers also forget their sacrifices and simply drop back into the old business world which they left. But it is quite another thing if three and a quarter million American citizens, sobered and not forgetful, do take up the flung torch and say that the dead of Flanders shall rest content — not merely for a day or so remembered — not merely for a year or two revenged, but for all the centuries verified and made of worth and justified in their sacrifices.

A part, only a small part, of the work of the American Protective League is done. We who silently pass back yet further beyond recognition, are not disbanded at all. The flung torch is especially in our own hands. We have been only pretenders in this League, we have been only mummers and imposters in this League, if we do not individually carry on the work for the future. That work, as we take it, is to make America safe for Americans, and to leave each man safe in his own home, in a country of his own making, at a table of his own choosing.

When work on this book was first begun, it seemed to all concerned that the great matter was to accumulate instances of shrewdness in catching criminals; stories of plots foiled and villains thwarted. We all of us wanted to see stalk by with folded arms a tall, dark, mysterious stranger in a long cloak, with high boots, and a wide hat pulled low over his brow. We wanted him, in the final act, to pull off his hat with the sweeping gesture of one hand, his false moustache with the other, and stand revealed before us, smooth-faced and fair of hair, exclaiming "It is I — Clarence Hawkshaw, the young detective!" We shared the American thirst for something exciting.

It became obvious, as the great masses of sober, conscientious revelations from the very heart of America came rolling in and piling up in cumulative testimony, that what had at first seemed the most desirable material was the least desirable. If this record is to have any ultimate value — and it should have great historical value — that must be, not because of a few flashy deeds, but because of a great, sober, underlying purpose. Our final figure of the A. P. L. man is not to be a Hawkshaw, but — an American.

When the time came to call a halt and to disband, there was not a member of the League who did not lay down his work sober and grave of heart. The sum of the reaction of all these reports, large and small, from the hundreds of centers where the League was active, leaves any man acquainted with the facts convinced that America has done her part splendidly, here at home, in the war. It is splendid — what America has done. Far more splendid, what America is. Still more splendid, what America is to be.

The best reading for any American in these days is the

census map of the United States. Next year we shall have a new one, for by then, ten years more of our history will have been completed. The census map comes out once every decade, printed in different colors, showing the location of the foreign-born in the United States. The American-born regions have appeared in steadily lessening areas as the decades have passed.

It is only with a grave heart that any real American can face the census map to-day. The conviction is inevitable that we have been too long careless of our racial problems. If we are to have an America now, we must change. Our golden age of money-making is not a double decade in extent. We cannot go that road another twenty years. If your son is meant to be an American, have him study the census map and the story of the A. P. L. Then he will learn something about his own country. He has not known. His father has not known.

The English came early in our history and the Scotch-Irish, the finest of frontier stock. The Pennsylvania Dutch came and built homes. Then came the Irish, facile and quick to blend. Our immigration before the Civil War was north-European — sturdy stock, fit for the forests and prairies and the vast new farm lands of the West. Now we began to mine and manufacture more, and our immigrants changed the colors of the census map. We began to import work cattle, not citizens, for our so-called industrial captains. Steamship companies combed southern and southeastern Europe. Our miners could not speak English. The Irishman worked no more on the railroads, the sewers, the streets — he shrank from the squat foreigner as the lean Yankee shrank from him — as the Italian, in turn, will shrink from the Russian bolshevist, if we allow him to swarm in.

The map shows you all these things inexorably. It shows the shrinking of the American-born regions to-day to only a small spot on the tops of the Cumberlands in Kentucky, Tennessee, North Carolina and a corner of Alabama and Georgia. Now check up this rough census outline with the reports printed in these pages from all over America. We soberly must conclude that America is not America. We find that the great states of each coast are practically foreign — New York most of all; that the Bolsheviki abound in the mines of Pennsylvania, Michigan and Montana, where coal and copper and iron are found; that Southern Europe has not yet moved its center of population west of the Mississippi; that the Scandinavian and German element occupies Wisconsin, Minnesota and parts of upper Iowa. And the American — where is he?

Would to God that the chameleon record, that fatally accurate census map, could show us the American hue spreading decade after decade, and not these other colors of the map of America, showing the extension of the foreign-born! It is time now, old as we are, that we should seek a far more normal balance of the increase of our foreign-born.

Something is wrong. The census map shows that it is time to put up the bars at Ellis Island. They ought to go up for ten years at least. Twenty — thirty — lo! Then this would be America, and all inside our gates would be Americans. The gates ought never to go down as they have in the past. We ought to pick and select our foreign-born population. If we have not the courage to do that, we are lost.

Give us a generation of selected immigration; deport the un-Americans who divide their loyalty; revoke the naturalization of every man interned in this war and of every other disloyal man, — every adherent to the law of violence and destruction, — and then, and then only, the result may be an American population and a real America.

The best possible news for America would be that of the deportation of more than 300,000 false and foresworn citizens who have acted as German spies in America during this war. Send that many away from America, and those remaining soon would learn that the hyphen must go for all time. If not, let them also go. We do not need Germans now. The world is done with Germans. We want Americans now.

It is by no means impossible that some such action will be taken very soon. In his last annual report, the Attorney General of the United States recommends that all aliens who were interned during the war should be deported and that Congress shall pass a law to that effect. This would deprive us at once of a select society, estimated to number from 3,000 to 6,000, who have been taking their ease in their inn at our expense. Banded or disbanded, when the American Protective League says that law must be passed, it will be passed. And then we shall begin to have an America and not a mining camp with open doors. Hunt out Americans for your leaders. Vote for them. Where have we ever found better leaders?

The Department of Justice officials are on record to the effect that these interned aliens should not be left in this country to make future trouble and to serve actively as German agents. They were often trained propagandists; men involved in bomb plots; men who plotted against our shipping, against the transportation of our troops. We have no law by which we can punish those men further. Are they good citizens to retain? Our Department of Justice thinks not.

Among these interned prisoners are bank presidents, exporters and importers, college professors, merchants, musicians, actors, former officers of the German army and navy and merchant marine. Many of the names which have appeared in the testimony of the Senate Overman Committee appear also on the internment rolls. There are consuls, officials and noblemen, so-called, who also have been in our internment camps. Do we want them in our homes? The Department of Justice thinks otherwise.

Not less disloyal than these greater figures are thousands and hundreds of thousands of minor figures, paid or unpaid propagandists of Germany in this country during the war, pro-Germans, hyphenates, silent or outspoken, who are not Americans at all. Do we want them in our citizenship? If we cannot get rid of them, ought we to import any more of them?

Already Americans stir uneasily under the revelations of treachery within our gates. They ask of themselves, — Since these things were true but now, what guarantee have we for the future? How can America protect herself against the future treachery of so large an element of her population?

The answer to that question is very easy for bold men. Let us clean house. If the existing broom is not sufficient for that, let us make another broom. The revocation of citizenship for acts of disloyalty to this country is a remedial agency which will be applied more frequently in the future. A law should be, and probably will be, placed upon our statute books which will hold over the head of every foreign-born citizen attaining citizenship in this country a warning that he must come into this court with clean hands and must keep his hands clean forever thereafter. That is to say, there shall be no more an absolute patent of citizenship, nothing irrevocable any more in the citizenship of the foreign-born. We will hold a first mortgage — we will give him no deed. Four years ago, doctrine like this would have been scouted. Four years hence it will be accepted, perhaps, as the truth; indeed, the tendency has already begun. In eight years it will be a law. In twenty years, America will be a nation, and the strongest on the globe.

In New Jersey, Frederick Würsterbarth, who had a certificate of American citizenship, perjured himself and remained true to his foreign birth. He declared he would do nothing to help defeat Germany, and had no desire to see America win. He would not contribute to the Red Cross or to the Y. M. C. A. He added the old hyphenated plea that to support the war against Germany would be like kicking his mother in the face. The Federal courts canceled the certificate of citizenship of Würsterbarth. In the New Jersey case, the judge said of Würsterbarth: "Before he could be admitted to citizenship, he must declare under oath that he would support the Constitution of the United States and entirely renounce and abjure all allegiance and fidelity to any foreign sovereignty. Public policy requires that no one shall be naturalized except he exercise the utmost good faith in all the essentials required of him; and where the government is shown that good faith in any of the essentials is questionable, the burden must be on the respondent to dispel that doubt."

In addition to the statute which shall make false citizenship papers revocable, little doubt exists that we also shall have a law requiring the immediate deportation of any foreigner who has failed to take out his second naturalization papers within the prescribed time. The A. P. L. investigations during this war uncovered countless cases of these pseudo-citizens. Of what use can any Monroe doctrine be to America if it is our constant practice to nullify that doctrine and stultify ourselves by allowing practical colonization? And if you do not believe that we have foreign colonies, study your census map and the history of the American Protective League.

Is it bitter, such a belief? You think we still need the German language in the United States? One hundred and forty-two Illinois schools eliminated the study of German from their curriculums during the last year, while twenty schools reduced the courses offered in that subject. Ninety-six schools introduced the study of French for the first time and twenty-one schools added it to their curriculum in that one state.

You still think this is rabid? Read from the report of the Secretary of the Interior of the United States.

> There is even a larger problem than this that challenges our attention, and that is the teaching of the English tongue to millions of our population. Dr. John H. Finley, president of the University of the State of New York, in a recent speech presented this picture which he found in one of the cantonments:
>
> "How practical is the need of a language in this country common to all tongues is illustrated by what I saw in one of the great cantonments a few nights ago. In the mess hall, where I had sat an hour before with a company of the men of the National Army, a few small groups were gathered along the tables learning English under the tuition of some of their comrades, one of whom had been a district supervisor in a neighboring State and another a theological student. In one of those groups, one of the exercises for the evening consisted in practicing the challenge when on sentry duty. Each pupil of the group (there were four of Italian and two of Slavic birth) shouldered in turn the long-handled stove shovel and aimed it at the teacher, who ran along the side of the room, as if to evade the guard. The pupil called out in broken speech, 'Halt! who goes there?' The answer came from the teacher, 'Friend.' And then, *in as yet unintelligible English* (the voices of innumerable ancestors struggling in their throats to pronounce it), the words 'Advance and give the countersign.' So are those of confused tongues learning to speak the language of the land they have been summoned to defend. What a commentary upon our educational shortcomings that in the days of peace we had not taught these men, who have been here long enough to be citizens (and tens of

thousands of their brothers with them), to know the language in which our history and laws are written and in which the commands of defense must now be given! May the end of this decade, though so near, find every citizen of our State prepared to challenge, in one tongue and heart, the purposes of all who come, with the cry, 'Who goes there?' "

Who are you, new man at Ellis Island? Are you a demobilized German soldier looking for easy money in America? Let us see your hands. *Qui vive!* Advance, and give the countersign! And don't let it be in German.

What all the world is fearing to-day is the growth of Bolshevism. It has ruined Russia — and we must pay for that; it is blocking the peace parliaments in Germany — and we must pay for that. It is beginning in America and may grow swiftly in the turbulent days after the war — and we shall have to pay for that. Nobody knows what the Bolshevist is nor what are the tenets of Bolshevism — least of all the Bolshevists themselves. They have recruited their ranks from the most ignorant and most reckless — from the dregs and scum of the world. Their theory is that of force; of government they have nothing. They use the force of law without any surrender of privileges to the law. Their theory of life is self-contradictory. None the less, since they cannot be reasoned with, they constitute a menace to any country. The mischief makers of all classes make recruits for Bolsheviki — socialists, radical I. W. W.'s, anarchists, the red flag rabble of every country united in the general ignorant greed of the wolf pack.

Bolshevism may come to America through the Socialists, through the I. W. W. or through the Non-Partisan League — which in the State of North Dakota to-day hold a two-thirds majority of both House and Senate. It will grow out of the ignorant and discontented foreigners unassimilated in this country. We must expect it naturally to come from these and from the pro-Germans in this country, because those people never have been satisfied with what we did in the war. In general, Bolshevism lives only on its own excitement, its own lack of plans, its own eccentricities. It finds its opportunity in any time of unrest and of slackened government.

We have troublesome days of reconstruction ahead in America. Food prices and wages cannot go up forever, but it will be difficult to reduce wages and food prices. We shall have unemployment in this country. We shall have soldiers in this country dissatisfied because they find themselves and their deeds so soon forgotten. These things all are among the menaces of America, and they must be faced. It will require a united America to face them successfully.

Shall we import more such problems, or shall we dispense with certain of those which we now have? Besides all this irresponsible and sporadic Bolshevik propaganda, we may count upon the old, steady, undying, well-conceived and well-spread propaganda of Germany after the war as much as before and during the war. We shall meet— indeed, this very day are meeting — propaganda against the Allies intended to split us from France and Great Britain. Germany is going out after her lost markets all over the world as best she can. She will need all of her propaganda to help her crawl back even into a place in the shadows of the world and not in the sun of the world's respect. While the war was going on, some firm in America bought a shipload of German toys. Who wants such blood-reddened toys in his home? Soon we shall see German goods in our markets. Who wants such goods? Soon we shall hear the subtle commercial scoff, "It's all bosh to refuse German goods, for they are better and cheaper." Is it so? Is it our duty to be unsentimental in business? Germany was quite unsentimental when she tore up the Belgian scrap of paper. It now would seem to be time that we had some sentiment of the old sort. Sentiment rarely is fundamentally wrong. So-called common sense quite often is no more than common selfishness.

As these pages go forward, the Allies' declaration is that the Hun shall not be allowed in the peace conference nor in any League of Nations whatever that may be drawn up. One thing is sure. No League of Nations ever will be stronger than the individual thought of the countries combining. Our League of Nations will be no stronger than our feelings against pro-Germanism. If we forget that, and take up the game at the old place, our League of Nations is dead at its birth.

The Department of Justice, having removed restrictions on enemy aliens, and having wiped out the barred zones and the necessity of passes or permits, has released a great many pro-Germans who will slip back into their old places in America. In Great Britain the German waiter — so frequently the German spy — is not going to be allowed to take his old place. It may cause some inconvenience, but Great Britain is going to get on without him. That is what we must learn in America — to get on without some of the stolid or the obsequious labor that we have had. With the barring of alien labor, we should suffer many inconveniences in our personal lives. If we cannot endure those inconveniences, then we can have no League of Nations. With the refusal to buy any article made in Germany, we should be letting ourselves in for a considerable individual loss. Unless we are willing to accept that loss, we can have neither a League of Nations nor an America worthy of the name.

Germay is crippled, but not beaten and not repentant. The Germans regret the sinking of the Lusitania only because it was the thing which brought America into the war. For the war itself they are not sorry. If defeat did not make them repentant, heavy indemnities may help teach them something of their real place in the world. That lesson will be all the stronger if we in America shall make more stringent importation and deportation laws — if we shall deport more Germans and import less German goods. There is many and many an American home where German goods never again will enter the doors.

Prince Carl, of the House of Hohenzollern, when speaking of the war, said he thought that Germany ought not to have started her submarine warfare "without being absolutely sure it would succeed." He said he regretted the German propaganda in the United States — because it had been carried out so clumsily; he said that Germany ought to have started her propaganda here on a larger scale, and ought to have spent millions of marks instead of thousands! There you see the German idea and part of the German policy in America. They have learned some lessons, but not the great lesson of the humble and the contrite heart.

Maximilian Harden has been a voice crying in the Hun wilderness for most of the time of the war. He says that now there is no real revulsion of feeling against the men who have caused Germany's name to be a stench in the nostrils of the world. The soldiers returning from the front are cheered as heroes, though their hands are caked with the blood of innocent women and children. Not one of the groups scheming for advantage at Berlin has expressly repudiated the war. Not one has expressed horror at the violation of treaties.

Are these pages indeed bitter? They cannot be made bitter enough! We cannot sufficiently amplify and intensify the innate American horror at the revealed duplicity of this nation which we have fought and helped to beat. We find their spirit to have been one of fiendish ingenuity, their intellect of that curiously perverted quality to which attention has been called. Germany never has exulted more in the success of her armies in open warfare than in her success at stealth and treachery. Are these the men we wish to see marking our coming census maps?

We have nothing to fear from Germany. We have beaten the Germans at every game they have produced, and we can continue to do so. We are the victors and they are the vanquished. They made the vast mistake of being beaten in this war. There is no reason why we should fear them in the future, on either side of the Atlantic. Major H. C. Emory, a former professor at Yale, in a late address, rather colloquially voiced something of this feeling of confidence in his own country:

> Let us get sane! Get over this German bug of thinking that somehow or other the Germans are superior. Morally they are greatly inferior, but people have thought that somehow, intellectually or in organization, they are better than the rest of the world. We have shown them that we can smash the German military organization, which we have smashed. There is an idea that the Germans can do us in business; that somehow this is a race that we cannot compete with on normally fair terms. Put that out of your head! They are a patient, hard-working race; they will work fourteen hours a day where a Russian won't work four. They will plod faithfully. But, gentlemen, they are dumb; they are stupid. They do not understand things. They do not get the psychology of anybody else; and a large part of their

science and their supposed superior way of doing things is bluff and fake. They have done some good work, but no better work, and they are not doing better work, in the field of economics than the English, the French, and the Americans. In the field of business they have nothing on you. For the love of Mike, don't be afraid of them! You can put it over them every time.

We need not fear either the arms, the arts or the artifices of Germany. What we need to fear, really, is our easy-going, unsuspicious American character, our tendency to forget everything else in the great game of affairs. It is time now that from the great mass of the American people there shall appear silently, standing shoulder to shoulder and side to side as they have in their old organization, a new American Protective League. Our old League determined that our homes and our property should be saved. Let the new League determine that our country and our principles shall be saved. All the eyes of the world turn to America to-day. The remainder of the world is distracted. In Berlin, radicals coming up from the dregs are doing their best to get control of a ruined country. "Bismarck's structure was wonderful while it lasted," says an editorial in an able American paper, "but it was a nation without a soul. It was made of blood and iron, and it could not live because the spirit was left out." Neither can our civilization or our citizenship live if they are made of silver and gold, and if the spirit be left out.

It is time to look at the census map of America. We must revise those colors in the next ten years, or we have lost the war. This distrust of Germany in America, in South America and in Europe, is something which should excite no sympathy and no pity whatever. Wars are not cleared up, for example, on any basis of sympathy. There is no use figuring what we can do to show Germany how sorry we are. The thing to do is to leave Germany sorry. She has coal, iron, timber, copper, potash, phosphate, abundant other natural resources. If she cannot handle them, others can handle them for her. Marshal Foch has threatened repeatedly that if Germany continues cynically to disregard the terms of the armistice, he will march again on Germany. That is hard doctrine? Yes. But it was Germany that lost the war.

It is altogether likely that not the best writing in the world, not the most partisan history in the world, will ever be able to give a clean bill of health to America's conduct of this war, or to restore the old American confidence that we were the one great people of the world. The scales have fallen from the eyes at least of our soldiers. They know, and presently all the world will know, our shortcomings. Three million men will have something to say about the politics of this country. Perhaps they will say that our next war shall not find us so unprepared. Perhaps they will say that our next war shall not find us with an army of 2,000,000 spies, propagandists and pro-enemies who claim American citizenship. The Army man is the worst foe of the censorship which has held back the truth from America for so long. Perhaps the Army man will be able to settle accounts with that politician whose stock in trade is the holding back from the American people of the knowledge of themselves. It is time to raise the real banner of America. It will take courage to march under those colors. But if we cannot march side by side and shoulder to shoulder, then we have lost this war, we have lost the Monroe Doctrine, we have lost the League of Nations.

Why should we try to avoid the truth? Nothing is gained by that. The truth is that the reckoning of this war is not yet paid. Eventually it must be paid through the resolution and individual courage of those citizens who are not ashamed to be called American. Ostracism of the hyphen, where it is known still to exist; fearlessness in the boycott of blood-soaked German goods; rejection of the blood-soaked German hand; the wiping out of the foreign languages in the pulpit and press of America; the revocation of citizenship based on a lie; the deportation of known traitors — those are some of the things which must go into the oath of the next A. P. L. Until we can swear that oath and maintain it, we have lost the war.

It is a far cry enough. We have not shot one German spy out of those thousands whom we have found working here in America. We have not deported one man. We have revoked the citizenship of only two men — the above mentioned Fred Würsterbarth, who had been a citizen of America for thirty years, and Carl August Darmer, of Tacoma, Washington, who had been a citizen in America for thirty-six years. Do you think these two men were any worse than a one hundred thousand others who worked as spies of Germany? Hardly. The war remains still to be fought against these men who still are under arms. Apply this test to your friends and associates — to your lawyer, your doctor, to your grocer, above all, to your alderman, your councilman, your mayor and your representatives in Congress. Why not? It is only the same test which the United States District Court in New Jersey applied to Würsterbarth.

Eight years ago an American minister of the gospel who had lived much abroad, especially in Germany, came back to this country and wrote a book which perhaps never was very popular. He held up the mirror of America to herself. His views to-day would not be so much that of one crying in the wilderness. Let us follow along, in a running synopsis of the pages of his book, a hint now and then from page to page, and see what one man thought in that long ago before war was dreamed of; before the German army of spies, military and industrial, had been unearthed; before the plans of Germany for world conquest had been divulged. That writer says:

> In fifty years New York will be what the Italians make it. . . . In New York there is only one native American to twenty foreigners. Waterbury, Connecticut, has a population of 30,000, 20,000 being aliens. . . . New Haven and Hartford, cities of long-established colleges, have an un-American population which in ten years will outnumber the natives. . . . Parts of New Jersey are more hopelessly de-Americanized than New England. Perth Amboy has at least three to one non-Americans. Cincinnati and Milwaukee have been German cities for a quarter of a century; Chicago hardly less so. . . . Wherever I take a meal I am served solely by foreigners. . . . It seems odd that I should seldom ever see or meet Americans except in a social or professional way, and the professions are being rapidly filled by men of foreign names. . . . The Yankee no longer counts in the industrial and commercial life of New England. In his place is to be found the Italians, Hungarians, French, Polocks, Scandinavians and Jews. . . . Thoroughness, therefore, must now

be the watchword of the native American if he hopes to survive in the terrific commercial battle now waging all over the world. . . . This sort of thing must be stopped at once or we are lost. . . . Take the half-past-seven Sunday morning train from the New York Grand Central station, and you will see at every way-station a swarm of dark, sturdy foreigners entering or quitting the train at the little towns along the way — for this is a local train and makes all the stops — and these people are thus enabled to visit their friends and acquaintances. And there appears to be no town, however small, where these foreigners have not gained some footing as laborers, farmers and small tradesmen. I should say that more than half of the Sunday railroad traffic in New York, New Jersey and New England is foreign. I took a train from New York some thirty miles into New Jersey one Sunday morning in October and the conductor told me that he did not think the native Americans constituted ten per cent of his passengers. I asked him whether that was the usual thing on Sundays, and he said, "No, not quite so bad as to-day, but we always have more foreigners than natives on Sunday." . . .

Six millions of aliens are necessary, we are told, to the development of the resources of our country. Now, it is perfectly plain that these foreign hordes are necessary to the development of the multi-millionaires, the trusts and the monopolies; but it is not so plain that they are necessary to the peace, happiness and prosperity of this country. . . . The normal increase of the native American population in the last forty years would have been amply sufficient for the proper and healthy development of this country. Had not the foreigner been called in in such hordes, we should have been forced to do our own work ourselves and would have been all the happier and richer for it. . . . There must be a check put upon immigration. Self-preservation is the first law of nature, and the time has come when we must resort to it. . . . We need time to train our children to compete with these people and during that time the foreigner must be held at bay. Immigration must be checked. The resources of this land are being too rapidly developed by means of these aliens. . . . Some radical change for the worse has taken place in the last quarter of a century in the fibre of our life, our manhood and our national character. . . . Indiscriminate and immoderate immigration is, I believe, the main cause of this deterioration. We have ceased long since to assimilate the vast hordes of heterogeneous peoples who have been

> dumped down upon our shores and who swarm all over this land in the eager pursuit of the mere physical necessities of life. This is the object, the sole ambition of nine hundred and ninety-nine out of every thousand. Such an invasion is actually as disastrous to a country as the invasion of Germany by the Huns who were impelled solely by hunger (the very same motive that brings the vast majority of immigrants to this country) and whose ravages devastated the whole of Germany and scattered its inhabitants beyond the Alps to the Rhine and to the borders of the Mediterranean. . . . Such masses of crude humanity as pour in upon us cannot possibly be taken up into healthy circulation, but must lie undigested in the stomach of the nation, seriously affecting its health and happiness. . . . The curse these immigrants bring upon themselves is plainly to be seen, for it is immediate. They form a body incompatible with the healthy growth of this country. The greater curse of this country is that they do the work that should not be done by them at all, the work that should be done by natives. They take the work and the bread out of the hands and mouths of native Americans, and the question of their means of living must soon become one of the most pressing economic and social problems of the day.

Such extended quotations are made from one writer (Mr. Monroe Royce; "The Passing of the American") only because these truths of ten years ago are equally true to-day and more true. In the past ten years our census map has changed yet more. And now into this crude population of ours we have inducted all the seeds of discord of this war. We have learned a sudden distrust of a large number of our citizenry. Our returning soldiers will bring us yet more problems. The spirit of unrest in this hour of anarchy will add to all these problems.

It is time for another oath, sworn indeed for the protection of America.

AT THE PEACE TABLE

Who shall sit at the table, then, when the terms of peace are made —
The wisest men of the troubled lands in their silver and gold brocade?
Yes, they shall gather in solemn state to speak for each living race,
But who shall speak for the unseen dead that shall come to the council place?

Though you see them not and you hear them not, they shall sit at the table, too;
They shall throng the room where the peace is made and know what it is you do;
The innocent dead from the sea shall rise to stand at the wise man's side,
And over his shoulder a boy shall look — a boy that was crucified.

You may guard the doors of that council hall with barriers strong and stout,
But the dead unbidden shall enter there, and never you'll shut them out.
And the man that died in the open boat, and the babes that suffered worse,
Shall sit at the table when peace is made by the side of a martyred nurse.

You may see them not, but they'll all be there; when they speak you may fail to hear;
You may think that you're making your pacts alone, but their spirits will hover near;
And whatever the terms of the peace you make with the tyrant whose hands are red,
You must please not only the living here, but must satisfy your dead.

—*Edgar A. Guest.*

CHAPTER II

THE PEACE TABLE

The Price of Peace — The First Days After the Armistice — Ferocious Treachery of Germany in this Country — The Test of the Citizen — The New America.

To the merely morbid mind, the white faces of the starved, the moans of the maimed, the black habiliments of those who mourn, may be thought parts of a drama whose terrible appeal has found no counterpart in the human emotions. For the average man, soon to settle back to the grim struggle of making his living, perhaps even these scenes will fade, the world turning from them because the world can endure no more. But someone must make the peace, must bind up the wounds. Someone must point out the future to the staggering peoples, dizzy from their hurts. And it is not alone Europe which has a future to outline. Our own history is not yet written; our own problems lie before us still.

What shall a just peace be? If it must be tempered with mercy, to whom shall we show mercy — to the foe whom we have beaten, or the coming generation of Americans whom that foe has done all he could to betray and ruin? Shall we fight this war through now until it actually is done; or shall we face an indeterminate future, with possible further yet bloodier and more appalling wars?

Now the dead arise and demand their justice. The world leans over the rail of the arena, cold-faced, thumbs down, pitiless of the armed bully who lies vanquished and whimpering. A race which would fight as Germany has fought, and for such reasons, will fight again when possible. Such a race understands nothing but force. Mercy is mistaken with a people which knows not the meaning of mercy. Britain has a huge war bill against Germany; that of France is larger still. What of our own bill? And what of the total of all these sums, added to that which the war has cost Germany herself? If the Germans should be serfs for centuries, they could not pay the reckoning in silver and gold alone. But that is not the great question. What of the silent dead, demanding also their due before Almighty God?

Germany never can pay her bill. So long as her language is spoken, it will be the tongue of a debtor race whose account never will be paid and never can be. And why should the world forgive that debt or that debtor, even should it find it impossible to collect the debt. What outlaws such a debt in the just belief of the world? Shall continued arrogance and treachery serve to outlaw that unpaid debt? Shall a continuance in America of the old German ways in America serve to outlaw her awful and eternally unpaid debt?

Why does such feeling as this exist in the minds of the most chivalrous of foes against whom Germany ever fought? Why should America and France and Britain feel an implacable hatred against a helpless enemy? In other wars the sign of submission has arrested the wrath of warriors. But not in this war. The world looks on beaten Germany to-day with cold scorn and with no feeling of relenting. It is the way that she fought — it is the spying that she did, the brutality that she showed, which has awakened the ice-cold wrath of the world to-day. That wrath means to exact its pound of flesh from the heart of Germany itself. What of the dead who died unfairly? What of the innocent and the unarmed dead? Only in her own tears of blood could Germany learn the humble and the contrite heart. She has not yet learned her lesson. It must be taught her for a century yet and more.

More and more as the facts shall come from Europe, uncovering the real Germany, showing her ferocious treachery all over the world, her utter insensibility to any feeling of responsibility, her abysmal ignorance of such a term as honor, shall we be ready to make fair conclusions; for these must be our only premises.

It is only those who really know Germany's methods in America — those who know her treachery, her duplicity, her efforts to undermine our country — who can make up a fair judgment as to how Germany should be treated in the future.

The members of the A. P. L. have drawn aside the masks and found hundreds of thousands of two-faced "citizens" amenable to no sense of honor and fair play, hating the flag they have sworn to honor. America does not need those people. America needs only the facts about them. The judgment thereon will be written in the next two generations of American history.

The plea of Germany for food after the Armistice was only part of her old propaganda. Her attempts to split this country away from the Allies is now carried on only as a part of her old systematic propaganda. It behooves us to be well aware of such methods, since we once have known them. Germany will not be allowed at the peace table. She will not be allowed in the League of Nations. Why? Because she has lost the right to shake the hand of honorable soldiers. How about honorable citizens?

There is not so much bitterness as cold and relentless reason in all such statements. But you may get a trace of bitterness from the press of Europe, suffering as Europe has all these years under the ruthlessness of German war. There is indeed "every reason for belief that other pledges would be as treacherously shattered did not the victors control the only agency which Germany understands — sheer material force. There can be no compassion based on any code of sound morality for people so despicable as to snivel for help in the midst of an orgy of cowardly iniquity. Germany in this last and most loathsome of her ugly roles should excite about as much legitimate sympathy as a hungry snake."

The murders of Liebknecht and of Rosa Luxemburg have excited certain strange comment in the German press. "What will the world think of us?" asks the German paper *Vorwaerts,* "if we commit murders such as this?"

That certainly is a purely German question! It is a trifle academic. What in Germany is the murder of one woman or one man? The seventh of May, 1915, was proclaimed a national holiday in Germany. On the seventh of May in 1916, 1917, 1918, the German people closed their shops and their factories, and in holiday attire paraded the streets to celebrate that glorious German victory when a submarine sank an unarmed vessel and murdered more than a thousand persons, many of them women and children. And now Germany asks what the world will think of her for killing one or two of her own people!

The whole truth will never be known, but more than 100,000 citizens of Belgium and France were put to death on various pretexts; thousands of women made the sport of violent beasts who wore the Kaiser's uniform; thousands of little children maimed and tortured and every conceivable barbarity and infamy committed upon them. And yet Germany apologizes for killing two more persons! And Dr. Dernburg counts upon the future friendhip of America!

It must be the just men and brave men of America who shall constitute the court to determine the treatment of the foreign element in America. All of those men within our gates who retain their sympathy for Germany are enemies of this country after the war as much as they were during the war. They must share then in the defeat of Germany and must pay the losses of the loser. The victor decides. We are the victors. Let the foreign element reflect on that — we are the victors, not they, in this fight which they elected. It is only the man who makes the dollar his Ten Commandments who will feel toward Germany in America after the war as he did before.

What we Americans need is not so much a League of Nations as a League of Americans. The soul of the American Protective League — renamed, rechristened and reconsecrated — must go marching on even though the League be disbanded, its unseen banner floating no more over a definite organization. As citizens we must unite in a common purpose, or the war will have been lost for us no matter what shall be the treaty at Versailles. If we open our hearts and homes again to the former traitors at our own table, then we have lost this war. It is of little consequence what is done with the Kaiser — he is too pitiable a figure to be able to pay much, even with his life. But Kaiserism in America, still growing, still reaching out in the old ways — that is a different thing. We were leagued against that once, and must be leagued against it forever.

It is accurate enough to say that this war was no lofty thing in any phase. It was much like any other war, based on the biological impulse of nations to go to war almost rhythmically, almost periodically. Commercial jealousy brought out the war, and that it was " forced on " Germany was never anything but a pitiable lie. Germany wanted to control the Suez Canal, to enlarge her possessions in East Africa, to obtain the rich Indian possessions of Great Britain. All this was to follow her defeat of England and France, her absorption of Belgium, Denmark and Holland, her consolidation of Middle Europe, her subjection of the mujik population of Russia, already suborned and bought and beaten by German propaganda. It was indeed a grandiose scheme of world conquest. Nothing that Alexander planned could have paralleled it. But it failed!

In our own country, we of the A. P. L. have seen treason weighed and bought like soap or sugar, and the price was ready in German gold, no matter how high. Our morale was continuously assailed. Through our colleges, our schools, our churches, Germany always intended to undermine America and to break down her patriotism. On the list of men of intellect whom Germany had bought, there are, besides a long list of college professors, fifty other names, including judges, editors, priests, men of large affairs. The German satyrs of diplomacy juggled huge figures carelessly in a cold-blooded commerce which dwelt in hearts and souls and honor. That was done merely in the hope to divide and conquer the United States, all in good time. German-American citizens? Why, no. Why use even that hyphen? If they were not Americans during the war, they are not Americans now. They are no more demobilized than Germany's army is demobilized. Their hearts are no more changed than the heart of Germany has changed. If they were not at one time above prostituting the most sacred offices in the world, they are not above that now.

Let the dead speak at the peace table! Let them tell of the simplicity and worthiness of the German character, the German "love of liberty." We are often told about Germany's part in our Civil War. We are not fighting that war now — we are fighting this war. We are asked to distinguish between the German rulers and the German people; but the obvious truth was that Germany was more united for this war than we were united for it, more than Great Britain or France was united for it. She planned it as the exact working out of a business system — she made it her industry, her ambition, her business enterprise for this generation. Is such an ambition as this stifled forever in her soul, on either side the Atlantic? Let us not be too easy and too foolish. We are just beginning to learn about our own citizenship. If Germany struck medals to commemorate its gallant dead, each dead man of ours at the peace table ought to bear that medal in his hand which would serve as proof of Germany's oneness with her Kaiser in this war!

In these merciful and liberty-loving terms a German apostle of "kultur" writes:

> Let us bravely organize great forced migrations of the inferior peoples. Let them be driven into "reserves," where they have no room to grow . . . and where, discouraged and rendered indifferent to the future by the spectacle of the superior energy of their conquerors, they may crawl slowly toward the peaceful death of weary and hopeless senility.

Superior energy! Thrift! Efficiency! Let dead lips at the peace table spell out those words. We remember the *Alamo*. We remember the *Maine*. Shall we forget the *Lusitania?*

That statesmanship is not acceptable American statesmanship which plans mercy for such a people, or which tolerates the thought of unsafely letting in more of that breed within our country's gates. It is a false and weak statesmanship to mince matters in days like these. Had Germany's war been fought out honestly by soldiers in uniform only, against soldiers in uniform, in accordance with the customs among warriors, then that war might one day be forgotten. But Belgium and France, plus von Bernstorff and von Papen and Scheele — No, no, and again, No! We Americans can not forget.

The propaganda campaign is beginning again here, now, in America, even in the existing confusion of our industries, in the hurrying of our own plans for demobilization. We shall soon hear stories intended to make us believe that France robbed us commercially, that Britain does not love us and only used us. Can you not hear now the German song: "The war is over now. We are at peace. Let us forget. Kamerad!"

But we are not at peace. Our dead stand at the table with all those other gallant dead, to demand their hearing through all time. We must be done with foresworn citizenship in America. We could forgive a soldier; but we cannot forgive a naturalized German who foreswore himself when he took the oath of allegiance to our country. That treachery is one thing which must go — that is one thing which shall never be forgotten or forgiven in America. Such men as these lost their war. There is no injustice, no unfairness in any of these words, which sound so harsh. They set lightly on the innocent, heavily on those who have guilt in their hearts.

It is for every man of foreign blood to know his own heart — we cannot know his heart for him. He alone knows whether he is German or American. He knows which he wants to be. We know that he cannot be both. That is the one test — the impossibility of a man being both a good German and a good American. Let him choose. Let him read his own heart. And let him remember that he is not the victor but the vanquished in this war.

One great American — I fancy even his enemies will allow him that title now — wrote as his final message to America the real answer to this war as it applies to us in America. Colonel Roosevelt's last plea was for Americanism. It was read at an All-American Benefit Concert by a trustee of the society, because of the Colonel's indisposition:

> I cannot be with you, and so all I can do is wish you Godspeed. There must be no sagging back in the fight for Americanism merely because the war is over. There are plenty of persons who have already made the assertion that they believe the American people have a short memory, and that they intend to revive all the foreign associations which most directly interfere with the complete Americanization of our people.
>
> Our principle in this matter should be absolutely simple. In the first place, we should insist that if the immigrant, who comes here in good faith, becomes an American and assimilates himself to us, he shall be treated on an exact equality with everyone else, for it is an outrage to discriminate against any such man because of creed, or birthplace or origin.
>
> But this is predicated upon the man's becoming *in fact an American and nothing but an American.* If he tries to keep

segregated with men of his own origin, and separated from the rest of America, then he isn't doing his part as an American.

There can be no divided allegiance here. Any man who says he is an American, but something else also, isn't an American at all. We have room for but one flag, the American flag, and this excludes the red flag, which symbolizes all wars against liberty and civilization, just as much as it excludes any flag of a nation to which we are hostile.

To that doctrine, and to that alone, can the dead at the peace table nod their voiceless assent. By that doctrine only, continually kept alive, continually enforced, can their deaths ever be justified and made glorious indeed. Under that doctrine and for that purpose, we, who have our war to fight out here in America for a generation and more, can continue the battle, knowing that it is for a good cause, and knowing that we shall win.

The old oath of the American Protective League exists no more. The silent army has disbanded. But now it remains the privilege of each of those men, and their sons and brothers, to enlist again in a yet greater army, and to swear a yet greater oath, each for himself, at his own bedside, gravely and solemnly:

THIS is my country. I have no other country. I swear to be loyal to her always, to protect her and to defend her always, and in all ways. In my heart this is the truth, the whole truth, and nothing but the truth. So help me God!

THE END

APPENDICES

APPENDIX A

HISTORICAL STATEMENT OF HINTON G. CLABAUGH, DIVISION SUPERINTENDENT, U. S. BUREAU OF INVESTIGATION

Shortly after the severance of diplomatic relations between the United States and Germany on February 1, 1917, Mr. A. M. Briggs, then vice-president of a poster advertising company of New York, Chicago and elsewhere, whom I had met in connection with several official investigations, called at the office of the Bureau of Investigation, and made substantially the following statement: "Diplomatic relations have been severed and in all probability this country will be drawn into the European war. I am physically unable to join the active fighting forces, but I would like to help in some way, and it has occurred to me that a volunteer organization might be of great assistance to an investigating bureau such as the one with which you are connected. I hereby pledge all my time and all my resources. I am not a man of much wealth, but the Government is welcome to every dollar I possess, as well as my time, and I earnestly hope that if you can think of any way in which I can be of assistance to this Bureau you will command me."

In the meantime I had a conference with the late Herman F. Schuettler, then General Superintendent of Police of Chicago, and attended a meeting of prominent citizens of this community in the Federal Building.

Subsequently, or a few days after the first conversation, I told Mr. Briggs I had been thinking about his idea and believed that an organization of volunteers would be of very great help to the Department, and as a first step in connection with such organization we could use some automobiles, which would enable the agents to cover several times as much territory, to say nothing of the time thus saved, but that there was no appropriation from which the Government could pay for the upkeep of such cars. I also explained to him the substance of some telegrams which I had exchanged on the subject with Mr. A. Bruce Bielaski, Chief of the Bureau of Investigation at Washington.

Mr. Briggs on February 26th tendered the Chicago office three good cars, and offered to furnish a car, or cars, for the New York and Washington offices, as per my telegram to the Chief of the Bureau, dated February 27, 1917.

On February 27, 1917, I wrote the following letter to Mr. Bielaski, Chief of the Bureau:

"This letter will introduce to you Mr. A. M. Briggs, concerning whom I have already telegraphed and written you. Please be sure to have Mr. Briggs meet Mr. Wrisley Brown, Mr. Horn and Mr. Pike; and I should also like to have him meet Mr. Suter if he is in."

The Mr. Wrisley Brown referred to was Special Assistant to the Attorney General, and is now Major Wrisley Brown of the Military Intelligence Division. Mr. Raymond Horn, Mr. A. H. Pike and Mr. John Gardner were assistants to the Chief of the Bureau. Mr. Suter was Private Secretary to the Attorney General.

On February 28, Mr. Bielaski sent me the following telegram:
Department Justice, Washington.
"Hinton G. Clabaugh,
Bureau of Investigation, Chicago.
"Wire immediately whether acceptance offer automobiles would be used as advertisement in any way. Believe Congress opposed any advertisement feature. Bielaski."

On February 28, 1917, I wired Mr. Bielaski as follows:
"A. B. Bielaski,
Department Justice, Washington.
"Telegram received. Offer of four automobiles for Chicago, four for New York, three for Washington, referred to in telegram, not intended in any way as advertisement. In fact, specifically stated to contrary. Clabaugh."

Mr. Briggs also tendered a gift of fifty to seventy-five automobiles, to be divided up among the various offices of the Bureau, in the principal cities, where they could be used to best advantage, without any cost to the Government whatsoever, as per my letter to the Chief of the Bureau of February 27, 1917.

On March 14, 1917, I sent a personal letter to Mr. Bielaski, Chief of the Bureau, enclosing a letter addressed to me by Mr. Briggs under date of March 14, a copy of which I have and which is as follows:
"Hinton G. Clabaugh,
Bureau of Investigation, Chicago.
"My dear Mr. Clabaugh:
"Believing that the Department of Justice is at this time in need

of possible assistance in their work and that a volunteer organization, properly built and controlled, could render valuable and efficient service, I beg to submit the following for your consideration:

Its Purpose: A volunteer organization to aid the Bureau of Investigation of the Department of Justice.

The Object: To work with and under the direction of the Chief of the Bureau of Investigation, of the Department of Justice, or such attorney, or persons as he may direct, rendering such service as may be required from time to time.

Membership: This organization is to be composed of citizens of good moral character who shall volunteer their services and who are acceptable to your Department.

Construction: It is proposed that national headquarters be established either in Washington, or perhaps Chicago, because of its geographical location, and that branch organizations be established in such cities as your Department may direct.

Finances: It is proposed that headquarters organization and branch organizations shall finance themselves either by outside subscriptions or by its members.

Control: It is proposed that each unit of this organization shall be under the control of the Government but will report to and be under the direction of the nearest Department of Justice headquarters.

Trusting you will give the foregoing your consideration,

(Signed) A. M. Briggs."

On March 19, 1917, Mr. Bielaski telegraphed me as follows:

"Hinton G. Clabaugh,
Bureau of Investigation, Chicago.

"Replying your letter fourteenth Briggs should be encouraged in organization volunteer association. Be glad talk with him about matter. Letter follows. Bielaski."

Mr. Bielaski confirmed his telegram by letter under date of March 20th, which reads in part as follows:

"Hinton G. Clabaugh, Chicago.

"In reply to your letter of the 14th, with respect to letter addressed to you by Mr. A. M. Briggs of Chicago under date of 14th, I beg to advise you that this Department is encouraging the organization of volunteer associations to aid the Government in securing information as to the activities of foreign Governments or unfriendly aliens.

"In the pressure of business your desire for an immediate answer was overlooked, but I have just telegraphed you the gist of this letter. This organization should be handled as confidentially as practicable, and care taken that nothing is done by it to unnecessarily alarm aliens in this country or cause them any apprehension as to the fair manner in which they will be treated, and no arrests should be caused, except after consultation with the federal authorities, in order that there may be no confusion.

"I will take no further action in this matter until I hear from Mr. Briggs or yourself."

On March 20, I telegraphed Mr. Briggs as follows:

"A. M. Briggs,
Hotel Claridge, New York City.

"Just received following telegram from Chief Bielaski: 'Replying your letter 14th, Briggs should be encouraged in organization volunteer association. Be glad talk with him about matter. Letter follows.' Personally, foregoing makes me very happy, as it does you, I am sure. Please wire what day you will confer with Chief. Clabaugh."

On March 20, I received the following telegram, dated New York, from Mr. Briggs:

"Hinton G. Clabaugh,
Bureau of Investigation, Chicago.

"Great news. Will see Chief Washington Thursday morning nine thirty. Please arrange appointment. Briggs."

I then wired the Chief of the Bureau, and on March 22, Mr. Briggs wired me from Washington as follows:

"Hinton G. Clabaugh,
Bureau of Investigation, Chicago.

"Very satisfactory interview. Chief has approved. Organization, our original plan, to be formed immediately. See you Saturday. Briggs."

Thus it was that Chicago was the first city in the United States to have such an organization. It was the idea of Mr. A. M. Briggs, and of no one else. Although in public speeches, letters and upon other occasions he has been generous enough to credit the idea to me, I want it positively understood that the whole scheme was his thought, and it is due to his untiring energy and sacrifice that the organization was started and put on its feet during the early period of its history, when many people were inclined to look upon it and ridicule it as "a bunch of volunteer detectives, etc." Mr. Briggs personally defrayed all expenses in the early history of the organization. National headquarters were here in the Peoples Gas Building and the Chicago Division was formed as well. Thomas B. Crockett was Assistant Chief of the national organization prior to the time, or until the time, he was made a Major in the Army, and assigned to the Intelligence Branch, Central Department.

At the beginning of the war, the Bureau of Investigation handled all complaints of violations of so-called federal war laws, the enforcement of which were not specifically charged to other departments or bureaus by statute. In time, however, the military authorities established a bureau of Military Intelligence, and the Navy established in Chicago the Aid for Information and Naval Intelligence Bureau.

Under the direction of the Bureau of Investigation, a War Board was formed, consisting of representatives of the following Investigating Bureaus:

Chairman: Hinton G. Clabaugh, Division Superintendent, Bureau of Investigation, Department of Justice.

Colonel Carl Reichmann, former Military Intelligence Officer, Central Department, War Department.

Major T. B. Crockett, Military Intelligence Officer.

Lieutenant Edwin L. Reed, Aide for Information, 9th, 10th and 11th Naval Districts.

Lieutenant Commander Clive Runnells, Naval Intelligence Officer.

General James E. Stuart, Post Office Inspector in Charge.

Colonel L. G. Nutt, Supervising Agent, Internal Revenue.

H. R. Landis, Inspector in Charge Immigration Service.

John J. Bradley, U. S. Marshal.

Charles Howe Bradley, Special Agent in Charge, Treasury Department.

Davis S. Groh, Special Agent in Charge, Plant Protection Division, War Department.

John H. Winterbotham, Chairman, Chicago Division, American Protective League.

Robert A. Gunn, Chief, Chicago Division, American Protective League.

John H. Alcock, former Acting General Superintendent of Police.

John J. Garrity, General Superintendent of Police.

Morgan Collins, former First Deputy, Superintendent of Police.

By degrees the League, through the Bureau, tendered its services to these several branches.

In this necessarily brief and naked sketch of the early days of the American Protective League, I ought to add just a word or so regarding the composition and the purposes of this War Board. I called a meeting of the heads of the various federal investigation bureaus of the several departments of the Government, having to do with investigation involving the detection and prosecution of crime under Federal laws, and the general superintendent of police, who represents the local authorities. The purpose of this meeting of the committee was to discuss various matters relating to individual bureaus, with the idea of coördinating the work and to have maximum efficiency with minimum confusion and expense, and thus to avoid unnecessary duplication of work. A committee representing two or three departments was appointed, which met almost daily for many months. This committee was of invaluable assistance. It kept the various heads of bureaus working together in harmonious coöperation, and many constructive ideas were put into effect.

Chief Thomas I. Porter, Operator in charge of the Secret Service Division, Treasury Department, nominated me for Chairman. The nomination was seconded by Colonel Carl Reichmann, Military Intelligence Officer, and unanimously approved, although I favored the selection of one of the older men. Captain Charles Daniel Frey, later of the Military Intelligence Division at Washington, and one of the National Directors, attended the first meeting, and was selected secretary of the committee.

The Chicago Bureau, assisted by the American Protective League, has conducted some of the most important investigations in the country. It is my judgment that the convictions under war laws in the Chicago district will equal that of any three cities in the country. While comparisons are odious, I am referring to the record as a matter of pride rather than egotism.

Topping the list with the famous I. W. W. trial, as late as May, 1917, it was believed that the I. W. W. situation was one which should be handled by the state authorities, but their activities and the history of the organization were such that the Government undertook to follow it up officially shortly after that time.

I was placed in charge of the investigation at Chicago. A branch bureau was established in the McCormick Building, and assisted by a number of Special Agents, we worked there continuously, not coming near the Federal Building for eight or ten weeks, until on September 5, 1917, the Government, through search warrant process under the Espionage Act, raided I. W. W. headquarters in approximately one hundred different places throughout the country simultaneously. The prosecution was in charge of Special Assistants to the Attorney General, Frank K. Nebeker, Frank C. Dailey and Claude R. Porter, as well as Oliver E. Pagan, Indictment Expert and Special Assistant to the Attorney General, and U. S. District Attorney Charles F. Clyne.

Indictments were subsequently returned. A trial, lasting a number of months, was had, which resulted in convicting about one hundred, or practically all of the active leaders of the I. W. W. movement, ninety-seven of whom were sentenced by Federal Judge Landis and are now serving sentences in Leavenworth Federal Penitentiary. Cases are pending, as this is being written, against other leaders of the I. W. W. in Sacramento, Kansas City, Omaha and elsewhere.

In connection with the preparation of the evidence at Chicago, I take this occasion to commend most highly the efficient, untiring assistance of Special Agent George N. Murdock, of the Indianapolis office, who was assigned to Chicago and relieved me of the investigating detail work in December, 1917, and he continued to assist those in charge of the case throughout the trial. Mr. Murdock is still Special Agent of the Department of Justice, in active charge of the investigating work at Sacramento, Kansas City, Omaha and elsewhere.

The Bureau of Investigation and the American Protective League are very greatly indebted to the late Herman F. Schuettler, then General Superintendent of Police of Chicago, for his competency and very great assistance personally, also his entire Police Department, in helping make the American Protective League a success in Chicago. The same is true of John H. Alcock, former Acting General Superintendent of Police, Morgan Collins, First Deputy Superintendent of Police, and other officials of the Police Department.

I shall therefore not burden this memorandum except to call attention to the famous Rockford draft cases, which resulted in the conviction of about one hundred persons. (Rockford is the entry-point for Camp Grant Cantonment.)

After war had been declared and during the discussion in Congress of the Draft Act, the I. W. W. members and their sympathizers carried on an active campaign against the Act, and when the Act was passed, simply advised their members not to register. They were particularly active in the Chicago Division, as well as around Rockford. To insure carrying out their plans at Rockford, an all-day meeting and picnic was announced for June 5 at Blackhawk Park for the purpose of keeping their members and sympathizers together until after the close of the registration booths in order to prevent their registration.

On June 6, 1917, Wait Talcott, Chief of the American Protective League at Rockford, presented the facts to me and he was directed to request the local authorities in Rockford to take steps to apprehend all those who had not registered. Late in the afternoon three were apprehended and locked up in the county jail. This act enraged the leaders of the I. W. W. Meetings were held, demanding the release of the persons in custody. Upon adjournment of the meetings the members marched in a body through the principal streets of Rockford to the jail, about a mile and a quarter away, and a demand was made to release the prisoners. Upon the Sheriff's refusal to do so, the mob incited a riot, as a result of which, arrests were made of the leaders and persons known to be in sympathy with the I. W. W. and placed in jail. About one hundred and thirty-five arrests were made. At the time standing room only was available in the jail. Sheriff Guy Ginders of Rockford arranged with the Sheriffs of Boone and Stevenson Counties to accept some of the prisoners. With this end in view special interurban cars were chartered. Thirty-five were taken to Boone County, forty-five to Stevenson County, and about thirty remained in the Rockford city jail. Before the transfers were made all the glass in the windows of the jail was broken and most of the plumbing wrecked. The leader, James Cully, was indicted by the Federal Grand Jury, tried in the federal court, found guilty, and sentenced to Leavenworth Penitentiary. A majority of the balance were indicted by the federal grand jury for failure to register, and about 107 were sentenced to a maximum of one year in the Bridewell at Chicago.

This case, together with the I. W. W. case at Chicago, makes a total of 212 defendants convicted in two cases — a record, I believe, in the Federal Courts of this country. The American Protective League aided the Department in both of these important cases.

As I understand it, "The Web" will be a history of the League as an organization rather than a work referring to any individuals connected with it, but, nevertheless, I desire to say that in addition to Mr. A. M. Briggs, both Captain Charles Daniel Frey and Mr. Victor Elting, who later became National Directors at Washington, but who were Chief and Assistant Chief respectively of the Chicago Division in its early days, deserve the highest possible praise for the work done by them and the sacrifices they made in putting the League on its feet. Mr. Robert A. Gunn, formerly Assistant Chief, later Chief of the Chicago Division, is also entitled to highest possible praise for his untiring devotion to the service. Mr. John H. Winterbotham, Chairman of the Board of Governors at Chicago, who was one of the first members of the League, and who aided it in its financial development and other work, besides traveling through a number of cities in the middle west, appointing local chiefs of the League, etc., has done as much as any other man to perpetuate and make the League a success. The League will never be able to repay Mr. John F. Gilchrist, its Chief for many months during a very trying period, for his able leadership and devotion to the work. He was ever available, at all hours of the day and night, and with his assistants is entitled to the credit for making the Chicago Division what it is.

Without exaggeration, I think the Chicago Division of the American Protective League did seventy-five percent of the Government investigating work throughout the war. It seems to me that this one sentence covers the situation.

When Captain Charles Daniel Frey was Chief of the Chicago Division, there was never a more active, energetic worker, and while I am not personally familiar with his work at Washington, I feel sure it was in keeping with what I know he did at Chicago.

In addition to working for all Government bureaus, and helping in thousands of investigations, the League conducted a famous so-called "Slacker Drive" in Chicago during the period July 11 to 15, inclusive, 1918, and apprehended, or caused to go to the local boards to straighten out their records, 40,167 delinquents. The total number of deserters and delinquents apprehended during the period of the war, or taken to the local boards and inducted into the service, or permitted to file their questionnaire, or register, totaled approximately 67,000. Not one word of criticism was heard of the Chicago raid. During the four days, approximately 200,000 persons between the ages of 21 and 31 were questioned. Hotels, cafés, saloons, baseball parks, moving-picture theatres, railroad depots, and other places where people are wont to congregate, were visited systematically and simultaneously throughout the district. A few who were unnecessarily detained, or believed they should not have been detained, instead of filing a protest, congratulated the Department and stated that their slight inconvenience was nothing to compare with the duty they owed to the community in aiding the authorities in apprehending those who had not complied with the law. The press, throughout the period of the war, aided the League and the Bureau of Investigation in every possible way.

In addition to the automobile service rendered free of charge to the Government by the American Protective League, there grew out of this idea an organization known as the Emergency Drivers of Chicago, composed exclusively of women who devoted their entire time and machines, without cost to the Government, to driving the agents around this vicinity. They maintained, from the beginning of the war down to the present time, an office in the Rookery Building, and furnished this Bureau with an average of fifteen to twenty automobiles per day. Mrs. Frederick D. Countiss, whose husband, Mr. Frederick D. Countiss, was also active in the American Protective League work, was responsible for this organization, and subsequently Miss Florence Spofford was Chairman of the Chicago Division. The organization was afterward taken over by the American Red Cross, and is now known as the American Red Cross Automobile Drivers, although, because of the manner in which it originated, it has always maintained an independent branch in the Rookery Building, over which Miss Spofford presided and which continued to furnish assistance to this Bureau. Personally, I doubt whether there is a single member of the American Protective League or emergency driver who appreciates just how much this volunteer assistance has meant to the Government during the war.

(Signed) HINTON G. CLABAUGH

Chicago, December 15, 1918.

APPENDIX B

CONFIDENTIAL CONSTITUTION OF THE AMERICAN PROTECTIVE LEAGUE AS FIRST OUTLINED TO MEMBERS

Executive control of the organization is centered in a Board of National Directors operating from National Headquarters at Washington, D. C., in coöperation with the Department of Justice, and through it with other departments and agencies of the Government; this Board being established to coördinate the activities of the local branches throughout the country.

Divisional headquarters are established in the various States to coördinate the work of local branches operating throughout the divisional territory; to keep in touch with the work of each; to promote their efficiency and to render them practical assistance; and to establish and maintain ready communication with Agents in Charge of the Bureau of Investigation of the United States Department of Justice; and to develop methods of operation.

The work of the American Protective League in the field is performed through the local branches. The Chief of the Local Branch is appointed, and is subject to removal, by the Board of National Directors. He is the directing head of the organization and responsible therefor. He will appoint an Assistant Chief; and, in his discretion, an Advisory Committee.

Members of the organization must be American citizens of legal age, of good character and absolute loyalty, who undertake to serve from patriotic motives and without compensation. The reward of a member is the opportunity to serve the Government in a responsible way in matters of grave importance. The selection of members is a most important duty devolving upon the Chief, both because the future efficiency of the Local Branch is dependent upon its personnel, and because of the potential danger involved in mistakes in enrollment. The interest of the Government and the ability of the candidate to render efficient service are the first considerations and are paramount to any considerations of business, family or friendship.

Every member of the organization must subscribe and swear to the formal oath before enrollment. This rule will be rigidly enforced and no member will be recognized as such until this action has been taken. The candidate will be sworn in before an officer qualified to administer oaths.

Strict observance by members of the rules and regulations of the organization is required. The Government must not be embarrassed by unauthorized action of members in the attempted performance of their duties. Experience has demonstrated the value of a Trial Board consisting of disinterested and responsible members of sound and unprejudiced judgment.

The Bureau of Finance procures the funds necessary for the work of the organization from voluntary contribution of citizens, and has charge of all expenditures. It is important that an accurate system of requisition and voucher be installed and that all contributions be strictly accounted for. Periodic audits should be made at regular intervals. No volunteer member of the League should be allowed to profit through his service.

Local Branches should not derive their revenue from any single person or interest, but should secure them from various sources so that no individual or business interest shall at any time be in a position to dictate as to the personnel, policy or activity of the Local Branch. Great care should be exercised that no alien enemy, or person in sympathy with the cause of the enemy, be allowed to contribute money and thereby discredit the organization. Experience has shown that through appreciation of the protection afforded the community by a competent local organization, adequate funds may readily be secured from responsible citizens. Each Local Branch is self-supporting, and will be requested to make its proportionate contribution toward defraying the expenses of the National and Divisional Headquarters. The efficient operation of these Headquarters, and their usefulness to the Local Branches, require adequate quarters, equipment and clerical assistance; and involve large expense for printing and distribution of bulletins of instruction and other literature.

The Bureau of Law maintains an adequate corps of competent lawyers. It advises operatives upon all matters relating to their work, including questions of right and authority, the competency of evidence, etc. It assigns individual attorneys to direct particular investigations, and gives advice as to the construction of laws. It revises the reports of operatives, and briefs the same for submission to the Bureau of Investigation of the Department of Justice. In large and thickly populated communities a zone or district system of organization has proven most effective, members being assigned according to their residence. Under this plan the territory is divided into inspection districts, each under the command of an inspector. Each inspection district is in turn subdivided into convenient territorial units, each under the direction of a captain. Under each captain is a company consisting of the requisite number of platoons, each under the command of a lieutenant. No platoon should exceed ten men in size. Each inspector is definitely responsible to the Chief for the territory in his district, and each captain is responsible to his inspector for the territory assigned to him. Cases for investigation within a district are assigned to the inspector for that district and by him through a captain to the men best fitted for the work. An auxiliary squad for emergency work may operate directly from headquarters.

Experience has shown that a company under a captain should not exceed fifty men. The organization of a company is indicated in the general chart.

The Investigation Bureau should establish and maintain a close association with the Agent in Charge of the Bureau of Investigation of the United States in order to render the greatest possible assistance to the Department of Justice. In the larger cities and wherever possible it is highly desirable that a Special Agent of the Department of Justice be assigned to the Local Branch to direct the work of investigation.

It is the duty of each division chief to extend the organization throughout the city within the lines of his department in such manner as to attain so far as practicable the following ends: (1) the enlistment of responsible persons of sufficient number in each bank, business house and industrial plant of importance, whose sworn duty it will be to promptly report through the proper channel all cases of disloyalty, industrial disturbance, or other matter likely to injure or embarrass the Government of the United States; and (2) the establishment of an organization, through such means, which will at all times be ready and able to assist the operation of the Investigation Bureau of the Local Branch and of the Department of Justice when their investigations shall require an entrance into and the securing of information from such banking, business or industrial establishments.

In this Bureau large numbers of citizens will be enrolled, forming *a WEB of communication* throughout the community, by means of which quick and responsible report will be made of any and all matters affecting the welfare of the country during the present crisis. The duty of members to report will extend to all industrial, social or political plans or conspiracies, and to all other activities or utterances, designed to embarrass the Government in the prosecution of the war.

In extending the organization each Division Supervisor, after his enrollment, will prepare a comprehensive plan covering the ground of his division. He will then proceed to enlist as Deputies under him, a responsible man in each plant or business house within his jurisdiction, such deputies to be executive officers of their respective business concerns if practicable. The deputies after enrollment will select as aids a reliable man in each department of the business, preferably a superintendent, foreman or other man filling a responsible position in his department. The deputies will then confer with the aids and explain to them the nature of the organization and the scope of their duties. The aids will suggest to the deputies the names of several trusted employes in each department who are American citizens of legal age and who, on account of their long service and general character, can be relied upon for loyal service to the country and the employer. The men so suggested as Reporters will not be approached in the matter by the deputies or aids. After the selection of the aids and reporters, the deputy will report his complete plan of organization to the Chief of the Local Branch, and upon approval of the organization the aids and reporters will be directed by the Chief to attend at convenient times for the purpose of being sworn in.

The Real Estate Division reports all information secured by its members, and furnishes investigators with facts connected with the construction of buildings and occupations of and removals from office buildings, houses and apartments.

The Financial Division includes banks, stock and bond houses and safety deposit vaults, reports all information coming to its members, and furnishes to investigators facts with regard to foreign transactions, use of alien enemy funds and transactions with Germans. The department will furnish valuable information in connection with the use of safety deposit vaults by alien enemies.

The Insurance Division provides useful information through insurance inspectors of the character and use of buildings and plants, and reports upon casualties; it also provides life insurance data upon individuals and details of marine insurance.

The Professional Division includes engineers, accountants, physicians and other professions, and in addition to reporting information coming to the knowledge of its members, is called upon for professional assistance and advice in connection with work of the investigators.

The Hotels Division includes hotels, restaurants and theatres. The division is organized so that responsible persons will be enlisted in all departments of all of the hotels and restaurants. They will be able to make prompt and reliable reports on the doings of all transients and others connected with the hotels and restaurants.

The Transportation Division covers all railroads, shipping, taxicabs and teaming. This division will report information and assist in investigations throughout these interests.

The Public Utilities Division includes all lines and methods of commuication, including telephone, telegraph, wireless, electric light, gas, elevated and traction lines and other local transportation.

The General Merchandise Division includes mail order houses, department stores, retail and wholesale houses.

The Division of Industries is subdivided as follows: munitions, war equipment, metal trades, lumber trades, electrical, packing houses, grain, foodstuffs, chemicals and paints, and miscellaneous. The Miscellaneous Subdivision will include, under separate deputies, automobiles, building material, cigars and tobacco, coal, contractors, leather, motion picture producers, paper trades, photographers, and printers and engravers.

Any one of these subdivisions may be of sufficient importance in a given community to constitute a separate Division. On the other hand, many of the above divisions when locally unimportant may be included in "Miscellaneous."

The work of each Local Branch is under the responsible direction and control of the Local Chief. He is responsible for the efficiency of the work. It is essential that an Assistant Chief be appointed to counsel with the Chief and to act with authority in his absence.

In cities of larger size an office in good location, convenient to the Department of Justice, is desirable. An efficient organization will readily command adequate financial support, and the work will be carried on with less publicity and greater efficiency in an independent office, suitably equipped. Adequate clerical and stenographic help should be provided so that investigations and reports may be promptly made.

In connection with the central office the services of volunteer interpreters should be available at all times for translating papers and interviewing witnesses.

Full coöperation with Government and police officials should be promptly secured so that they may be quickly available in all cases of emergency.

The work of the various Branches and Divisions should be coordinated through the central office so that information or assistance of any kind may be promptly secured at any time by any member from any other department through the established channel.

Each Local Branch will operate in close coöperation with and under the general direction of the Government Agent in charge of the nearest office of the Bureau of Investigation of the Department of Justice, and all reports of investigations, unless otherwise directed, will be made to him. The Local Branch will coöperate at all times, through the Department of Justice, with other Governmental Departments and agencies, but will undertake no work from them by direct assignment except with the knowledge of the Bureau of Investigation of the United States Department of Justice, or by instruction from National Headquarters. It is the desire of the organization to render useful service to all Departments of the Government.

Members will always be mindful of the fact that they are acting in the interests of the Department of Justice of the United States and conduct themselves with dignity, tact and discretion. They must refrain from words and conduct in any way calculated to bring the Government or the organization into disrespect.

The work of the members must be carried on wholly without publicity or personal advertisement.

Members will not discuss cases assigned to them with other members or officers of the organization, but will make their reports to their immediate superiors. Members will not take outside individuals into their confidence.

Members must not permit the source of information of any complaint, or the name of the complainant, to be disclosed under any circumstances. They will state in all cases where opportunity offers that neither the American Protective League nor the Department of Justice will disclose directly or indirectly to any person the name or the complainant or any person giving information with regard to the suspect. This cannot be too strongly impressed upon all persons with whom the organization comes in contact.

No member shall inform the suspect or his family of the fact of the investigation, or interview them regarding the subject of inquiry, without direct authority from his Captain or Chief.

Members will not disclose to suspects, or to persons not connected with the organization, the names of other members or officers of the League. It is important that the work of the League be impersonal. The enforcement of this rule is likewise necessary to safeguard the officers and members of the League in their work.

Abuse of their credentials by members by public exhibition or otherwise will be ground for immediate discharge from membership. The use of such credentials under an assumption of authority for the purpose of escaping penalties for automobile speeding, or otherwise, or to secure special privileges in theatres, street cars and other public places is likewise ground for dismissal. No member will be permitted by such means to embarrass the organization in its work and in its relation with public officails.

Members are not privileged through membership in the organization to carry firearms or other weapons forbidden by law. The carrying of such weapons at any time is wholly upon the responsibility of the individual.

No member will be exempt from military service under the requirements of the Selective Service Regulations, or otherwise, by reason of his membership in the organization.

Members will carefully avoid any representation, direct or indirect, that they are Government officers; and will particularly avoid any statement or implication that they are members of the "Secret Service Department of the United States." The American Protective League is organized with the approval and is operating under the direction of the United States Department of Justice, Bureau of Investigation. It is not connected with the Secret Service Division of the Treasury Department.

When making investigations after receipt of instructions members of the American Protective League are authorized to state that they are making the investigation "for the Department of Justice."

Members of the American Protective League have no general powers of arrest. They are investigators only, and have no greater power than private citizens in the matter of arrests. As a general rule a citizen can make an arrest without warrant where a felony has been committed in his presence, but there is no authority for a citizen to make an arrest without a warrant to prevent the commission of a misdemeanor, or for a misdemeanor committed in his presence which does not amount to a breach of the peace. At common law, and except where changed by statute, it is the duty of every citizen to assist in preserving the public peace and safety. Any citizen may arrest without a warrant one who commits a breach of the peace in his presence, or where there is reasonable ground for apprehension that the arrested person is about to commit a breach of the peace. It is essential to justify such an arrest that the offense committed shall amount to a breach of the peace, that such offense shall have been actually committed or attempted in the presence of the person making the arrest, and that the arrest be made at the time when the offense was committed. No private person has the right to make an arrest for a misdemeanor without a warrant after the event or upon mere information or suspicion. The term "breach of the peace" is a generic one, and includes riots, unlawful assemblies, riotous and wanton discharge of firearms in the public streets, affrays, assaults, the use of profane, indecent and abusive language on the street, and in the presence of others, and other acts destroying public order and tranquility. The right of citizens in this regard, however, depends somewhat upon the Statutes of the several States and members should be advised by their Local Chiefs of their authority in the premises. They should act only where the regular police officers are not reasonably available and where inaction may be productive of serious results.

Under the laws of the United States (Act of August 29, 1916; C. 418, Sec. 3) it is lawful for any civil officer having authority under the laws of the United States or of any State, Territory, District, or possession of the United States to arrest offenders, summarily to arrest a deserter from the military service of the United States. Under the opinion of the Judge Advocate General of the Army (C. 17327-1) a citizen acting under an order or direction of a military officer may apprehend a deserter, but a citizen, and this term includes a member of the American Protective League, has no authority as such to arrest a deserter from the army in the absence of a special request or direction of a military officer.

It is seldom that the necessity for arrest arises. In such a case the member will notify his Chief who will secure prompt action by the proper authorities.

Cases will be assigned for investigation by the Chief to inspectors and by them transmitted through the captains to the lieutenants, who will assign them to the members best qualified for the particular work. All reports must be submitted in writing through the lieutenants and captains to the inspectors, and by the inspectors to the central office. All reports of a confidential nature should be brought to the office by the inspectors in person or by private messenger. In the smaller cities where inspection districts are not created, the above rules will be accordingly modified.

All investigations and reports are the business of the League and must become matters of permanent record. They may not be suppressed or destroyed, but must be disposed of in regular course through the established channels of the Bureau of Investigation of the United States Department of Justice.

Great opportunity for service is afforded the American Protective League in reporting promptly and accurately all evidence of enemy propaganda throughout the country. The League is in a peculiarly advantageous position to secure this information and present it to the authorities at Washington.

APPENDIX C

THE ORIGINAL CALL

The following was the first national summons sent out by Mr. A. M. Briggs in the early days of the American Protective League:

I have been authorized by the United States Department of Justice, Bureau of Investigation, to organize confidentially in your town, a division of the American Protective League. You have been recommended to me as a man possessing the necessary qualifications to successfully organize and command the organization, and I will be glad to have you accept the responsibility of building the organization in your town and acting as its Chief.

The object of the American Protective League, which is entirely a patriotic one, no member of which receives any compensation whatever for his services, is to work under the direction of the United States Department of Justice, Bureau of Investigation, in assisting the Department in securing information of the activities of agents of foreign governments, or persons unfriendly to this government for the protection of public property, etc., and any other work that may be assigned to us by the Department at any time.

Each local organization or Division of the American Protective League will work under the direction of the Government Agent in charge of the nearest office of the Department of Justice—and as Chief of your local Division you will report daily or as often as necessary, personally or by telephone, telegraph or mail, to your nearest Special Agent of the Department of Justice.

Your organization should be made up only of American citizens of high moral character and good standing in your community who are willing to serve the organization from a purely patriotic motive and without compensation. Your organization will be in your charge as Chief and you will properly enroll and swear in each member of your organization on enrollment blanks which you will keep on file in your office. As soon as your organization is complete you will please forward me a duplicate list of your entire organization, with your name as Chief, with your Captains and Lieutenants and the men enrolled under each Captain.

It is essential that the greatest possible secrecy be maintained, both in forming the organization and in conducting it, and that all arrangements must be kept as confidential as is practicable, and, further, that great care must be taken by your entire organization at all times that nothing is done by it or by any member of it to unnecessarily alarm aliens in this country or cause them any apprehension as to the fair manner in which they will be treated, and that no arrests should be caused excepting after consultation with the local Government Agent or his assistants.

You will personally administer the oath to each member you enroll and accept and at the same time assign to that member a number,—enter his number on his enrollment blank, his commission card and on the list you will later forward to this office. Start with Number One, which is your number as Chief.

It is advisable that you consult with the Chief of your local Police or ask your Government Agent to do so, so that the Chief of Police may instruct his officers fully in reference to our organization so that the commission card will be recognized by the Police in cases where such recognition is desired. You will, undoubtedly, find that your local Chief of Police will be very glad to work with your men wherever his assistance may be necessary in forwarding the interest of the Government.

It is the desire of the Government that every possible source of information that may be of value to the Department of Justice be thoroughly and efficiently covered by your organization in your town and you will please use great care in the selection of the Captains, Lieutenants and members of each Company so that each Company can be depended upon to efficiently handle the work assigned to it.

In forming your organization, bear in mind the great variety of investigation that you are likely to be called upon by the Government to make, and make your organization large enough to thoroughly cover every business, manufacturing and other interests in your town that in your opinion should be covered — so that you will be immediately informed of any activity that may prove directly or indirectly unfriendly to the best interests of the Government.

You will handle the organization work along the most effective lines possible. If convenient to do so please confer with your Government Agent on the entire organization work. It is unnecessary to call your attention to the fact that the greatest possible speed consistent with thorough and efficient organization is greatly desired by the Government.

Yours very truly,

(Signed) A. M. BRIGGS,
General Superintendent.

The selection of Chiefs was inaugurated by the following communication:

Acting under instructions from Bureau of Investigation, Department of Justice, we are required to organize a separate branch of the American Protective League in each town. Our method is to secure the name of a live, aggressive patriot who is willing to undertake the responsibility of organizing and acting as Chief of our branch in his town, and then send him the enclosed letter which explains the organization work and ask him to undertake the work. I will be very glad indeed to have you act as the organizer and Chief of the Branch of the American Protective League if you can and will do so. Otherwise, I will be very glad to have you turn the enclosed letter over to the man in your town whom you select as the best fitted for this responsibility and have him write me at the above address so that I can authorize him immediately to go forward with the organization work.

We are sending you under separate cover enrollment blanks for the enrollment of your organization. You will please personally fill out one of these blanks and swear to it before a Notary signing the oath in the presence of the Notary, then forward the card to this office. After you have taken the oath yourself you will then proceed to administer it to your men.

Enclosed herewith you will find your commission card as Chief of your Division, which you will please sign at the same time you take your oath, and retain. When you fill out your commission card, please use the date on which you were appointed Chief.

As each member takes the oath, you will issue him a commission card, filling in his rank either as Captain, Lieutenant or Operative, and have him sign his card in your presence.

As each man is sworn in, you will please place his number on the commission card. Please use great care that no commission card leaves your possession until it is given to a member of your organization after having been signed by him in your presence at the time he takes the oath.

The matter of credentials was at first covered by a letter of instruction from the Superintendent to all Chiefs:

The badges to be worn by the members of the American Protective League will be ready for shipment within a few days. Your members are not required to wear a badge if they do not care to do so. In delivering the badges to your men, please caution them to wear the badge concealed at all times and not to display it unless it is necessary to do so while making their investigations. It is advisable that you consult with the Chief of your local Police or ask the local Government Agent to do so, so that the Chief of Police may instruct his officers fully in reference to our organization so that the badge will be recognized by the police in cases where such recognition is desired. You will, undoubtedly, find that the local Chief of Police will be very glad to work with your men wherever their assistance may be necessary in forwarding the interests of the Government.

It is directed that each member of your organization be sworn in by you, taking the oath printed on the back of the enclosed enrollment blank. Paste the oath at the top of a sheet of paper, and as your men take the oath have them sign on the paper below, together with the number that you will assign to each man. This list you will retain in your possession, but as soon as you have sworn in your entire membership, please send this office a complete list of your members with their new numbers.

APPENDIX D

DIGEST OF THE AMENDED ESPIONAGE ACT AS PRINTED IN "THE SPY GLASS," JUNE, 1918

Signed by President Wilson on May 16, the amended espionage laws opens a new chapter in the work of the American Protective League. For the first time we have an inclusive law under which to operate—a law broad enough in its scope and classifications to cover and define as serious crimes a multitude of offenses which were classed as minor by our peace-time code but actually offered serious hindrances to this country's military operations and preparations.

For the first time, too, heavy penalties have been provided for acts and speeches which before could hardly be punished at all under the law. Maximum sentences of twenty years imprisonment and $10,000 fine are not to be taken lightly either by disloyal and pacifist citizens or by unfriendly or enemy aliens who have made it their business, since war was declared, to invent and circulate discreditable stories about almost every phase of America's war activities.

Disloyalty Now a Crime

No distinction is made between the disloyal talk or act of a citizen and the hostile speech or deed of an alien, enemy or otherwise. The act or speech is the offense and whoever commits it must pay the penalty — though the law allows a good deal of latitude to the court in determining the latter.

All this means a tremendous simplification of every member's labors. So far-reaching and important are the provisions of the amended law — so clearly does it indicate the chief kinds of spying and of propaganda which the League must combat, that the whole catalogue of crimes may well be set down here for study and ready reference in months to come. Omitting the preliminary enacting clauses and breaking up the main section into handy paragraphs, the amended law now reads as follows:

OFFENSES:

I — False and Interfering Reports

SECTION 3. Whoever, when the United States is at war, shall willfully make or convey false reports or false statements with intent to interfere with the operation or success of the military or naval forces of the United States, or to promote the success of its enemies, —

II — Obstructing Bond Sales, etc.

— whoever shall willfully make or convey false reports or false statements, or say or do anything except by way of bona fide and not disloyal advice to an investor or investors, with intent to obstruct the sale by the United States of bonds or other securities of the United States or the making of loans by or to the United States, —

III — Inciting or Causing Mutiny

— whoever, when the United States is at war, shall willfully cause or attempt to cause or incite or attempt to incite, insubordination, disloyalty, mutiny, or refusal of duty, in the military or naval forces of the United States, —

IV — Obstructing Enlistments

— whoever shall willfully obstruct or attempt to obstruct the recruiting or enlistment service of the United States, —

V — Attacks on Government, Flag, etc.

— whoever, when the United States is at war, shall willfully utter, print, write, or publish any disloyal, profane, scurrilous, or abusive language about the form of government of the United States, or the Constitution of the United States, or the military or naval forces of the United States, or the flag of the United States, or the uniform of the Army or Navy of the United States, or any language intended to bring the form of government of the United States, or the Constitution of the United States, or the military or naval forces of the United States, or the flag of the United States, or the uniform of the Army or Navy of the United States into contempt, scorn, contumely, or disrepute, —

VI — Encouraging Resistance

— whoever shall willfully utter, print, write, or publish any language intended to incite, provoke, or encourage resistance to the United States, or to promote the cause of its enemies, or shall willfully display the flag of any enemy, —

VII — Curtailing Production

— whoever shall willfully by utterance, writing, printing, publication, or language spoken, urge, incite, or advocate any curtailment of production in this country of anything or things, product or products, necessary or essential to the prosecution of the war in which the United States may be engaged, with intent by such curtailment to cripple or hinder the United States in the prosecution of the war, —

VIII — Defending or Teaching Disloyalty

— whoever shall willfully advocate, teach, defend, or suggest the doing of any of the acts or things in this section enumerated, —

IX — Supporting the Enemy

— and whoever shall by word or act support or favor the cause of any country with which the United States is at war, or by word or act oppose the cause of the United States therein,—

THE PENALTY:

— shall be punished by a fine of not more than $10,000 or imprisonment for not more than twenty years, or both.

An additional section of the amended law provides for the instant dismissal of any official or employee of the United States who commits a disloyal act or utters disloyal or unpatriotic language. This is as follows:

Any employee or official of the United States Government who commits any disloyal act or utters any unpatriotic or disloyal language, or who, in an abusive and violent manner criticizes the Army or Navy or the flag of the United States shall be at once dismissed from the service. Any such employee shall be dismissed by the head of the department in which the employee may be engaged, and any such official shall be dismissed by the authority having power to appoint a successor to the dismissed official.

No Mail For Propagandists

Plotting or propaganda by mail is made punishable by immediate withdrawal of postal privileges from any individual or firm, against whom satisfactory evidence is brought that he is violating any provision of this new law. Conviction is not necessary: evidence satisfactory to the Postmaster General is enough to close the mails to the offender. Here is the amended section:

SEC. 4. When the United States is at war, the Postmaster General may, upon evidence satisfactory to him that any person or concern is using the mails in violation of any of the provisions of this Act, instruct the postmaster at any post office at which mail is received addressed to such person or concern to return to the postmaster at the office at which they were originally mailed all letters or other matter so addressed, with the words "Mail to this address undeliverable under Espionage Act" plainly written or stamped upon the outside thereof and all such letters or other matter so returned to such postmasters shall be by them returned to the senders thereof under such regulations as the Postmaster General may prescribe.

An All-Embracing Clause

Read over the ninth clause of section 3 again: "whoever shall by word or act support or favor the cause of any country with which the United States is at war, or by word or act oppose the cause of the United States therein —." That clause alone serves to make enemy propaganda or native-born sedition a hazardous undertaking in any community where League members are awake and on the job.

Gone is the necessity of arguing and pleading with the pro-German, the pacifist and the native-born disloyalist to speak with straight tongues. Loyal citizens retain the right to free speech and to honest and reasonable criticism of the Government's actions and policies. But indiscriminate abuse and lying reports of what is happening here at home or overseas are going to stop. The amended law is a powerful weapon put into our hands for that very purpose.

Notice also that the word "willfully" is omitted in Clause Nine. To convict a man of disloyalty or sedition, you will not have to prove his disloyal or hostile intention. Like murder or burglary, espionage and sedition are become positive crimes. No one who commits them can plead innocent intent.

APPENDIX E

REMOVAL OF ALIEN ENEMIES

R. S. SEC. 4067 (as amended). Whenever there is a declared war between the United States and any foreign nation or government, or any invasion or predatory incursion is perpetrated, attempted, or threatened against the territory of the United States, by any foreign nation or government, and the President makes public proclamation of the event, *all natives*, citizens, denizens, or *subjects* of the hostile nation or government, *being of the age of fourteen years and upward*, who shall be within the United States, and not actually naturalized, shall be *liable to be apprehended*, restrained, secured and removed, as alien enemies. The President is authorized, in any such event, by his proclamation thereof, or other public act, to direct the conduct to be observed, on the part of the United States toward the aliens who become so liable; the manner and degree of the restraint to which they shall be subject, and in what cases, and upon what security their residences shall be permitted, and to *provide for the removal* of those who, not being permitted to reside within the United States, refuse or neglect to depart therefrom; and to *establish any other regulations*, which are found necessary in the premises and for the public safety. (Act of July 6, 1798, Chap. 66, Sec. 1, Stat. 577. As amended by Act of April 16, 1918: Public No. 131 — 65th Congress: H. R. 9504.)

APPENDIX F

PRESIDENTIAL PROCLAMATION REGARDING REGULATION OF ALIEN ENEMIES

Pursuant to the authority vested in me, I hereby declare and establish the following regulations, which I find necessary in the premises and for the public safety:

(1) An alien enemy shall *not have in his possession* at any time or place any fire-arm, *weapon* or implement of war, or component part thereof, *ammunition*, maxim, or other silencer, bomb, or explosive or material used in the manufacture of explosives;

(2) An alien enemy shall not have in his possession at any time or place, or use or operate any aircraft or *wireless apparatus*, or any form of signalling device, or any form of *cipher code*, or any paper, document or book written or printed in cipher or in which there may be invisible writing.

(3) All property found in the possession of an alien enemy in violation of the foregoing regulations shall be subject to *seizure* by the United States;

(4) An alien enemy shall *not approach or be found within one-half of a mile of any Federal or State fort*, camp, arsenal, aircraft station, Government or naval vessel, navy yard, *factory*, or workshop for the manufacture of munitions of war or of any products for the use of the army or navy;

(5) An alien enemy shall *not write, print, or publish any attack or threats against the Government* or Congress of the United States, or either branch thereof, or against the measures or policy of the United States, or *against the person or property* of any person in the military, naval, or civil service of the United States, or of the States or Territories, or of the District of Columbia, or of the municipal governments therein;

(6) An alien enemy shall *not commit or abet any hostile act* against the United States, *or give information*, aid, or comfort to its enemies;

(7) An alien enemy shall *not reside in* or continue to reside in, to remain in, or enter any locality which the President may from time to time designate by Executive Order as a *prohibited*

area in which residence by an alien enemy shall be found by him to constitute a danger to the public peace and safety of the United States *except by permit* from the President and except under such limitations or restrictions as the President may prescribe;

(8) An alien enemy whom the President shall have *reasonable cause* to believe to be aiding or about to aid the enemy, or to be at large to the danger of the public peace or safety of the United States, or to have violated or to be about to violate any of these regulations, *shall remove to any location designated* by the President by Executive Order, *and shall not remove therefrom* without a permit, or shall depart from the United States if so required by the President;

(9) No alien enemy shall *depart from the United States* until he shall have receive such permit as the President shall prescribe, or except under order of a court, judge, or justice, under Sections 4069 and 4070 of the Revised Statutes;

(10) No alien enemy shall *land in or enter the United States*, except under such restrictions and at such places as the President may prescribe;

(11) If necessary to prevent violations of these regulations, all alien enemies will *be obliged to register;*

(12) An alien enemy whom there may be *reasonable cause* to believe to be aiding or about to aid the enemy, or who may be at large to the *danger of the public peace or safety*, or who *violates*, or attempts to violate, or of whom there is reasonable ground to believe that he is *about to violate*, *any regulation* duly promulgated by the President, or any criminal law of the United States, or of the States or Territories thereof, will be subject to summary arrest by the United States Marshal, or his deputy, or such other officer as the President shall designate, and to *confinement* in such penitentiary, prison, jail, military camp, or other place of detention as may be directed by the President. This proclamation and the regulations herein contained shall extend and apply to all land and water, continental or insular, in any way within the jurisdiction of the United States.

NOTE—Made applicable to *females*, who are natives, citizens, denizens or subjects of Germany, by President's Proclamation of April 19, 1917, except that Regulation 4 was not to become effective until such time as might be fixed and declared by the Attorney General.